I0866542

A COALITION OF LINEAGES

A COALITION OF LINEAGES

The Fernandeño Tataviam Band of Mission Indians

DUANE CHAMPAGNE & CAROLE GOLDBERG

THE UNIVERSITY OF ARIZONA PRESS
TUCSON

The University of Arizona Press
www.uapress.arizona.edu

© 2021 by The Arizona Board of Regents
All rights reserved. Published 2021

ISBN-13: 978-0-8165-4223-9 (hardcover)
ISBN-13: 978-0-8165-4222-2 (paperback)

Cover design by Leigh McDonald
Cover photos: Fernandeño Tataviam Bird Singers performing in front of LA City Hall on Indigenous Peoples Day, photo courtesy of The Fernandeño Tataviam Band of Mission Indians (FTBMI) [top]; Burro Flats photo by Albert Knight [bottom]
Typeset by Sara Thaxton in 10.25/14 Minion (body) and Abolition (display)

Library of Congress Cataloging-in-Publication Data
Names: Champagne, Duane, author. | Goldberg, Carole E., author.
Title: A coalition of lineages : the Fernandeño Tataviam band of Mission Indians / Duane Champagne and Carole Goldberg.
Description: Tucson : University of Arizona Press, 2021. | Includes bibliographical references and index.
Identifiers: LCCN 2020048354 | ISBN 9780816542239 (hardcover) | ISBN 9780816542222 (paperback)
Subjects: LCSH: San Fernando, Rey de España (Mission : San Fernando, Calif.)—History. | Indians of North America—California—San Fernando—History.
Classification: LCC E78.C15 C46 2021 | DDC 979.4/9301—dc23
LC record available at https://lccn.loc.gov/2020048354

Printed in the United States of America
♾ This paper meets the requirements of ANSI/NISO Z39.48-1992 (Permanence of Paper).

CONTENTS

Preface vii

Introduction: Lineages Then and Now 3

1. Cultures and Communities Before the Mission (pre-1797) 17
2. Lineages Within Spanish Colonization (1797–1821) 49
3. Continuity and Dispossession (1821–1850) 69
4. Statehood to Eviction (1850–1885) 97
5. Federal Recognition (1885–1904) 145
6. Lying Low but Laying Groundwork (1900–1950) 171
7. Captains, Tribal Government, and Community (1950–2019) 207

Conclusion: A Recognizable Tribe 241

Appendix A: Captains and Lineage Leaders at San Fernando Mission 245
Appendix B: List and Analysis of the Forty Petitioners 267
Appendix C: Genealogies of Progenitors 277
Appendix D: Names of Tribe and Nonprofit 281
Glossary 283
Notes 289
Bibliography 357
Index 377

PREFACE

This book was produced with the support and encouragement of the Fernandeño Tataviam Band of Mission Indians. Their support includes resources to hire archival and genealogical researchers and oral history interviewers; clippings, photos, and documents from the tribe's own files; sponsorship of tribal community gatherings where we presented work in progress and solicited interviews, personal memorabilia, and photos from individual tribal members; and introductions to elders and other culture bearers for purposes of interviews. As the tribe has pursued its petition for federal recognition, filed in 2009, we have provided background research and assisted with responses to questions from the Office of Federal Acknowledgment. We are immensely grateful to the tribe and its members for allowing us this opportunity to foreground their history, perspectives, and voices.

Additional support for production of this book came from the Rockefeller Foundation's Bellagio Center, which awarded us a joint writing fellowship for the entire month of May 2010, and from the Dean's Discretionary Fund of the University of California, Los Angeles, School of Law, which has funded several research assistants over a period of years in collaboration with the UCLA Hugh and Hazel Darling Law Library. We also want to thank the following individuals who conducted research and assisted with the manuscript: Dr. Heather Daly (archival research), University of Southern California professor Gelya Frank (oral history interviews), John Schmal (genealogist and Spanish translator), Demelza Champagne (archival researcher and bibliographer), Kimia Fatehi (researcher), Maria Montenegro (Spanish translator and research assistant), Jamie Lee Wright (archival researcher), Colin Hampson (attorney for the Fernandeño Tataviam Band of Mission Indians), William Wood (attorney and graduate student in history), Heather Singleton (researcher), Nicole Johnson (researcher), Caroline Mayhew (researcher), James Kirkpatrick (researcher), Orode Nanna (research assistant), and Marcus Tippens (research assistant).

A COALITION OF LINEAGES

Introduction

Lineages Then and Now

As a dry heat overtook the valley on the afternoon of Monday, September 1, 1845, six bells rang out from the tower beside the chapel of Mission San Fernando Rey de Espana, one of the largest missions in the territory Mexico called California. Two fifteen-year-olds, Rita and Benigno, both from prominent Indian families, had just been joined in marriage at the mission's altar, a rococo display of carving crowned by a massive wooden statue of St. Ferdinand III ablaze in gold paint. As the young couple emerged from the church into an open area encircled by the dormitories for the unmarried Indians, many individuals from the San Fernando Mission Indian community were there to greet them. Among them was the mayordomo (manager) of the mission, Pedro Lopez. Lopez was Mexican of Spanish descent, not Indian, but he had made a point of cultivating good relations among mission Indian leaders.

The Indians at San Fernando Mission were a diverse group, recruited to the mission from a network of lineages and villages in the surrounding regional valleys, mostly within a fifty-mile radius. The lineage members spoke distinct dialects from one of at least four different languages that were distributed among them: Tataviam, Chumash, Kitanemuk, and the language dialects that linguists later called Fernandeño-Gabrieleno.[1] For millennia, members of these lineages had intermarried, traded with one another, and shared stories and ceremonies.

Although Rita and Benigno's wedding day was a joyous and important occasion for the Indians of San Fernando Mission, it was not a good time for the mission itself. Founded by the Spanish in 1797, San Fernando Mission had a spacious church, an impressively long convent, with twenty roman arches where mission staff and travelers stayed, quarters for the resident Indians and soldiers, and a cemetery. In its heyday, between 1810 and 1820, the 120,000-acre mission housed about 1,200 Indians, producing wine from over thirty thousand grapevines and tending more than twenty thousand head of livestock. The growing pueblo of Los Angeles, only twenty miles to the south, provided a ready market.

But since 1830, when Rita and Benigno were born, the world around the mission had changed drastically, signaling the decline of its economy and way of life. In 1833, twelve years after securing independence from Spain, the Mexican Congress initiated legislation to secularize the California missions. Secularization meant that the lands and property held in trust by the missions for the Indians were to be distributed to the Indians for farmland and for establishing self-governing pueblos or town governments. Parish priests and a bishop would administer the new Indian parishes rather than missionary friars.[2] Indians would retain enough land for their livelihood, and most of the land would be returned to the Mexican state for distribution to Mexican citizens. The implementation of Alta California secularization, however, was fraught with political struggles among the landed class, the missions, the central Mexican government, and the Indians. In the mid-1830s, against the directives of the central Mexican government, the California landed classes took administrative control of the missions, which they, in most cases, pillaged, dismantled, and greatly destroyed.

Friar Francisco Ibarra, the resident friar who baptized both Rita and Benigno, had refused to renounce loyalty to the Spanish, and by 1835, unable to bear the hostility of the Californio civil authorities, had left. Two years later, Friar Blas Ordaz, a missionary who had served up and down the Alta California coast, was assigned to San Fernando Mission. Friar Ordaz recited the marital blessing for the young couple. He knew, however, that the Californio leaders wanted to destroy the missions and turn the Indians into laborers for the ranches. Officially, Indian lands were held in trust by the church until such time as the church succeeded in converting and "civilizing" the Indians.

In 1843, under orders from the central Mexican government, California governor Manuel Micheltorena restored management of all the missions, including San Fernando, to the friars, much to the dismay of the Californio landed class. Then in February 1845, just seven months before Rita and Benigno's wedding, Micheltorena was forced out of office by the local landholders. The new governor, Pio Pico, didn't care whether the missions had been established to hold land for the future benefit of the Indians. He wanted to sell or rent the mission lands immediately—to reward his political allies, to enrich his own family, and, at least for public consumption, to raise money for the impending war with the United States.

The Indians were well aware of this turn of events. For the preceding ten years they had been leaving the missions in droves and returning to their ances-

FIGURE 1 Sketch of San Fernando Mission in 1856 by Henry Miller. Courtesy of University of California, Berkeley, Bancroft Library.

tral homelands and villages, seeking freedom and avoiding mismanaged and exploitive mission administration, unsure of what would come next. As of 1845, no more than 365 Indians remained in residence at San Fernando Mission.[3] In 1843, forty of them petitioned the Mexican government for a grant of land, and Governor Micheltorena gave them a deed to one square league, over four thousand acres, with the condition that they could not sell it and they must continue working to support the mission. But Pico threatened to retract the grant.

The wedding celebration for Rita and Benigno was reason enough to put aside these fears, at least for a day. Rita and Benigno's marriage continued the long-time practice of women from one small lineage marrying men from another, even if the lineages were located more than a day's walk apart through the many mountain passes that crisscrossed the country between the desert to the east and the ocean to the west. All but the Chumash-speaking lineages spoke related languages, held similar beliefs, and organized their communities in similar ways. The Chumash speakers had intermarried with the Tataviam and others for so long that they had figured out ways to communicate, some speaking multiple languages. And all the lineages accommodated cultural differences, especially since women dominated in the Chumash-speaking lineages and men in the other, mainly Takic-speaking, lineages.

Each lineage was formed around a primary village, and Rita herself epitomized the knitting together of these family lines. Rita's father, Francisco Papabubaba, was born at the mission. But his father came from the Tataviam-speaking village of Chaguayanga, located fifteen miles north and slightly west of the mission. Rita's mother, Paula Cayo, had maternal ancestors from Siutcabit, the lineage based at Siutcanga (what the Spanish called Encino), due south of the mission, about ten miles. Paula's paternal ancestors were from the Chumash-speaking village of Tapuu, in the Simi Valley, fifteen miles northwest of the mission. Tiburcio Cayo, Paula's father, and therefore Rita's maternal grandfather, was an important person—a master shoemaker and a leader of his extended family.

Several years before the wedding, Tiburcio negotiated with San Fernando Mission to secure a grant for Rancho Encino, the site of his wife's ancestral village, for his family and relations. Siutcanga/Encino had long been a village site because of its pools of fresh water and bubbling warm springs. Tiburcio and the others in his group were growing crops and raising forty to fifty head of cattle there, supplying the mission's needs as well as their own. Although the mission had approved the grant, Tiburcio needed confirmation from the California governor in order to obtain a deed. He was corresponding with the Mexican government toward that end when on April 9, 1844, he died at the age of fifty-one. Two of his sons-in-law, including Francisco Papabubaba, Rita's father, finally parlayed Tiburcio's negotiations over Encino into a deed from Governor Pico, dated July 18, 1845. Having title to Encino was worth celebrating, along with Rita's marriage.

Considering Benigno's family history, his marriage to Rita pulled the web of village relations even tighter. Benigno's father, Cosme, was Cabuepet—a member of the lineage that comprised the village of Cahuenga, which was ten miles east of Encino and about fifteen miles southeast of the mission. Cosme was one of the forty Indians from San Fernando Mission who had petitioned Governor Micheltorena for a grant of one league of mission lands. His mother, Esperanza, was from the village of Tusina, which was located in the mountains about fifty miles north of the mission.

Looking around at the guests at their wedding, Rita and Benigno could see respected people from all the closely linked family lines.[4] The witnesses and wedding guests were doubtless pleased to see these two well-connected young people united in marriage. But their parents had another reason to hurry them into matrimony. None of the guests would have been able to notice, but the bride was three months pregnant with Benigno's child. It wasn't clear how the two had gotten together. Most likely, it had been at one of the Indian festivals held at the mission in the summer of 1845.[5] Indians came to these gatherings from

FIGURE 2 Restored San Fernando Mission altar. Photograph from Getty Images/iStock.

a circumference of one hundred miles, traveling from distant villages, such as Tehachapi in the northern mountains and Soboba in the south.

After the wedding celebration, Rita and Benigno settled in Encino with her parents. By this time, Rita's father, Francisco Papabubaba, had taken on Tiburcio's leadership role, along with the other two co-owners of Encino, Roque and Ramon. With its rich water supply, Encino was a place where Francisco Papabubaba,

Roque, and Ramon could amply display their ranching skills. Roque, from a Chumash lineage near Santa Barbara, had married Agueda, aunt to Rita, daughter of Tiburcio, and sister-in-law to Francisco. Ramon, sometimes given as Roman, was a farmer and was probably partnered with Teresa, Tiburcio's widow.

In late 1845, just a few months after the wedding, Governor Pico set in motion a series of land transactions that soon left the Indians dispossessed and evicted from the mission lands.[6] For some, the place of refuge was Encino. In February 1847, however, Francisco Papabubaba died, leaving Rita as his sole surviving child and heir to a one-third interest in Rancho Encino, with the other two-thirds interest held by Ramon and Roque. Along with that inheritance came the role and responsibilities of a captain. Roque left for the goldfields in the late 1840s, never to return, leaving his wife, Agueda, to manage his one-third share of Rancho Encino.

The Mexican American War of 1846 shifted control of California to the Americans. The changeover brought new threats to the Encino land, including newly imposed property taxes and a costly process for proving up title under Mexican law.[7] With one child born just six months after the wedding and another arriving a year later, Rita and Benigno formed a household with Rita's aunt Agueda. Benigno took ill and died some time in 1861 or early 1862. By then, Rita had taken up with Fernando Ortega, a Yaqui Indian who lived not far from them. In March 1862, Fernando and Rita married. In all, they had four children together. Of the four offspring, two survived to adulthood and built families of their own.

Nearly 165 years after Rita and Benigno's marriage, descendants of that wedding party gathered in the same courtyard of San Fernando Mission for a less joyous occasion—the funeral of Rita's great-grandson, Rudy Ortega Sr. As the mourners left the chapel at San Fernando Mission on the afternoon of August 14, 2009, ushers distributed small black umbrellas for protection against the harsh sun blasting its dry heat on the grounds of the mission's cemetery. Rudy Ortega Sr., grandson of Antonio Maria Ortega and great-grandson of Rita, was being laid to rest at the age of eighty-two. As the casket was brought to the gravesite, more than two hundred people gathered to show their respect for the man, also known as Chief Little Bear, who had been their leader since the 1940s. At the funeral service in the chapel, a new generation of tribal leaders, including Rudy Ortega's sons, spoke emotionally, providing the community with recollections, solace, and a commitment to carry on Chief Little Bear's legacy.

FIGURE 3 San Fernando Mission Cemetery, where lineage captain Chief Little Bear (Rudy Ortega Sr.) was buried in 2009. Photograph by Sierra Pope.

It had been Rudy Sr.'s life's work to sustain the sociopolitical networks of the Indians who know themselves as Fernandeño, which means Indians descended from those brought to and baptized at San Fernando Mission.[8] Rudy's primary purpose was to persuade the federal government to give formal recognition as an Indian tribe to the coalition of lineages that came to be known as the Fernandeño Tataviam Band of Mission Indians. For a variety of reasons, federal agents had never included the Indians of San Fernando Mission in treaty negotiations and land distributions in Southern California. Most egregiously, even though the plight of Indians of San Fernando Mission had figured heavily in the efforts of late nineteenth-century reformers to secure land for California's Mission Indians, the Fernandeños never received a tract of their own through that process. The heavily urban character of the San Fernando Valley was one of the most serious obstacles in their way. Land was thought to be way too precious to set aside for an Indian homeland. It was also difficult to apprehend the Indian presence in such a densely settled area, even though the Fernandeños still concentrated their homes in the eastern part of the valley, not far from the mission.

In 2007, the Fernandeño Tataviam Band accumulated significant resources to begin the research needed for a successful petition to the United States. Though in failing health, Rudy Ortega Sr. provided critically needed material for the project: oral history interviews, documents and news clippings, and personal photos long stored in boxes in the dusty shed in his backyard. It was a huge task for the elderly leader, but on July 26, 2009, the research team reassured him that they had gone over everything he had given them and his work was done. As he drove home from the session with his wife, his heart gave out and he died.

The gathering of Fernandeño Indians at the funeral, the traditional bird songs that accompanied his funeral service, and the easy political transition upon his death showed that Rudy Ortega Sr.'s mission had been largely accomplished. What remained unfinished was the federal recognition effort. If the Fernandeño Tataviam Band of Mission Indians succeeded in achieving federal recognition, the gains would be many. They could receive social services and health-care benefits under federal Indian programs. They could gain greater control over their children through a 1978 federal law that gives tribes precedence over states in foster care and adoption proceedings. They could make claims for repatriation of ancestors' remains and sacred objects in federally funded museums. And they could purchase territory that the federal government would hold in trust for them—territory that could serve as the base for economic development and

FIGURE 4 Chief Little Bear, Rudy Ortega Sr. (1926–2009), lineage caption. Courtesy of Fernandeño Tataviam Band of Mission Indians.

cultural practices. Other people thought federal recognition was all about tribal gaming, a form of economic development that became a multibillion-dollar industry after the federal government enacted the Indian Gaming Regulatory Act of 1988,[9] which affirmed inherent rights of Native nations to conduct that activity within their territories. Certainly the San Fernando Valley would be a prime location for a tribal casino. But Rudy Ortega Sr. and the Fernandeños had begun their federal recognition effort long before the advent of tribal gaming, and, unlike some other tribal groups pursuing federal recognition, they were not beholden to gaming interests to finance their efforts.

Federal recognition requires proof that members of the lineages composing the Fernandeño Tataviam Band of Mission Indians descended from "a historical Indian tribe" that existed before 1900 and maintained continuity as a community—socially, politically, and genealogically—since the time of the mission or since any later time when the federal government already supplied what is called "prior recognition."[10] It also requires proof that outsiders have identified the group as a tribe. In 2007, the Fernandeño Tataviam Band engaged us to research the tribe's history and document, where possible, this continuity and prior recognition. We have presented this research through the tribe's petition for federal recognition and its responses to queries from the Office of Federal Acknowledgment and now in this book. Although we are allies of the tribe, convinced of the justness of their claim for recognition, we are also academic researchers. And our research has drawn us to an understanding of the Fernandeño Tataviam Band that challenges much received wisdom about so-called California Mission Indians.

We found that if one is looking for a "tribe" with a single social hierarchy and a highly centralized political leadership—the imagined tribes of the Great Plains, for example—it won't be found in the San Fernando Valley. The Indian lineages brought to San Fernando Mission (as well as the Indians of the Plains) were never that kind of people. They were a network of diverse lineages, each a small tribe by present-day definitions and each associated with a particular territory but linked by intermarriage, economic interdependence, shared ceremonies, and world views.[11] Their political leadership was decentralized and largely noncoercive, resting on knowledge of history, community culture, and kinship ties. When the Spaniards moved Indians from their different villages to the mission, the physical circumstances of Indian life changed, producing new common experiences and introducing new political and economic systems. But the underlying world views, sociopolitical systems, values, and lineage organization continued to coexist with and accommodate these more centralized identities and political arrangements.[12] After the mission disbanded, when urban sprawl overtook the San Fernando Valley, several lineages continued to live near the mission and share identity, kinship ties and obligations, and an alliance of cooperation. That shared identity incorporated their historic links to San Fernando Mission, reflected in their construction of a political community labeled Fernandeño. Like so many Indigenous North American groups, the Fernandeños became multicultural, accommodating to new religions and new social, economic, and political systems, without abandoning their precolonial institutions.[13]

The Indian lineages formerly at San Fernando Mission, originally numbering in the hundreds, have not disappeared. Although the numbers declined steadily during and after the mission period, several coalitions of surviving lineages live in the city of San Fernando, Ventura County, near Tejon Ranch (north of Los Angeles), in Santa Clarita, and elsewhere. One coalition, with headquarters near

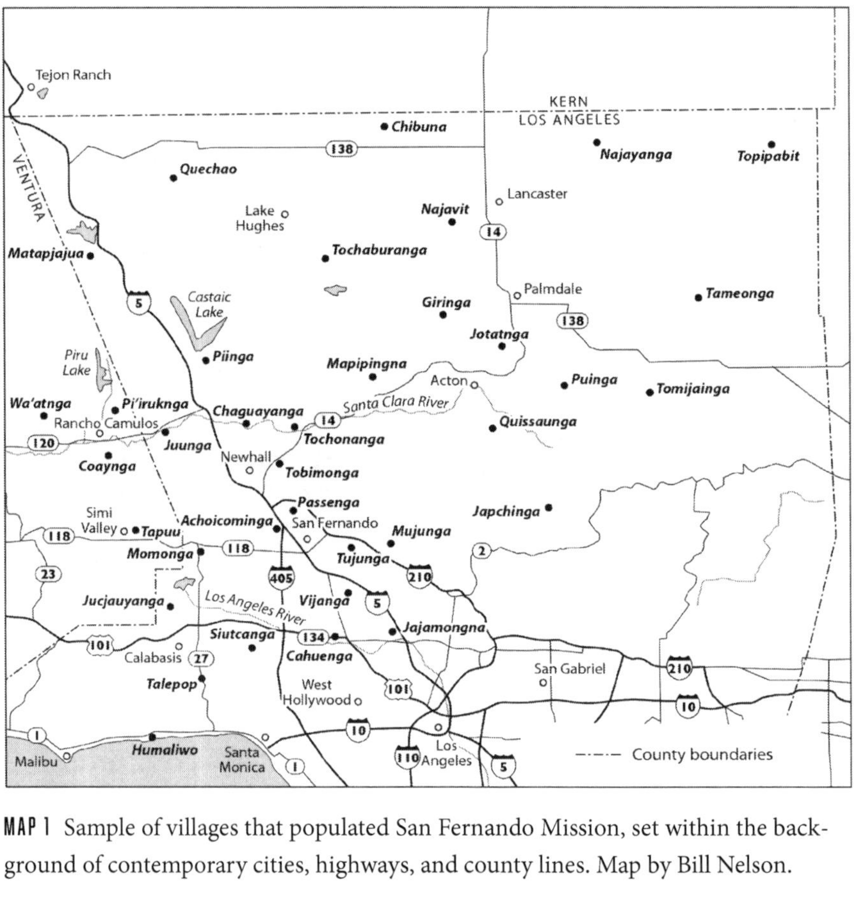

MAP 1 Sample of villages that populated San Fernando Mission, set within the background of contemporary cities, highways, and county lines. Map by Bill Nelson.

San Fernando Mission, is the Fernandeño Tataviam Band of Mission Indians. The tribe includes the word Fernandeño in its name to reflect the shared historical experience of governing tribal affairs at the mission. Its cooperating lineages—generally labeled Ortega, Ortiz, and Garcia, after their progenitors in the modern period[14]—have sustained relationships of mutual dependence and still rely on valued leaders who provide the guidance, cultural knowledge, and resources they need to survive in the contemporary world. Descendants of other lineages that trace back to San Fernando Mission are welcome into the tribe because of their shared connection to the larger Fernandeño historical tribe. This is the collective story of the Fernandeño Tataviam Band of Mission Indians, told through interviews with their members as well as through an extensively researched documentary and genealogical record. Driven by the framework this book uses to understand and relate their experience, the story also includes accounts of the dispossessions and assimilationist efforts pursued by successive colonizers—the Spanish, Mexicans, and Americans.

The historical narrative presents the story of the struggles of Indigenous peoples seeking to preserve their cultures, self-government, land, and social order while being subject to successive assimilative policies from Spanish, Mexican, and American nation-states. In our view, the processes of change, resistance, and inclusion can be better understood by examining multiple levels of institutional organization: cultures, governments, social communities, and economies. In sociology, this type of conceptualization is called *multidimensional social action theory*.[15]

Social change actions or choices are a result of multiple political, cultural, economic, and social interests. Complex social change is created within a framework of multiple interests or dimensions. This framework invites the researcher to examine empirical social organization and identify accompanying interests of individuals, groups, and institutions. A historical narrative traces the social action and pattern of events that form the processes and extent of cultural, political, economic, and social change. Because of overlapping institutional relations, any Indigenous nation will attempt to retain cultural, political, economic, and social traditions while at the same time adapt to specific institutional changes that address the transformative orientations of expanding nation-states.[16]

The narrative of social change consists of tracing changing structural differentiation and reintegration of social, cultural, economic, and community institutions and relations. In general, less differentiated social orders are less adaptive, productive, and powerful than more differentiated social orders. Our focus is not on evolutionary change but rather on the responses of Indigenous social orders to the expansion of colonizing social orders. Spanish, Mexican, and American social orders are themselves struggling with colonization and increasing internal demands for more democratic and market-based societies with private property.

The presently known Fernandeño Tataviam Band of Mission Indians consists of a coalition of three lineages whose ancestors were brought to San Fernando Mission and who once lived at Siutcanga, Cahuenga, and Huwam/Jucjauybit (Escorpion), although they also had kinship ties elsewhere. The institutional differentiation of Indigenous nations tends toward nondifferentiated social orders consisting of kinship ties that form overlapping relations of political identity, economy, ceremonies, and after-life beliefs honoring lineage ancestors.

The Spanish, Mexican, and American colonizing states sought complete transformation of the social and cultural order of the Indigenous peoples, supplanting Indian ways entirely with the ways of the colonizing states and societies. From that colonial point of view, incorporating and reeducating Indigenous peoples would be successful only if those peoples entirely abandoned their own social orders and entirely adopted those of the colonizer. Colonization is a conflict between two differing social orders with differing institutional arrangements and beliefs about religion, land, government, membership, and political autonomy. Spanish, Mexican, and American nation-states wanted to remake Indigenous peoples into their own ways of life, which meant those peoples had to reject their own histories, social orders, and cultural beliefs.

The historical narrative of colonization and resistance presents the contending actions of differing social orders and beliefs. Who and why there are winners and losers is contingent on the conditions present during the historical period. The forces of the emerging colonial states dominated over the decentralized Indigenous political orders of Southern California. However, military conquest does not necessarily mean the Indigenous people gave up their sociopolitical orders and cultural beliefs. In this book we present an empirical exploration of events and patterns of change as seen through lenses of social orders with divergent configurations of institutional differentiation. Both sides may see the world differently and continue to adhere to their separate values, beliefs, and institutional directions.

The narrative presented in this book departs from conventional scholarly accounts of California Mission Indians in several ways. First, although it depicts and demonstrates the unjustness of three different dispossessions, by Spain, Mexico, and the United States, this account focuses far less on Indians as victims. Much of the writing about Mission Indians, especially in recent decades, has attended to either the cruel treatment of the Indians or the Indians' periodic resistance movements aimed at that treatment.[17] In contrast, this book concerns itself with the world views, identities, and social and political organization of specific

Southern California lineage groups and how those groups sustained and adapted their cultures over centuries into the present day. In a turn consistent with our book, some contemporary scholars have shifted focus to cultural persistence, Indigenous agency, and adaptation.[18] But their emphasis has frequently been on material culture and ceremonial practices, not on direct evidence of social and political organization, which is the heart of this book.[19] To the extent scholars such as Kent Lightfoot and Steven Hackel have attended to continuity of social and political organization,[20] particularly the persistence of traditional leadership systems, their work has typically ended with the collapse of the mission system and the onset of American colonization in the middle of the nineteenth century. In contrast, this book documents continuity and adaptations into the twenty-first century. Furthermore, the present work centers Indian voice and agency with the aid of multidimensional tools that identify complex social relations and interpretations. The multidimensional lens enables greater understanding of political, cultural, economic, and social change within and between colonizing and Indigenous social orders. Persistence outcomes should be complex, multidimensional institutional actions that give us enhanced understanding of both Indigenous and colonizing social orders.

Second, some scholarly literature has treated the missions as sites of cultural obliteration, including consolidation or amalgamation into a common Mission Indian identity of the scores of village-based lineage communities that were relocated there for purposes of conversion.[21] The research presented in this book shows that distinct lineage identities, commitments, practices, and leadership survived through the mission period and beyond, coexisting with a broader San Fernando Mission Indian identity and political community. As in the past, lineages are autonomous, each one deciding whether to join with others for social, ceremonial, economic, or political purposes. The present-day Fernandeño Tataviam Band of Mission Indians reflects one such set of choices, made within the umbrella of San Fernando Mission historical experience.

As this story unfolds, several terms appear that require explanation, especially because they are so often misunderstood and misused today. The glossary defines and explains these terms.

Historian James Sandos has observed that the hidden or suppressed stories of subordinate groups are site specific, "meaning that in California one would need to study carefully the elite-written documents and histories of all twenty-one missions to reconstruct the many hidden native stories."[22] This book pursues such a project for the Indians at one particular mission, Mission San Fernando Rey, augmenting and correcting Spanish, Mexican, and American sources with oral histories, memoirs, photographs, and other materials drawn directly from Indian descendants that extend the story into the present. It is a story of adaptation and persistence, not just resistance. Although the experiences of Indigenous people at each of the missions likely diverge in some ways, a common feature, at least in Southern California and probably statewide, was the displacement of Indians from politically autonomous lineage-based villages. Those lineages, in turn, had for centuries formed multiethnic coalitions for ceremonial, marriage, trade, and other purposes. Because these arrangements were always consensual, the postmission political developments may vary, with some groups, like those that formed the Fernandeño Tataviam Band of Mission Indians, choosing to join forces politically and others uninterested in doing so. Whatever those choices might be, understanding contemporary Mission Indian formations and federal recognition efforts requires a fundamental understanding of the lineages and their relations with one another over time, as well as the impact of shared experiences at the missions. It also requires acceptance of the unjustness of the successive dispossessions that colonizers Spain, Mexico, and the United States inflicted on those lineages, among others. In 2019, California governor Gavin Newsom issued a formal apology on behalf of the state to California Indians, citing the history of state involvement in "violence, exploitation, dispossession and the attempted destruction of tribal communities."[23] As this book will show, the government of the United States was California's partner in these injurious policies. Federal recognition of the Fernandeño Tataviam Band of Mission Indians would be a step toward remedying that harm.

CHAPTER 1

Cultures and Communities Before the Mission (pre-1797)

The dead are born again. The souls of the dead go to the west.

FERNANDO LIBRADO, *BREATH OF THE SUN*

For thousands of years before Europeans arrived, people lived on the land now commonly called Southern California. Chumash speakers have lived in the region for at least ten thousand years. According to anthropologists, Takic- or Uto-Aztecan-speaking peoples were relatively late comers who migrated from eastern locations about 2,500 years ago. All of these peoples had their own creation stories, cultures, social arrangements, governments, and territories that marked them as independent and enduring nations with their own traditions.

Those who occupied the deserts, mountains, and coastal lands of the present-day San Fernando Valley, Santa Clarita Valley, and surrounding area, including ancestors of the Fernandeño Tataviam Band of Mission Indians, were no exception. Defense of their communities, lands, cultures, and diverse identities is threaded throughout the prehistory and history of the peoples indigenous to this region. Understanding their institutions of kinship, culture, government, and religion before European (Spanish) contact is the critical first step in understanding their beliefs, practices, adjustments, and continuity after European intrusion.

Nearly all of what we know about precontact Southern California Indigenous cultures and communities comes from sources developed after Europeans arrived. These sources include information recorded by anthropologists, linguists, journalists, and diarists, as well as from Indian people who lived through both periods—information passed down intergenerationally within tribal communities, records kept by the Spanish and, later, Mexican missionaries, and information gleaned from the material culture of earlier periods. The portrait that emerges inevitably reflects a moment in time, and it is important to keep in mind that no culture is static. Such a portrait is also likely to suggest a unitary system of beliefs and practices within communities that downplays internal differences. Nonetheless, the dominant world views and sociopolitical systems prevailing among Southern California Indians at the time of contact retain importance

MAP 2 Sample of villages that populated San Fernando Mission, set within the background of lakes and rivers. Map by Bill Nelson.

because those the Spanish called Indias or Indios adhered to them and were attached to them at the time the Spanish arrived. Later Spanish, Mexican, and U.S. efforts to assimilate and transform the Indians, evoking the Indians' resistance, cultural persistence, and different forms of adaptation and multiculturalism, should be understood within the context of prevailing cultures at the time of contact.

KINSHIP AND COMMUNITY

The Indians of Southern California lived in villages and associated settlements based on kinship, with kinship reckoned through descent from a common ancestor. Several nuclear families formed an extended family, and several extended families formed a lineage or, if large in size, typically 200–250 people, what modern-day anthropologists sometimes call a *clan*. Early twentieth-century anthropologist A. L. Kroeber called groups composed of multiple clans *tribelets*.[1] Whatever label is applied to them, all the people in a kinship group were interrelated blood relatives who shared a common ancestor.

Throughout Southern California were numerous politically sovereign,[2] ethnically specific, linguistically diverse[3] landholding lineages and clans. Each clan or lineage held recognized territory encompassing several settlements and a central village.[4] Unlike much of the rest of the world, where villages are composed of several clans or multiple lineages,[5] Southern California Indian villages and their associated settlements were occupied by a single extended lineage. Hence, the terms for *village* and *lineage* or *clan* are largely interchangeable, though in Takic dialects the ending *bit*, *vit*, or *pet* referred to the lineage or clan, and the ending *anga* referred to a place or territory of that lineage or clan.[6] To varying extents, each of these lineages shared ceremonial, economic, and marriage exchanges with other lineages.

FIGURE 5 Drawing of Tataviam village by Larry Ortega, president, Fernandeño Tataviam Band of Mission Indians, 2009–2015. Courtesy of Fernandeño Tataviam Band of Mission Indians.

Villages ranged in size from 10 to 600 inhabitants in the historical period, averaging about 220.[7] Oral history suggests that village populations were at one time larger.[8] Southern California Indians most likely were reduced in number by diseases introduced through trade among tribes, originating from direct and indirect contact with European traders, explorers, and colonists during the period before 1769.[9] However, much of what is known about Southern California Indians comes from sources recorded during the postcontact colonial record, after 1769.

LANGUAGE AND IDENTITY

Indian languages spoken in the region included the commonly named Gabrieleño, Ventureño, Kitanemuk, Fernandeño, and Tataviam, as well as other dialects. Ventureño, not a Native expression, is a dialect of the Chumash language.

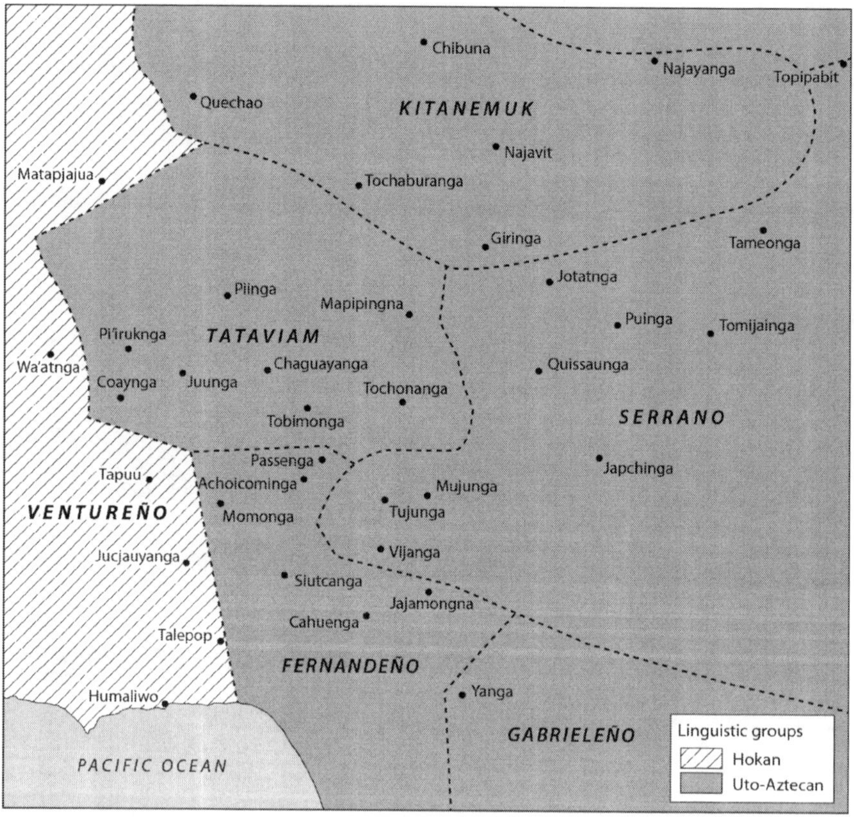

MAP 3 Sample of politically autonomous villages showing predominant languages and dialects. Map by Bill Nelson.

Kitanemuk and Tataviam are Indian names of dialects related to the Takic Serrano language. Fernandeño and Gabrieleño were related Takic dialects, varying only in tone and a few words. Many of the now commonly used language names were not used by the Spanish or Indians during or before the mission period but were developed later, in the early twentieth century, by American linguists.[10] For convenience, we use many of the commonly used language terms but with the understanding that the Indians themselves did not use these specific expressions for identifying their own linguistic, social, political, or cultural groups.

These language groups were subdivided into local dialects that were often shared by several lineages. The linguistic diversity required that some individuals speak multiple languages and dialects. Because of intermarriage practices among villages, one of the partners of a newly wedded couple often moved to a new lineage, where either the wife or husband needed to learn a new language or dialect. Multilingual persons were useful for interpreting during regionally shared ceremonial gatherings, visits, trading, and conflict resolution.[11] Lineages that spoke a common language or dialect did not form language-based political entities, though they might share similar norms, cultural rules, leadership, and ceremonies.

CLANS, LINEAGES, VILLAGES, AND GOVERNMENT

Much of the written knowledge of the Indians of the greater Los Angeles region comes from the accounts of Hugo Reid, a Scottish immigrant who published a series of articles about Indians of Los Angeles County in the *Los Angeles Star* in 1852. His observations date back to the 1830s, and he documented continuities with the premission period. Reid reported that the Indians in Los Angeles County were composed of independent lineage groups led by local lineage leaders or captains:

> Before the Indians belonging to the greater part of this (Los Angeles) county were known to the Whites, they comprised as it were one Great Family under distinct Chiefs. . . . Being related by blood and marriage, war was never carried on between them. When war was consequently waged against neighboring tribes of no affinity, it was common cause. . . . The government of the people was invested in the hands of their Chiefs: each Captain commanding his own lodge. The command was hereditary in a family. If the right line of descent ran out, they elected one of the same kin, nearest in blood.[12]

As Reid explained, the Indians were led typically by hereditary leaders, called *captains* by the Spanish. Each *lodge* (Reid's word for a lineage or clan) had leaders and elders, who managed lineage affairs. Marriage was exogamous since marriage within one's birth lineage was forbidden and was punished by death. Relations among lodges were guided by marriage and in-law ties. The lineages were independent and decentralized and did not constitute shared government. Each clan or lineage made its own rules and maintained its own government and territory.[13] Reid's mention of a Great Family referred only to the universe of friendly, interacting, politically autonomous lineages.

Reid gave the names of forty lodges or rancherias (a *rancheria* being the Spanish name for the village of a lineage community) as a sample of lineages or villages. Each lodge or village had a name. For example, Cahuenga and Passenga were mentioned as two of the villages in the San Fernando Valley. The latter village names correspond to names given in the San Fernando Mission records. The terms *lodge*, *rancheria*, *tribelet*, *lineage*, and *village* can be used interchangeably in the San Fernando Valley region.[14] Among Southern California Indians, all these expressions refer to the same social and political entity. For many Native nations outside California, these terms may not mean the same thing or be interchangeable in the same way.[15]

If one knows the village or clan name of a lineage entity, then one knows the name of the lineage.[16] There is no other name for nation or sovereignty, such as the United States of America.[17] The name and location of a lineage designate collective rights to land, self-government, culture, and distinct lineage membership. For example, several village-lineages are Chaguayabit, Tujubit, Siutcabit, and Cabuepet. The latter four lineages are also recognized by the place-names of Chaguayanga, Tujunga, Siutcanga, and Cahuenga and are currently well-known geographic locations in the eastern San Fernando Valley and Santa Clarita Valley. Cahuenga means *Place of the Hill*, and Tujunga means *Place of the Old Woman*.[18] Although the location and group designations are often used interchangeably, the group marker, such as Siutcabit, is preferable when addressing group activity, whereas the expression Siutcanga is better when addressing a place or location.

In his 1852 series of articles, Hugo Reid made important observations about the absence of large-scale political centralization among Southern California Indians, observations that have informed much subsequent anthropological work. Addressing both the presently named Gabrieleño- and Fernandeño-speaking Indians and alluding to other nearby "tribes," he wrote that

> it probably may not be out of place here to remark, that this tribe had no distinguishing appellation. And it is almost certain that many other tribes were similarly situated; for the so-called *Cahuillas* have been named by the Spanish

> Missionaries through the mistake of taking the word to designate the people. Whereas *Cahuilla* signifies nothing more than *master*.[19]

His point is that while each lineage had a name, there was no "tribal" name for all the lineage groups as a collection or a whole, at least before 1852. The absence of a collective name for an entity or government above the separate village or lineage suggests there was no unified political or religious entity with authority above the village. There were no tribal councils of chiefs or religious leaders with authority or responsibilities or power above or outside of the lineage group. Villages or lineages were responsible for their own members. When multiple lineages met, no lineage was in a position to force action from any other lineage. Therefore, agreements required consent from lineage leaders and ultimate consent from the individual lineage members. As Friar Zephyrin Engelhardt, early twentieth-century historian of the California missions wrote,

> In pagan times the Californians had no general government. Each rancheria had its own chief and was absolutely independent of all others. The chief would take the lead in time of war, make peace, appoint feasts, and give good advice; but beyond this he had little power.[20]

The chiefs or captains were assisted by elders and culturally knowledgeable individuals who had considerable influence and power. These shamans and assistants to the captains helped organize ceremonies, assisted with funerals, coming-of-age ceremonies, and commemoration events, and carried on some administration. The shamans were trained as healers, and some had knowledge of astrology and taught young people about ceremonies and advised about earthly and spiritual life. There was often conflict among rival shamans. Since spiritual gifts or powers were given by the creator, competition and actions among shamans were carried on outside the jurisdiction of the lineage-based government.[21] A shaman's power came from the spirit level, and the lineage captain had limited power over such individuals.[22]

The tribes of Los Angeles County had territory and were led by chiefs or captains. The people made laws, captains judged disputes, individuals were executed for crimes such as incest, murder, or treason, and the tribal members belonged to a single lineage. The legitimate use of force is usually considered a defining characteristic of a state or governing organization. Using this definition, historical tribes in the premission era were state-like structures because they exercised legitimate use of force.[23] According to Reid,

> The government of the people was invested in the hands of their chief: Each Captain commanding his own lodge (village/lineage). The command was hereditary in a family. If the right line of descent ran out, they elected one of the same kin, nearest in blood. Laws in general were made as required . . . war was declared and conducted by a council of the whole.[24]

The tribal community, or council of the whole, had inherent rights to elect chiefs or captains, make laws, and declare and conduct war. If appropriate leaders or captains were not available, then community members appointed temporary captains.[25]

Since lineage members were of common ancestry, marriages normally took place with persons from other villages or lineages. A village was populated by the lineage members and their spouses who were born to other lineages or villages. Spouses who married into a lineage usually did not become members of the host lineage, since only persons of the lineage bloodline were members. A married-in person remained a member of his or her birth lineage-village.

Chumash speakers were matrilineal, and therefore a man usually left his birth lineage to live with his spouse in another village. The Tataviam, Kitanemuk, and Fernandeño-Gabrieleño language speakers, or Takic speakers, were patrilineal. Generally, among the Takic speakers, once a woman married, she left her home lineage and went to live in her husband's lineage community. In Chumash-speaking villages, the children belonged to the lineage of the mother, and in Takic-speaking villages, the children belonged to the lineage of the father.

LINEAGE LEADERS

Each lineage or clan had a headperson who was the leader of the lineage community. There may also have been sublineages or settlements that had a leader who was a lineage elder. The Spanish identified lineage leaders as *captain* and recorded this information in the mission baptismal records. However, each lineage had its own name for the leader, such as Tomiear among some Tataviam lineages and Taari among the Topipabit (Tejon Ranch area) and other clans.[26] Many of the names are markers of esteem, honor, and influence. Leadership names were usually granted to people who were in certain hereditary lineages but who also demonstrated experience in and knowledge of clan history, culture, and ceremonies.

Among the lineages of the Fernandeño-speaking Cabuepet and Siutcabit, some lineage leaders were named Chari.[27] At the Tataviam village of Tochonanga, the terms Mu, Nu,[28] and Nuguit were leader titles, and at another Tataviam village,

Chaguayanga, the name Genu was used for chief. At the western Gabrieleño-speaking village of Tujunga, the names Nu and Cunu were used for chief.[29] For example, Jose Maria (?–1840), whose Indian name was Seuyeuyeminasu, was captain of the lineage at Tochonanga. His two children also held chiefly names such as Nu and Mu, and relatives held the name of Cheri or Chori.[30] The variety of chiefly names at Tochonanga suggests that the village may have been a significant ceremonial center. Tomearunasjum (1767–98), the first Indian person buried at San Fernando Mission,[31] had the chiefly root name of Tomear, a name (also Tomiear or Tomiar) that was used among the Kitanemuk, Tataviam, and Gabrieleño and is presently used among the Fernandeño Tataviam Band of Mission Indians.[32]

Francisco Xavier (1752–1821), from Chaguayanga, was another important captain from the premission period. His Native name of Chachaguayuba reflected his leadership association with that lineage-village.[33] Genu (1768–1803), whose later baptismal name was Jacob, was a leader among the Chaguayabit lineage.[34] Genu was probably an assistant to the captain and had obligations to help organize and participate in a range of ceremonies and act as a messenger.

The leaders in all these lineages were typically elders, who by seniority and experience shared their knowledge and advice with other lineage leaders and the community at large. They did not command. As Kroeber explained, "A successful chief was an ornament to his people and must conduct himself with considerable dignity when the situation demanded it. He had however next to no authority. His role was supposed to be essentially one of using moral influence on the side of wisdom and coordination, and of preventing dissension and trouble from coming up."[35]

The captain position was usually hereditary. If a man was captain, then one of his sons, often the eldest son, was typically recognized as future captain and succeeded his father in the role. In the Chumash-speaking lineages, a female captain was generally succeeded by her oldest daughter. If a possible successor candidate was considered unfit or the customary successor was unwilling, other candidates of near kinship were considered. If the captain and lineage elders agreed on a particular successor and the lineage members did not disagree, the choice was secured by general consensus. Usually the successors were members of the leading families of the lineage. If the original leadership family line ran out, a near kin member was appointed.[36] The lineage also had the right to choose the captain by general consent, if necessary.

Lineage captains typically arranged marriages of their children or siblings to leading families in other lineages.[37] The practice of marriage among leadership families usually enabled closer relations among regional lineage leaders and allied lineages.

THE LINEAGE AS MINISTATE

If a state is defined as the organization that controls the legitimate use of force,[38] then each Southern California Indian lineage group could be deemed a state because of its rules allocating use of force, leadership, and decision-making. Each kinship-based lineage community had a well-understood hierarchy based on knowledge, age, respect, ceremonial participation, and past service. The rules were consensual, but elders had a certain amount of political and social influence. The lineage community was a kind of gerontocracy, led by elders who were experienced, knowledgeable, respected, and understood to be working for the well-being of their lineage kin.

Elders were deferred to and always given preference to sit by the fire. Deer meat was reserved for the elders.[39] Maintaining harmony and order within the community was a major goal for leaders and elder kin. A person who misbehaved was chided by elder kin. If harm was done, then the leader or captain decided the issue and the forms of restitution.[40] The captain and elders made decisions and laws as needed, addressing any discussion or dissent within the lineage community and resolving any quarrels among lineage members.[41] Murder and incest were punished with death by shooting of arrows.

Conflicts between villages were managed through negotiation between the two lineage captains. In cases where no agreement could be reached, a third lineage captain decided, without appeal.[42] Long-term conflict between families was often deflated by singing contests. In an eight-day ceremonial space, a hostile lineage sang sarcastic, funny, and insulting songs about their opponent, and their enemies did the same. The song contests continued on a regular basis for many years, and direct physical violence was avoided.[43]

A lineage captain, elder, or group who enforced a law or imposed a sanction for a transgression, such as murder or incest, was acting on behalf of a government according to its norms and values. Lineage leaders and elders and the lineage members carried out the law whenever a person was punished, put to death, or compelled to provide restitution. The captain and elders defined the rules and procedures for arriving at a decision about crime, punishment, and restitution. The lineage leaders' determination of criminal actions and punishment and requirements of restitution, supported by community consent, were acts of collective or state government. The lineages each had traditions and laws the leaders had to obey, execute, and administer. All persons born to the lineage were expected to follow the rules of the lineage tradition and faced punishment or other consequences from the captain or the larger group if rules were broken.

The traditions, rules, and laws of the lineage were its constitution, and the captain and elders carried out the rules, enforced the rules, and maintained order. Members received their laws and norms from their lineage's creation teachings. A right to inherent self-government suggests that lineages, as *ministates*, held all rights and powers of sovereignty over their people and throughout their territory. No other group was recognized to have competing rights to govern the land or people of a lineage or clan. The cycle of ceremonies renewed agreements and relations with the creator and ancestors and renewed the separate governments and territories of each lineage.

Although each lineage was an independent political entity with a distinct kinship identity, friendly coalitions often formed for purposes of marriage, trade, and ceremonial obligations. When politically sovereign lineages formed friendly alliances, the lineages remained sovereign and independent from each other and did not subordinate their identities or political powers to the other lineage. They formed a coalition of equal sovereign entities. No one lineage would be able to force its powers onto the other. The suppressed group would simply walk away and decline further interaction with the aggressive clan, or the lineages might agree to the kind of singing contest described earlier.

If a charismatic leader arose in a particular lineage, persons from other lineages might come under his or her influence. Nevertheless, all lineage members owed ultimate loyalty and allegiance only to the leaders of their own lineage.[44] Lineages were not responsible for the well-being of members of other lineages. Decision-making within a lineage community ultimately required general consent, ratifying ideas or proposals presented by leaders or lineage elders. Consent was not taken by a group vote but by discussion and consensus-building among elders and lineage members. Leaders and elders accommodated the thoughts and complaints of their kin persons and accordingly adjusted actions or proposals.[45] Lineage, community, and clan political relations were tightly interconnected, if not one and the same.

TWO LAYERS OF COMMUNITY: LINEAGE-CLAN AND REGIONAL

Among Southern California Indians of the San Fernando Valley and elsewhere, there were two types of community: one based in the lineage or clan and the other regional in nature. The lineages or clans, functioning as the first and primary layer of community, exercised power over territory, maintained self-government, managed a justice system, and participated in a selected network of social, economic, and political ties to other lineages over an extensive regional area.[46] Lineage life consisted of direct face-to-face interactions among members, the married-in spouses, and their children. Many lineages were organized into multiple settlements. For example, the members of the Portola expedition in 1769 observed the community of Chaguayabit, which was composed of five relatively large settlements.[47] The various settlements, or sublineages, lived on assigned portions of the clan land base and ran their own local issues and affairs. The entire clan gathered together at various times throughout the year during regular ceremonies and lineage gatherings.

Each lineage was an internally sovereign ministate that managed relations among the lineage members and hosted the intermarried spouses. Lineages each had their own spiritual identities and regular calendars of social and cultural activities, meetings, festivals, and political gatherings.[48] Lineage members and their spouses attended the regularly scheduled internal ceremonies and community interactions.[49] Everyone in the lineage knew everyone else or could identify lineal ties to everyone else. Those who married into a lineage participated in day-to-day activities but were not considered members of the lineage for purposes of consensus-building, leadership, and administration of justice.[50] They remained political participants in their own ancestral lineages. The lineage-villages had intense internal social and political interactions. The unification of all lineages was a foreign concept; political-ancestral membership and identity belonged to a specific lineage. Lineage members also did not try to convert individuals from other lineages, since lineage ceremonies were unique to each lineage. The sacred bundles and ceremonies were different and would only work for the benefit of the lineage communities for which they were intended.

A second level of community was the engagement of each lineage with other lineages in the region. Arranged marriages, some ceremonies, and trade took place at gatherings that included participation from multiple friendly lineages or clans. Gatherings of lineages would also occur on the occasion of dispute resolution.[51] Relations with other lineages were generally amicable, redistributive, and formal and sometimes carried on through leaders.

The regional community was like present-day international space. Other lineages with different languages and specific cultural and political identities were tolerated and invited to participate. The regional area was a crossroads of multiple cultures and languages and numerous sovereign political entities in the form of lineages or clans organized as villages. There was no sovereign political power or religious power above the lineages. Each lineage continued to exercise its own sovereignty and apply its own rules.

Although the lineages were connected by friendship, marriage, and in-law relations, the gathering of lineages did not have a political, linguistic, or religious name. When lineages from the region gathered for multilineage events and exchanges, there were some shared common rules. The regional community consisted of a voluntary group of lineages, something akin to the present-day United Nations, where many sovereign lineages participated in trade, ceremonies, and intermarriages, and no lineage had power or sovereignty over another lineage or over the whole regional collection of lineages. There were strategic reasons for a lineage to encourage its members to marry individuals from a range of external lineages because such relations opened opportunities for political alliances, trade, and ceremonial cooperation.

In sum, the village community was composed not only of lineage blood relatives but also spouses who were normally expected to be treated well and to live their days among the lineage community of their husband or wife. There was little ethnic purity, and ethnic purity was not a goal. The inclusion of persons who married into the lineage supported tolerance for different village cultures, religious views, and political identities. "They don't quarrel with their neighbor's mode of worship, but they consider their own the best."[52] Perhaps as many as 20 percent to 30 percent of the residents among a lineage community were people who had married in from "foreign" lineages. The demography of the village communities reflected the diversity of regional cultural, linguistic, and ceremonial relations.

REGIONAL ECONOMY AND ECONOMIC ETHIC

Fernando Librado, a Chumash source for linguist John Harrington, recounted the following statement by Naiyait, a Chumash elder, reflecting the community's economic ethic:

> I am thankful for what had been done for me in the world, and for what has been given to me to eat. You have given to me, however, not for me but for the world. . . . Now after thanking you for what you have done for me, I will say to you to remember that it is not to me that you have given this, but to our god, for it is he who gives us everything that the earth produces, which is the earth, and when it rains it gives all the earth produces. . . . And I want to tell you that you must be industrious in gathering all that your mother earth gives us for our subsistence; those that are not lazy will always have plenty to eat. It will be

> the lazy one, who will go with another lazy one, that will try to see if they can find somebody from whom they can take their property.[53]

For Southern California Indian lineages, groups held land as a collective asset, although various parts of the lineages occupied specific land areas for settlements, hunting, fishing, and gathering. With permission, lineages could share land resources with each other.[54] Lineages understood and respected territorial borders. Sometimes agreements were made for passage through the land, and some landlocked lineages had the right to pass through the territories of coastal villages to fish in the ocean. Agreements might be made for sharing of specific oak groves or berry or root patches.[55]

Lineage members cooperated in hunting, fishing, and gathering excursions to find food. Using bows and arrows, clubs, and sticks, the inland and desert lineages hunted animals, gathered plants, and caught fish in rivers. They hunted bears, rabbits, gophers, squirrels, and deer for their furs and for food. Lineage members collected and ate acorns, wild blackberries, currants, wild plums, gooseberries, roots, seeds, and jicamas. The pits of wild plums were ground into meal. Yucca cabbage and mescal were made into drinks. The nopal cactus, or prickly pear, was harvested for both food and medicinal purposes. The tender paddles of the nopal cactus were cut and their needles removed with a stone scraper, then the paddles were diced, washed, some residue removed, and cooked in water. Pots were made from soapstone. Sometimes the cactus was toasted over

FIGURE 6 Fernando Librado, photo taken by Gerald Cassidy (ca. 1912). Courtesy of the General Charles McCormick Reeve Collection, Autry National Center Archive.

a fire. The tunas, or fruit, which also grow on the prickly pear cactus, were peeled and eaten.[56] The western coastal and island groups supplemented their diets with ocean animals, including seals, whales, seagulls, abalone, fish, and other sea creatures. Coastal lineages used plank canoes, sealed with tar that accumulated on sandy beaches, for travel, trade, and fishing. All adults knew how to build houses and participate in conflicts and generally used healers, who were also members of their own lineage. Regarding their economy and media of exchange, Hugo Reid recounted,

> Although money in the strict sense of the word did not exist among them, they had an equivalent, consisting of pieces of thick rounded shells. . . . They had thereby a circulating medium and legal tender to transact business, when barter could not be employed. Considerable barter and trade was carried on between those of the coast and those of the interior, the latter furnishing deer skins and seeds in exchange for money (sea shells), fish, sea otter skins, and soapstone pots.[57]

SHAMANS, CEREMONIES, AND COMMUNITY

Every lineage community had a specific ceremonial bundle, associated with a distinctive teaching about its meaning, uses, and purposes.[58] The sacred bundles provided unique ways in which each lineage community communicated directly with the spirit world.[59] Although some linguistically related villages shared similar ceremonies and beliefs, the details of creation teachings and ceremonies varied from lineage to lineage. The unique spirituality of the lineage fostered a desire to preserve a specific lineage community and identity by maintaining the land, ceremonies, and self-government.[60]

The lineage leader usually conducted ceremonies and was aided by special assistants, typically experienced healers. The lineage leader and his or her close family kin were keepers of the sacred bundle, which was central to the main ceremonies and to leadership. If the ceremonies and songs were not sung in proper ceremonial cycle, the world would be out of order, illness and disease would spread, plants and animals would not multiply, and other misfortunes would be visited on the lineage.[61]

Each lineage community included a ceremonial space or big house. Depending on the place, either the political leader of the community or a related kin person served as the ceremonial leader. For all the lineages within the region, no organization or person and no central government, church, or regional interlineage organization stood between the lineage community and ceremonial communication with the religious or spirit world.[62]

Ethnohistorian William McCawley has noted that

> California Indian shamans increased and consolidated their political influence by organizing themselves into associations that cut across lineage boundaries and provided a regional framework of religious and political authority. Through these organizations shamans controlled the recruiting, testing, and training of candidates and established rules of conduct. . . . Shamanistic associations are reported to have existed among the Cahuilla Indians as well as the Chumash. The Gabrielino participated extensively in the Chumash organization, which was known as the *'antap*, and in their own association, which has been called the *yovaarekam*, a reference to the *tovar*, or sacred enclosure. A Kitanemuk Indian . . . told Harrington that the *'antap*, "the religion of the coast in which they knew all things . . . was very strong at San Gabriel."[63]

That same Kitanemuk source informed Harrington that his people had an organization of shamans similar to the Ventureño *'antap*. "The *'antap* was a regional assembly consisting of community leaders who conducted important rituals and festivals and advised provincial leaders."[64]

"Members of [a subgroup of the *'antap* known as] the *shan* served as assistants to the *'antap*, traveling throughout the provinces and relaying important information back to the leaders."[65] Shamans of different groups, later identified by linguists as the Ventureño Chumash–, Kitanemuk-, Tataviam-, Gabrieleño-, and Fernandeño-speaking lineages, had regular contact with the 'antap community of healers and shamans, ceremonial leaders, and lineage political leaders. Often political leaders were also shamans and participated in the regional activities of the shaman associations. Conflict among the shamans was held in check by other shamans or by members of the shaman associations. The healers and astrologers of many clans met at various intermittent interethnic ceremonies and discussed issues of the day. There were no regular meetings and no formal organization, but the shaman groups were devoted to the ceremonial life and were active and influential in the political and ceremonial activities of their own local clans. Messengers, functioning as assistants to captains and ceremonial leaders, often traveled with important news to inform the various clans of significant regional events or issues.[66]

FIGURE 7 Human symbol pictograph from a Tataviam dwelling site in the Vasquez Rocks County Park in Agua Dulce, California. Photograph from iStock.

TEACHING THE YOUNG

Gift giving and sharing were often done with children present, "so they will learn the lessons of helping others."[67] Boys and girls at ages eight to ten were admitted into the mourning and other ceremonies where they learned the purpose and meaning of the ceremonial cycle. "When they have grown up they have learned it all."[68]

Before puberty, the child lived within the discipline of his or her father and mother. After puberty or coming-of-age ceremonies, however, the child was regarded as a full member of the lineage and was under the jurisdiction of the captain or lineage leader.[69] Boys and girls had separate coming-of-age ceremonies.

As part of the coming-of-age ceremony among the Ventureño Chumash speakers, young boys and girls were given a drink made by taking fruit from the plant the Spanish called *toloache* (also known as *datura* or *jimsonweed*), drying it, pounding it into powder, and mixing it with water and other ingredients. The drink was also used for medicinal purposes, including curing snake bites and treating colds, influenza, and other maladies.[70]

The toloache drink, called *pespivat* in Takic dialects, also caused hallucinations and euphoria.[71] When young initiates consumed the drink during the coming-of-age ceremonies, they were each watched over by a guardian. The drink made

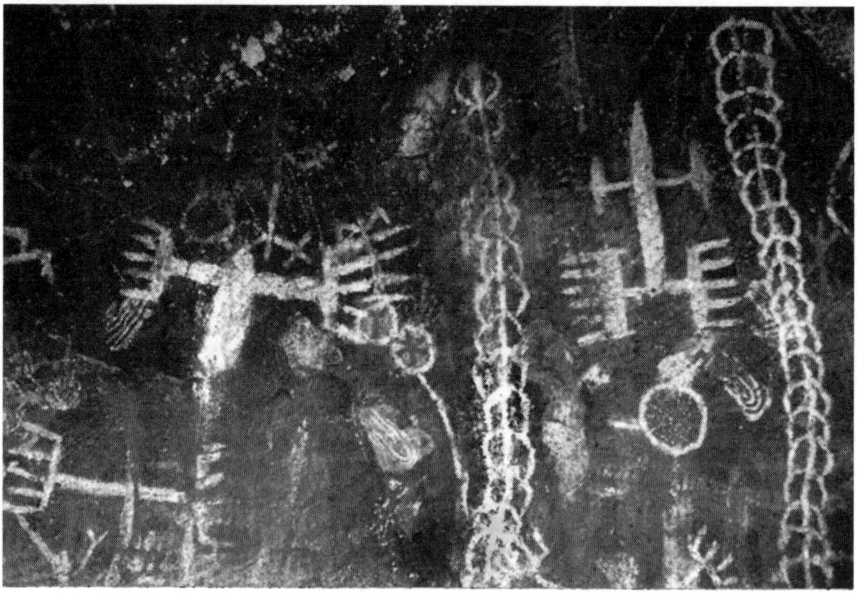

FIGURE 8 Pictograph art from a Chumash site in eastern Ventura County, California, known as Burro Flats. Photograph by Albert Knight.

the youngsters unconscious and released their dream spirits and put them into a dream state where they experienced visions. After the toloache wore off, the initiates shared their visions with the elders, and the elders then interpreted the experience and meaning of the visions to the young initiates. This experience was understood as a message providing the young initiate with information about his or her goals and directions in life. A spirit helper or guardian was asked to provide guidance and protection to the initiate.

The young people were instructed to eat moderately, exercise, obey lineage rules, and participate in and materially support ceremonies. The young initiates were instructed in how to live long lives and the best ways to ensure a successful transition after death to the land of spirits or the upper world. Those who took on the lives of healers, leaders, or ceremonial participants and supported collective community life gained experience and knowledge that enabled them to reach the land of the dead or even become embedded as a celestial object in the upper world.[72]

MULTIPLE SPIRITS

Many American Indian peoples, including those in Southern California, believe that a person has at least two spirits. One is a dream spirit, which is liberated when a person sleeps, and the other is the awake conscious spirit. When a person dies, the dream spirit takes over and liberates itself from the physical body and prepares for the journey to the Land of the Dead. The Chumash believed in a third soul or spirit, which inhered within a person's bones and merged with the regenerative life forces of mother earth after burial.[73] In the Ventureño Chumash way, the spirit or soul is immortal, and if properly managed with respect, knowledge, and ceremonial participation, an individual's spirit will be reborn back on earth.[74] The multiple Indian souls or spirits contrast with the single Christian soul, which upon death departs for heaven, hell, or purgatory, which are in otherworldly locations, according to the life led.

VENTUREÑO CHUMASH WORLD VIEW

Chumash and various Takic speakers held to different creation teachings and different views about the afterworld.[75] Whereas the Ventureño Chumash–, Gabrieleño-, and Fernandeño-speaking lineages believed in the possibility of selected rebirth, there is little evidence that the Tataviam and Kitanemuk held similar beliefs. Beliefs about rebirth are found among many hunter-gatherer Indigenous communities in North America and elsewhere.[76]

The Chumash have a well-documented belief in rebirth. After a person's death and funeral ceremonies, dream spirits travel to the Land of the Dead, which is located across the western ocean. Some of these dream spirits are reborn. The Chumash did not cremate their dead but buried them after five days of mourning. According to their beliefs, the spirit of the bones of the dead reunites with mother earth and helps replenish the spirits and life of plants and animals.[77]

Multiple obstacles could keep the dream spirit of a newly deceased person from crossing the final bridge to the Land of the Dead. Those who had murdered or poisoned people were turned to stone before reaching the bridge and forced to watch the parade of spirits traveling to the Land of the Dead and Milky Way.[78] Those who had lived in ignorance of sacred life, did not participate in rituals, lacked knowledge of the teachings, and did not drink toloache would be dropped into the water below and transformed into various water beasts, fish, sea creatures, or sea monsters. Any spirit that drowned in water could not be reborn.[79] The foremost scholar of Chumash spirituality, Dr. John Anderson, has written that

> the educated Chumash did not weep at funerals for the dead, because they knew that death was not a tragedy for most souls. They wept instead for their personal grief at losing a loved one. In some cases, they also cried in fear that the soul of the newly dead would not be successful in finding the Path of the Dead and would therefore wander the earth as a dangerous ghost (angry soul of the dead).[80]

Guaranteed passaged to the Land of the Dead and possible rebirth were for those who upheld ceremonial life and lived according to normative social and spiritual rules.

A well-educated Chumash person would have enough knowledge and courage to pass by any obstacle on the way to the Land of the Dead, which was located in the west, across a large ocean and over the rainbow bridge, and farther, to the upper world. Journeying spirits began their ascent at the time of the winter solstice, when the sun dies and is reborn. A Chumash spirit had to earn passage to the Land of the Dead and to the possibility of rebirth or reincarnation. Only well-educated practitioners of Chumash culture could make their way across the vast seas and, in some versions, negotiate the obstacles of the underworld and finally reach the rainbow bridge, which they would cross to enter the Land of the Dead, en route to the upper world. The spirits of the most culturally knowledgeable shamans, healers, and lineage leaders and members found the pathway and rose to the upper world and manifested as stars in the Milky Way, the backbone of the upper world's canopy.[81] There, in the form of a star or some other celestial object, the spirit lived on. Those who passed through to the Land of the Dead and into the Milky Way slept in a form of hibernation in the upper, or sky, level. Then sometime, often years later, they underwent rebirth back on the middle level, or earth.[82]

There was a cycle of birth and rebirth. Some spirits—of those who had not been committed to ceremonial activities or had not become knowledgeable about Ventureño Chumash interpretations of the world—left the cycle, so there could be no unbalancing or destructive overpopulation of the middle level of the world, the earth. The invention of death ensured that the world did not become overcrowded with people and prevented overexploitation of hunting and gathering resources.[83] The Chumash most likely lived for thousands of years in their present locations west and north of the present-day San Fernando Valley. They kept an ecologically sound environment and had a deep spiritual ethic for preserving the resources of the land.[84]

A notable Chumash elder instructed, "You must not be in love with what you have, for these things will someday disappear. You are also going to disappear, and so will it be with everything and everybody else."[85] The Chumash did not yearn to accumulate property and wealth. Much of what was owned was redistributed to other lineage members and often contributed to ceremonies and festivals. It was proper to be industrious and share, but the destiny of humans was to pass away. If a person had been properly educated and was culturally knowledgeable, that person's spirit would find its way to hibernation and rebirth. The world would be different then, and past wealth would not play a role in future rebirths. The goal was to be reborn again and again, and that required generosity and redistribution for the well-being of people and the preservation of the world in accordance with the ceremonies.[86]

Among the Ventureño Chumash, some of the main ceremonies were the winter solstice, summer solstice, funerals, boys' and girls' coming-of-age ceremonies, and mourning. All the latter ceremonies played a role in education and action of the spirit according to maintenance of a sustainable world.

KITANEMUK AND TATAVIAM WORLD VIEWS

The Takic-speaking Kitanemuk and Tataviam shared a similar language and a similar tradition of a dying god who bestowed knowledge at his deathbed. The dying-god theme was also shared by other Indian nations in Southern California, such as the Luiseño, Cahuilla, Serrano, and others, though the names and details differ.[87] In the beginning, the god created the first peoples or lived among the first peoples. After some time, the god committed crimes or otherwise the people grew tired of him. He was poisoned through trickery with the help of a frog. While dying, he offered information and knowledge to anyone of the first peoples who would listen.

After the death of the god, the first peoples regretted their deed. The death of the god was the first death of any being, and thereafter all beings were subject to death. In some traditions, the trickster coyote suggests that the old people be put into a lake with the power to restore life. However, other beings argued that too many immortal spirits would soon overcrowd the world, which was a finite place of three levels—upper, middle, and under.[88] An analogous story of the origin of death and the avoidance of death was also given by the Ventureño Chumash.[89]

In the stories of the Kitanemuk and Tataviam, the world was transformed by a great flood. Many of the first peoples were killed in the flood, but some survived by climbing to the top of the highest mountains, where they avoided the rising waters. The first-people survivors of the flood were reshaped into the animals of the present world or, as among the Kitanemuk, regenerated into present-day humans.[90]

Some people became pine trees or oak trees, which supplied food for future people. The pine trees and oak trees were seen as reincarnations of the bones of ancestors. The oak trees, in particular, were believed to be ancestors of present-day people. The spirit of their bones melded with the force of mother earth and contributed to the generative powers of trees and other plants. People ate acorns and understood they were having communion with their ancestors.[91] There is some hint that community members who died sometimes returned as reincarnated animals and visited with their family members.[92]

For some lineages, the burial ceremony included a painted pole, which represented the spirit of the deceased. A fire dance, consisting of a forward jump, then a long step, and then a backward jump, was performed while circling around a fire. Americans who later observed the fire dance thought it was a war dance.[93] It appears likely that when the lineages cremated their dead, the fire dance was related to cremation or commemoration ceremonies.[94]

Mission historian Friar Zephyrin Engelhardt reported that

> if a pagan Indian dies, they dig a deep hole. In this they put a pot, a basket, an otter skin, and two or three dollars' worth of beads. On this they place

> the corpse and then cover it with earth. Immediately they send notice to the rancherias of the district, so that all, old, young, and children may paint themselves for the general feast, during which they serve all kinds of pinole, meat, etc. Thereupon the chief earnestly commends all present not to mention the name of the deceased lest he come to haunt them. All must come weeping. Finally, they burn the hut and everything the deceased possessed.[95]

The Tataviam and Kitanemuk had similar views of the world encompassing several levels and the land resting on a large body of water.[96] As in many Chumash accounts, the spirit place, or land of the dead, "lay across many seas to the west."[97] According to John Harrington's source, Eugenia, persons going to the Land of the Dead were not reborn in the human land again.[98] Eugenia related a story of a boy who had a near-death experience and recovered after four days without movement during his funeral activities. The boy recounted his experience in the Land of the Dead:

> The people there turned their faces in the other direction—not toward this world—and were happy—laughing and dancing and some cried too. Had a good place there—danced all dances. . . . They turned their faces away from this world so as not to think of the people here. Also so that they would not make the people of this world attracted thither so they would die and cause sorrow. . . . When it is daytime here all is quiet there, but that as the evening comes on their activity begins. . . . It was so good that he wanted to stay there, but his relatives who greeted him there and with whom he spoke quite a little said why should he grieve his mother so.[99]

Among the Tataviam and Kitanemuk, the organization of influential healers, shamans, and lineage leaders formed a hierarchy based on traditional knowledge and activities. Only those initiated could enter the "church," or ceremonial space, during memorial mourning ceremonies and dances.[100] Both males and females were among the initiated. Participation in ceremonies and access to healing and astrological knowledge were not made available to those kin and village members who by choice or exclusion were not among the initiated.

Both the Kitanemuk and Tataviam initiated the boys from influential families into a coming-of age ceremony and included use of toloache (*datura* or jimsonweed). Over a period of weeks, the boy initiates were taught songs and dances, and their dreams and visions from the toloache drinking were interpreted. A sand painting explaining the organization and purpose of the world was shown and interpreted for the initiates, and the concepts of afterlife and organization of the world were explained.[101]

GABRIELEÑO AND FERNANDEÑO WORLD VIEWS

The Fernandeño-Gabrieleño speakers[102] believed in a creator named Qua-o-ar, who sang the sky and earth into existence. Originally the world was chaos, and Qua-o-ar gave it its present order. Qua-o-ar made the plants and animals and then formed male and female humans who were ordained to live together. Soon after forming the world, Qua-o-ar ascended to the upper world, the canopy of the world including stars and other celestial objects.[103]

In Reid's account, the creator ascended to "heaven";[104] but that is far too Christian an interpretation. Heaven and earth are two different and contrasting worlds in Christian theology. Southern California Indians generally have upper, middle, and lower sectors that compose one world. The upper world is the abode of celestial beings, the middle world is the earth, and the underworld is beneath the earth. The underworld consists of monsters and shape-shifters and is visited at night by humans in the form of active dream spirits. "They had no bad spirits connected with their creed; and never heard of a 'Devil' or a 'Hell' until the coming of the Spaniards."[105]

There was no belief in resurrection of the spirit or soul. The same words were used for *life*, *soul*, and *spirit*. The Christian view of resurrection suggests that at the end of time, at the Last Judgment, the bodies of worthy people will rise to life again. For many of the Southern California Indians, the dream soul or spirit is immortal and continually moves between the levels of the world, including the earth, the underworld, and the upper world.

Fernandeño-Gabrieleño speakers believed the spirits of some seers and powerful shamans could transmigrate into animals. Seers often were reincarnated as bears, eagles, and other strong animals with special powers and significance. For example, in Reid's telling,

> the Indians make "feasts" to the Eagle on account of a tradition, which states it formerly to have been a *remarkable clever*, *industrious man*, chief of a large tribe, and who, when dying, told his people that he intended becoming an eagle, and that he bequeathed them his *feathers*, from henceforth to be employed at their feasts and ceremonies. Feasts are in consequence held in *honor of his memory*; and great reverence is shown to the bird.[106]

The eagle ceremony was often a prelude to mourning ceremonies, in which dead persons were remembered and sent gifts. During the eagle ceremony, a young captured eagle was bloodlessly sacrificed, releasing the eagle's spirit.

Upon death, Gabrieleños and Fernandeños traveled to the Land of the Dead, far across an ocean to the south or west. Even individuals who were considered quite unruly were thought to be admitted to the Land of the Dead. Among Fernandeño-Gabrieleño speakers, a spirit took three days to extract itself from the body and move on to the journey to the Land of the Dead. Mourning activities proceeded until the body started to show decay. The spirits of individuals who were learned in Fernandeño-Gabrieleño ceremonies, healing, and knowledge could ascend to the upper world as stars, comets, and other celestial beings. When shape-shifted into a celestial physical being, a star for example, the person kept one spiritual identity and consciousness.

Among the Ventureño Chumash, preparation for a similar spiritual journey took five days. Among both lineages, the spirit of the deceased, if dissatisfied or angry, might not want to start the journey to the Land of the Dead and would remain to seek revenge for an injustice. Angry spirits could upset and harm living people, so families, both friends and foes, wanted to hurry them on their journey. The mourners cut their hair and put on paint to scare the spirits to let them know they needed to leave soon and that they were no longer welcome within the community.

Reid provides a story about a child who claimed to be the son of God and argued about diverse topics with old men and seers. "The chiefs and wise men of the tribe at length determined to put him to death."[107] This story and the eagle ceremony seem to invoke a remembrance of a dying-god theme that is less explicit among the Gabrieleños and Fernandeños but more widely shared among the Tataviam, Kitanemuk, Luiseño, Diegueños, and many other Southern California communities and traditions. In the end, the local leaders decided to kill the unruly boy. They believed that burning the boy's body destroyed his spirit.

After the boy's death and cremation, some people said that there was no God, because the boy was cremated into dust. But most Fernandeño-Gabrieleño people said, "No! We have only destroyed his body, for his soul ascended to Heaven (the upper world)."[108] The young boy broke rules about disrespecting elders and, probably, community government. He suffered physical death as punishment, but his dream spirit lived on, and he took a place among the stars.

Upon entry into the upper world, individual spirits often gathered around the star of a captain or lineage. Those stars sometimes grouped together to form a constellation. Reid provides the illustrative story of the seven sisters whose husbands were all hunters. The rule was that hunters may not eat their own food but must share the bounty of their hunt with the local kinship community.[109] Among the seven hunters, only the husband of the youngest sister shared his game with his wife. When the sisters found out they were not being supported by their husbands, they decided they must do something. They discussed, but rejected, the possibilities of transforming themselves into water, stones, or trees. Eventually they accepted a proposal by the youngest sister that they change into stars. As stars, the sisters reasoned, they would be seen from the earth but would be out of reach of their hunter husbands. The sisters built a machine that enabled them to ascend to the upper world, and there they formed the constellation known by Europeans as Pleiades. The youngest husband, who was faithful to hunting obligations and shared his meat with his wife, asked to join the seven sisters. He was instructed to use the machine and was allowed to join the constellation Taurus, as known by Europeans.[110]

In this story, the hunters, save one, broke the rules of sharing the products of their labor, the animals they killed. Six of the hunters were punished when the women became stars that their husbands could see but not reach. The youngest hunter, who shared his food, was allowed to ascend to the upper world and transform into a star, but in a different constellation. There were rules and punishment.

Hugo Reid was well informed about Gabrieleño and Fernandeño culture and world view, and he chose to share that knowledge through stories. One of the themes in the stories about the next life is that spirits of dead persons among Fernandeño speakers cannot be resurrected. Powerful shamans or doctors might be reincarnated as animals, but spirits of dead people were not resurrected as human beings.

The theme of trying to recover the human form of a loved one who has passed away is known in many cultures. Sometimes such stories are called Orpheus myths. Orpheus lived in ancient Greece, and he loved his wife, Eurydice, dearly. One day she was killed by a snake bite. So Orpheus traveled to the underworld to reclaim Eurydice. With pleas, music, and poetry, he persuaded the gods to grant Eurydice the right to return to the earth world. Orpheus was instructed not to look at his wife until she was in the sunshine. Eager to see Eurydice again, Orpheus looked at her too quickly as she emerged from underground. Then he only saw the image of Eurydice fade back into the underworld. Unconsolable, Orpheus wandered aimlessly the rest of his days.

Reid presented a similar story, where a man lost his wife and sought to follow her to the Land of the Dead. After her burial, the husband lay on the wife's grave for three days and nights. On the third day, the spirit of the wife arose in the shape of a whirlwind. She advised her husband not to follow her, but he insisted. The wife traveled south. "They passed over an immense sea, and ultimately reached the land of spirits."[111]

The spirits, who could be heard but not seen by the husband, insisted he leave. The wife argued for his remaining in the spirit land. The spirits suggested a series of trials for the husband to prove himself worthy of staying with his wife. With the help of his wife, the husband passed all the trials.

Nevertheless, the spirits did not want to allow the husband to remain in the spirit land and suggested that the wife accompany her husband back to earth. The husband was given the condition that he was forbidden to have sexual relations with her over the next three days as they journeyed back to earth. The husband agreed, but during the journey home, as his wife's image became more visible, the husband could not resist and had relations with his wife. Since the three days had not passed, the wife turned into a bundle of logs and likely returned to the land of the spirits. The husband wandered dejected for the rest of his days.

The spirits preferred that the husband live out his days on earth. He had broken the rules in the first place by entering the land of the spirits as a live human being. He then broke the rules again by having sexual relations with his wife before the end of their three-day journey home to the land of the living. As a consequence, he was punished with the loss of his wife's company. However, because the husband was a worthy person who had passed all their trials, upon his death his spirit could join his wife's and the ancestral spirits in the celestial upper world.[112]

The central ceremonies for the Fernandeños and Gabrieleños were the coming-of-age ceremonies for boys and girls, funeral ceremonies, eagle ceremonies, and memorial mourning ceremonies. In the coming-of-age ceremonies, the girls and boys in separate ceremonies were given toloache, taught songs and dances, and shown a sand painting and instructed about the cosmic order and purpose.[113] There is very little if any mention of winter or summer solstice ceremonies, but such information may have been lost or not passed down.

THE WORLD IS GOD

When the missionaries arrived in California, they observed that as measured by their own Christian understandings, the Indians did not have moral rules, religion, or centralized government. It should now be evident, however, that Ventureño Chumash, Kitanemuk, Tataviam, and Fernandeño-Gabrieleño speakers had their own forms of government, norms, laws, and views of god and afterlife. Demonstrating their lack of comprehension and the narrowness of their definitions, the missionaries claimed that the "California savages had no Religion whatever."[114] The California Indians for centuries, if not for thousands of years, had their own forms of government, landholding, spiritual conceptions, rules, and norms.

The Indians and missionaries, however, understood religion, history, government, community, and other views in specific and different ways. A Christian definition of religion is "the bond between the Creator and creature, the reverent acceptance of whatever the Creator had revealed directly or indirectly, and the eager endeavor of the creature to praise, thank, propitiate, and petition the Creator for the purpose of being united with Him in everlasting bliss."[115]

Within the San Fernando Valley region, Indians believed they had multiple immortal spirits and access to an afterlife. There was no belief in heaven or that there was any existence outside of the present world. "There are no forces, beings, or places beyond man's ken."[116]

Instead of heaven separated from the earth, or the existence of heaven, hell, or purgatory, the Indians believed in three, or sometimes five, levels of a world floating on a great ocean and supported by giant beings. The universe is closed, finite, and with clear boundaries. The upper world is populated by the spirits of ancestors in the physical form of stars and other celestial beings. Death is justified by the need to not overcrowd the space available in the world in order not to overexploit the world's finite resources. In the Chumash version, the transformations of life and death reoccur through the transmigration of spirits and in some cases rebirth in human form. In other versions, upon death, an individual's dream spirit journeys to the land of spirits and takes up life there. The land of the spirits is in the same world but distant from the land of the living. Matter is finite and is not created or destroyed but transformed into different shapes or beings.[117]

The Indian view of several levels of the world is in effect one world formed by the connections of levels—upper world, earth, and underworld. This view can be expressed as a *this-worldly* interpretation. The Christian view holds that earthly existence is temporary and that the real world is in heaven in the company of the creator God. Through morally good behavior, individuals earn salvation and the right to gain heaven and avoid hell or purgatory. Otherworldliness is a physical and spiritual escape from earth—a place of death, sin, pain, and harm and only a stepping-stone to the real world, which is heaven, a place beyond and outside of worldly existence. The earth is rejected and heaven is embraced. People live to escape earth and to live eternally in the next world.

The absence of orientations or commitments to an otherworldly Christian God or similar deity among the Southern California Indians was quickly recognized by the missionaries at contact. In this way, the friars' view was that the Indians did not have religion and that they lived a life that greatly needed Christian instruction. The Christian friars comment throughout the mission period about the carnality and absence of Christian spirituality among the Mission Indians. "As he, brutelike, only aimed at filling himself and gratifying his animal instincts, the subject of (Christian) Religion did not interest him . . . and that he existed for something higher than eating, drinking, sleeping, and amusing himself. . . . If a man's conception of God be low, material or carnal . . . then will such a man's moral ideas be naturally low."[118]

The Indians of the San Fernando Valley region gave little emphasis to personal salvation in an alternative universe. They believed there was no escape from this world to a heavenly otherworld. Indians embraced the world and its gifts. A person's dream spirit was immortal and lived within the world, or universe. The conscious spirit of waking life disappeared at death. The spirit of a person's bones was united with mother earth and helped to regenerate the world. The dream spirit was a shape-shifter and could be transferred into different beings.

Many rules and laws governed the Indian communities, and the world was full of powerful beings, plants, and animals, all of which had to be respected. Breaking rules, not performing ceremonies properly, lacking cultural knowledge, or disturbing powerful beings led to this-worldly punishment. This-worldly punishments included loss of hunting and gathering opportunities, defeat in war, defeat by personal enemies, death or injury to loved ones, and other earthly trials. However, misdeeds or misfortunes did not prevent a person, after death, from traveling to a land of the spirits, such as Land of the Dead.

"Fernando replied that an old man told him we are all brothers, and our mother is one: this mother earth. He has always believed what the old people told him when he was a boy—that the world is god."[119]

PRECONTACT PROGENITORS OF THE ORTEGA LINEAGE

Later mission records show that Tiburcia (1755–1837) was born at the village of Taapu (Tapuu or Tapu), located in the present-day eastern Simi Valley. She spoke the language now known as the Ventureño dialect of the Chumash language and was engaged in the Ventureño Chumash culture. Tiburcia's Indian name was not recorded. Her husband did not become a Christian and there is no record of him. During much of Tiburcia's lifetime, Salvador (1758–1813) was captain of Taapu. Salvador's Chumash name was Yalasuit. The Chumash reckoned descent and relations through the mother. Tiburcia and Salvador were relatives through their common female ancestor. Tiburcia had a son, Tiburcio Cayo (1793–1844), who was born at Taapu village.[120]

Juana Josefa (1765–1819) was born to the community of Siutcabit. The village's location is in the southeastern portion of the San Fernando Valley and is known today as Encino. The inhabitants of Siutcabit spoke the Fernandeño dialect. Juana Josefa's husband did not become a Christian, and there is no information about him in mission records. In 1797, the same year San Fernando Mission was established, Juana Josefa gave birth to Teresa (1797–1850?) at either Siutcanga or Cahuenga. Tiburcio and Teresa later married at San Fernando Mission, ultimately becoming grandparents to Maria Rita (or Rita), progenitor of the Ortega lineage in the present-day Fernandeño Tataviam Band of Mission Indians.[121]

Leocadia (1760–1837) was born at Tochonabit, a Tataviam-speaking village located in the present-day Santa Clarita Valley.[122] Her Indian name was not recorded, and her partner did not accept baptism and did not become a Christian. Therefore, his name was not recorded at all. Leocadia had one child, also born at Tochonabit, a girl later named Francisca Xaviera (1784–1822) by the friars.[123]

Juan Maria (1778–1831) was born to the Tataviam-speaking community of Chaguayabit, not far from Francisca Xaviera's home village of Tochonabit in the present-day Santa Clarita Valley. Juan Maria's father was named Lenmans and his mother was named Yantuna. Both are remembered by their Indian names, since they did not enter the mission.[124] Like Tiburcio and Teresa, Francisca Xaviera and Juan Maria later married at San Fernando Mission, becoming the other set of grandparents to Maria Rita, progenitor of the Ortega lineage.[125]

PROGENITORS OF THE GARCIA LINEAGE

Zenona (1751–?) was born to the Topipabit community located near present-day Victorville, California. Her Indian name was Purichi, and her people at Topipabit spoke the Kitanemuk language, a dialect of Serrano. Her husband's name was not recorded. Purichi was the mother of Paulina (1773–?), who also was born to the Topipabit community and came to San Fernando Mission as an adult. Paulina's Indian name was Yupjuiban. Most Indians did not take surnames until the American period, after 1850. Paulina married Taari, which was a chief's name, similar to Chari. Taari and Paulina had several children, who became chiefs. Taari and Paulina were progenitors of Indians who are members of the present-day federally recognized Tejon Indian Tribe. The present-day Garcia lineage among the nonfederally recognized Fernandeño Tataviam Band of Mission Indians count Taari and Paulina as progenitors as well. Many members of the present-day Tejon Indian Tribe and the Garcia lineage among the Fernandeño Tataviam Band of Mission Indians are descendants of Paulina and Taari through their great-granddaughter, Leandra Leyva, and her husband, Jose Juan Leyva.[126]

PROGENITORS OF THE ORTIZ LINEAGE

Maria Encarnacion (1783–?) was born at Rancho Cabuepet, also known as Cahuenga, which was located on the southeastern corner of the present-day San Fernando Valley. Her Indian name was not recorded. The villagers of Cabuepet spoke the Fernandeño dialect. Maria Encarnacion was baptized at San Fernando Mission in 1803. About 1806, Maria Encarnacion partnered with a man of mixed Gabrieleño Indian and Spanish descent named Miguel, who lived at San Gabriel Mission. Information about Miguel's background is scarce. Maria Encarnacion had at least twelve children, nine of whom died at ages less than one or two years. Maria Encarnacion's son, Jose Miguel Triunfo, and her granddaughter, Rosaria Arriola Ortiz, are progenitors of the Ortiz family within the Fernandeño Tataviam Band of Mission Indians.

SUMMARY

Before European contact, the Indians possessed world views, political and community traditions, beliefs about the afterlife, philosophies of how to live, and ways to achieve the good life before and after death. The Indian world view emphasized that the world or universe was finite and was a unity of upper world, middle world, and underworld levels. The only place of being is within one of the three layers of the world. There is no heaven, rather, the spirits of the dead traveled to live in other parts of the world. Punishments for transgressions and rewards for good acts came not in the next world, in hell or purgatory or heaven, but in the world where people still lived.

The this-worldly orientation of the Indian philosophies contrasts sharply with the otherworldly orientation of the missionaries and Christian society. The Indians preferred sharing, this-worldly rewards, and collective land ownership. They focused on traditional knowledge and skills, lacked interest in personal accumulation, and believed that a successful transition to the next level was possible for most community members who had command of traditional knowledge. Traditions and institutions enabled Indians to live for thousands of years before European contact. Values and institutional arrangements did not prepare Indians to prefer or enter into Christian or Western civil society.

The tribe as lineage, village, rancheria, government, community, landholder, and ceremonial entity was tightly interrelated and overlapping and for practical purposes the same. In theoretical terms, the lineages had strongly nondifferentiated institutional relations among government, economy, religion, and community. Such a strong and inclusive set of interconnected, if not contemporaneous, institutional relations suggests that lineage members were highly motivated to uphold and preserve the traditionally given and interrelated kinship, leadership, land, ceremonies, and community relations. The expectations within a multidimensional social action framework are for cultural persistence but also for continuity or persistence of nondifferentiated relations of political, economic, and kinship institutions, as well as of cultural order. This framework envisions that lineages will strongly resist the transformative efforts of colonial nations to remake nondifferentiated lineage-based communities in their own image.[127]

A regional layer of culturally knowledgeable shamans and lineage leaders organized and conducted major multilineage ceremonies, shared knowledge with initiated shamans and leaders, distributed news, and gave advice to leaders and communities. This layer of shamanistic regional relations, a loose and intermittent coalition, stood ready to defend and maintain order according to their own agreement and understanding of traditional knowledge. According to social action theory, these carriers of traditional knowledge and beliefs will oppose change to their world views and institutional orders.

Left to their own way of life, undisturbed by colonial contact, the lineages would not readily change their ways. When kinship, government, ceremonies, land rights, this-worldly values, and community are tightly interrelated or nondifferentiated, change requires reorientation and movement in several overlapping institutional relations at the same time. Such change is possible, but it usually faces strong resistance and requires powerful forces and events to make it come about.

CHAPTER 2

Lineages Within Spanish Colonization (1797–1821)

> I have gone through many stages in life, the last one being with the priests. They told us their God would give us our share, but we have received only a G-string once a year, much work, and some lashings.
>
> FERNANDO LIBRADO, *BREATH OF THE SUN*

SPANISH COLONIZATION AND DISPOSSESSION OF THE INDIANS

Throughout the eighteenth century, as Russia pursued colonial ambitions for trade and political control in Alaska and Northern California, imperial Spain moved to secure its claims to Alta California. The Spanish plan was to establish missions to reeducate and "reduce" (in landholdings) the Indians by concentrating them in settlements, to build forts or presidios for military control of territory, and to create towns or pueblos for settlers to build a Spanish government, society, and economy. The Indians, being pagans in need of Christianization, supplied a justification for colonization. Most of their labor and land were to be conscripted in service of the Spanish Empire.

When the pope conferred the right to colonize most of the "New World" on Spain, Spain understood that it could lay claim to all the land within its new domain.[1] Even theologians who insisted on reasoning from "natural law" contended that Christianity's obligation to convert the Indians included the right to dispossess them of and assert dominion over their territories.[2]

The Indians of California were hunters and gatherers who needed and utilized large territories to hunt, fish, and gather berries, roots, and other foods. Because Indian hunting and gathering practices left little room for Spanish settlers, the Spanish did not attempt even a pretense of consensual dealings by treaty, as the English and later the Americans did.[3] Such dealings would presuppose the Indians' legal rights to all or nearly all the land. Under British and American treaties, Indians typically ceded large tracts of land in exchange for guaranteed reservations (hence the term) of smaller tracts for their perpetual, undisturbed occupation. In contrast, the Spanish claimed all the land for the Crown, offering Indians future unspecified rights to property for communal and individual agricultural communities and limited self-government as municipalities once they became assimilated Catholics.[4]

Spain justified its policy partly in economic terms. Spanish policy used the missions to gather the Indians together at one or more local places so they could teach them to be laborers in the Spanish colonial economy. Once the Indians learned to use animals for growing grains and to raise sheep and cattle, they would not need their former extensive lands. Friar Zephyrin Engelhardt explained that

> as soon as the territory of California was occupied by Spain in 1769, the absolute title to the land vested in the King. . . . The natives were recognized as the owners, under the King, of all the territory needed for their subsistence; but the civilizing process to which they were to be subjected would greatly reduce the area from that occupied in their savage state; and thus there was no prospective legal hindrance to the establishment of Spanish settlements.[5]

The missionaries took the land into trust for the Indians and were to manage it until the king provided laws or directives that allocated the land to settlers and away from mission and Indian use and control. When the Indians and missions were ready, the mission Indians were to be organized into pueblos or Indian towns. These Indian pueblos would have limited powers of self-government, which meant they could keep any local or traditional laws, rules, or norms that did not conflict with territorial or national law.

Until that time, the Alta California missions were granted management of Indian land as well as responsibility for organizing the production and distribution of food, clothes, and other material comforts. Friar Serra, who led the Franciscan missionaries, argued that the Indians could be converted only if their new god provided greater and more stable material support than their old god or religion. Both Spanish civil authorities and Franciscans believed that an agricultural economic base would introduce a more stable, reliable, and productive way of life for the Indians than hunting and gathering did. Once this-worldly oriented Indians could see that for themselves, they would be won over.[6]

The task proved far more difficult than Serra expected. Mission difficulties in converting the Indians of southern Alta California into the Catholic religion and integrating them into Spanish government became evident in October 1785 when several dozen Indians attacked San Gabriel Mission, near the pueblo of Los Angeles. Among the leaders of the attack were Toypurina, daughter of the captain

FIGURE 9 Map of California missions, with dates and order of establishment. Photograph from Shruti Mukhtyar/Wikimedia Commons.

of the lineage at Japchavit, and Nicolas Jose, born to the Sibapet lineage and a prominent baptized member of San Gabriel Mission. Toypurina was a shaman gifted with powers, and Nicolas Jose was a ceremonial practitioner with knowledge and understanding of history, culture, and ceremonies. Both were among the elite of their lineage communities. The details of the rebellion are recounted elsewhere.[7] Here we explore the motives and voice of the Indians.

The rebel Indians were captured and tried. Nicolas Jose testified that he was angry because the San Gabriel missionaries would not allow him to return to his lineage community and engage in ceremonies and dances. Toypurina complained that the hunting-and-gathering economy of her lineage and other lineages was disrupted by the resettlement of lineages near San Gabriel Mission.

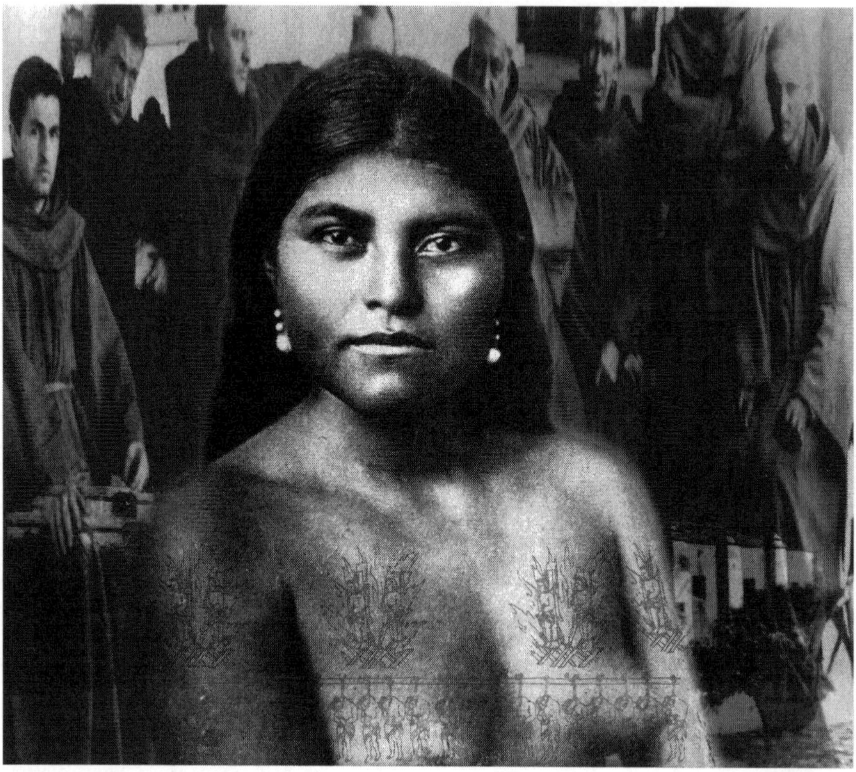

FIGURE 10 Toypurina, leader of a 1785 rebellion against San Gabriel Mission, as imagined by artist Judy Baca. Reproduced by permission from Judith F. Baca, "Witnesses to Los Angeles History," ©1996. Image courtesy of the SPARC archives sparcinla.org.

She said the Spanish did not respect lineage land boundaries or lineage political leadership. "Both [Toypurina and Nicolas Jose] wanted land to live on, and the freedom to move within it; both wanted the freedom to become Christian or continue to dance, or both; both wanted to be able to decide when and if they would cross back and further from one world to the other, and to what extent those worlds could be one."[8] The rebellion leaders preferred to have multicultural choices rather than to be forced to abandon lineage traditions in order to demonstrate full acceptance of Christianity. Multicultural choices toward both traditional and Christian world views were common among the Indians. Each lineage upheld specific ceremonial traditions and respected and often participated in ceremonies of other lineages. Similarly, many mission Indians were willing to practice both traditional and Christian ceremonies.

For Nicolas Jose the dances and ceremonies were important to continue. In traditional beliefs, nonperformance of ceremonies can lead to this-worldly punishments, such as lack of rain for food, disease, losses to enemies, and other misfortunes. The emphasis on this-worldliness contrasted with Catholic otherworldliness. Toypurina sought to preserve ancient lineages and their territories. She challenged the claim of only one true religion offered by the Spanish friars and civil government. The Spanish saw the rebellion as a challenge to the one true religion and questioned the dissidents' loyalty to the Spanish king and government. Both Toypurina and Nicolas Jose had accepted baptism but at the same time wanted to practice their own traditions on their own terms.[9] Unwilling to accommodate a multicultural approach to beliefs and political loyalty, the Spanish banished Toypurina and Nicolas Jose, sending them to missions far from their homelands.[10]

INDIAN ALCALDES AND LEADERS

After the death of Friar Serra, Friar Fermin Lasuén became president of the Alta California missions, serving from 1785 to his own death in 1803. He helped to create nine California missions, including Mission San Fernando Rey. Lasuén, a veteran friar, was wary of the progress of conversion in the missions. "The majority of our neophytes have not yet acquired much love for our way of life and they see and meet their pagan relatives in the forest, fat, and robust, and enjoying complete liberty."[11]

On September 15, 1796, Diego de Borica, governor of Alta California, informed Friar Lasuén that annual elections of Indian alcaldes and regidores, or councilmen, must be held. These elections were to further a policy of advancing the shift from a mission-based economy to one in which Indians lived in pueblos and worked as laborers on Spanish-owned ranchos. Friar Lasuén passed a circular to the friars requesting that they comply with the order to hold elections for Indian pueblo officers. The friars, however, were unwilling to acknowledge the administrative authority of Indians elected to pueblo government office. The missionaries insisted that they would honor Indian pueblos only when the missions were secularized, the Indians transferred to the authority of a bishop, and parish priests assigned to minister to their spiritual needs.

The Franciscans argued that if the Indians were to stay in the missions, under mission jurisdiction, then the elected officers should be subject to mission rules and authority. "The elections were to be considered mere object lessons which were to prepare and instruct the natives to appreciate full citizenship in time; but as for allowing the missions to be governed by such Indians, that was out of the question until the king himself should declare that these establishments ceased to be missions and become pueblos or curacies. In that event the friars would withdraw."[12]

In a letter written December 20, 1797, Viceroy Branciforte ordered the Alta California missions to allow the election of Indian alcaldes and regidores. Friar Lasuén replied on April 3, 1798, that the elections had been held for the year 1798.[13] When Governor Borica received Lasuén's report, he agreed with the missionaries that the elections served only a long-term training purpose and did not delegate civil government powers to elected Indian alcaldes and officers.[14] Management of elections and powers of local law and civil government would belong to the missionaries. The Indians would take up pueblo self-government only after the king directly gave orders to secularize the missions, establishing Indian pueblos, providing suitable land, and directing the Alta California governor to assume civil jurisdiction over the Indian pueblos.

For the next forty-eight years, the missions held elections on January 1 of every year and reported election returns to the president of the missions, who reported to the governor.[15] Throughout the period from 1798 to 1846, Indian alcaldes and councilors at the missions were not empowered to govern directly. Elected Indian officials were subject to the management of missionaries, except for murder cases, which were brought to the governor's attention. The Indians' ability to elect alcaldes and other pueblo officials did not lessen mission everyday control and did not establish a tribal organization or multilineage tribal government.[16] Mission alcaldes remained under the control of missionaries for the rest of the mission period, ending in the middle 1840s.

Although the missionaries and civil government of Alta California would not recognize the power of elected Indian leaders, the Spanish government and missionaries recognized that the Indians had rights to self-government and rights to land under Spanish law.[17] These rights would be recognized in the future when secularization laws and rules empowered elected leaders of Indian pueblos to report to the governor and Territorial Assembly. The Indians' right to hold a reduced portion of land was protected by the Alta California governor.

By 1797, missionaries had gained spiritual jurisdiction over soldiers and colonists living in California.[18] The missionaries managed local civil law for both baptized and unbaptized Indians. The missionaries often objected to civil government and military actions but generally did not directly disobey civil or military authorities. While Indian land was under the responsibility of the missions, land owners and other settlers fiercely envied the missionaries' control and active economic engagement. In various instances, missionaries protected Indian land from settler expansion. Without a direct command or grant from the king or his administrative agents, most land was off-limits to settlers. By 1800, the missions had significant agricultural and craft industry, operated by Indian workers who could not choose to leave once they were baptized. The friars organized labor into specialized tasks, akin to the assembly lines of future factory production. These relatively productive enterprises generated significant goods and services that supplied the missions and almost entirely supported the soldiers and California civil government. Without taxes, California government and military were heavily, if not entirely, dependent on the missions' management and Indian labor.

INDEPENDENT LINEAGES AND CHRISTIAN CONVERSION

Throughout the Spanish period in Alta California, missionaries and government leaders wrestled with the question of how best to make lasting Christian conversions among the Indians. Was it best to baptize the Indians in their rancherias and let them continue to live on their homeland territories? Should the Indian converts resettle at new locations under management of the missionaries? In 1803, Friar Lasuén made an argument that prevailed among most California missions and was applied in the management of the new Mission San Fernando Rey.[19] Friar Lasuén was about eighty years old and a veteran of missionary work in Mexico and both lower and upper California. He observed that for the missions in Baja California and Colorado, the Indians lived in their lineage homelands. He argued that when the missions allowed baptized Indians to remain in their rancherias, the Indians did not develop strong or enduring commitments to Christianity. The more contact the baptized Indians had with pagan Indians, the more the baptized Indians quickly lost their Christian learning and ways.[20] The pagan Indians invited the baptized Indians to continue practicing traditional ceremonies, norms, and values.

Friar Lasuén viewed the mission at San Diego as a great failure, attributing that failure to the fact that most Indians in the area lived in their rancherias, each composed of a patrilineal lineage, and attended teachings and church events at San Diego Mission only periodically.

According to Friar Lasuén, the Indians of Alta California were much harder to convert than the Indians of Baja California. "I know both! Those of the peninsula are less intractable and much more attached to Christianity, and decidedly more willing than those of Upper California to extricate themselves from their heathen habits and customs . . . to let them live thus is thought to be a smaller evil than to let them remain pagans . . . and the result is disastrous."[21]

By 1803, despite twenty-eight years of exposure to the California missions, the Indians were not ready to give up their way of life and pursue the civil and religious alternative offered by the Spanish missionaries and civil government. Friar Lasuén wrote,

> Generally the neophytes have not yet enough affection for Christianity and civilization. Most of them are excessively fond of the mountains, the beach, and of barbarous freedom and independence, so that some show of military force is necessary, lest they by force of arms deny the Faith and law which they have professed. It is hoped that the easy and frequent intercourse with pagans may cease. This has been effected in the new missions with regard to the surrounding savages.[22]

Very few Indians in Alta California rejected their traditional cultures and sociopolitical identities or fully accepted Christian teachings and customs. The Indians continued to exercise traditional political and normative ways and made only partial accommodation to the norms and values of the missions or Spanish civil government. According to Friar Lasuén, the Alta California missions would need another ten years, if not more, to complete the religious transformations desired by the Spanish. The Alta California missions continued to exercise power over Indian alcaldes and manage economic and religious affairs while holding Indian land in trust. The missionaries asserted that the Indians were not ready to join Spanish religious or civil life and needed the direction and guardianship of the missionaries for an indefinite period.

MISSION SAN FERNANDO REY

The rebellion of 1785 at San Gabriel Mission prompted the Franciscans to establish a mission between San Gabriel and San Buenaventura Missions. Those two missions were so far apart—more than two days' walk—that many Indian communities in the surrounding area managed to elude their grasp. Over the next decade, explorations were made and a site chosen for a mission in the present-day San Fernando Valley.

Mission San Fernando Rey was established on September 8, 1797, close to a lineage whose territory was called Achoicominga.[23] A short distance away was another lineage at a place called Passenga. Both lineage communities were patrilineal and speakers of a Takic dialect that in the early twentieth century came to be called Fernandeño.

The friars at San Fernando Mission gathered members from at least four regional linguistic groups in the surrounding area. The Native people became known as the Indians of San Fernando Mission, or Fernandeños. At San Fernando Mission, about 25 percent of the Indians spoke a Takic dialect known as Tataviam, 40 percent spoke a related dialect called Fernandeño, 9 percent spoke a Serrano language later labeled Kitanemuk, and about 24 percent spoke a Chumash dialect, later known as Ventureño.[24] The friars and Indians did not use the four linguistic group names of Fernandeño, Tataviam, Kitanemuk, or Ventureño Chumash, but they, in their own languages and dialects, differently recognized the names and places of the various lineages in the area.[25]

In the records of San Fernando Mission, more than 175 distinct village, rancho, or settlement names are listed, although there is considerable variation in spellings in some cases.[26] Most lineages were very small, under ten people, and often did not have a captain named in the record. It is possible that many of the smaller settlements were attached by kinship to other settlements and lineages, but such information has not survived.

Several lineages provided relatively large numbers. Among the Ventureños and Chumash speakers, Humaligo contributed 67, Escorpion 69, Tapuu 61, and Sujuiyojos 27. Among the Tataviam-speaking villages, Chaguayabit contributed 45, Piru 68, and Tochonabit 50. Among the Fernandeño-speaking villages, Cabuepet contributed 73, Passenga 25, Siutcabit 49, and Tujubit 86. One might expect that the larger lineages played a stronger role within Fernandeño mission internal politics.

By 1810, most baptized Indians at San Fernando Mission had been removed from their lineage homelands and relocated to the mission. Over time, the missionaries built some adobe apartments for Indian families to live in. Children were kept in boys' and girls' dormitories, and unmarried adults also lived in gender-separated dormitories. Some married people were granted a room to live together, but most adult baptized Indians lived about a half mile northwest of the mission, in an Indian village arranged in the Spanish style around a central village square. This Indian village was composed of many lineages that retained their captains and lineage allegiances.[27]

From the beginning of the missions, Indians were inclined to run away and return to their home lineages to rejoin their kin. They retained strong attachments to their own lineage leadership, communities, cultures, and ceremonies. The Indians tended to quickly forget the Christian religious and social ways and to readily reenter lineage life. Needing a break from the mission, the Indians often asked permission to hunt, fish, or collect roots and berries, even at some distance from the mission. The missionaries frequently gave their permission since the Indians left without it anyway. Pagan (unbaptized) kin and friends of baptized Indians often encouraged them to leave the mission.

By moving Indians to live near the mission, away from unbaptized Indians, San Fernando Mission seized economic control over the region's Indian lands, primarily in the San Fernando and Santa Clarita Valleys. The friars also centralized the daily economic tasks for the mission community. Women wove clothes for all the mission members, prepared three meals a day, and performed other tasks for the community. Men assumed a variety of occupations as farmers, shoemakers, cowboys, shepherds, carpenters, metalworkers, and any tasks necessary to sustain the largely self-reliant mission economy. In addition to building the mission church, the Indians built workshops, adobe apartments, dormitories, farms, orchards, and other related projects. Each worker was assigned production of a certain number of pieces or tasks per workday, such as a specified number of tiles. Artisans from Mexico worked at the missions to cultivate the necessary skills, expertise, and training among Indian workers.[28] The friars assumed the role of collective economic managers so they could produce enough to supply all those dependent on the mission, including the Alta California civil and military authorities.[29]

The movement of Indians to the mission and away from their villages and settlements was an attempt to discourage kin-based lineage relations, erase lineage land ownership, and displace lineage leadership. Traditionally nondifferentiated lineage territories, kin-based leadership, and kin-organized economy were disrupted and congregated into land-trust relations and a more differentiated economy that was managed and controlled by the missionaries. Especially as more lineage members were born at the mission, a more unified Fernandeño identity and sense of community began to emerge, albeit without supplanting the lineage-based system.[30]

CAPTAINS AND LEADERS

When Indians entered San Fernando Mission, acceptance into the community required the ceremony of baptism. The friars, according to Spanish tradition, made written records of each baptism and, when possible, included the names of parents, the lineage of origin, the homeland name, and other information. The friars often indicated on the baptismal record whenever a person was known as captain of a lineage. The record gives the names of at least forty captains who were baptized and moved to San Fernando Mission. The friars also recorded many leadership names, such a Mu, Nu, Chari, and others.[31] If a child was born at San Fernando Mission, the friars recorded San Fernando Mission as the birthplace, in an attempt to erase knowledge of the child's traditional homeland.

THE SPANISH SECULARIZATION ACT OF 1813

In 1813, the Spanish legislature, or Cortés, passed a secularization law that became the model for the landed class in Alta California. The act took aim at the enduring issue of the amount of time some missions took to transform the Indians into culturally assimilated Spanish subjects. At some missions, "[Indians who have been living there] for thirty, forty, fifty and more years have already been converted from paganism . . . and should be delivered to the Bishop of the Diocese."[32] Under the act, which applied across the entire Spanish Empire, including the Americas, wherever Indians had been converted by missions for at least ten years, the missions would be required to surrender their Indians to local civil government authorities and local parish priests:

> The missionaries from Religious Orders must immediately surrender the government and administration of the estates of those Indians, leaving it to the care and choice of these Indians, by means of their Ayuntamientos and under the supervision of the civil governor, to nominate among themselves those who would be to their satisfaction, and may have more intelligence for managing them, the lands to be divided and reduced to individual ownership in accordance with the Decree of January 4, 1813, concerning the reduction of the Valdios [vacant lands] and other lands to private ownership.[33]

Indians who were baptized and lived in a mission for ten years or more were to organize pueblos, farm private land, and take up religious practice with the local bishop and parish priests. Mission lands were to be reduced to individual allotments, which Indians and their leaders could choose, and the Indians were to form a pueblo government, retaining their community councils and reporting to the civil governor of the state or territory. This decree applied to most, if not all, mission Indians in Alta California, including the Indians at San Fernando Mission.

Circumstances soon challenged implementation of the secularization law. When the War of Independence erupted in central Mexico in 1810, there was little direct military action in faraway Alta California. The most immediate effect of the Mexican Revolution was the withdrawal of Spanish government support for the territory's civil administration, missions, and military. The turmoil of the revolution led to considerable uncertainty and the absence of clear direction from Mexico City.

THE RESPUESTA OF 1814

As it pursued secularization, the Spanish government realized it needed more information about the condition of the Indians living at the missions. In the fall of 1811, the Spanish government directed each California mission to respond to a thirty-six-question survey regarding the Indians subject to their dominion. In 1814, two friars at San Fernando Mission returned a response that contained firsthand information about Indian cultural and political norms and values. Both the civil governments and the missionaries understood that Indian cultures, leadership, government, and kinship communities were obstacles to assimilation. At San Fernando Mission, Spanish officials learned, the Indians outwardly conformed to the ways of Spanish government but also retained many fundamental aspects of their traditional lineage kinship-based forms of government and social relations.

The friars at San Fernando Mission reported the following: "There are no Caciques or governors. The Indians respect only those who were the chiefs of their rancherias in paganism; and these do not molest them at all, nor do they demand any service from them."[34] "Neither men nor women give any personal service."[35] "They still preserve the customs of their forefathers."[36] "All work in community, and from its products they eat and dress."[37] "All are dressed alike and partake of the same food."[38] They worked and shared the product of their labors collectively. The Indians did not perform personal service, meaning that they did not work for one another and did not want to perform personal service to Spaniards or others. The Indians were not willing to sell their individual labor, but they were willing to work in a collective economy and share in the common production. The Indians, male or female, did not believe they owed service to their captains, or leaders, except by personal and group consensus. In essence, the Indians at San Fernando Mission continued to be organized politically, economically, and socially through kinship as they had before the mission.

Regarding religion, the friars noted that "the Indians are inclined to idolatry; for it is observed that in their race-courses they make a great circle, in the center of which they raise a pole covered with bundles of feathers from the crow and adorned with beads. As many as pass the pole pay homage to it, and returning round about blow to the four winds, thus asking relief of their necessities." Their gods, according to one report, were five with one goddess.[39]

According to the friars' response, the Indians continued to recognize their own gods, and they were this-worldly, looking to the sacred for "relief of their necessities." The pagan or gentile Indians said they have "no idea of eternity, of reward or punishment, of heaven, purgatory, and hell. The Christians say they believe these truths." "They no longer burn the corpses, as at the beginning of conquest; but they still put seeds with them in the grave."[40] The Indian lineages at San Fernando Mission maintained this-worldly, non-Christian orientations.

At San Fernando Mission, each year on January 1, the Indian community elected an alcalde, councilmen, and other positions. There is no surviving record with information about the annual election results. A handful of San Fernando Mission alcaldes are known from baptismal and marriage records, mainly from the middle and late 1840s. What is known is that the mission friars had great influence over the Indian leadership and used the municipal government to organize work, keep order, and mete out punishment. The Indians in their lineage communities did not elect leaders but chose them based on a combination of heredity and ability through a process of consensus among elders and community members.[41] Alcaldes were instruments of the mission and did not have legal status or political power within colonial Spanish governance. Influential alcaldes were those who enjoyed consensual support from numerous lineages. With this support, the alcalde system gradually became institutionalized among members of the Fernandeño lineages, contributing to the sense of shared identity.

The friars' Respuesta response noted in 1814 that the number of neophytes dying at San Fernando Mission was greater than the number of Indians being born there. In precontact times, the Indian lineage communities maintained an equilibrium of population, territory, and food resources. This balance of life and resources persisted for several thousand years before the mission period. However, after 1814, the Indian population at San Fernando Mission began to decline steadily. The visible population decline and the loss of many young children had a depressing effect on individuals, families, and lineages.[42]

The outbreak of the Mexican War of Independence against the Spanish Empire triggered years of political instability. The mission friars were mainly of Spanish origin and preferred to remain in the Spanish fold. In 1818, many Indian men at San Fernando Mission were commandeered into forming a military force armed with spears, bows, and arrows. A feared attack, however, never materialized.

Alta California was a great distance from Mexico City and on the edge of focus for the central government. Distances were long and communication slow. Some efforts toward secularization emerged from Governor Pablo Vicente de Solá, the last Spanish governor of Alta California, who served from 1815 to 1822. Solá developed a plan to move well-trained, more economically self-sufficient Christian Indians and their families near to one of two missions. The proposed site in the south was close to San Fernando Mission. The friars at San Fernando were to provide spiritual leadership to the new pueblo.

The idea of moving the best Indian workers to territories unfamiliar to them, away from their lineages and homelands, met with opposition. Also, it was thought that moving the best Indian workers would weaken production at the other missions. The plan to build a new Indian pueblo town and government was not implemented. Nevertheless, the idea was raised again in the 1820s after the Mexican government assumed control of Alta California.[43]

The California missionaries moved to comply with the secularization law. The missions' president, Friar Payéras, wrote that "the missions do not have to continue forever; they must endure only so long as necessary to transform them with success into civilized pueblos."[44] The Mexican Revolution derailed the missionaries' plans to turn over their charges, however, and no missions in the Americas complied with the 1813 secularization law. In California, the missionaries and mission Indians waited to see what directions the emerging Mexican government would offer.[45]

THREE LINEAGES AT SAN FERNANDO MISSION

The three lineages of the present-day Fernandeño Tataviam Band of Mission Indians are descended from Indians baptized at San Fernando Mission in the years before Mexican independence, each of whom belonged to a lineage upon entering the mission.

Lineage Ancestors of the Ortegas

Tiburcio Cayo, born in the Ventureño Chumash village of Tapuu, was baptized at San Fernando Mission in February 1803.[46] Teresa, daughter of Josefa, from the Fernandeño-speaking village of Siutcabit (present-day Encino), was baptized at the mission in December 1800.[47] In 1810, Tiburcio Cayo and Teresa married at San Fernando Mission. Tiburcio was by occupation a master shoemaker. Since

Teresa and Tiburcio were from two different cultures and languages, there is some question about which culture prevailed for social and cultural obligations. Tiburcio eventually went to live at Encino, where he became a land owner. Such a move suggests compliance with the Chumash tradition where the man goes to live with his spouse's people, in this case the people at Encino. However, the Siutcabit traditions were such that the woman went to live with her spouse's people. People were respectful of each other's ceremonial and social obligations. It appears that most culturally mixed couples tried to accommodate the requirements of dual ethnic traditions. Couples of mixed marriages often honored ceremonial and social obligations of both traditions to the extent possible or convenient. Teresa was active in the church, was godmother to six children, and was a strong figure in family affairs into the early 1850s. She and Tiburcio Cayo had seven children, two of whom lived to adulthood. One of them, Paula Cayo (1813–49?), married Francisco Papabubaba (1806–47), son of Francisca Xaviera and Juan Maria.

Francisca Xaviera, daughter of Leocadia, from the Tataviam-speaking village of Tochonabit, was baptized at age fifteen at San Fernando Mission.[48] At her baptism, Juan Francisco Reyes, land owner and alcalde of the pueblo of Los Angeles, stood as Francisca Xaviera's godfather. Settlers often acted as godparents and took on the responsibility of spiritual guidance within the Catholic community, including the godparenting of mission Indian children.

In 1800, Francisca Xaviera married Juan Maria, of the nearby Tataviam-speaking village of Chaguayabit, in a Catholic ceremony. Juan Maria had been baptized six days later than Francisca, in December 1799. A year later, in December 1800, the two were married. Juan Maria and Francisca Xaviera had eight children. Only two children, Francisco and Felipa, lived to adulthood and had children. Francisco (1806–47) was born at Chaguayabit, and Felipa was born in 1817 at San Fernando Mission. Francisco's Indian name was Papabubaba.

Papabubaba married Paula Cayo (1813–49?), daughter of Tiburcio Cayo and Teresa, in 1827. The couple had three children. Two of their children died in childhood, and their daughter, Maria Rita (1830–69?), lived to maturity and raised a family. Her extended family moved from the mission to present-day Encino (Siutcanga). Francisco Papabubaba took up farming and cattle raising with his father-in-law, Tiburcio Cayo, and other members of Tiburcio's family and in-laws. Rancho Encino was part of several agricultural ranches that supplied food in support of San Fernando Mission.

Maria Rita is a progenitor of the present-day Ortega lineage within the Fernandeño Tataviam Band of Mission Indians. She had eight children and two husbands. Her first marriage, to Benigno, a descendant of Cabuepet on his father's side and of the village of Tusina on his mother's side, did not yield surviving children. Her marriage to and partnership with Fernando Ortega, who was of mixed Mexican and Yaqui descent, resulted in five children, with two surviving to have families of their own. The families of survivors Antonio Maria Ortega and Luis Eduardo Ortega constitute the Ortega lineage.

Lineage Ancestors of the Garcias

The Garcia lineage can trace its ancestry to Paulina, born in the Topipabit community near present-day Victorville, California, and baptized upon arrival at San Fernando Mission in 1811, at the age of thirty-eight.[49] She had earlier married Taari, a chief from her village, who died around 1811. Most likely as eldest son, Kawana (?–1873) became chief following his father, Taari. Later, about 1850, Kawana took a Spanish name from his brother Vicente Francisco. Vicente Francisco got his Spanish baptismal name at San Fernando Mission in 1819. His Indian name was Tinoqui. After 1850, Kawana was also known as Vicente, and his brother retained the name Francisco. In 1873, after his brother Kawana/Vicente's death, Francisco became chief of the Tejon Indian Tribe.[50]

Paulina also had a daughter, Teofila (1799–1819), whose Indian name was Gigiuco. Like her parents, Teofila was born among the Topipabit. She came with mother Paulina to San Fernando Mission in 1811. At San Fernando Mission, Teofila gave birth to a girl baptized as Eugenia (1817–1928). Eugenia's father was Francisco del Espiritu Santo (1799–1830), who was born at Tujunga, a Fernandeño-speaking village community in the present-day eastern San Fernando Valley.[51] Eugenia lived to a very old age and late in life became an informant to the anthropologist John Harrington in 1916–17.[52] Her daughter, Leandra Leyva (1840–65?), partnered with Jose Juan Leyva, descended from the Ventureño Chumash village of Escorpion on his father's side and the Tataviam-speaking village of Piru on his mother's.[53] A daughter of Leandra and Jose Juan, Josefa Leyva Garcia (1865–1952) partnered and bore children with Isidoro Garcia, a mixed Mexican-Yaqui Indian. Josefa (also Josephine) is known to be a progenitor of the Garcia lineage of the present-day Fernandeño Tataviam Band of Mission Indians.

Lineage Ancestors of the Ortizes

The Ortiz lineage counts among its ancestors Maria Encarnacion, born in the Fernandeño-speaking village of Cabuepet, or Cahuenga, in the southeastern

FIGURE 11 Eugenia Mendez, a progenitor of the Garcia lineage, ca. 1924. Photograph by Edward Curtis, Library of Congress, Prints and Photographs Division, Edward S. Curtis Collection, LC-USZ62-115825.

corner of the San Fernando Valley. She was baptized as an adult at San Fernando Mission in 1803 and soon thereafter formed a household with a man from San Gabriel Mission named Miguel, of mixed Spanish and Gabrieleño descent. Among Maria Encarnacion and Miguel's surviving children was one child baptized as Jose de Todos Santos (1814–58?). Jose did not use his full baptismal name but adopted his father's name to yield Jose Miguel. He also took on the honorific title of Triunfo, and was sometimes known as Jose Miguel Triunfo. Jose Miguel was a prominent manager for a farm at Cahuenga that supported San Fernando Mission. In the 1840s, because of his contributions to the mission's economy, he was awarded land near his ancestral lineage site of Cahuenga. In the Fernandeño language, Cahuenga is the name of the village territory for the community of people called Cabuepet. Jose Miguel is a progenitor of the Ortiz lineage of the present-day Fernandeño Tataviam Band of Mission Indians. The daughter of Jose Miguel, Rosaria Arriola (1840–1911), partnered for a few years with a man named Ortiz, but they did not share children. Nevertheless, Rosaria and her children adopted and used the surname Ortiz.

The friars baptized and moved their converts to the grounds at San Fernando Mission. They thought that by bringing the converts together at the mission they could discourage the independence of lineages, but this effort was thwarted by the shortage of housing on mission grounds. By 1810, a multiethnic mission village formed about a half mile northwest of the mission where many families, perhaps a majority, lived. The Indian village was composed of many lineages that had been formerly independent and self-sufficient. While living in the San Fernando Mission village, the Indians retained their captains and lineage-clan allegiances, even as the common experience prompted the emergence of a shared Fernandeño identity, especially among those born there.[54]

SUMMARY

The Spanish aimed for total transformation of cultural, political, economic, and community relations among the Indians. The king of the Spanish Empire sought to transform San Fernando Mission Indians into workers or individual farmers, Roman Catholics, political subjects, and Spanish speakers. The Spanish secularization plan envisioned the removal of Indians from temporary missionary tutelage and their resettlement in self-governing pueblos composed of Indian farmers with access to private and collectively held land.

At San Fernando Mission, the removal of Indian communities from ancient traditional homelands to a mission village near the mission itself was designed to forcibly differentiate Indian lineages away from a hunting-and-gathering economy as well as away from culturally and politically significant homelands with the intention to erase lineage-based self-government, eradicate ceremonial practices, and dislodge lineage control over economic production and distribution.

San Fernando Mission Indians participated in the Catholic religion, but at the same time they engaged in their own lineage ceremonies and religious beliefs. The Indians lived in communities with long traditions of respect for and participation in varied lineage ceremonies and world views that were supported by nondifferentiated institutional relations. Political, economic, and cultural activities were embedded in kinship and lineage relations.

Few Indians learned to speak or write Spanish, so much of the day-to-day administration of mission activities was carried on in Indigenous languages. Lineage participation and relations remained central to the lives of most Indians at San Fernando Mission, where they continued to honor the ancient norm that all persons marry outside their lineage and that each marriage partner remain a member of his or her birth lineage.

The annual election of an Indian alcalde and other officers, though managed by the friars, composed a layer of tribal government at San Fernando Mission. The election of alcalde officers was regarded as training for when mission Indians would adopt self-governing pueblo governments. Although the establishment of pueblo governments never came to pass, the alcalde system left a lasting impression on Fernandeño identification and government experience. Nonetheless, the Fernandeño lineages remained loyal to their decentralized captains, elders, and relatives.

At San Fernando Mission, the Fernandeños were taught to work within a more differentiated, factory-like economic organization and specialized division of labor that engendered greater productivity. Both males and females were encouraged to abandon their hunting-and-gathering economy. Hunting and gathering, however, remained a backup or alternative means to supplement mission-based food production.

The Fernandeño workers, nevertheless, did not experience an equitable distribution of goods or benefits. The Spanish rancho economy and small-scale farmers failed to produce significant surpluses to support the territorial government and military. The missions and Indian laborers became the primary economic producers in Alta California during the Spanish colonial period.

Not surprisingly, the Fernandeños showed little, if any, acceptance of the secularization plan through the Spanish period. California missionaries often commented on Indian reluctance to accept Christianity, Spanish government, or subject status or to enter into the Spanish community. Spanish secularization plans implied that mission Indians should be ready for emancipation from missions after ten years. At San Fernando, by the end of the Spanish period, many lineage members had been at the mission for more than twenty years. Missionary observers commented that the mission Indians were culturally, politically, and socially still very far from accepting and entering into Spanish society.

Christian and lineage world views clashed. Lineage members preferred a multicultural path and adhered to Christian and various traditional lineage world views. Spanish civil authorities and missionaries encouraged lineage members to accept only Christian and Spanish national identities and world views. The missionaries and Spanish authorities, however, had to tolerate an extensive and open ceremonial calendar carried on by the lineages at San Fernando Mission.

Among the Fernandeño lineages, nondifferentiated relations of leadership, kinship, ceremonial beliefs, and now-limited kinship control of hunting and gathering suggest continued resistance to change and institutional persistence during the period of Spanish colonization. Political leadership, community, and cultural relations remained tightly interrelated with kinship or lineage organization. The most significant changes during the Spanish mission period came in the economic sector with some handicraft manufacture and large-scale estate-style agriculture and husbandry and in politics with the advent of the alcalde system. The missionaries assumed control of most economic production and distribution for the numerous lineages that populated San Fernando Mission. Most economic activities were removed from lineage control and managed by missionaries. In politics, the new alcalde system had to be negotiated with the Fernandeño captains but emerged increasingly as a form of shared community and governance.

CHAPTER 3

Continuity and Dispossession (1821–1850)

> When all the Mission Indians heard the cry of freedom, they said, "Now they no longer keep us here by force." Some people stayed on the mission lands and some went home to their Rancherias. . . . It was General Figueroa who took all that belonged to the Indians, the livestock, the land without survey, and everything. He distributed these things among the people and the newcomers.
>
> FERNANDO LIBRADO, *BREATH OF THE SUN*

Struggles between central-federal parties and state parties were rife in early Mexican political history. Liberals, who called themselves the party of progress, favored more differentiated or secularized government with separation of church and state, equality before the law, and elimination of economic privileges held by the church, Indians, and military. Indians were to be integrated into the Mexican government and economy by granting them citizenship and encouraging them to become small-scale farmers. The liberal position did not allow for Indian reservations or Indian pueblo self-government. Citizenship in the Mexican state offered Indians individual political inclusion but did not sustain Indian tribal self-government or tribal control over traditional land.

Centrists favored conservative alliances between the Catholic Church, landed classes, and the army. The Catholic Church managed many Indians within their missions in Mexico and Upper California. The centrists supported the Catholic Church and upheld Spanish colonial laws of secularization that provided Indians with rights to some land and self-government.

The Mexican conservatives predominated in the national government until the late 1850s. In Alta California, liberals and national centrist administrations struggled over the definition of Indian ownership of land, the administration of Indian affairs, and the meaning and scope of secularization among California Indian missions. Most of the Mexicans living in Alta California, or Californios, were liberals who challenged mission and centrist views until Mexican government ended in 1848. Unfortunately for the Californios, centrists controlled the national government from 1830 to 1845 and protected missionary control over the California missions and management of mission Indians. The Californio liberals contested centrist policies favoring the missionaries and exiled virtually all governors appointed by the centrist governments during the 1835 to 1845 period.

MEXICAN SECULARIZATION AND INDIAN EMANCIPATION IN THE EARLY YEARS

On October 4, 1824, Mexico adopted its first constitution, establishing the Mexican Republic as a federation of nineteen states and four territories. Alta California and Baja California constituted one territory, with its capital at Monterey. The territories were to be ruled by a governor appointed by the president, with a territorial legislature elected by the people, all under the general supervision of the Mexican National Congress.

What did this new government portend for the Alta California missions? The Mexican plan for California was to secularize the missions, which meant emancipating the Indians from control of the friars and putting them under municipal government, redistributing the missions' economic assets, and providing the Indians with parish priests and land held in trust by the Mexican government. A confluence of forces, however, operated against rapid secularization,[1] prominent among them being resistance by the missionaries themselves.

The missionaries, many of them Spanish citizens, were reluctant participants in Mexican secularization. The friars believed that Indians were critical for the economy of Alta California. The labor of mission Indians supported the civil government, soldiers, and missions, as well as the Indians themselves. Emancipation of the best workers threatened the entire economy of the territory because emancipated Indians could leave the mission at will.

Missionaries also did not believe the Indians were ready to become independent farmers or Mexican citizens.[2] The friars suggested that the transformation of Indians to Mexican citizens should be done slowly, and it would require decades.[3] In contrast, the Californio Liberals wanted secularization to proceed quickly. The time needed to assimilate was long past the ten-year mark given by the 1813 Spanish secularization law. These Californios sought swift dismantling of the missions, allotment of land to the Indians as private property, creation of Indian pueblo governments, emancipation of the Indians, and citizenship for those Indians who qualified. All in a matter of a few years. Further "tutelage" under the missionaries was pointless and only delayed the advancement of Californio interests.

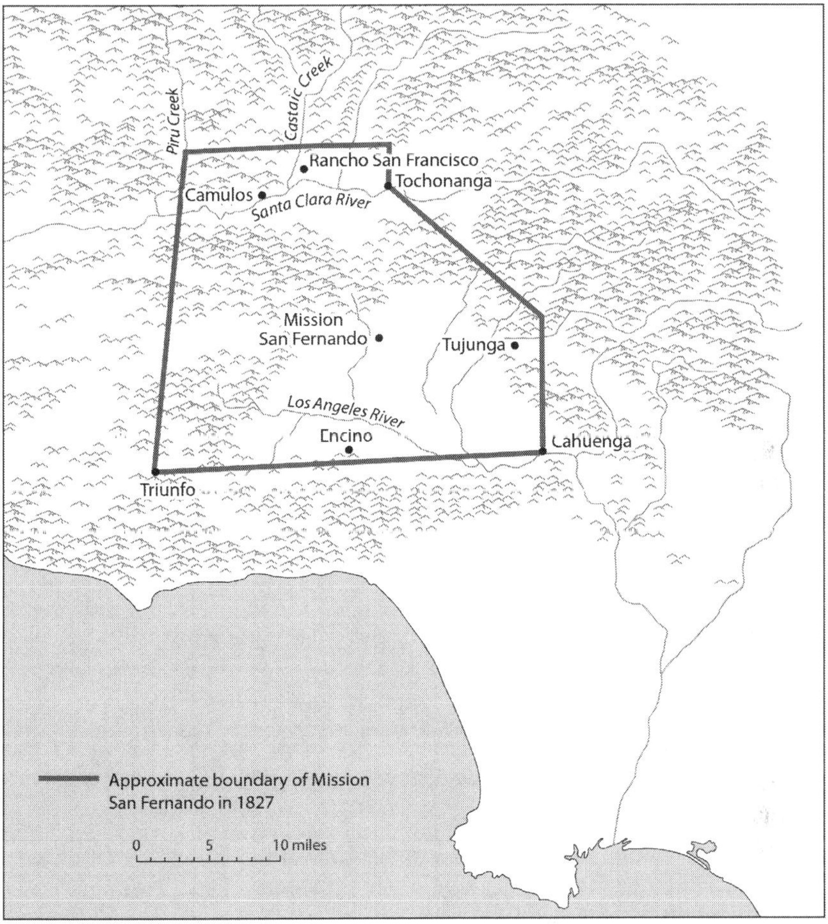

MAP 4 Approximate boundary of San Fernando Mission in 1827 as described by Fr. Ibarra in a report to the Alta California Territorial Assembly. (Zephyrin Engelhardt, *San Fernando Rey: The Mission of the Valley* [Chicago: Franciscan Herald, 1927], 46–47.) Map by Bill Nelson.

Expressing that impatience, Pio Pico, a prominent Liberal landowner and future Alta California governor, wrote to General Mariano Vallejo and others on May 15, 1832. Pico noted his distrust of the Spanish friars because of their actions supporting the Spanish king during the Mexican Revolution and then commented on the condition of the Indians: "What program have [the missionaries] made in more than 60 years with their neophytes when these show the same knowledge and habits as the heathens? And how is the inclination to a civilized life they have been taught shown when they prefer to live in their old Rancherias than in the establishments?[4]" According to Pico, after sixty years for the older missions and about thirty-five years at San Fernando Mission, the missions had made little progress in transforming the Indians into Christians and Mexican citizens. Indians living in the missions still shared the same cultural identities and habits as Indians living in their traditional villages and lineages.

EMANCIPATION AND SECULARIZATION (1832–1835)

In late 1832, the Mexican government appointed Jose Figueroa governor of Alta California. Figueroa intended to carry out a policy of slow secularization and land grants, but the newly elected Mexican president, General Santa Anna, deferred on policy to his vice president, the Liberal Valentin Gomez Farias. Consequently, Governor Figueroa moved quickly to implement the now-liberal views of the Mexican leadership.

On July 15, 1833, Figueroa issued a Provenciones Provisionales, or a tentative plan for the emancipation of mission Indians in California.[5] According to the plan, emancipated Indians had to have twelve years of mission experience, established families, and trade skills to ensure a livelihood. If there were at least twenty-five families ready to join, the liberated Indians could form pueblo governments and elect their own officials, at which point they would be granted Mexican citizenship and the right to vote and hold office.[6] The Indians were to be granted individual plots of land, from seven to twenty-eight acres, and share in the use of a common land area. Any liberated Indian who neglected his farmwork would be given three warnings and time to reform. Such persons, if they did not reform, were subject to reassignment to a mission.[7] A little over a year later, after the Mexican Congress enacted a secularization law putting parish priests in place of the missionaries,[8] Figueroa issued further regulations for the administration of mission lands by civilian appointees, distribution of property, and other elements of secularization.[9]

Friar Durán, president of the California missions, disagreed with the emancipation plan, stating that the Indians would not take to emancipation and citizenship but would rather reclaim their traditional ways of life.[10] In other words, the government wanted the Indians to form agriculturally based pueblo communities under Mexican rule. The landed classes went even further, preferring the Indians as wage laborers without pueblo self-government. And the Indians continued to favor their own hunting-and-gathering economy and lineage-based political decentralization. Very few Indians applied for or received emancipation under Figueroa's provisional rules.[11] The Indians generally were not interested in emancipation or secularization. When occasionally they were given a choice, very few agreed to either. Most preferred to return to their villages or to stay at the mission.[12]

The Californios appointed new salaried administrators to the missions by late 1835. One of the most knowledgeable Californios, Pablo de la Portilla, understood that the Indians would resist relocation as a group to lands not their own. This comanager of Mission San Luis Rey wrote at the time that they "don't form a nation."[13] They were organized by lineages, situated on different ancestral lands, spoke different languages, and recognized different leaders.

The Mexicans, as the Spanish before them, wanted the Indians to reform or, better yet, abandon their own cultures and take up Spanish Mexican pueblo local government under the power of territorial and central governments. The Indians were to gain economic self-sufficiency through a transition to sedentary agriculture so that they would no longer need a large land base necessary for exploiting a variety of ecological environments for their subsistence.[14] The transfer from kinship-based lineage member to Mexican citizen required giving up considerable territory referred to as "empty land," traditional economic life, and kinship-based government.[15] As citizens of Mexico, the Indians would not have

FIGURE 12 Families of secularization administrators occupying the padres' quarters at Santa Barbara Mission, after a drawing by Alexander Harmer (ca. 1900). Colorized © 2014, Pentacle Press LLC. Reproduced by permission from Mission Resource Center and Pentacle Press.

rights to their traditional land and would have little freedom to practice their own religions or the right to manage their own kinship-based governments. The Indians resisted by not conforming to the expectations of the Spanish, and later Mexican, colonists. Many Indians preferred village life and were unwilling to participate in the Mexican government, economy, and religion in ways that the colonists wanted and ultimately expected.

Secularization of the missions over the 1834–45 period greatly impaired mission economies and Indian livelihood. With some exceptions, the appointed managers and protectors of the mission Indians stole the assets of the mission. They acquired "horses, cattle, sheep and other animals, thought of little else and accomplished little else than enriching themselves. It cannot be said that the spoliation was immediate; but it was certainly rapid."[16] Some Indians and friars reacted to the new secular mission administrators by killing cattle, selling tallow, and destroying vineyards. Many Indians deserted the missions, and others refused to work and cooperate. The predictable consequences were mission decline and political and economic instability.

STRUGGLES OVER SECULARIZATION (1835–1842)

On November 7, 1835, the increasingly conservative Mexican Congress passed a law restoring control of the missions to the friars and suspending implementation of the 1833 secularization act until the friars assumed possession of mission properties. The mission friars were to resume mission administration and "maintain things in the state in which they were when the said law [1833] was made."[17] The Californio Liberals declined to obey this congressional act and tightened their control of mission administration. The friars were treated as parish priests and granted a salary.

Californio leaders feared an Indian insurrection in response. In 1836, Pio Pico wrote to Mariano Vallejo that "so many rumors of war, so many fantastical stories, have produced their effect; for the Indians, who were formerly so satisfied with their lot, and who labored with such pleasure, have become bad. Instead of taking care of cows, they kill them, and sell the hides and tallow."[18] Many Indians believed their work farming and raising livestock formed a collective mission Indian economy.[19] Other Indians just abandoned the missions, returning to their ancient villages if they were still populated by their Indian lineage relatives. In an effort to stop runaways, Governor Chico issued a command requiring that mission Indians secure and carry passes when traveling. The order backfired, prompting more Indian resistance and desertions.[20]

Ignoring the decree of November 1835, the rebellious Californio government declined to restore mission administration to the friars. In 1836, Californios rebelled against Santa Anna's appointees, sending both Governor Chico and Governor Gutiérrez into exile. Antonio Coronel, a prominent Californio, later noted that many demoralized neophytes died and most "went back to villages of wild Indians."[21]

SAN FERNANDO MISSION INDIAN CULTURE IN THE LATE MISSION PERIOD

The number of Indians remaining at San Fernando Mission in 1841 was about four hundred, approximately twice the average for all twenty-one missions.[22] Indians chose to remain at San Fernando Mission at a higher rate than at most other missions.[23]

Nonetheless, a major complaint by the Fernandeños was that Rancho San Francisco, located in present-day northern Santa Clarita Valley, was being granted to Don Antonio del Valle. They said that the rancho, which encompassed several traditional lineage settlements,[24] was "in ordinary years the only place where there is any certainty of harvesting a crop."[25] Del Valle had been commissioned to administer San Fernando Mission in 1834 but was relieved of his post in 1837. When he petitioned acting governor Juan Alvarado for the land grant, his successor "called the proposed grant an outright theft of mission lands by a man . . . trying to take advantage of his previous position as mission administrator for personal gain."[26] With the help of bribery and connections, however, Governor Alvarado granted Rancho San Francisco to del Valle on January 22, 1839, without seeking permission from the Indians or the friars and, probably, in violation of Mexican law.[27] The Fernandeños continued to complain so bitterly about the loss of Rancho San Francisco that Don del Valle feared for the safety of himself and his family while living on the ranch.[28]

During this time the missionaries could not suppress Indian social and cultural activities, and so they chose to overlook them. There is no record of the missionaries participating in or materially supporting Indian ceremonies. Such events probably were viewed as unchristian, pagan, and forbidden to the friars. The missionaries were looking to transform the Indians into Christians for the

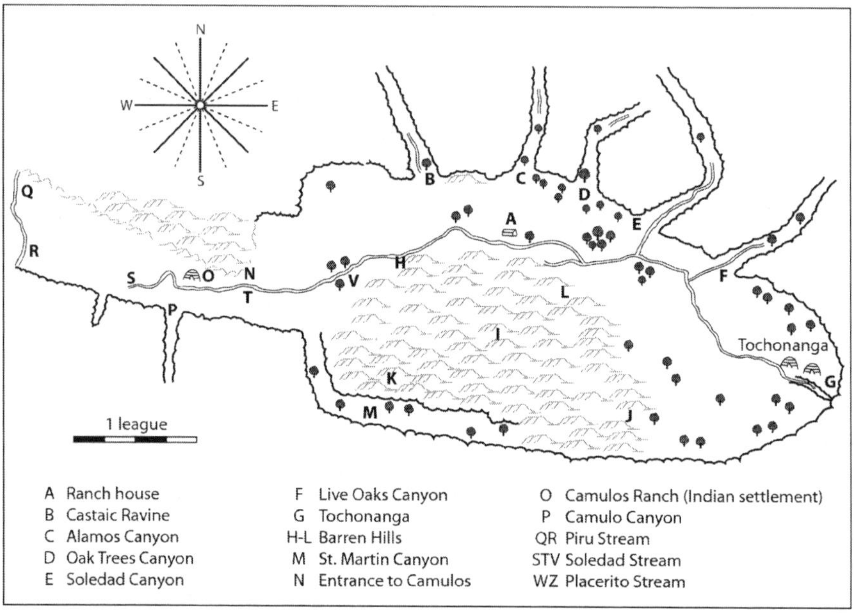

MAP 5 Translated diseño of Rancho San Francisco, 1838. Map by Bill Nelson.

church and citizens for the Mexican state. Nevertheless, the Indians continued to resist speedy acculturation.

Direct observations of continuing ceremonies at San Fernando Mission, and regionwide multicultural Indian participation, came from a variety of sources, both Indian and non-Indian. The practice of numerous ceremonies was reported by Catalina Lopez and recorded by her granddaughter, Isabel Villegas Brooks. Catalina's father was Don Pedro Lopez, the mayordomo of San Fernando Mission, who lived at the mission with his family from 1837 to 1846. In 1853, Catalina Lopez, by then married to Geronimo Lopez, returned to live near the mission. The couple built a ranch and a stagecoach station. The Lopez family were friends to the Fernandeño Indians living in and around the town of San Fernando.[29] Another source is Hugo Reid, who wrote a series of newspaper articles in 1852 covering the late mission period for Los Angeles County, including Indian ceremonial practices. Still another source is Eugenia, an Indian born at San Fernando Mission in 1817.[30]

Regarding Indian ceremonies, as Catalina Lopez related through her granddaughter, there were many regional Indian and Christian festivals at San Fernando Mission in the 1830s and 1840s. In particular, Saint Ferdinand's Day on

May 30 brought people to San Fernando Mission from all of Southern California. According to Lopez, "The Indians had special fiestas of their own." The Indians practiced various ceremonies known to the mission staff and missionaries. Unfortunately, information on the exact ceremonies that took place during the late mission period is largely missing. Likely possibilities include coming-of-age ceremonies, burial ceremonies, solstice ceremonies, wedding ceremonies, and the eagle ceremony mentioned by Hugo Reid as current.

One ceremony related by Catalina Lopez[31] is quite recognizable as the image ceremony, also known as the commemoration ceremony, which was practiced throughout most of Southern California.[32] The tribes, or lineages, formed a periodic, decentralized, regional ceremonial community to perform the commemoration ceremony, an important regional ceremonial activity.[33] Hugo Reid also provided a description of the eight-day commemoration ceremony for the Indians of Los Angeles County, including Indians from San Fernando and San Gabriel Missions. Additionally, Eugenia reported to John Harrington that she had attended commemoration ceremonies at Saticoy, Piru, and San Fernando Mission. The ceremonial ground at San Fernando Mission was the largest of the three. Eugenia most likely attended commemoration and other ceremonies as early as the 1830s and 1840s.

The commemoration ceremony indicates the processes of political leadership. A host, usually a prominent person related to a recently deceased person, takes on the task of supporting and managing the commemoration ceremony. The host invites neighboring lineages to the event. As early anthropologist C. Hart Merriam explained, the host also

> chooses from each tribe or village a prominent man to serve as captain for that tribe or village. These captains, called to-me-arr' (Tomear), must be actual mourners. . . . It rarely happens therefore that the to-me-arr' is the real chief of the tribe or band which he represents. Each to-me-arr' selects from his relatives two or three men (if possible, a son, brother, or uncle) to do the necessary work. These workers . . . like the captains, must be actual mourners.[34]

The passage suggests that leaders could be appointed for specific tasks or situations, and people were selected from the same lineage.[35] In the face of declining populations, removal from traditional territory, and loss of direct access to a hunting-and-gathering economy, the lineages exploited flexibility in their traditional system of recognizing leaders to accommodate changing political and economic circumstances. The commemoration ceremony itself validated and maintained the social and political organization of the lineages, as well as each lineage's connections to the other groups.

The continuing practice of the commemoration ceremony through and beyond the end of San Fernando Mission in 1845 was a sign that the Indians acted on their own world views and did not wholly accept the Christian views of heaven, purgatory, and hell. According to Reid,

> They have at present, *two* religions—one of custom and another of faith. . . . They don't quarrel with their neighbor's mode of worship, but consider their own the best. The life and death of our Savior is only, in their opinion, a distorted version of their own life. Hell, as taught them, has no terrors. It is for whites, not Indians, or else their fathers would have known it. The Devil . . . makes his appearance on all occasions. Nevertheless, he is only a bugbear and connected with the Christian faith; he makes no part of their own. The resurrection they cannot understand, but a future state of spiritual existence is in accordance with their creed.[36]

The Indians selectively adopted parts of Christianity but retained critical ceremonies and understandings of spirits and the afterlife that did not accord with Christian faith or beliefs.

Reid's account suggests that the Indians of Los Angeles County became multicultural. They did not fully accept Christian ways, political organization based on individual citizenship, or the centralized, hierarchical administrative government of the Spanish and Mexicans. Nevertheless, the mission Indians tolerated the Christian religion, just as they tolerated the varied beliefs of Indians in their regional ceremonial alliances. The San Fernando Mission ceremonies were part of the regional multicultural alliances of government and religion. However, from the Indian point of view, neither the Christian religion nor the Mexican civil government was supreme over their lives, affairs, or communities.

Writing in 1852, Reid commented on the continuity of religion and world view.[37] "No standing Church remains nowadays; it is made yearly and consecrated when required, on any spot they choose to select."[38] According to anthropologist Robert Heizer, "Reid is describing here the great annual mourning ceremony (Fernandeño-Tataviam), held in the *yoba*, an unroofed brush-walled enclosure which he calls the 'church.'"[39]

Reid believed that the American, Mexican, and Spanish colonizers did not have a good understanding of Indian social and political relations. He wrote that "it probably may not be out of place here to remark, that this tribe had no distinguishing appellation. And it is almost certain that many other tribes are similarly situated; for the so-called *Cahuillas* have been named by the Missionaries through the mistake of taking the word to designate the people. Whereas *Cahuilla* signifies nothing more than *master*."[40] By tribe, Reid meant what we have called interchangeably in reference to Southern California Indians in the period, *lineage*, *village*, or *clan*. Life in San Fernando Mission added another layer of tribal experience and identity to this traditional form but did not erase it.

FINAL YEARS OF MEXICAN CALIFORNIA: FURTHER DISPOSSESSION

The final years of Mexican rule in California witnessed efforts by the central Mexican state to protect at least some mission lands for eventual distribution to Indians through the secularization process. Local liberal forces in California mobilized against that effort, disregarding the trust attached to mission lands. Well-connected Californios wanted large ranchos, preferably the most productive lands, granted to them as private property. Mission lands, among the most bountiful in the state, were not off-limits. In the end, although territorial governors of Mexico made a few small land grants to Indians, most of the mission lands were conveyed to non-Indians. The legality of such conveyances became an important question during the American period. The unjust dispossession of mission Indians of mission lands—really a second dispossession after the original Spanish seizures of their original territories—would not be rectified.

On November 17, 1840, Mexican president Anastasio Bustamante, a conservative, granted requests by Bishop Garcia Diego for restoration of mission property, Indian land in trust, and administration of the missions by the church,[41] relying on "the decree of Congress of November 7th, 1835, which commands that the missions should be restored to their ancient state." "To this end," the president directed, "a general order will be dispatched to the Governor of California . . . without delays or obstructions, the possession and property, which used to be under their management for the conversion of the pagans, be restored to the Missionary Fathers."[42] The Californio governor, Territorial Assembly, and members of the landed class ignored Bustamante's decree.

California governor Manuel Micheltorena, appointed in 1842, proceeded to grant land to Californios on nonmission lands and to make some grants to Indians living on mission-held land. In April 1843 at San Fernando Mission, the governor granted two hundred acres to Samuel, of the Chaguayabit lineage. Samuel had been working as a farm manager, and he was awarded the land for good services to the mission. Samuel was a relative of Papabubaba and his daughter, Maria Rita, and they all had patrilineal ancestry at Chaguayanga, site of the Chaguayabit lineage.

In 1843, Jose Miguel Triunfo was awarded a land grant of 388 acres at Rancho Cahuenga, on the site of his mother's lineage village.[43] Like Samuel, Triunfo was granted land as a reward from the mission for past good service. Triunfo had managed the mission farm and stock at Rancho Cahuenga from the late 1830s.

In 1839, Tiburcio Cayo, from the Chumash lineage of Tapuu in present-day Simi Valley, managed a farm and about sixty head of cattle at Rancho Encino. One of his daughters was Agueda, who married Roque, a Chumash-speaking Indian from a village near Santa Barbara Mission. Agueda's godmother was Paula, her older sister. In late 1843, Agueda and Roque had a child named Francisco Xavier. Francisco Xavier's godmother was Marcelina, the wife of Urbano Chari, the Indian leader and keeper of the keys at San Fernando Mission for many years. Thereafter, Urbano Chari was a chief at Rancho Escorpion until his death, about 1860. Marcelina was the daughter of Odon, a Ventureño captain at Rancho Escorpion for many years. In 1843, the lineages at Ranchos Encino, Cahuenga, Escorpion, and Samuel's grant were connected by relations of kinship, marriage, in-laws, and godparenting.[44]

In spring of 1843, Tiburcio and his two sons-in-law, Francisco Papabubaba and Roque, sent a letter to Governor Micheltorena requesting a land grant at Rancho Encino. Micheltorena approved the request by stamping the letter with his official seal. The letter is lost, but most likely the petitioners asked for a square league of land, close to 4,500 acres.

A month later, in early May 1843, forty petitioners from San Fernando Mission received a grant of one square league from Governor Micheltorena. Missionary friar Blas Ordaz approved the transaction. Pedro Joaquin, first alcalde for the year 1843, represented the forty petitioners.[45] Among the petitioners were many chiefs and many leaders and elders of now-decimated lineages, including Odon, Emiterio (Emeterio), Camilo, and Melchor. The list also included Rogerio and his father German (Jerman), the latter then a chief. Rogerio would follow as chief or captain after his father's death, around 1850. Another on the list, Vicente Francisco, would later become first alcalde and chief among Tejon Indians. He was uncle to Eugenia, a progenitor of the present-day Garcia lineage. Also listed were Cornelio and his son, Ramon, the latter married to Eugenia. Eugenia and Ramon's daughter, Leandra, is another Garcia lineage progenitor. Cosme represented Cabuepet (Cahuenga), the lineage of Triunfo's mother. In September 1845, Cosme's son, Benigno, married Maria Rita, daughter of Francisco Papabubaba, although none of their children survived to have families.[46] The marriage of

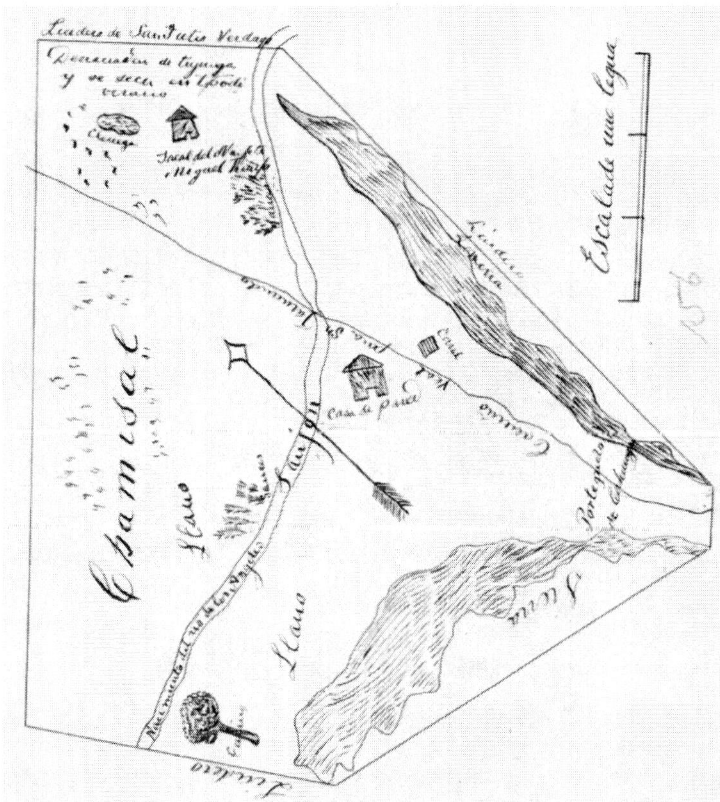

FIGURE 13 Diseño of Rancho Cahuenga. Courtesy of UCLA, Library Special Collections, Charles E. Young Research Library.

Maria Rita and Benigno bound together ancient relations between Cahuenga and Chaguayanga, which included in-law relations with Triunfo and his lineage.[47]

The forty petitioners, representing the central San Fernando Mission site, were seeking enough land to plant for support of their families. They feared, with good reason, that the mission land would soon be rented to Californios. In a letter dated May 3, 1843, Governor Micheltorena wrote to Friar Ordaz instructing him to clarify to the forty Indian petitioners, now joint owners of the designated square league of land, that they could not sell the land. It would continue to be held in trust by the Mexican state and no longer held in trust for the Indians by the missionaries of San Fernando Mission.[48] Both the fact of the joint petition and the provision for land in trust reflect the growing cohesion, both socially and politically, of the Fernandeño tribal community.

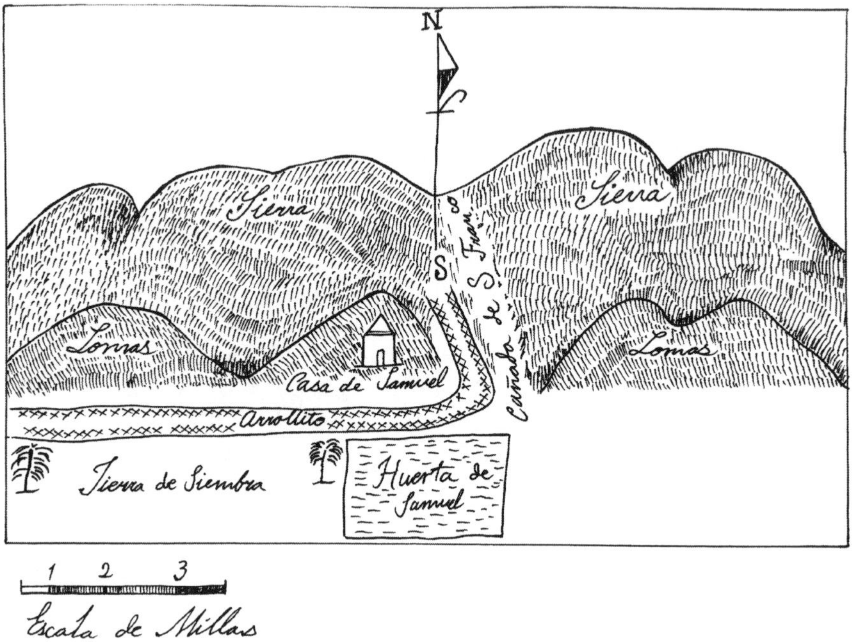

FIGURE 14 Diseño of grant to the forty petitioners. Drawing by Brandon Francis. Original courtesy of the U.S. National Archives.

THE FALL OF SAN FERNANDO MISSION

Governor Micheltorena's measures to reinstate friars as administrators of the missions, ordered directly by President Santa Anna, caused an uprising among the Californio landed class. When the Californios took up arms against him at the Battle of Providencia, February 19–22, 1845, Micheltorena ceded the governorship and left for Mexico City.[49]

Pio Pico was leader of the California Assembly and therefore next in line to become acting governor, subject to approval by the central Mexican government. He and the other Californios, or California landholders, wanted to dismantle the missions and distribute the land and stock among themselves. They were staunch Mexican-style liberals, violently opposed to the powerful role of the Catholic Church in the central Mexican economy and government. The Californios wanted to establish rights of individual citizenship and make land a commodity accessible to a free market. However, they were far from recognizing consensual political institutions or organizing competitive markets based on

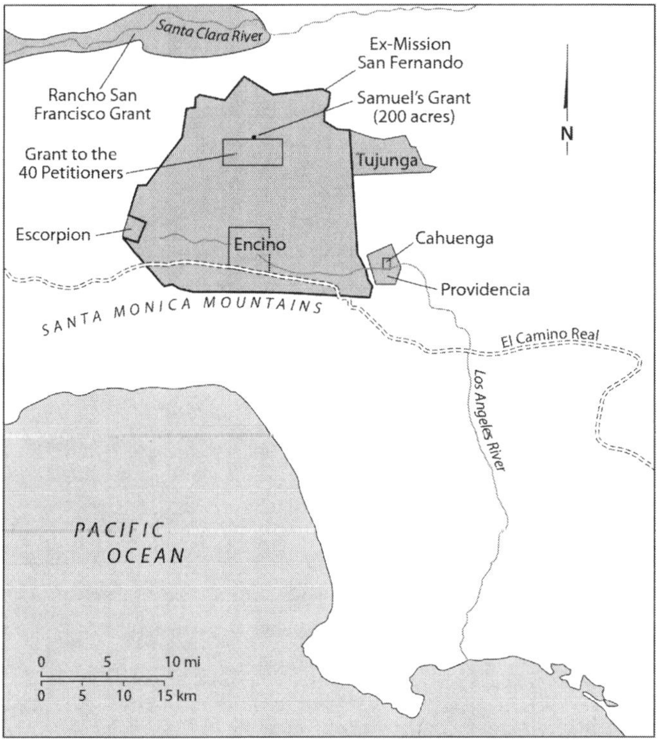

MAP 6 California territorial government grants of land associated with San Fernando Mission, 1839–1845. Map by Bill Nelson.

individual entrepreneurship. Instead of land in trust and pueblo self-government for the Indians, the Californios sought an arrangement of private land ownership of grand ranchos that would be served by skilled, missionary-trained Indian wage laborers.

In pursuing these goals, the Californio leadership was in direct conflict with the centrist Mexican governments that supported a stronger central government and alliance among the Catholic Church, the military, and wealthy Mexican landed classes. Through different administrations with different ideologies, the Mexican government had always held to the position that Indian land and rights to pueblo government should remain in missionary trust until some future date when secularization could be completed. Nevertheless, the Californios immediately proceeded to break up and destroy the missions, including San Fernando Mission, by renting or selling the lands to non-Indians and "liberating" the Indians from mission control.[50]

Pico and his followers took little care to preserve Indigenous rights to land and self-government that were inherent within the centuries-old secularization laws. Abruptly liberating the mission Indians without their own consent was a way to deprive Indians of their land and rights to self-government, contrary to secularization laws—a second dispossession after the original Spanish displacements.

Writing to Pico on March 26, 1845, Friar Durán, president of the California missions, expressed opposition to the government's plan of "placing the immovable property of the Indians into the hands of private citizens" and turning the Indians into Mexican citizens, without land in trust protection under Mexican law. The Indians held protected minority status and were legally minors, he contended. As he had argued before, Durán did not think the Indians were ready for private property ownership.[51]

On May 28, 1845, the Territorial Assembly and acting governor Pio Pico issued a decree: "Renting of Some and for the Converting of other Missions into Pueblos." San Fernando Mission was designated for rent, and the Indians were free to work for the lessee, work their own land, or work for private persons. Article 5 stated that one-third of the rent funds collected would go to the Indians, one-third would go to the church, and the last third would go to the California government.[52] This funding plan did not come to fruition, but it recognized that Indians had an ownership interest in the land. Under Mexican secularization law, Indians could not retain all the land held in trust by San Fernando Mission, but they were entitled to the amount of land that would sustain them when they organized into pueblo governments.

LAND GRANTS IN FEE SIMPLE

In the summer of 1845, Governor Pico issued two land grants to Fernandeño tribal members (see map 6). These were fee simple grants, without any option for the lands to be held in missionary or Mexican government trust. Francisco, Roque, and Ramon received a grant for one square league (just under 4,500 acres) at Encino on July 17, 1845, in effect renewing the earlier grant from Governor Micheltorena.[53] The next month, Odon, Urbano, and the latter's son, Manuel, received their own fee simple grant of one square league of land at Escorpion.

Pico's land grants deliberately excluded individual or collective trust protection by the missions or Mexican government, leaving the Indians in difficult economic and political circumstances. Most Indians did not read, write, or speak Spanish or English but continued to speak their Indian languages. Furthermore, Indian landholding traditions favored joint or collective ownership. All members of a kinship community worked on the land and collectively shared its bounty.

In 1845, Triunfo traded Rancho Cahuenga for Rancho Tujunga. Triunfo and his buyers treated the land as fee simple, without Mexican government or mission trust land impediments. In 1850, Triunfo sold Rancho Tujunga in two half interests, leaving him without land. He moved to Rancho Encino and took up residence near Maria Rita and her aunt Agueda. In 1851, Samuel gave or sold his land to Ildefonso Triunfo, Jose Miguel Triunfo's stepson, and to Antonio Triunfo, Jose Miguel's son. Samuel, who did not have children who survived to adulthood, took up farm management at Rancho Escorpion.

INDIAN COMMUNITY AT SAN FERNANDO IN LATE 1845

Vicente Francisco was elected alcalde at San Fernando Mission for the year 1845. He bore official witness to the marriage of Benigno and Rita at San Fernando Mission church on September 1, 1845, as one of his duties. Benigno was the son of Cosme, who was descended from Cabuepet (Cahuenga) and was one of the forty petitioners attached to the land grant from Governor Micheltorena in 1843. Rita is a progenitor of the present-day Ortega lineage. She inherited a one-third share of the Encino grant after her father, Papabubaba, passed in 1847. Vicente was the patrilineal uncle of Eugenia, a progenitor of the present-day Garcia lineage. Vicente was also one of the forty petitioners, and his participation declared his intention to remain at the mission rather than return to his kinship community near present-day Rancho Tejon. The wedding brought together many Fernandeños still living in and around San Fernando Mission.[54]

The Fernandeños, numbering no more than 365 in 1845, still adhered to political and social relations based on traditional lineages, augmented by a tribal superstructure derived from their common mission experience. Most likely, one of the reasons the Indians continuously rejected Spanish Mexican pueblo government was that it presupposed complete abandonment of their lineage organization. In contrast, Mexican pueblos were organized around individual citizens joined in a single unified municipal polity.

CAPTAINS IN 1845

It is possible to count leaders and captains among the Fernandeños as the Mexican period came to a close. Counting each of the forty petitioners from 1843 as a leader or captain, and including the five Indian land grants at San Fernando Mission, the total number of leaders, or co-owners, yields forty-seven distinct individuals. The captains were mostly men, who participated in and negotiated land grants from 1843 through 1845. Some individuals among the forty petitioners, such as Rogerio and his father, German, were from the same lineage. Others, however, such as the well-known leader Pastor Cano of the Pimu lineage, did not receive a land grant. Counting all the captains present and future who were alive during the 1843–45 period and who were not party to the seven land grants to Fernandeños, there are at least twenty-three more captains.[55]

A total of seventy captains or lineage leaders can thus be counted at San Fernando Mission during the 1843–45 period. This large number of diverse leaders reflects the traditional regional network of politically distinct lineages and sublineages. These seventy leaders were associated with no more than 365 individuals counted at San Fernando Mission in 1846, a pattern reflecting decentralization with many leaders and relatively few followers per leader. These leaders and their kinship lineage members also shared a Fernandeño tribal identity.

LIBERATION AND SAN FERNANDO MISSION LAND

The wedding of Rita and Benigno took place nearly one month before Governor Pico and the Territorial Assembly, consisting of four members, proclaimed the rental and sale of various mission lands in late October 1845. "The Mission of San Fernando . . . shall be rented to the highest bidder for the term of nine years."[56] That same month, most of the mission land was rented in a nine-year lease to Andres Pico, brother of Governor Pico, and to Juan Manso, an associate. The leased land encompassed most of the San Fernando Valley, except for land already granted at Ranchos Encino, Tujunga, Cahuenga, Escorpion, and Providencia. Rancho Ex-Mission San Fernando consisted of 116,858 acres.

The governor also proclaimed the following: "Article 17. The Indians are free from their neophyteship, and may establish themselves in their missions or wherever they choose. They are not obliged to serve the renters, but they may engage themselves to them, on being paid for their labor, and they will be subject to the authorities and to the local police."[57] Pico later recollected, "My principal object which guided me in my actions respecting these establishments was to abolish completely the regime of missions, and to establish pueblos in their stead. . . . I was determined to put an end to the mission system at all cost, so that the properties could be bought by private individuals, as was set forth in the law of colonization."[58] The acting governor's plan did not recognize or organize self-governing Indian pueblos with property under Mexican government trust. No Indian pueblos were formed, and no land was provided for collective and individual trust ownership that was sufficient to support the Indians in 1845 or later.

Lineage leaders provided guidance to families and lineages that were now much reduced, but each lineage and individual made an independent decision about whether to leave the mission or stay. Whether lineages or individuals stayed or left the San Fernando Mission area would be very important in the years ahead because political identity and community continuity depended on whether lineages remained living near San Fernando. Rogerio remarked about his father that "he never went away."[59] The Fernandeños in 1845 were interconnected through marriage, godparent relations, witnesses at marriages, common Catholic rituals and holidays, traditional regional ceremonies, and a common mission experience and identity.[60] The mission friars argued that the Catholic Church was holding the land in trust for the Indian neophytes and protested Pico's efforts to sell and rent mission land. Into the 1850s, the Franciscans insisted that the Indians owned the land in and around San Fernando Mission.[61]

INDIAN LAND AND THE MEXICAN AMERICAN WAR

The Mexican minister of justice and public instruction, Demetrio Montesdeoca, issued an order dated November 14, 1845, to the governor of the Department of the Californians:

> His Excellency, the President [Jose Joaquin de Herrera] has received information that the Government of your Department has ordered to be put up for sale all the property pertaining to the Mission of said department which your predecessor [Micheltorena] had ordered returned to the respective missionaries for the management and administration of their temporalities. Therefore, he has been pleased to direct me to say that the said Government will report upon those particulars, suspending immediately all proceedings respecting the alienation of the before-mentioned property until the Supreme Government has reached a resolution.[62]

President Herrera, a political moderate working with both Mexican liberals and conservatives, moved quickly to stop Governor Pico from selling or renting land held in trust by the missions for the Indians.

With this letter, the Mexican government denied Governor Pico power to sell or rent mission trust lands. Between 1835 and 1845, the California government had been repeatedly instructed by Mexican authorities to suspend processes of secularization and return administration of mission trust lands to the friars, who managed them for the future benefit of the Indians and claimed only specific buildings and grounds for the church. At some point, Indians would form pueblo governments and acquire trust land sufficient for their material necessities, based primarily on agricultural labor. The land not needed by Indian farmers and pueblos would be distributed to Mexican citizens.

Governor Pico received the order to suspend land rentals and sales on April 15, 1846. Instead of following it, Pico and the California Assembly pocketed the letter in committee. Pico's biographer suggests that the order was rightly disregarded because "by that time the Herrera government had been overthrown, and the California assembly had advanced its mission policies beyond the point of return."[63] However, in 1864, during the American period, the U.S. Supreme Court had occasion to consider the binding nature of the Herrera/Montesdeoca suspension order and readily found that it invalidated any sales or leases that Pico may have subsequently made of mission lands.[64] Unfortunately, the Supreme Court made that ruling after the confirmation of the sale of San Fernando Mission was final.

At the time the suspension order arrived in California, in April 1846, it wasn't too late to return San Fernando Mission to trust status. The land had been rented for nine years but not sold. Appropriate land distributions to Indians could have been made and Indian pueblo governments formed. Nonetheless, disregarding the suspension order, Pico seems to have sold San Fernando Mission, now described as Rancho Ex-Mission San Fernando, to Eulogio de Celis on June 17, 1846, a month after the United States declared war against Mexico.[65] The transaction was dubbed a "pretended purchase" in an 1851 article in the *Los Angeles Star*, which claimed that de Celis never actually paid for it,[66] but his title was later confirmed in American courts. This sale of mission land that was promised in trust to Indians contravened standing and recent orders from the central Mexican government, flouting centuries of laws and policies governing Spanish Mexican and Indian affairs.[67]

Lease and sale of Rancho Ex-Mission San Fernando also dispossessed the forty petitioners of the grant from Governor Micheltorena in May 1843,[68] depriving them of their political and territorial heritage under Spanish and Mexican secularization laws. These petitioners, representing the vast majority of Indian lineages still living at the central rancho of San Fernando Mission and the associated Indian village,[69] had requested and received their grant in joint or collective ownership with the provision that they could not sell the land. Governor Pico leased and then sold the one square league (nearly 4,500 acres) of land held by the forty petitioners without seeking their consent or even annulling the grant to them. It was highly unusual, perhaps unprecedented, that a California governor, without explanation, rented and later sold land that had been granted by a previous governor.

Pico argued that he needed to raise funds to hold off the American invasion and to wage war against the United States and that this need provided him with authority to rent and sell San Fernando Mission.[70] The document he relied on, discussed below, did encourage resistance to the American forces, generally, but it did not expressly authorize the sale of Indian land held in trust by the missionaries as a means of financing that resistance.[71] The Mexican government had the responsibility to provide pueblo governments and sufficient land for Indian cultivation. Yet Pico's land sale to Eulogio de Celis encompassed the square league of land granted to the forty Fernandeño petitioners in May 1843. As American forces were forming to invade southern Alta California, Pico quickly sold the Rancho Ex-Mission San Fernando. The sale did not leave any land available within the San Fernando Valley for an Indian pueblo or for the economic support of an associated Indian community.

During the American period, when grantees of mission lands sought confirmation of their titles, Pico testified that he was acting under authority of a document from the Mexican government dated March 10, 1846, that empowered him to take measures necessary to repel the imminent American invasion.[72] The decree stated, "The governors of the departments are authorized to act expeditiously in extraordinary cases, and with due justification to preserve the great interests of the independence and the integrity of the national domain, and to secure tranquility and public order, without which these inestimable blessings cannot be sustained."[73] Governor Pico argued that he needed to raise funds to wage the war—an argument that some American adjudicators later accepted in confirming Mexican title, including the Board of Land Commissioners, which addressed Eulogio de Celis's title to Rancho Ex-Mission San Fernando.[74] Ultimately, the U.S. Supreme Court rejected that justification, and with good reason.[75] Pico's claim that the money was needed to mount a defense of Mexican California rubs up against the fact that the Californios gave little active military resistance to American advances throughout California. Almost without a shot fired, the Americans captured Monterey on the Northern California coast on July 7, 1846. Some months later, the American army engaged the pueblo of Los Angeles, which surrendered in January 1847 at Campo de Cahuenga, near present-day Universal Studios, after several months of sporadic failed cavalry charges and limited fighting.[76]

Governor Pico fled to Baja, Mexico. The meager military resistance mounted by the Californios during the 1846 American military campaign in California suggests that the funds he raised from selling land were not used effectively or used at all. Some authors state that Pico spent the funds fighting with his Mexican political enemies rather than resisting the Americans. The same authors suggest that Pico forged numerous grants.[77] Governor Pico's policies defied the central Mexican government, destroyed the missions, and politically and economically dispossessed the California Indians while failing to mount material military opposition to the Americans. A further casualty of those policies was the Indians' rights to form limited self-governing pueblos or governments.

CALIFORNIA INDIANS AND THE QUESTION OF MEXICAN CITIZENSHIP

By the Treaty of Guadalupe Hidalgo, February 2, 1848, all Mexican citizens living in California at the time of the treaty could elect to become U.S. citizens. The treaty did not mention mission Indians or their citizenship status. But treatment of mission Indians under laws of Mexico and Alta California suggests they were not considered citizens of Mexico until formally "emancipated" from the missions, which would occur upon satisfaction of conditions demonstrating sufficient assimilation or at the time of land distribution in trust and the formation of an Indian pueblo.[78] Until then they were akin to minors or wards. Although many mission Indians, possibly as much as 60 percent, left the missions and returned to their villages after 1830, most, if not all, were not emancipated and therefore were not citizens of Mexico. For the no more than 365 Fernandeños living at San Fernando Mission in 1845, there is no record of emancipation or Mexican citizenship.[79] Usually, emancipated Indians left the mission.

At the time of the treaty, few Indians were willing to abandon their own kinship-based political, religious, and social orders for the more hierarchical Mexican government and citizen-caste society. Until such time that they accepted Mexican government, economy, and citizenship, the Indians remained in protected minority status, waiting to receive the land and self-government promised to them as far back as colonial Spanish law.

FERNANDEÑOS IN THE EARLY AMERICAN PERIOD, 1846–1850

By late 1846, most of the Fernandeños could not survive at the mission. Deploying ranching skills and trades they had acquired there,[80] many sought employment on ranchos in Los Angeles County and others found work as servants.[81] Some returned to their lineages in their original tribal communities and territories and later sought American recognition through treaties and reservations.[82]

The effort to detribalize Fernandeño lineages was not successful. Despite fifty years of living and working at San Fernando Mission, Fernandeños had not given up on their own forms of government, religion, community, and economy. Although they had acquired an overlaid identity as Fernandeños, had operated under a tribalwide political regime of alcaldes and other officers, and had begun to act collectively to protect their land rights through the forty petitioners, their system of lineage relations and captains remained.

Contemporary observers noted the persistence of Indian cultures.[83] In a letter dated October 30, 1847, well-known military commander Marino Guadalupe Vallejo wrote to the American military governor:

> This race of people appear to be a singular race, and although in their youth capable of the best education, when they pass this age there is no moderate way of inducing them to leave their miserable manner of living like brutes, and consequently they are incompatible with our manners and customs.
>
> The young Indians seeing this example are naturally included to their customs, and it is very difficult to break them of the habits which they have practiced in their tender age and the attraction toward them is irresistible. . . . I, governor, have been for many years the protector of this singular, unhappy, and degraded race.[84]

Vallejo recounted the failure of missionary and Mexican policies to fully assimilate Indians into the Catholic religion and Mexican government and society, recommending use of force if necessary. "In spite of my vigilance and profound meditations, I have no other (solution) but rigor."[85] Vallejo suggested prison for Indian wrongdoers, public labor for prisoners, elected Indian alcaldes to keep the local peace, special cavalry units assigned solely to keep order among the Indians, and the rounding up of seditious Indians.

Many Fernandeños returned to their traditional homelands and lineages. Some quickly became recognized as leaders.[86] Their experiences and contact with Spaniards, Mexicans, and now Americans enabled them to move quickly to leadership roles in their own lineage groups. In 1959, the Indian Claims Commission found, "At any rate, we gather from the evidence that with few exceptions no tribelet voluntarily completely abandoned its tribal home and upon secularization many, if not a majority, of the missionized Indians returned to their ancient habitats."[87]

As the mission system crumbled, the Fernandeños maintained their own lineage communities, leadership patterns, and religion, which had never been destroyed. Even as they were required to participate in Christian and Mexican practices, Fernandeño lineages remained part of a regional network of ceremonial and other relations that long predated arrival of the missions. Baptisms, godparenting, kinship ties, and commemoration ceremonies continued to strengthen and formalize relations among and ties within the lineages and the Fernandeño tribal community. San Fernando Mission Indians still mostly married other mission Indians, upholding their kinship rules by marrying outside their lineage communities as they had done before the mission period.

At this same time, the vast majority of Fernandeños continued to speak Indian languages. Most did not speak Spanish well, and few could read and write in that language. Virtually none of the San Fernando Mission Indians spoke or were literate in English. The friars did not educate Indians at all, let alone for citizenship, and most Fernandeños were not eager to participate as citizens in either Mexican or American political life, about which they knew very little.

After 1846, the Fernandeño community consisted of those Indians who chose to remain and live in the San Fernando Mission area, maintaining friendly social and ceremonial relations with other local kinship groups. The U.S. census of 1850 identified many Indians living in the San Fernando Valley. However, only 113 can be identified by name and traced in the baptismal, marriage, and death records of San Fernando Mission. Many others went to live and work for ranchos or returned to their nonmission family lineages in the mountains or to Ranchos Escorpion and Encino, which were still owned by Fernandeños.

CALIFORNIA CONSTITUTIONAL CONVENTION

By December 1848, it was clear to those in California that the U.S. Congress could not agree quickly on creating a territorial government. The Californians and military government moved to organize a state constitutional convention, called for from September 1 to October 13, 1849. The growing population of American citizens, especially in Northern California, wanted a system of laws and government similar to American states.[88] Under the Mexican governing arrangement of a governor, a small assembly, and local alcaldes, markets and law had never developed. Debts and contracts went unenforced and clear title to land could not be acquired. Individual security was not guaranteed as there was a constant flow of murders, robberies, and other outrages.[89] The new constitution would protect and enforce property and contract rights, introducing a system of local property taxation sufficient to support a proper legal system.

Although the Indian population was at least one-third the entire population of California, Indians were not represented at the Constitutional Convention nor were they parties to the California constitution. Only a few of the elected convention delegates, such as Hugo Reid from Los Angeles, were familiar with Indian affairs or cultures.

The convention granted voting rights to white male citizens of the United States, disenfranchising women and Indians who had become American citizens by virtue of their Mexican citizenship. Of course, most mission Indians were not Mexican citizens, as only a small number were emancipated or held private land.[90] Indians were not granted citizenship or voting rights in the new California government. Several members of the California Constitutional Convention thought, in terms of voting and citizenship, the mission Indians "had not been dealt with fairly."[91]

Although Indians were practically excluded from participation in the Constitutional Convention, most still preferred their own political, economic, and cultural ways of life. Indians voted with their feet, returning to their villages whenever possible. As in the Spanish and Mexican colonial periods, the gulf separating cultural, political, and territorial understandings held by the California Indians and the new California government and community remained vast. The Indians faced a government and society that at best was bent on transforming them into free laborers and at worst was committed to exterminating them.[92] As far as possible, most Indian lineages resisted the new government by holding on to their cultures, communities, and identities, including new tribal identities developed at the mission, such as Fernandeño.

For California Indians, the new state constitution brought competitive markets, the English language, American laws and political institutions, property taxation, and no voting rights. Mission Indians had rights under Spanish Mexican secularization laws for a share of trust-protected land and self-government. However, it was not immediately clear how the new California government and society would address their rights. Most Indians were considered culturally incompatible with the new California government and society, still strongly adhering to their kinship, ceremonies, and hunting-and-gathering ways. Some legislators, a minority, realized that Indians had long-standing traditions and social political orders that would persist into the foreseeable future.[93] These legislators advocated for respect for Indian social organization and integration of Indian labor into the California economy. A majority, however, wanted to eliminate culturally nonconforming Indians from the state through removal or more violent means.[94]

SUMMARY

The Mexican period features a continuing struggle between conservative centrists and liberals. The centrists supported the missionaries and offered the Spanish version of secularization, which meant keeping California Indians in missions until they were ready to accept a new system. Under this version of secularization, individual Indians would be granted farming land and political membership in pueblos where they could practice self-government within Mexican territorial and central authorities. The liberal Mexican alternative featured quick transformation of the Indians into farmers on private property or wage laborers, coupled with a grant of citizenship.

Neither centrist nor liberal plans gained broad support from the California Indians generally or from those at San Fernando Mission. The centrist secularization plans held out hope for land and self-government. However, the land usually was not located in areas of traditional meaning for the Indians. And the proposed Mexican pueblo governments did not recognize the lineage captains' power and government. The Mexicans proposed pueblo governments where kinship was differentiated from government organization and where elected officers represented the entire body politic as individuals rather than as their own lineages. The early Spanish and mission attempts to create centralized tribal government succeeded only insofar as preexisting lineage leaders and communities consented to incorporate them. The long tradition of voluntary coalitions of lineages provided a foundation for broader Fernandeño identity and collective action.

The Mexican liberal plan for liberating Indians at San Fernando Mission was no more appealing to the Fernandeños. Mexican citizenship forcibly differentiated Indians from collective tribal land, traditional spiritual life, and lineage government. Mexico was a Roman Catholic nation-state and citizenship required Catholic membership. The lineage captains, however, were knowledgeable about traditional history and ceremonies.

The nondifferentiated political, spiritual, and kinship relations of Fernandeños and their leaders were not acceptable to either political branch of the Mexicans. For Mexican centrists, Indian pueblo governments had to be secular and not dominated by kinship. For liberals, land had to be individually owned and not collectively owned, as in lineage-based communities. Religion was also a problem. For both Mexican political parties, religion had to be Roman Catholic. Although the Fernandeños knew how to practice Catholicism, they retained their traditional ceremonies as well.

Most Fernandeño and California Indians did not openly favor the centrist or liberal secularization plans. In the early 1830s, the emancipation law laid out strict rules for individual emancipation. Few mission Indians were individually emancipated. However, about half of the California mission Indians, including San Fernando Mission Indians, decided to leave their mission and return to their home villages. Missionaries and Californio liberals were puzzled by the significant movement to return to home lineages. Some Californio liberals had begun to believe that the mission Indians, even after several decades of mission life, would reject their lineage traditions and fully accept Mexican or American citizenship.

The Indians who left the missions returned to and took up life in their home villages. These villages remained relatively nondifferentiated. Captains, lineages, ceremonies, and a hunting-and-gathering economy were all tightly interrelated and continued to reign in the "wild" Indian homelands. Most returning Indians sought life without direct Mexican control and carried with them a modified lineage economy. They brought new skills to their homelands, with the ability to farm, participate in seasonal rancho employment, and hand manufacture some goods. Nevertheless, with some economic innovations, the returning Indians reentered lineages with overlapping nondifferentiated institutional forms of kinship, government, spirituality, and economy.

At San Fernando Mission, lineages remained forcibly differentiated from traditional homelands and places. Economic relations were managed by missionaries and alcalde leadership and other officers. Nonetheless, numerous lineages continued with captains, traditional ceremonial life, mission economy, and lineage-based community. They adopted and practiced the Catholic religion but generally did not abandon their own traditional world views and ceremonies. Cultural, political, and kinship relations remained nondifferentiated and persistent, though overlaid with a collective Fernandeño identity and tribal organization.

After San Fernando Mission closed, the much-reduced number of former mission Indians, hardly more than one hundred, used their acquired work skills to supplement hunting-and-gathering economies and to enter into seasonal and wage-labor agricultural work on American farms and ranches. The nondifferentiation of captains, world view, and lineage remained in adapted form, modified to incorporate the new Fernandeño identity that built on traditions of interlineage relations.

CHAPTER 4

Statehood to Eviction (1850–1885)

> Some people had the idea that liquor killed most of our Indians. But it is entirely a mistake. Lots of them never drank at all, and few had anything to sell or trade for liquor, because all of their possessions, game, land, and foodstuffs were taken away from them without pay.
>
> FERNANDO LIBRADO, *BREATH OF THE SUN*

Only two years after the Treaty of Guadalupe Hidalgo ended war with Mexico, the U.S. Congress granted statehood to California in 1850, dispensing with the standard prerequisite of territorial status. National controversy over slavery prompted the haste. California was admitted to the Union as a supposedly "free" state under the Compromise of 1850. For the Indians of San Fernando, however, this label was a travesty. For them, the shift of colonial authority from Alta California, Mexico, to the U.S. state of California launched an era of disenfranchisement, further dispossession, and discrimination. State-sponsored murderous rampages against Indians did not occur as widely in Southern California as they did in the northern part of the state, but there were Indian slave markets in Los Angeles, mocking the state's claim to be "free." Moreover, American economic designs on Southern California portended a major shift from large ranchos to smaller farms and urban development, threatening, and ultimately ending, Indian landholdings in coveted regions such as the San Fernando Valley.

Both Indian land rights in trust under Spanish Mexican secularization laws and the small number of Indian land grants in fee slipped from the Indians' grasp. In 1875, special U.S. commissioner Charles Wetmore, appointed to report on the condition of mission Indians, wrote, "When [the Mission Indians'] lands became valuable and coveted by whites, they were speedily made paupers and vagrants to accommodate the white brother whose laws had been promised for their protection and improvement. . . . They have begged in vain for legal rights."[1] He included in this indictment the Indians of "Mission San Fernando Rey, September 8, 1797."[2]

Facing down this law-driven catastrophe, the Fernandeño lineages struggled to maintain their territorial, social, and political ties. For example, marriage patterns, and therefore lineage identities, now coupled with a broader Fernandeño identity, adapted to the new challenges of population and land loss. Normally, when two persons from matrilineal Ventureño-speaking lineages married, the children belonged to the mother's lineage. Among the patrilineal Takic speakers, when both marriage partners were Takic speakers the children belonged to the father's lineage. In the case of a mixed marriage, when the marriage partners were from different matrilineal and patrilineal traditions, complications arose. If a Ventureño woman married a Takic-speaking man, both traditions claimed the child, and some resolution had to be negotiated between the lineages. If a Ventureño man married a Takic-speaking woman, the child belonged to neither lineage. In such cases, the practice was for the parents to honor both lineages for ceremonial participation and lineage membership. Mixed marriages were known from traditional times and probably increased during the mission period. At the mission, the various lineages were in much closer proximity than when they lived in their traditional homelands.

The parents of captain Rogerio Rocha, one of the forty petitioners, provide an interesting example of a mixed marriage. Rogerio's father was a captain from the Ventureño-speaking lineage of Quimishag, and his mother was from the village of Tujunga, a Takic-speaking lineage. Nevertheless, Rogerio participated in both lineages. Rogerio succeeded his father as captain of the Quimishag lineage and was very influential among the Tujuabit.[3]

The Spanish, Mexicans, and Americans introduced a system of bilateral kinship relations, with the children belonging to both the mother's and father's families. During and before the mission, marriage to non-Indians had been almost unknown. After the end of San Fernando Mission in 1845, Indians came in contact with and married Americans (including ethnically Mexican Americans), especially as the pool of Indian marriage partners declined because of epidemics, natural disasters, and dislocation. When a Mexican American or other American man or woman married a former San Fernando Mission Indian, the children belonged to both parents. Adapting to this new system, the lineages began treating their children, who were blood descendants of the lineage of the Indian mother or father, as members of that Indian parent's lineage. Because Fernandeño tribal lineage membership required a direct blood tie to the lineage ancestors, the non-Indian parent was excluded. Thus, Fernandeño lineages continued to understand themselves as distinct entities and to enforce membership rules as modified to fit the new harsh realities.

A CROSSROADS OF LEGAL SYSTEMS

Supporting the assault on the Fernandeños was a new legal regime connected to American and California rule. The mission system that Mexico inherited from Spain had both exploited the Indians and provided a measure of rights and protections tied to conversion and forced assimilation. Those rights included allocations of mission lands in trust for individual and collective use and municipal rights of self-government as pueblos subject to Mexican law. Mexican law conferred some semblances of citizenship on the small number of former mission Indians who had become emancipated, and briefly espoused universal citizenship, regardless of race or indigeneity. The short-lived period of Indian citizenship and equality offered scant material benefit to Indians. The trope of Indians as citizens, however, would be used by the Americans and Californios to commodify the land and ignore Mexican colonial law, which upheld Indian self-government and claims to modest amounts of land.[4] The Indians' rights to occupation and future ownership of former mission lands were jeopardized as greedy and corrupt governors sold those very lands to their cronies, almost certainly in violation of Mexican law.[5] Mexican authorities also made limited grants of tracts in the Ex-Mission, Encino, Escorpion, and Tujunga ranchos to important figures in Fernandeño lineages, but the Ex-Mission grant was conveniently disregarded by later gubernatorial rental and sale of the same land to non-Indians. And the land that was granted to individual Indians was not granted as "collective Indian property" but as private property and therefore without trust protection by the missionaries or the Mexican California territorial government.

California statehood displaced the Mexican system, leaving only those rights protected under the Treaty of Guadalupe Hidalgo. The results for Fernandeños and other mission Indians were disastrous. Even though the treaty promised American citizenship to Mexican citizens, including at least some emancipated Indians, California proceeded to include in its first constitution a provision limiting the vote to "white male citizens."[6] A statute enacted shortly thereafter criminalized Indian "vagrancy" and prohibited Indians from testifying in legal proceedings. To secure a cheap workforce, authorities in the Los Angeles area arrested Indians for "intemperance" that was tolerated in the whites, and allowed landowners to "purchase" their release in exchange for their labor[7]—hence the acknowledgment at that time of "Indian slave marts."[8]

Indian land rights fared no better than Indian citizenship under American and California law.[9] In theory, tribal lands should have been at least as securely protected under the new system. The U.S. Supreme Court, in some of its earliest decisions, had upheld Indians' federally protected possessory rights (known as "Indian title" or "aboriginal title") to their ancestral lands.[10] According to the Supreme Court, tribes could lose those rights only by ceding their lands in a treaty, voluntarily abandoning them, or being defeated in a "just war." It was unclear whether Spanish or Mexican colonial law offered even this limited guarantee, although it did offer the prospect of distributions of land in trust, carved out of lands of the missions where Indians labored. Furthermore, the U.S. treaty with Mexico had promised that "property of every kind, now belonging to Mexicans . . . shall be inviolably respected. The present owners, the heirs of these, and all Mexicans who may hereafter acquire said property by contract, shall enjoy with respect to it guarantees equally ample as if the same belonged to citizens of the United States." Thus, any grants made by the Mexican government that included protections for Indian occupancy, as well as any grants to Indians individually or for the benefit of their lineages, should have remained valid and received protection by the U.S. courts. Furthermore, mission lands that were unlawfully granted to non-Indians and never properly taken out of trust should have been treated as still belonging, at least partly, to the Indians for whom they had been maintained.

Not only federal law but also state law purported to extend protection to Indian land rights. In its first year of statehood, the California legislature passed An Act for the Government and Protection of Indians, which recognized Indians' rights on rancho lands previously granted by the Mexican government. Under section 2 of that act,

> persons and proprietors of lands on which Indians are residing shall permit such Indians peaceably to reside on such lands, unmolested in the pursuit of their usual avocations for the maintenance of themselves and their families; provided the white person or proprietor in possession of such lands may apply to a Justice of the Peace in the Township where the Indians reside, to set off to such Indians a certain amount of land, and, on such application, the Justice shall set off a sufficient amount of land for the necessary wants of such Indians, including the site of their village or residence, if they so prefer it, and in no case shall such selection be made to the prejudice of such Indians; nor shall they be forced to abandon their homes or villages where they have resided for a number of years; and either party feeling themselves aggrieved can appeal to the county court from the decision of justice, and then, when divided, a record shall be made of the lands so set off in the court so dividing them; and the Indians shall be permitted to remain thereon until otherwise provided for.[11]

This language promised protection for Indians' rights to continue occupying their lands, subject only to the possibility of minor relocation within a larger tract.

Because of local hostility and lackluster federal support, however, the reality of tribal land and personal rights was far worse under the new regime. Newcomers to Northern and Central California, besotted by the promise of the 1848 gold rush, opposed Indian land rights anywhere in the state. They found common cause in Southern California with newly arrived land-hungry developers, who greedily eyed the vast ranchos and former mission domains with a very different economy in mind. There was no place for Indian land rights, or even the Indians themselves, in the views of those seeking gold and land. Federal authorities weakened by the conflict over slavery and operating at a huge distance—as yet untraversed by railway or telegraph—did little to protect or enforce tribal rights. Ultimately, Congress, capitulating to local interests, joined the state in fashioning a legal system that thoroughly dispossessed the Indians of California—a third dispossession following those effected by Spain and Mexico. The Fernandeños were certainly not spared.

An array of legal enactments and practices converged to produce this regrettable end. These measures took three distinct forms: (1) a failed federal treaty process, (2) a federal claims process that reinforced unlawful Mexican grants and swept Indian lands into the U.S. public domain, (3) and a system of state property taxes that pressured Indian holders of Mexican land grants to sell to non-Indians.

A FAILED TREATY PROCESS

Initially, in accord with American legal theory, federal treaty commissioners were sent to California to negotiate treaties that would set aside federally protected territories for the tribes and extinguish their possessory rights (their aboriginal title) to much of the remainder of the state. Eighteen such treaties were negotiated at various points throughout California, securing approximately 7.5 million acres of land for poorly understood groups of Indians. As anthropologist Robert F. Heizer observed more than one hundred years later, "Rarely, if ever, in United States history, have so few persons without authority been assumed to have had so much, and given so much—for so little in return—to the federal government."[12]

The closest treaty to Los Angeles was still seventy miles away to the north. Directed at the southern end of the Central Valley, the Treaty of Tejon was signed in June 1851, with most of the signatures coming from local Kitanemuk Indians. Not only did this treaty set aside 763,000 acres between Tejon Pass and the Kern River for Indian occupancy, it ceded all other lands to which the signatory Indians might have laid claim to the federal government. Exactly how far the ceded lands went was unspecified, but the U.S. government had its own maps suggesting that the Tejon treaty ceded all lands due west of the coast range of mountains, including Los Angeles and the San Fernando Valley.[13] There is no basis for believing that the signatory tribes had any interest in or right to such extensive territory or any power to make cessions to the United States. Most of the villages within the so-called ceded lands on the map were controlled by coastal Chumash, Tataviam, Fernandeño, Serrano, and Gabrieleño speakers, not the Indians who signed the treaty.

For Indians in the Los Angeles area, the treaty process was abortive. Federal treaty agents were unable to carry out their plans to engage with local tribal groups because of lack of funds.[14] As Commissioner George W. Barbour later reported to Commissioner of Indian Affairs Luke Lea in September 1851,

> I remained [in the San Joaquin River area] until I received intelligence that the Indians in the vicinity of Los Angeles and San Diego were expressing dissatisfaction in not being treated with, and producing some alarm among the whites, lest they might commence hostilities, Col. Johnston the subagent for the district of the San Joaquin Valley being on the ground, and having received and turned over to him the beef before spoken of and the Indians throughout the San Joaquin and Tulare Valleys being quiet and satisfied, I determined to return to San Francisco, and if I could make the necessary arrangements for the purchase of goods for presents to the Indians and procure the money necessary to meet other incidental expenses, to proceed by sea to San Pedro the Embarcadero for Los Angeles, and from thence proceed to the Indian Country in the vicinity, and enter into Treaties with them.
>
> On reaching San Francisco I received a letter from the Department advising me of the fact that only the sum of $25,000 had been appropriated for the object of our mission, and that so soon as that amount had been expended we were to cease our negotiations. . . .
>
> Disappointed in my intended trip to the Indians in the neighborhood of Los Angeles and San Diego, everything connected with my duties as agent being arranged and moving on harmoniously under the management of Agent Johnston who was left in charge, and the "rainy season" about to set in, when business of every description would in all probability be suspended, I deter-

> mined to visit Washington City, Report to the Department, and visit my family in Kentucky, accordingly after making the necessary arrangements I left San Francisco on the 4th day of October 1851.[15]

Barbour's failure to pursue treaty negotiations in the Los Angeles area, and at San Fernando specifically, finds another explanation in an article that appeared on June 21, 1851, in the *Los Angeles Star*, asserting that "San Fernando is too near the valley of Los Angeles for an Indian Reserve."[16] In other words, the potential for development of the area—not the absence of Indian aboriginal claims—justified creating reservations farther from a future metropolis.

Had the California treaties been ratified, Commissioner Barbour's change of plans would have deprived the Los Angeles–area Indians of a relatively decent arrangement for protecting their land rights. What happened instead was that the U.S. Senate refused to ratify the eighteen treaties, citing pressure from the California congressional delegation, and ordered the treaties hidden away. News of the Senate's actions was withheld from the Indians, who had placed their names and invested their faith in agreements with the United States. In the end, there were no federal treaty rights ensuring territories for California Indians, even though many Indians moved to the places they mistakenly believed would be protected for them by the United States. As California attorney general Robert Kenny stated nearly one hundred years later,

> The results of the rejection of the treaties left the Indians of California exposed, helpless and largely unprotected to ruthless evictions, unprovoked aggression, bitter persecution, conscienceless exploitation, dispossessed and despoiled of their property without recourse, to become homeless wanderers in the land of their fathers. . . . In the bitter struggle for existence thousands perished in despair as the result of unprovoked war, massacre, disease and famine.[17]

A MISLEADING, MISGUIDED LAND CLAIMS PROCESS

Under U.S. law, the absence of treaties meant that Indian possessory rights to their land—their aboriginal title—remained intact, potentially complicating future real estate transactions and thwarting the appetites of non-Indian developers. Under U.S. law, the Indians' aboriginal title could be lost only by abandonment or by agreement between the United States and the Indians. Abandonment could be found only if the Indians voluntarily left their ancestral territory to live elsewhere. But in the case of former mission Indians, such as the Fernandeño lineages, the movement from traditional settlements to the mission was hardly voluntary. As the federal Indian Claims Commission later determined in 1959, "With few exceptions no tribelet voluntarily completely abandoned its tribal home and upon secularization many, if not a majority, of the missionized Indians returned to their ancient habitats."[18]

In the absence of ratified treaties or abandonment, it is unclear whether Congress ever properly eliminated the aboriginal title of California Indians. The matter is much disputed. Even as treaty negotiations designed to extinguish aboriginal title were underway, Congress passed, on March 3, 1851, An Act to Ascertain and Settle the Private Land Claims in the State of California.[19] Section 8 of the act provided that all persons "claiming lands in California by virtue of any right or title derived from the Spanish or Mexican government" must present their claims to the Board of Land Commissioners in San Francisco by March 3, 1853. Any petitioner whose claim was upheld by the commissioners would receive a patent (a kind of deed) from the United States. The issuance of such patents was not to affect any rights of "third persons" in the lands.[20] Under section 13 of the act, any lands for which claims were not presented or confirmed by March 3, 1853, would become public domain lands of the United States. Section 16 further provided

> that it shall be the duty of the commissioners . . . to ascertain and report to the Secretary of the Interior the tenure by which the mission lands are held, and those held by civilized Indians, and those who are engaged in agriculture or labor of any kind, and also those which are occupied and cultivated by Pueblos or Rancheros Indians.

There is no evidence that the Board of Land Commissioners ever conducted an inquiry into the land rights of Indians mentioned in the act,[21] or filed a report with the secretary of the interior. As legal scholar William Wood points out in his intensive study of the subject,

> It appears that the Commissioners ignored even the documented evidence that was before them, as well as Mexican and Spanish laws concerning Indian land and land use rights. This evidence included . . . the express provisions in the Mexican grants that they confirmed stating that Indians were not to be disturbed in the use and occupancy of their lands, waters, gardens, or grazing areas by any grantee or assuming grantee.[22]

The land commissioners also should have inquired into the rights of mission Indians under Mexican law that promised them future allocations out of the mission territories that were held in trust for them, both individually and collectively, for the purpose of forming self-governing municipalities.[23] Any such investigations would also have revealed that mission lands, including San Fernando Mission, had been sold to non-Indians in violation of Mexican law, leaving the trust status of those lands arguably intact.

In a separate act, passed on March 3, 1853, Congress confirmed the status of unpatented lands as public domain. Included in that second act, however, was language affirming that "this act shall not be construed to authorize any settlement to be made on any tract of land in the occupation or possession of any Indian tribe, or to grant any preemption right to the same."[24]

Under the 1851 and 1853 acts, were Indian landholders, whether claiming aboriginal title or rights under Mexican law or land grants, obliged to prove up their rights to the Board of Land Commissioners or lose their lands to the United States as public domain? In *Barker v. Harvey*, a 1901 case[25] pitting Indians' aboriginal title claims against non-Indian claims derived from a Mexican grant, the U.S. Supreme Court determined that aboriginal title was lost because the Indians had failed to present their claim to the Land Commission. Later judges have treated the Supreme Court's conclusion as established law.[26]

Unpersuaded by this weight of authority, Professor Wood argues that the Indians were under no obligation to present their claims to the commission and therefore could not have lost their lands and rights by failing to do so.[27] He notes, for example, that aboriginal title claims did not derive from Mexican law but rather from continuous occupation of the land and therefore did not even fall within the category of claims covered by the 1851 act. He also relies on the language in the 1851 act directing the commission to inquire into Indian land tenure, language that clearly puts responsibility to ascertain claims on the commissioners, not the Indians. Further, he points out the 1853 act specifically excluded land occupied by Indians from status as public domain, open for settlement. Finally, he notes that if Congress had truly intended the 1851 and 1853 acts to extinguish California Indians' land rights, it is difficult to understand why Congress simultaneously authorized treaty agents to negotiate treaties with the tribes for that same purpose.

California Indians, unsurprisingly, were not participants in the land claims process under the 1851 act. Apart from the language in the act itself, which indicated that they were not covered by its terms, there were other reasons. Indians who had signed treaties were unaware of the Senate's decision not to ratify and believed they had lands guaranteed to them under the treaties. Those who had not signed treaties were never notified of the act, and even if they had known of it, they would not have had the language skills, resources, or freedom of movement to hire attorneys and travel to San Francisco. The missionary friars had not even taught them to read and write in Spanish and did not act on the Indians' behalf to assert rights that the missions held in trust for them. Nonetheless, the Indians' failure to present claims to the Land Commission became an excuse, however flimsy, for dispossession under U.S. law. Any claims of aboriginal title were lost, at least according to the Supreme Court's later ruling, because of failure to participate in the process. And any Indians who had claims under Mexican law, including grants from the Mexican government, would find their rights to the land effectively erased if they had not participated.

Instead of attending to the rights of mission Indians, the Land Commission became an instrument of their third dispossession, this time under U.S. law. Interestingly, the Land Commission could have served to demonstrate the unlawfulness of the second dispossession, effected by Mexican officials when they granted mission grounds that were supposed to remain in trust for future distribution to the Indians and for the formation of Indian pueblos. But again, the game was rigged against the Indians. When Eulogio de Celis came forward to prove up his 1846 grant of the Rancho Ex-Mission San Fernando from Governor Pico, there was no one to speak up for the Indians and challenge Pico's authority to sell the land. The friars, who were supposed to administer the trust, had fled the crumbling missions. The United States wanted the land for sale or distribution as public lands, not for the Indians. De Celis, of course, wanted confirmation of his right to the vast quantity of Ex-Mission land. Former Mexican governor Pico, whose brother had an interest in the land and who had designs on the land himself,[28] provided a deposition in the de Celis proceeding, asserting (contrary to earlier newspaper reports) that de Celis had in fact paid $14,000 for the land[29] and that he (Pico) had authority to make the sale because of wartime exigency. Pico stated, "There was not any law in force at the time of the sale of the Mission lands of the government of Mexico prohibiting their sale."[30] The directive from the Mexican government suspending mission land sales was part of the record;[31] nonetheless, no one from the United States seems to have raised that as an issue or even argued that the central Mexican government had specifically withdrawn any authority Pico might have had to sell lands when those lands were part of a mission. In their decision confirming de Celis's title on July 3, 1855, the land commissioners opined, "The genuineness of the grant is clearly established, and the circumstances under which it was made so clearly explained as to leave no

FIGURE 15 Pio Pico, Mexican governor of California, 1845–1846. Photographer is unknown. Photograph from Wikimedia Commons, courtesy of Anaheim Public Library.

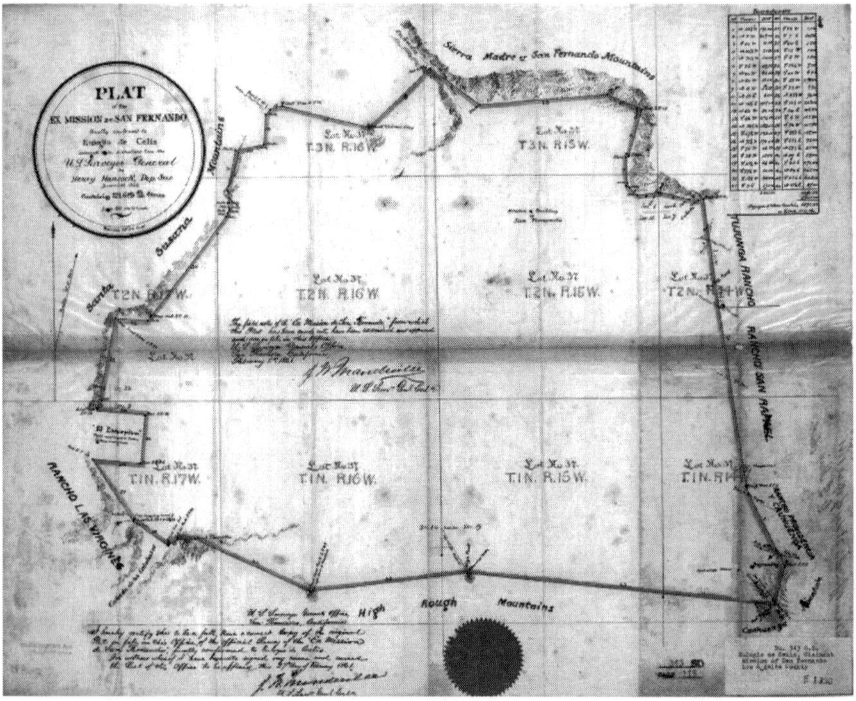

FIGURE 16 Plat of Ex-Mission San Fernando, finally confirmed to Eulogio de Celis (1858). Reproduced by permission from University of California, Berkeley, Bancroft Library.

doubt that it was done in good faith."[32] The United States chose not to appeal this decision.[33]

A successful appeal by the United States probably would have been more immediately beneficial to the United States than to the Fernandeños, since the alternative to de Celis's title under American law was U.S. government ownership. But at least a U.S. victory would have exposed the possible unlawfulness and definite unjustness of the sale to de Celis. There is every reason to believe such an appeal would have succeeded, as the United States did challenge a different wartime grant of mission land by Pico—this one of San Gabriel Mission—all the way to the U.S. Supreme Court, which ruled the grant invalid.[34] The Supreme Court's decision made it clear that the Mexican government had suspended Pico's authority to grant mission lands, and nothing in his war-making powers overcame that suspension.[35] Unfortunately, that 1863 decision came too late to upend the de Celis grant. Because of failure by the United States to pursue an appeal, the Board of Land Commissioners' decree in favor of de Celis had become final in 1857, and U.S. courts would not allow it to be reopened.[36]

DISASTROUS STATE LAW POLICIES

State law in practice was at least as detrimental to the land claims of California Indians as federal law was in practice, although in different ways. The 1852 California Act for the Government and Protection of Indians, quoted earlier, purported to guarantee Indians' rights to continued occupation of land on which they resided and worked. But that same law also disqualified Indians from testifying against whites in state courts and made it discretionary for judges to hear complaints brought by Indians. So if a dispute arose with the "proprietor" of the land they occupied, Indians had no way to defend their interests. Reporting to Commissioner of Indian Affairs Hiram Price in 1883, Helen Hunt Jackson and Abbott Kinney wrote that to their knowledge, "this act has never been . . . complied with in a single instance" and that "it would be held as of no value in the California courts."[37] As Professor Joel Hyer has pointed out, "Justices of the peace divested Indians of most of their lands, including choice land near San Francisco, Los Angeles, San Diego, and other communities that later arose as major cities."[38]

State law also operated against Indian land rights through the mechanism of property taxation. Property taxes were unknown under Spanish and Mexican law. As historian Robert Glass Cleland observed, "Prior to American annexation, the California government derived its meager revenue chiefly from port charges and import duties on foreign vessels."[39] The impressed service of missions also supported military and civilian governments. Under U.S. law of the mid-nineteenth century, in contrast, property taxes were the main source of government revenue. Property taxes therefore came into being along with California statehood in 1850. One goal and consequence of these taxes was to break up the large rancho holdings of Mexican grantees. Smaller Indian landholdings were threatened as well, however. Although U.S. law, even then, prohibited states from taxing tribal lands, California went ahead and taxed lands granted to Indians by the Mexican government. Inability to make these tax payments, compounded by lack of access to bank credit and hard times because of floods, drought, and disease in the 1860s, left California Indians, especially those in the south, vulnerable to loss of lands through tax foreclosure. This risk led many to sell rather than lose the land altogether.

California Indians also did not receive fair protection within California courts[40] and could be attacked without fear of government justice.[41] The courts bound out Indian children who were found homeless to families as servants and Indians who were arrested for alcohol and could not pay their fines to ranchers to work off the fines.[42]

LINEAGES AT THE CROSSROADS OF MEXICAN AND U.S. LAW

When California conducted its own census in 1852, Los Angeles County sprawled across 35,000 square miles, an area larger than the island of Ireland. Until losing much of its land base to San Bernardino and Orange Counties, Los Angeles County stretched from the Pacific Ocean on the west to the Colorado River on the east and from the southern end of the Central Valley on the north to Mission San Juan Capistrano on the south.[43] The 1852 census counted a mere 8,200 people occupying that expanse, slightly more than half of them labeled "domesticated Indians."[44] Livestock raising was the predominant economic activity, with orchard and field crops trailing far behind in scale and importance.

By that time, secularization and American colonization had taken a heavy toll on the mission-based economy, creating new challenges for the Fernandeño lineages. By 1850, most Indians who had been living at San Fernando Mission[45] had no choice but to leave the mission grounds, though a few who were older and infirm retired there, some remaining into the 1890s.[46] Many who left the mission grounds did not go far, settling and working on nearby ranchos.

For those who left, there were several possibilities under the new American regime. Already well trained as blacksmiths, masons, carpenters, winemakers, tanners, shoemakers, soap makers, millers, coppersmiths, bakers, cooks, brickmakers, carters, weavers, saddlers, constructors of adobe buildings, shepherds, horticulturalists, agriculturalists, and cowboys (among other trades),[47] some former San Fernando Mission Indians continued to pursue employment as ranch hands or servants on local ranchos. About a hundred remained on the Ex-Mission lands. Their skills, developed during years at the mission, were also in demand at these large estates, some of which were carved out of the former mission lands. As Indian agent B. D. Wilson reported to the Department of the Interior in 1863, "These same Indians had built all the houses in the country, planted all the fields and vineyards."[48] Living conditions for these workers were grim, however. According to historian Robert Glass Cleland,

> In return for simple but abundant food, primitive shelter, and a scant supply of clothing, scores of Indians, recruited chiefly from the fast-decaying mission communities, served as *vaqueros* [cowboys]. Many of these native families lived in the *Indiada*, a cluster of primitive huts built near the main adobe *casa*, while others dwelt in small villages, called Rancherias, widely scattered over the estate.[49]

As bad as it was for the Indians, even this economic arrangement became unsustainable over time, for rancho owners and Indians alike. The advent of the American period introduced an entirely different mode of economic organization, based largely on market forces. Through the 1850s and most of the 1860s, grantees of Mexican-era ranchos were pressed by taxes, high interest rates, collapsing market prices for cattle, devastating floods, sustained drought conditions, and smallpox epidemics that depleted the rancho labor force of its Indian workers. Ultimately, most grantees sold out to Americans, who increasingly turned from ranching and cattle raising to grain production and then to commercial and private development of the San Fernando Valley by the late 1870s and 1880s.[50] Once again, the Indians were displaced, often from the very mission lands that had been established, originally, on their traditional lands or held in trust for them. William H. Brewer observed in 1861 that "the natives . . . are slowly giving way before the Americans, with whom they do not assimilate."[51] Mission Indians who wound up in the town of Los Angeles quickly came within the grasp of the local peonage system—arrested for vagrancy and then forced to work off the amount paid by those who had bailed them out.

For some Indians who left San Fernando Mission after secularization and returned to their traditional homelands and lineages,[52] it did not mean going far, as the mission had been founded on the site of one village and near several others. Others headed for more distant ancestral territories in the mountains or along the coastal beaches, sometimes to their own village, sometimes to the village of their spouse's lineage. Upon their arrival, at the dawn of the American period, these survivors of the mission found that their acquaintance with non-Indian languages and cultures made them valuable to their own communities. Respected as leaders, some former San Fernando Mission Indians sought American recognition for their people through treaties and reservations.[53]

Several of these former San Fernando Mission Indians were signatories to the unratified treaty made near Fort Tejon in June 1851, known by the United States as Treaty 4 or Treaty D.[54] All of these signatories were from the Kitanamuk,

Yokuts, and Chumash lineages in that area or were married to women of those clans.[55] Although San Fernando Mission early on had brought in converts from these communities, signers of the treaty represented their lineage communities and not San Fernando Mission Indians as a whole. One such signatory was Francisco Tinoque Cota, who was baptized at San Fernando Mission in 1819.[56] He signed his name to the treaty as Francisco. His unbaptized brother, Kawana (later known as Vicente), signed the treaty as chief of the Tejon Indians.[57] Francisco's sister, Teofila,[58] was baptized at San Fernando Mission and married Francisco del Espiritu Santo, from the lineage at Tujunga. Their granddaughter, Leandra, is a progenitor of the present-day Garcia lineage of the Fernandeño Tataviam Band of Mission Indians.

Shortly after the treaty process failed and the California Land Claims Act dispossessed Indians throughout the state, the U.S. government created the Sebastian Reservation at Tejon Pass. The reservation's official name, Sebastian Military Reserve,[59] reflected its overriding objective: to pacify and subjugate the Indians. A military post rose up nearby. The reservation land was near both Kitanemuk and Chumash villages, but Indians from many California Indian communities were convinced or compelled to live and work there. Among those drawn to the Sebastian Reservation were Indians from San Fernando Mission, some of whom remained and married into Kitanemuk families, while others stayed only for a limited time.[60] The reservation lands were quickly in jeopardy from a competing

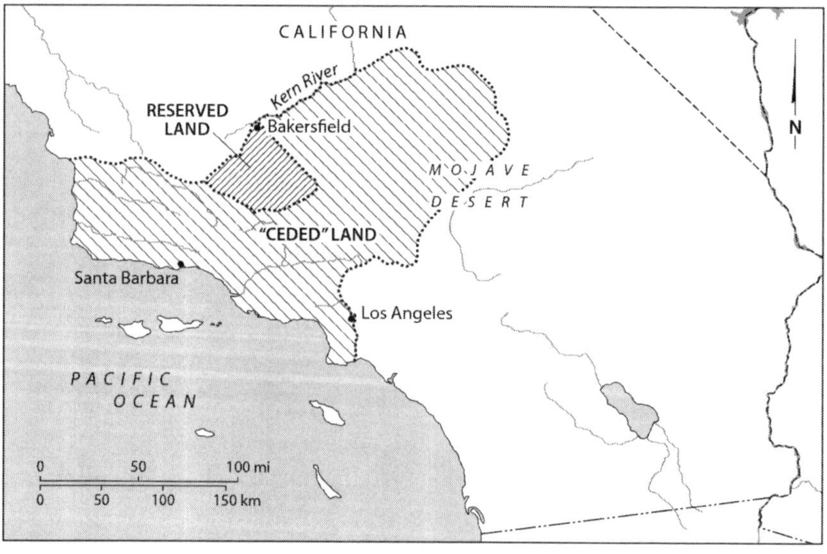

MAP 7 Reserved and "ceded" lands, unratified Treaty of Tejon, 1851. Map by Bill Nelson.

Mexican land grant claim, which eventually prevailed, forcing the closure of the reservation by 1864.

Soon thereafter, Edward F. Beale, first superintendent of the Sebastian Reservation, purchased the former reservation lands and other lands and formed Rancho Tejon. Since Beale knew many of the Indians personally, he invited them to work at the ranch and gave them considerable leeway to keep their own farms and manage their own sheep and cattle.[61] Beale promised the Indians, numbering about one hundred,[62] that he would allow them to live on the land as long as he was owner, and he kept his word.[63] Some of the Indians at Rancho Tejon worked there until Beale died in 1893 and through part of the ownership and lifetime of his son, Truxtun. The community at Rancho Tejon consisted of descendants of long-standing regional relations and intermarriages,[64] though distinct lineages tended to retain allegiance to their own political leaders.

Other Fernandeños entered the American period equipped with land grants they had received during the waning years of Mexican rule—grants that often overlapped with their ancestral lineage lands. These grantees, many of whom belonged to lineages of or tied to the present-day Fernandeño Tataviam Band of Mission Indians, tried to maintain their holdings under the new regime. They carried on ranching and cooperative relations with Native lineages and other people in the region and in the emerging town of San Fernando, near the old mission site.[65] Agent B. D. Wilson reported in 1852 that "a better crop and more commodious hut—perhaps, a table and chair or two—may distinguish them from the denizens of the mountain village. Everything else is quite after the Indian fashion. Still, with these, and the right to land, and honest conduct, they have made a broad step toward civilization."[66] The Fernandeños would soon find any such path blocked by the powerful forces of congressional acts and American property law enforced in the courts of the new state of California.

FERNANDEÑO LANDHOLDINGS AND LOCATION AS OF CALIFORNIA STATEHOOD, 1850

According to the first federal census conducted in California, dated 1850, approximately one hundred Indians lived within a twenty mile radius of the former San Fernando Mission. Those most closely connected with the present-day Fernandeño Tataviam Band of Mission Indians were located on their Mexican-era granted lands, still held at Encino, Tujunga, Samuel's grant, and Escorpion, or were living and working on the Ex-Mission lands, some of which had been granted to the forty petitioners and nearly all of which had subsequently been sold by Mexican governor Pico, flouting direction from the central Mexican government, to Spanish-born Eulogio de Celis. No matter where they lived, these Fernandeños were connected in social relations through godparenting, ancestral ties, lineage, and marriage.[67] Notable Fernandeño figures at this time include Maria Rita, Jose Miguel Triunfo, Jose Juan Leyva and his spouse, Leandra, Rogerio Rocha, Odon, and Pastor Cano.

It is impossible to know whether the Fernandeño lineages would have retained their landholdings and residences had Mexico held on to its colonial authority over Alta California. Once the United States and California assumed power, however, the Fernandeños were dispossessed within forty years through an assortment of legal and political processes.[68] Memory of these events remains within the Fernandeño lineages to this day. Grandparents pass the stories on to their grandchildren, reciting the injustices and conveying the feelings of loss.[69] Tribal member Stanley Salazar recalls the following:

> My grandma knew that land was stolen from them. My grandma told me that that land was taken and that there was nothing they could do about it at that time. My grandma knew in her heart and her mind that they were taken advantage of, that people were moved away, first of all, through taxes. And if you look at the Treaty of Guadalupe Hidalgo, this is from book learning, you know, they mentioned Natives like maybe two or three times very small. We're not even really mentioned in the Treaty of Guadalupe Hidalgo because it was between the United States and Mexico. They sold the land; they sold our land to them. So when that came out the Gold Rush wasn't far after that, right in and around the same time. So, whatever the Spanish didn't take then the miners from the Gold Rush took. So, we had to fight. We didn't have anybody to run to D.C. for us because no one was listening anyway.[70]

To understand what was lost, it helps to know the landholdings of San Fernando Indians at the advent of U.S. and California rule.

Though only twenty years old in 1850, Maria Rita had already inherited traditional leader status at Encino, previously held by her then-deceased maternal grandfather, Tiburcio Cayo, and her deceased father, Francisco Papabubaba.[71] Her powerful connections within the Fernandeño tribal lineages had only been strengthened through her marriage to Benigno five years earlier. And in 1847, as Papabubaba's only surviving child, she had inherited his one-third interest in the 1845 Mexican grant for Rancho Encino, a square league (nearly 4,500 acres) in size, as well as his position as captain. Rita by that time had two children with Benigno, a daughter born just six months after the wedding and a son born a year later. Co-owner Ramon (also called Roman) was in the household as well, along with Agueda (Aguila), widow of the third co-owner, Roque. Roque had gone to join the gold rush in Northern California a few years earlier and never returned. Like Roque, Benigno was not present in the 1850 census for Encino.

Ownership of land and water and the sharing of such resources with other community members as well as providing work and a place to live had reinforced the leadership of Francisco Papabubaba and the other joint owners of Rancho

FIGURE 17 Eulogio F. de Celis (1845–1903), San Fernando landowner. Courtesy of Los Angeles Public Library Photo Collection.

Encino.[72] Maria Rita continued in that tradition at a time of her community's desperate need. When Eulogio de Celis received a grant of the Ex-Mission lands in 1846 from Governor Pico, a provision in the grant allowed the Indians there to remain, undisturbed. For those who now felt insecure on the land, refuge was available at Rancho Encino, where many could be found in 1850. A year earlier, Ramon, Rita, and Agueda sold a one-third interest of Rancho Encino to a Mexican tavern owner and public official from Los Angeles, Vicente de la Osa, for $100. De la Osa may have known the Fernandeños from the time his father had been stationed with the Mexican military at the mission.[73] De la Osa came out very much ahead on the deal. He had recently sold Mexican-granted land of the same size as Encino, near present-day Burbank, for $1,500. For the $100 purchase of a one-third interest, he secured access to the entire Encino tract, which was well watered with warm and cold springs. As of 1850, however, Rita and Roque's widow, Agueda, both remained as co-owners.[74]

Early in that same year, Jose Miguel Triunfo was living at Rancho Tujunga, a tract of more than 6,500 acres that he had acquired in trade for his Mexican grant at Rancho Cahuenga in 1845. The trade was made with brothers Francisco and Pedro Lopez, non-Indian superintendents (mayordomos) at the mission who had received the original Mexican grant for Tujunga. Apparently, the brothers thought that Cahuenga, though less than a tenth in size, was more advantageous for ranching and farming because it had a more ample supply of water. Later in 1850, however, Triunfo sold a half-interest in Rancho Tujunga back to Francisco Lopez for $400 and then the other half-interest to two American-born Los Angeles merchants. Now owning no land of his own, he went to join Maria Rita and her family at Encino.[75] The move to Encino was a natural one, as the lineages at Encino and Cahuenga, where Triunfo had kinship ties, had long carried on social and political relations.[76] Jose Miguel Triunfo's last days were sorrowful. As one of John Harrington's informants, Setimo Lopez, recounted, after the loss of a son in 1849 and after "another son they carried to the isla . . . the old man went crazy."[77] He lived on until at least 1858,[78] consumed by grief.

In 1851, Samuel, the mission land grantee who was born in the Tataviam-speaking village of Chaguayanga,[79] was still living on his two hundred-acre ranch northwest of the mission at a site that would later be covered by the Upper Van Norman Lake reservoir early in the twentieth century. On March 1, 1851, he gave the land to Jose Miguel Triunfo's surviving widow, Maria Rafaela Perfecta, and Jose Miguel's surviving son, Antonio (age seven), and stepson, Ildefonso (age eleven), as a gift.[80] It's unclear why he did so, though it could have been because of inability to pay taxes or fear that he couldn't manage the land claims process

FIGURE 18 Setimo Lopez (1853–1930), informant to John Harrington and member of the Cano lineage. From Harrington Papers, National Anthropological Archives, Smithsonian, 91–31239.

necessary to sustain his title. This land, according to Setimo Lopez, John Harrington's informant, was called Sikwanga (a green place).

Jose Miguel's son and stepson planted orchards at Sikwanga, growing pears, oranges, and pomegranates. Samuel took up residence at the western end of the valley, where he served as manager of the Indian land grant known as Rancho El Escorpione, or just Escorpion.[81] Sadly, none of Samuel's children survived to adulthood.[82]

Already living at Escorpion in 1851, when Samuel arrived, were the original 1845 Chumash grantees: Chief Odon, his son-in-law, Urbano, and Urbano's son, Manuel.[83] These three joint owners of that 1,100-acre parcel, granted by the Mexican government, were recognized as chiefs or captains, and many Fernandeños worked on the Escorpion ranch. Odon was a Chumash chief at Humaliwa, near the south end of present-day Malibu, and for the Chumash people on the western end of the San Fernando Valley.[84] Married to Marcelina, daughter of the Ventureño-speaking Odon, Urbano had served many years as a trusted member of the San Fernando Mission administration. As of 1850, he was using the surname Chari, a chief's name. Urbano and his son had ancestral ties to Siutcabit, the lineage at Encino, where Maria Rita's maternal relatives lived. Marcelina was actively engaged in godmother duties within the Fernandeño community, and she was *madrina* (godmother) to the children of Roque and Agueda, who were joint owners at Encino in the late 1840s and early 1850s.[85]

Escorpion, in 1850, was also home to twenty-six-year-old Rogerio Rocha, an accomplished blacksmith raised at the mission who claimed ancestry from Tujunga on his mother's side and from Chumash villages of Quimisac (north of Simi Valley) and Lalimanu (north of present-day Malibu) on his father's side.[86] During the Mexican period, Rogerio's father, German, was a respected captain, cultivating a ten-acre plot on the vast mission grounds. The land and water were attached traditionally to the settlement near Tujunga village and used by the Tujubit lineage. The people of Tujunga were Rogerio's family on his mother's side. The land became known as Rancho La Cienega, or the swamp, in recognition of its good water.

Rogerio and German managed the distribution of water as a collective asset for the benefit of the Tujubit lineage and others in the Fernandeño community. Located northeast of the mission, the rancho had an ample water supply, allowing German and Rogerio to invite others to partake and reinforcing German's role as a captain, or leader. Rancho La Cienega was not far from the mission's Indian village, which was located due west. Both German and a young Rogerio had been among the forty Indian petitioners who collectively received an 1843 grant of one square league (nearly 4,500 acres) of mission lands from Governor Micheltorena.

German died sometime before 1850,[87] and Rogerio took up residence at Escorpion to be near an ancestral village of his wife, Maria Manuela.[88] The 1850 census records that Maria's brothers, twelve-year-old twins, were also part of their household. Around 1860, one of the twins, Jose Juan, married Leandra, the daughter of Eugenia and a progenitor of a lineage with both Tataviam and Escorpion ties that is later called Garcia. It is likely, however, that Rogerio continued to tend his father's farm, less than twenty miles away from Escorpion. The 1850 census suggests that most Indians left San Fernando Mission and found work at Escorpion, Encino, the ranch of Joaquin Romero near Escorpion, or among private ranches. In 1850, Rogerio worked as a laborer for Urbano Chari. Joaquin Romero, an employee of San Fernando Mission, was granted use of land from the mission. During the early 1850s, about thirty former mission Indians went to work for him, but the legal basis for his grant was not supportable.

Other Fernandeños, like the family of captain and ceremonial leader Pastor Cano, were still managing to live and work on Ex-Mission lands as California achieved statehood in 1850. Born in the Gabrieleño-speaking village of Pimu on Catalina Island, Cano married Josepha Leonisa Palma, who joined the mission from a Kitanemuk village near Tejon. They worked as wage laborers, first for Andres Pico, who initially rented the Ex-Mission lands for nine years starting in 1845, and later for Eulogio de Celis, who purchased the Rancho Ex-Mission San Fernando, and grew food from their own gardens.

LAND LOSS AND EVICTION, 1850–1885

The next three and a half decades brought natural disasters and profound demographic and economic changes to the Los Angeles area. The Fernandeño Indians were hard-hit—by nature, by ruthless developers, and by the now-controlling American legal system. Their numbers declined dramatically.

Natural disasters came in the form of disease and extreme weather, operating, unfortunately, in tandem. In the early 1860s and again in the mid-1870s, prolonged, severe droughts devastated livestock herds on the ranchos in the Los Angeles area. Hundreds of thousands of cattle and sheep were slaughtered for their hides and horns. Closely following each drought was a virulent smallpox epidemic.[89] Cattle and sheep ranching, which had flourished in Southern California, could no longer be sustained, depriving many Indians of a major source of their livelihoods. The toll from disease, however, was far worse. As historian Robert Glass Cleland described,

> Health conditions among the Indians and lower-class mestizos appear to have grown steadily worse after the American conquest. . . . Living conditions . . . were deplorable; no attempt was made to enforce quarantine regulations; patients stricken with the plague were often concealed from the authorities and attended secretly by members of their family; and almost nothing could be done to check the spread of the disease.
>
> The country had few physicians, all of whom resided in the larger towns, and consequently most ranch settlements and Indian communities were without medical attendance. Vaccine could be secured only by steamer from San Francisco.[90]

Deaths from the epidemic of 1862–64 nearly depopulated the Fernandeño communities, from seventy-eight members in the 1860 census to only thirty-four in 1870.[91] Far too many Indian children died or were orphaned and taken in by extended family or employers. The network of Fernandeño lineages, though severely weakened, rose to meet this challenge.

As periods of drought, alternating with ferocious floods, made ranching increasingly infeasible, it was unclear what other economic endeavors could take root in the lands around Los Angeles. Besides the inadequate facilities for irrigation, the area suffered from a chronic dearth of capital, prohibitive interest rates, uncertainty about land titles, lack of transportation for access to markets, and state legislation favoring grazing interests.[92] Many of these obstacles began to fall away in the 1870s. With the end of the Civil War and the completion of the transcontinental railroad, immigration to California swelled, bringing individuals with deep pockets and towering ambitions. The railroad also opened whole new markets for California goods, and by 1870 interest rates finally fell to more reasonable levels. The California Land Commission also rendered decisions that brought greater clarity to land titles, often by ignoring Indigenous rights. The upshot of all these developments was California's first big real estate boom. As land values soared, promoters acquired and subdivided the large ranchos into smaller plots for orchards, vineyards, and grain production. The increase in real estate values also brought sharp escalation in property taxes. For the Fernandeños, holding on to their land and homes became increasingly difficult.[93] In 1882, a *Los Angeles Times* editorial proclaimed that "the poor Neophytes, as they were called, were cut off from all resources and the remnant of a once large and industrious people have been driven to the mountains to starve."[94] Although they did not all flee to the mountains or starve, the Fernandeños lost much—lives as well as land—in the decades immediately following statehood.

Maria Rita and Encino

Once California became a state in 1850, counties began exacting property taxes—financial demands that had been unknown under Mexican rule. Indians such as Maria Rita and her Indian co-owners of Rancho Encino were unprepared for this new requirement. They had only about thirty head of cattle and no income stream they could tap to pay their tax bills.[95] Then in 1851, the new American government demanded that property owners undergo the lengthy, expensive process of proving their title to the federal commission and eventually to the federal courts. The treaty with Mexico had guaranteed property rights established under Mexican law, but the United States wanted proof that Mexican landholders actually held good title. Thus, even as the United States contested the rights of grantees under Mexican deeds, the local county of Los Angeles imposed property taxes on landowners such as Rita. Unlike other holders of Mexican deeds, however, Rita had Indigenous claims to her land and to exemption from state taxes. Congress had acknowledged the special status of mission Indians when it set up the Land Commission in the first place. But it never followed through to protect Indian rights, leaving Rita saddled with tax bills and legal obligations she could not manage.

In stepped Vicente de la Osa, the Mexican-born, Los Angeles-based politician and tavern owner who had designs on acquiring all of Rancho Encino. The property's critically important water resources, plentiful grazing land, and strategic location on the stagecoach route from Los Angeles to Santa Barbara made it a prized parcel. In 1849, for the pitifully low price of $100, he had become a co-owner, taking over Ramon's one-third interest in the land. De la Osa then managed the burdensome process of proving and securing good title before the American legal system. Early in 1855, the U.S. District Court for the Southern District of California affirmed title in Rita's, de la Osa's, and Roque's heirs, with Roque presumed dead because he had never returned from the gold fields. Although the U.S. attorney was intent on appealing to the U.S. Supreme Court, an appeal that ultimately failed,[96] de la Osa knew the property was now far more valuable. He waited for Rita's and Roque's heirs to fall behind on their taxes and then swooped in to buy their interests at the tax sales. For a little more than $20 in overdue tax payments, de la Osa acquired most of the remaining two-thirds

FIGURE 19 De la Osa Adobe (built 1849), at Rancho Encino. Courtesy of Los Encinos Docent Association.

of Rancho Encino.[97] By late 1860, Rita no longer had any ownership rights to the Encino property, and she soon moved her family the eleven miles back to San Fernando.[98]

During this period, Rita's personal life was equally turbulent. Her husband, Benigno, was not even around in 1850, perhaps gone to the goldfields with Roque. While living in Ramon's extended household she took up with a Yaqui Indian living nearby, Fernando Ortega. Fernando was an expert maker of carts, or *carettas* as they were called in Spanish, and worked first for Vicente de la Osa and later for Geronimo Lopez, whose father-in-law, Pedro, had been the mayordomo of the mission. Eventually, Fernando became the foreman of the prosperous Lopez Ranch. Over the next ten years, Rita and Fernando had five children together.[99] Even though Benigno returned during this period, he was probably in ill health, and he died some time in 1861 or early 1862. In March 1862, Fernando and Rita married. Interestingly, the marriage certificate presents her as Maria Rita Alipaz, a surname long associated with healers and leaders in the Chumash tradition.[100]

Rita probably taught her children a Fernandeño dialect learned from her mother and grandmother, the latter who was raised at Siutcanga, later known as Encino.[101] She also most likely taught some of her healing knowledge to her children, including her son, Antonio Maria. Antonio later practiced traditional healing and was well informed about local tribal history and knowledge.[102] Rita also maintained good relations with the Mexican and Mexican American families who had been connected to the mission, such as the nearby household of Geronimo Lopez, for whom her husband worked. Those good relations came in handy. Sometime between 1864 and 1870, both Rita and Fernando died, probably succumbing to the smallpox or diphtheria epidemics that raged through Southern California. Two of their children as well as Rita's two with Benigno also died during that time, and her remaining three children with Fernando became orphans. One of those orphaned children, baptized Jose Rosario in 1857 but known to all as Antonio Maria,[103] found refuge in the home of Pedro and Angela Reyes, close relatives of Fernando's employer, Geronimo Lopez.[104] Luis Eduardo Ortega, Antonio's younger brother, was taken in and cared for by the Geronimo Lopez family.[105] Antonio Maria Ortega and Luis Eduardo Ortega belonged to their mother's Chaguayabit lineage, later called Ortega in Spanish and English, after their mother's married name. The Ortega lineage is one of the main lineages in the contemporary Fernandeño Tataviam Band of Mission Indians.[106]

Once Antonio was old enough, Geronimo Lopez also employed him as a carreta maker at the Lopez Ranch and as a farmhand. Antonio's entire life was spent

FIGURE 20 Geronimo and Catalina Lopez, friends of the San Fernando Indian community. From Lopez Adobe Photo Gallery.

in San Fernando. He later married, rented a home, set up his own household, and raised a family.[107]

Jose Miguel Triunfo's Family and Samuel's Grant

Following California statehood, Jose Miguel Triunfo's young son, Antonio, and his stepson, Ildefonso, helped their mother tend the orchards on the land they had received as a gift from Samuel in 1851. Rose (Rosaria) Triunfo, the daughter of Jose Miguel Triunfo and Maria Perfecta, bore a son out of wedlock in 1861.[108] She baptized the child with the name Jose Abelardo Godey (Godoi). The father, Alexander Godey, worked closely with Edward F. Beale, who was superintendent of Indian Affairs and Indian agent at the Sebastian Reservation during the early 1860s. Godey did not take responsibility for the child. In the early 1860s, Rose

Triunfo[109] briefly partnered with Miguel Ortiz, a Mexican American who was widowed and already had a family. Rose left the relationship after only a few years, but her and Miguel's families continued on friendly terms. Rose renamed her son Joseph Ortiz,[110] preferring Miguel's surname to the name of his biological father. Through his mother and maternal grandfather, Joseph Ortiz was tied to the Cabuepet lineage, later called Ortiz in Spanish and English, after his mother's married name. The Ortiz lineage is one of the main lineages in the contemporary Fernandeño Tataviam Band of Mission Indians.

Unfortunately, the new American regime made the Triunfos' way of life unsustainable on Samuel's grant. Like Maria Rita Alipaz, they were hard-pressed to come up with cash to pay the property taxes they now owed. As Indians living on ancestral tribal land, they might have had a good claim to exemption from state taxation, but federal and California law denied them the political and legal standing they needed to enforce such rights. The only real alternative was to sell, and Jose Miguel's son and stepson, Antonio and Ildefonso, tried to stretch out that process as long as possible. Part of the land could be sold initially to pay taxes on the remainder. So, in June 1858, Ildefonso sold his one-half interest to Maria de los Angeles Felis de Burrows, a cousin of Geronimo and Catalina Lopez.[111] A little over four years later, in August 1862, Antonio sold his remaining one-half interest in Samuel's grant to the same Maria de los Angeles.[112] The background and identity of Maria de los Angeles is not well recorded. As a widow[113] engaging in real estate transactions on her own, she may have had a comfortable inheritance or been a front for other interests.

What is known is that Maria de los Angeles held on to that land during the difficult years of the floods, drought, and epidemics of the 1860s while her cousins, Geronimo and Catalina Lopez, developed forty acres of the site into the well-known inn and stagecoach stop Lopez Station.[114]

Located on the main land route between Los Angeles and points north, Lopez Station also housed the valley's first post office, English language school, and general store. The school was for the Lopez children but also for local Indian children, some of whom were orphaned by the epidemics that swept Southern California in the 1860s. Among the students was the orphaned Antonio Maria Ortega. Photos of the period show the station as an isolated outpost, surrounded by barren hills. Operating the station from 1862 to 1882, the Lopezes, whose family had longstanding godparenting ties to the Fernandeños, employed some of the Indians in their enterprises. Among the "boarders" listed in the Lopez household in the 1880 census is Luis Ortega, son of Maria Rita Alipaz and brother to Antonio Maria Ortega.[115] During this period, in 1871, Maria de los Angeles actu-

FIGURE 21 Lopez Station, built 1861, located under what is now Upper Van Norman Reservoir. Photo taken in 1890. From SCVhistory.com.

ally sold the forty acres to the Lopezes at a price of only $160. Then in 1872, she sold the balance of the Samuel/Triunfo tract to C. R. Rinaldi, a European-born American entrepreneur who was flush with cash from the sale of his successful Los Angeles furniture business.

Within a decade of these transactions, the Lopezes and Rinaldi were threatened by new claimants to the Ex-Mission: men with powerful political connections and prodigious financial backing, at least for that time. Most prominent among these men was Charles Maclay, a devout Methodist minister who had represented San Jose in the California State Senate during the 1860s. A florid public speaker with a reputation for eloquence, Maclay enjoyed the favor of railroad magnate Leland Stanford. In 1874, Maclay moved to Southern California, where he formed a partnership with another former state legislator, the well-to-do businessman George Porter.[116] Using their own funds and $60,000 borrowed from Stanford, they acquired 56,000 acres of Ex-Mission land in the northern San Fernando Valley, land still owned by the heirs of Eulogio de Celis.[117] The meager cost of $2.50 per acre belied the tract's propitious location.[118] A land boom was on in Los Angeles in the 1870s, and the Maclay-Porter acquisition included the southernmost station of the recently completed Southern Pacific railway line that ran between Bakersfield and Los Angeles. There, near the site of the old San Fernando Mission, Maclay and Porter laid out a new city of San Fernando, looking to profit handsomely from subdividing the land. Jeopardizing the success of that endeavor, however, were competing claimants to the land, such as the Lopezes and Rinaldi, both of whom traced their claims to Maria de los Angeles, who traced hers to the Triunfos and ultimately to Samuel. The deeds from the de Celis heirs did not include clauses protecting Fernandeño land claims and use, which had been honored before 1872. Seizing on this omission, Maclay and Porter turned to the California courts, bringing suits to evict those in their way and to establish clear title to their property. Some, like the Indians who still maintained farms on the Ex-Mission lands, had little financial capacity or legal standing to resist. Others, like Rinaldi and the Lopezes, fought back.

The lawsuit brought by Maclay and Porter against C. R. Rinaldi and others allows us to learn a history of the transactions relating to Samuel's grant, later the Triunfos'.[119] In their answer to the complaint, Rinaldi and his codefendants offered two defenses: first, that the de Celis heirs and Andres Pico, another person through whom Maclay and Porter claimed title, had previously consented to

FIGURE 22 Drawing of Andres Pico at San Fernando Mission by Edward Vischer (1865). Courtesy of University of California Berkeley, Bancroft Library.

the good title of Maria de Los Angeles; and second, that Maclay and Porter were prevented from challenging the title of Maria de los Angeles because Andres Pico and the de Celis heirs had deceived her at the time she purchased the land from the Triunfos.

The transactions relating to Samuel's grant are described in considerable detail in Rinaldi's answer.[120] As recounted by Rinaldi's attorney, in 1869, before Maclay and Porter entered the scene, the San Fernando Farm Homestead Association, organized by a group of wealthy San Franciscans, acquired a large interest in the Ex-Mission tract, tracing their claim to Pico's 1846 grant to Eulogio de Celis and de Celis's sale of a part interest to Pio's brother, Andres Pico. In financial trouble after the great Southern California flood of 1861, Andres sold his part of the vast tract to brother Pio in 1862, retaining about two thousand acres around the mission.[121] Seven years later, in 1869, Pio Pico wanted to liquidate his own landholdings to finance a grand new hotel in Los Angeles.[122] The Farm Homestead Association bought his half interest in the Ex-Mission—nearly sixty thousand acres of the San Fernando Valley—for $115,000[123] and proceeded to file a partition suit in state court against all claimants to the Ex-Mission, including Maria de los Angeles. The aim of the suit was to carve out a portion of the tract that would belong just to the association. In 1871, the district court obliged, and the Ex-Mission was carved horizontally along an east-west axis at what is now Roscoe Boulevard, with the Farm Homestead Association acquiring exclusive title to the southern half. The land that Maria de los Angeles claimed through Samuel and the Triunfos was in the northern part, but Rinaldi, who had bought the land from her, tried to argue that the partition suit included consent by de Celis and the Picos, through the judgment entered November 29, 1871, to the title claimed by Maria de los Angeles. This supposed consent constituted Rinaldi's first defense.[124]

Rinaldi's second defense, based on misconduct by Andres Pico and the de Celis heirs, required an even longer historical account, dating back to the days when the Triunfo family held the property:

> On the first day of March 1851, Yldefonso and Jose Antonio Triunfo were the owners in fee simple of the land described in the complaint under a deed of conveyance of that date of one Samuel an Indian of the Mission of San Fernando to whom prior to the grant to de Celis to wit on the 15th day of May 1843 said land had been granted by written grant by Manuel Micheltorena Governor of California. . . . [The subsequent transfers to Maria de los Angeles Felis de Burrows, Geronimo Lopez, and C. R. Rinaldi are recited.]

> The said grant to Samuel and all of the deeds aforesaid were duly recorded in the Recorder's Office of Los Angeles County, and the tract of land described in the complaint has ever since the date of said grant been in the actual, exclusive, notorious and adverse possession and occupation of the said Samuel and his successors in interest. . . .
>
> Ever since the date of the grant aforesaid to the said de Celis, deceased, he and his successors in interest the said Andres & Pio Pico, and San Fernando Farm Homestead Association, and the said Eulogio F. de Celis administrator of the said de Celis, deceased, respectively . . . have known of and acquiesced in the occupation and claim of title of said land by the said Samuel and his successors aforesaid and have repeatedly & expressly acknowledged their title.
>
> The said Triunfos were both unlearned and ignorant men and unacquainted with the laws and language of the Americans and were in the habit of advising with said Andres [Pico] who was a prominent man in the community; and after the passage of the Act of March 3rd, 1851, "to ascertain and settle . . . land claims in the state of California," the said Triunfos applied to the said Andres for advice and counsel as to what they should do about their land and there upon the said Andres, acting for himself and as agent for the said Eulogio, deceased, advised & counseled the said Triunfos that it was unnecessary for them to present their claim to the U.S. Land Commission as they, the said Andres and Eulogio set up no claim to said land and would protect them in their title. Relying on their assurances and in consequence of this advice the said Triunfos did not present their claim to their land, as they otherwise would have done.[125]

Another point in this defense was that "the said Maria de los Angeles was also ignorant and illiterate and unacquainted with the laws and language of the Americans" and had sought advice from Andres Pico regarding the title of the Triunfos before purchasing from them.

> Thereupon the said Andres for himself and as agent of the said Celis represented that the title of the said Triunfos was good and that she might buy the land of them safely, and she, relying upon said representations and assurances bought the said land and would not have otherwise done so.

The court was not persuaded by either of these defenses and ruled for Maclay and Porter. Rinaldi went on to acquire other property in the valley,[126] and the Lopez family abandoned Lopez Station for an adobe in town—a good move because the railroad in San Fernando had supplanted the stagecoach line. Maclay and Porter continued to pursue others who stood in the way of their ambitions as developers.[127]

Although no Fernandeños were parties, questions regarding Indigenous property rights and the applicability of the 1851 federal California Land Act to Indians were at the heart of this property dispute. Was the original grant to Samuel sound, regardless of subsequent grants by the Mexican government and the title-clearing impact of the 1851 act? The advice given by Andres Pico to Maria de los Angeles, namely that the Triunfos were not required to file a claim under the federal act, had support in the language of that law. It was decades later that the U.S. Supreme Court insisted otherwise.[128] Both de Celis and Andres Pico may also have led the Indians to believe that they did not need to file claims because de Celis and Pico would secure the land through the commission and then grant the Indians their claims. In the meantime, the Triunfos, lacking liquid assets to pay their property taxes, had to sell their land and orchards. Even worse, without affirmation from the U.S. Land Commission, they probably had to discount the price.

Having fully sold out to Maria de los Angeles by 1862, the Triunfo family likely found shelter with relatives on other lands of the Ex-Mission. Again on the move, Jose Miguel's widow, Rafaela Perfecta, daughter, Rosaria Ortiz, and Rosaria's child, Joseph, moved to Tejon Ranch in 1877.

Escorpion

Rancho El Escorpione (later called Escorpion), the land Pio Pico granted to Chumash captain Odon, his son-in-law, and grandson in 1845, extended over one thousand acres in the western San Fernando Valley. Armed with a supportive deposition from Abel Stearns, one of the wealthiest and most influential leaders of early Los Angeles, Odon and his family braved the rigors of the California Land Commission process, receiving American confirmation of their title in 1856.[129] In 1860, Urbano Chari and his son, Manuel Chari, both died.[130] Soon thereafter, management of Escorpion shifted to Miguel Leonis, a migrant from the French Basque country who formed a common law marriage with Espiritu, Odon's daughter, and later purchased Odon's interest. Throughout the 1860s, Leonis employed local Indians and Mexican Americans to tend his herds of sheep and cattle. Although large numbers of would-be homesteaders surged into the area, believing the land was available for free settlement, he enlisted the courts to oust them legally and his employees to oust them physically.[131]

None of the present-day Fernandeño Tataviam Band of Mission Indian members trace lineage descent to the owners or community at Escorpion, which was located around the old Chumash village of Huam.[132] However, Jose Juan Leyva, born to a father from the lineage at Escorpion, was himself father to Josefa, whose married name of Garcia has been associated with one of the tribe's lineages. There were very few descendants of the Escorpion lineage community.

Rogerio Rocha and the Ex-Mission Lands of "the Forty"

While Andres Pico and the de Celis family held the Rancho Ex-Mission San Fernando they honored provisions in the original 1846 grant from Pio Pico protecting the rights of Fernandeños who were then occupying the land to continue residing on and using it. This right was not transferable, and it expired at the death of those Indians. But Pico and de Celis made no challenges to the Fernandeño landholdings or the occupation of parts of the Ex-Mission. However, when the de Celis family sold their share of Rancho Ex-Mission San Fernando to land developers Charles Maclay and George Porter, the 1874 deed contained no language protecting the Indian occupants.[133] Both the de Celis family and Andres Pico advised the Indians that their land interests would be protected. Yet there was no way to compel the new owners, who were in business to develop and sell real estate, to recognize the Indians' rights. One of the Indians cultivating his plot on the Ex-Mission lands was Rogerio Rocha, whose 1885 eviction, along with the eviction of others living on the tract, epitomized and publicized the situation.

Sometime between 1852 and 1870, Rogerio Rocha left Escorpion with his family to resettle on his father's ten-acre farm Rancho Cienega, which supplied water to Tujunga village. The rancho is located at the present-day corner of Hubbard Street and Fourth Street in San Fernando, about nine short city blocks from the Lopez Adobe.[134] A fenced-in area and park now mark the place where Rogerio grew crops. Rogerio, whose sweeping curved moustache and neat beard were already turning white by the 1870s, was a recognized community captain at San Fernando. He was a financially successful blacksmith and silversmith, especially adept at making spurs "in the California style,"[135] who played the violin, sang in the mission church choir, and spoke an Indian language, probably Fernandeño, as well as Spanish and some Latin, but not English.[136] He was famous for his commitment to the Catholic faith and conducted the funeral ceremony for his wife following their brutal eviction.[137] Perhaps most important, the land he occupied and cared for, long attached to the Tujubit lineage, had water. By welcoming all Fernandeños to partake, he reinforced his leadership status. Several Indian men and women and their families came to live on his land in a compound that

FIGURE 23 Lopez Adobe, San Fernando, California, in 1883. From Los Angeles Department of Water and Power Site, Water and Power Associates.

included two adobe houses, several traditionally constructed tule houses, and two wood frame houses.[138]

Rogerio's father was a captain, and when his father died, Rogerio was pronounced captain by acclamation. Rogerio had people and cultural skills, wealth, land, and water, which he shared with the local Fernandeño community, earning their respect and validating his leadership. His status as a captain is widely attested. Fernando Librado Kitsepawit, who recounted Chumash history and ritual to John Harrington, named Rogerio among those at a gathering of captains in the 1860s to select a captain for the village of Muwu, near present-day Leo Carrillo Beach in Malibu.[139] Librado also identified "Captain Rogerio" and his family as participants in the first and only commemoration ceremony held by Pomposa, the captain who had been selected for Muwu, in 1869. Contributing greatly to Rogerio's stature was the fact that he had held on to the land. His wide network of kinship ties also reinforced his leadership role. In addition to his Chumash links to the village of Homaliwo (present-day Malibu), he had in-laws and social ties among the Cabuepet of Cahuenga (including the Triunfos) and therefore some relations with the later-named Ortega and Ortiz lineages. Through his mother, Rogerio also had ties to the Tujubit lineage of Tujunga,[140] a lineage also connected to the later-named Garcia lineage. In the 1928 California Judgment Roll, many in that present-day Garcia lineage recognized Rogerio Rocha as a captain of the Fernandeño Tribe as far back as the time of treaty-making in June 1852.[141] His position was that of a traditional captain who was widely influential because of his leadership and cultural skills.

Rogerio Rocha lived on his farm until 1885, claiming aboriginal rights and Spanish Mexican trust protection but also, on the advice of Eulogio de Celis, paying property taxes on his land as well as poll taxes and road assessments.[142] He never went to the Board of Land Commissioners to prove up rights under a Mexican grant, probably because he believed, with some justification, that he did not need to. As the *Los Angeles Herald* later reported,

> Was there not an agreement entered into between Pio Pico and Celis on the one hand and the Indians on the other, to the effect that the Indians were not

FIGURE 24 Panoramic view of San Fernando Mission looking south across a largely unimproved San Fernando Valley (1875). From Los Angeles Department of Water and Power Site, Water and Power Associates.

> to apply for patent and then convey to the Indians their portion of the lands? Was there not agreement between Eulogio F de Celis and Porter & Maclay, at the time the latter purchased the lands, that the Indians would be protected in their rights to these lands?[143]

But in November 1885, the California legal system denied the validity of his rights to the land, either under the de Celis grant or through aboriginal title. Rogerio Rocha and the others were summarily evicted in an ejectment lawsuit that had been brought by real estate developers Charles Maclay and George Porter in 1878.[144] At the time the complaint was filed, Rocha challenged it as a legal matter through a response known as a *demurrer*, but the demurrer was overruled, and Rocha was directed to file a more complete response, known as an *answer*. The answer was filed by attorneys Cameron Thom and Erskine Ross, but under the name "Rodrigo." After that, the case sat until the end of 1883. Then Maclay and Porter's attorney (and Maclay's nephew), R. M. Widney, asked the court to rule in their favor by default, as Rocha had supposedly never filed his answer. Despite the likely confusion of names, the court granted Maclay and Porter's motion and entered judgment for them by default, based on a technicality. Rocha's efforts to reopen the judgment and set aside the default, led by a specially appointed U.S. attorney, G. Wiley Wells, failed and a harsh eviction followed. As Rocha described in a deposition given ten years later,

> During the bad weather of that year two officers came down and put us out, my furniture and horses and farming implements and all that I had on my ranch. They threw all the stuff out in the open ground. The night that the officers put us out it rained. We were out in the open ground. The rain came out on us. My wife got sick afterward when we moved up to the mission. My wife died from the sickness she got that night.[145]

Rocha's was perhaps the most poignant of the evictions, but certainly not the only one. All the Fernandeños still residing on Ex-Mission lands received visits from the sheriff's office in early 1878 and were expulsed from the lands they and their ancestors had toiled on since the establishment of the mission, nearly one hundred years earlier. In the same year Maclay and Porter filed suit against Rocha, they also brought an ejectment action against a group of Indians, designated "John Doe, Palo et al." on the cover of the original complaint and later changed to "Pablo Cota et al.," as plaintiffs gained knowledge of the individuals they sought to evict.[146] The list of defendants eventually included, besides Pablo Cota, Felicita Villa, Josefa Palma, Jesus Ramirez, Teresa Ramirez, Jesus Capistrano, Antonio Maria Ortega, and Orticimo.[147] The defendants may well have been working for the Lopez Ranch or Station and decided to live on the land of the forty petitioners from the 1843 land grant, which was contiguous with Samuel's grant.

Tracking the allegations in the complaint, which followed legal formulas of the time, the judgment of the Los Angeles County District Court found that

> the defendants did on the 1st day of July 1876, wrongfully and unlawfully, and without right or title enter into and upon said lands and premises in said complaint described, and did eject and oust the plaintiffs therefrom, and ever since that day have wrongfully and unlawfully withheld and now do withhold the said premises and the possession thereof from these plaintiffs.

Translated into conversational English, this statement meant that the defendants were, as of the date in question, occupying the land and preventing plaintiffs Porter and Maclay from exercising their rights to ownership and possession. Lacking resources to hire an attorney of their own, the defendants failed to respond, and Judge Ygnacio Sepulveda entered judgment by default for Maclay and Porter on February 11, 1878.

The names of the defendants, as well as the fact that they were sued together, is significant in demonstrating connections among the Fernandeño lineages and their willingness to also embrace a common tribal identity. Two years after Porter and Maclay got their deed from the de Celis heirs, defendants were holding their ground, challenging the newcomers' right to specific pieces of land in Rancho Ex-Mission San Fernando. Antonio Maria Ortega, son of Maria Rita Alipaz, was one of the few survivors of the Chaguayabit lineage. Josefa Palma was the widow of Pastor (Josefo) Cano, a revered captain and ceremonial leader from Catalina Island who died sometime before 1870. Felicita Villa, their adult daughter, became or already was a recognized leader among the Fernandeños. Her husband, Jesus Capistrano, a non-Indian, appears as a defendant as well. Another of the defendants, Orticimo, was possibly a corruption of "Setimo," the name of Josefa and Pastor Cano's son, who was noted in the Cano household in the 1870 and 1880 censuses. Teresa Ramirez, married to non-Indian Jesus Ramirez, was a Fernandeño born after San Fernando Mission closed. There is reason to believe that Teresa was closely related (as child or sibling) to Pablo Cota, another of the defendants. She does not appear in any census after 1880 and likely died within the next twenty years. Further, mission records suggest that Pablo Cota was also identified as Francisco Pablo.[148] Francisco Pablo's godmother was Paula Cayo, who was married to Francisco Papabubaba. Both were progenitors of the Ortega lineage. The godparenting role suggests that Paula and the Ortegas may have had close social relations with Francisco Pablo Cota's family.

Cota, Ortega, Ramirez, and Josefa-Felicita-Setimo defendants came from four separate lineages. The defendants represented a cross section, or coalition, of lineages in the case challenging Porter and Maclay's land ownership and defending Fernandeño land rights. The defendants do not appear to represent all the descendants of the forty petitioners to the 1843 land grant given by Governor Micheltorena. Antonio Maria Ortega may have had a claim through his mother, Rita, who married Benigno, whose father Cosme, in turn, was one of the forty petitioners. The Cano family was well represented, showing a cooperative collective effort among the several lineages still living at San Fernando. As one well-informed but anonymous author wrote in the pages of the *Los Angeles Herald* a decade later,

> Rogerio and his band of Indians were robbed . . . and . . . floating somewhere within the exterior boundaries of the great San Fernando grant is a tract of 4000 acres of land that rightfully belonged to those Indians and of the ownership of which they were never rightfully divested.[149]

Porter and Maclay construed the judgment they received in the *Pablo Cota* case to mean that Fernandeño claims to the Rancho Ex-Mission San Fernando—claims that the land belonged to the group of Fernandeño Indians—were invalid and void. Judgment in hand, Porter and Maclay proceeded to send eviction notices to all the Indians and other occupants living on the Rancho Ex-Mission San Fernando property. Rogerio Rocha was the last to be evicted when he and his household were set onto the road forcibly and pitilessly in 1885. As a former deputy sheriff recounted in 1896, these legally disreputable evictions were part of a pattern of dishonesty and fraud, often abetted by the courts, designed to cheat local Indians of their increasingly valuable rights to land.[150]

AFTER THE LAND

The Fernandeños suffered loss of all their land by 1885 and became, in the official language of the time, landless mission Indians.[151] As early as 1866, a federal report on landless nonreservation Indians, which would include the Fernandeños, asserted that

> the Indians in this superintendency are placed, by circumstances over which they have no control, under peculiar hardships . . . with no lands, no treaties, no annuities, no power or means of extricating themselves from the influences with which they are surrounded.[152]

Evictions and tax foreclosure sales of the 1870s and early 1880s made matters even worse.

Without plots of their own to cultivate, the Fernandeños found employment as wage laborers on ranches and farms throughout the San Fernando Valley and in historically linked territory.[153] The Southern California economy was changing rapidly in the 1870s, with railroads replacing stagecoaches and thousands of new residents arriving in the wake of the Civil War. Development companies bought up and subdivided real estate, fueling a boom in land prices.[154] By 1874 most of the San Fernando Valley, about 131,000 acres, was owned by eight owners or companies of owners.[155] Only Indians with strong and stable connections to important landowning families could afford to remain in the area. Most Indian laborers in Los Angeles were paid about half as much as American workers.[156] Sometimes the pay was in whiskey rather than in cash.[157] Consequently, Indians had strong incentives to move to more rural locations and carry on ranch life where their skills and training, gained at the mission, were more highly valued. Each lineage had the right to choose its own economic future. Some, including the Ortega brothers and the Cano family, stayed in San Fernando, remaining as workers at the Lopez family ranch, station, and, later, their adobe. Josefa Leyva (later Garcia) and Rosaria Ortiz and her son, Joseph, left, at least for a while, and lived and worked at Newhall Ranch and Tejon Ranch, respectively, where there were Indian communities.

As the dispossession proceeded, census records of 1860, 1870, and 1880 list the declining number of Fernandeños in the small but growing town of San Fernando, near the mission, but also in Tejon, Newhall, and Saticoy, the sites of ancestral lineage territories, as well as other locales in and around San Fernando and into Ventura County. Ancestors within the lineages now represented in the Fernandeño Tataviam Band exemplify the spatial and cultural patterns among the Fernandeños of this period. Antonio Maria Ortega and his brother, Luis Ortega, who had many economic and social ties with the prominent Lopez and Reyes families of the San Fernando Valley, had relatively stable employment opportunities as farmhands and therefore did not feel compelled to move from their home at San Fernando. In 1878, Antonio married Isidora Garcia, a woman of Mexican-Yaqui descent who was also working in the household of Geronimo Lopez.[158] Christina Ortega, their first child, was born in 1881.

By the mid-1860s, also living in San Fernando were Leandra, descended from ancestors among the people of Tujubit, Chaguayabit, Tejon, and Topipabit,[159] and her husband, Jose Juan Leyva, who was of Jucjauybit-Escorpion (Ventureño) descent on his father Efren's side[160] and Piru (Tataviam) descent on his mother Maria Ygnacia's side. The signature of Jose Juan Olivas on a document later accepted by the federal Bureau of Indian Affairs affirmed that Jose Juan Leyva was a 4/4 Indian from San Fernando Mission.[161] Although the identification of Jose Juan has been a troubling issue, because of the missionaries' regular use of the first name "Jose" for males and their failure to use surnames,[162] there is a very plausible basis for understanding his identity. Jose Juan, who appears in the San Fernando Mission records,[163] was one of identical twin brothers who remained at the mission with their family until around late 1845. Because Leandra's family was there as well during that time, the two families most likely had contact with or knowledge of each other in the Fernandeño community of no more than 365 people. During the early 1850s, Jose Juan's family moved away from San Fernando Mission to their ancestral village of Escorpion. From there they found refuge in the nearby Ventureño Chumash–speaking village of Saticoy. The 1860 census shows Leandra, age nineteen, listed next to Jose, whose age is given as twenty-two, a correct age for the twin Jose Juan born at the mission. His twin brother, Jose Jesus, is listed next to him as well.[164] When the family had to choose a surname in the American period, they chose to honor Efren's godfather, a Spanish soldier named Rufino Leyba, or Leyva.[165]

Leandra and Jose Juan's only child, Josefa or Josephine, was born in San Fernando in 1865.[166] Josefa's Ventureño Chumash descendancy on her father's side helps explain a strong sense of Chumash culture among present-day Garcia family members and leadership. Josefa's paternal aunt, Manuela, the older sister of the twins, was married to Rogerio Rocha and hence had many political and cultural connections. The connection to Rogerio Rocha also helps to explain the illustrious godparents present at the baptism of Maria Josefa Leyva in 1865. Josefa's godmother was Maria Felicitas, the daughter of Chief Cano from Pimu, at Catalina Island. Felicitas had a close social and political relationship to Rogerio Rocha. Her godfather was Estanislao, who was a chief among the Tataviam in the 1850s at the Sebastian Reservation near Tejon Ranch. Both Felicitas and Estanislao were baptized at San Fernando Mission.[167]

After the baptism of Maria Josefa Leyva in 1865, both Leandra and Jose Juan disappeared from the record. Maria was five years old and living with Felicitas in the 1870 census. Most likely Leandra and Jose Juan died before 1870 from communicable diseases that raged throughout Southern California in the 1860s. Maria Josefa appears to have entered into the household of the Cano lineage under the care of her godmother, Maria Felicitas.

In 1882, (Maria) Josefa Leyva moved from San Fernando to Newhall with her partner, Isidoro Garcia, and their first child, Petra, born earlier that year. Isidoro was a Yaqui Indian and brother to Isidora Garcia Ortega, wife of Antonio Maria Ortega. The move made sense for Josefa because Newhall was near the site of her ancestral lineage village, Chaguayanga.[168] Josefa and Isidoro's second daughter, Frances Garcia, was born in 1884. In an affidavit given in 1928 in connection with the judgment roll for the California Land Claims Act, Frances Garcia (married name Cooke) stated that she was born in San Fernando, and since then she and her children had lived most of their lives in Newhall, California.[169]

Rogerio Rocha and his wife remained in San Fernando through this period, living on their ten-acre plot in San Fernando until cruelly evicted in 1885. The widow and children of Jose Miguel Triunfo did not last as long. Pressed to sell off their farm in the 1860s, they had taken refuge with community members in San Fernando. But by 1877 they had to pack up again. The timing of this move suggests it was related to the eviction suits of the late 1870s brought by new purchasers of the Ex-Mission lands. By that time, Triunfo's daughter, Rosaria, had separated from her husband, Miguel Ortiz. At Tejon, she remarried.[170] Her son, Joseph Ortiz, received some schooling, and between 1878 and 1893 he was employed at Tejon Ranch, where some San Fernando Mission descendants lived. J. J. Lopez, son of Geronimo Lopez, was his manager there. Families like the Ortizes in Tejon and the Garcias in Newhall were joining related communities in a regional network. They did not lose contact with the Fernandeño community and culture.

Though strained by population decline, land loss, physical separation, discrimination, and new economic demands the network of Fernandeño lineages held. Marriage and kinship relations adapted to the changed conditions. With fewer local Indians to marry and more Americans, including Mexican Americans and other Indians available as potential partners, the traditional pattern of outmarriage to a connected lineage, driven by ceremonial and economic exchanges,[171] was modified. Marriage within one's lineage was still prohibited, but nonlineage partners could be from any background. Extensive intermarriage with the newcomers, especially for the Fernandeño women, became common. The children of such unions remained identified with the lineage of their Indian parent and usually were taught Native languages, especially among the descendants of Maria Rita Alipaz and Leandra. As a result, exogamy did not deplete lineage ranks but over time enabled greater growth among the families, lineages, and Fernandeño tribal community. These marriage patterns conformed to the general patterns of Indian communities throughout Southern California and to the traditional Fernandeño norms of seeking advantageous social, economic, and political marriages outside the lineage. The old rules were applied to the new circumstances.

Although lineages remained the fundamental, largely nondifferentiated form of organization into the American period, dispossession, population decline, a market economy, intermarriage, and dominance of the English language required some changes in the way lineages were understood. Before the mission period, lineages were associated with a particular place and dominant indigenous language. Through the mission period, survivors from several lineages tried, unsuccessfully, to hold on to those land bases. When that failed, the lineages essentially rebranded themselves, associating with progenitor ancestors rather than specific places and using reconstituted rules of descent-based membership to regrow their numbers. Through those progenitors they were connected to more distant ancestors from a variety of premission villages. But there was often a particular place, such as Encino, Cahuenga, or Escorpion, to which the lineage had stronger ancestral ties, especially if those ties had persisted through Mexican land grants into the mission period and beyond. The progenitor ancestors foregrounded in this book were women, survivors of the early American period who married non-Indian or Mexican Indian men with Spanish surnames that became associated with their lineages going forward. Those lineages continued to produce leaders in the form of captains, who guided the lineages in perpetuating traditional knowledge and maintaining social solidarity.

Even within this new framework, marriage patterns, accentuated and extended by the adoption of Catholic forms of godparenting and witnessing, could serve to reinforce the network of lineage ties, sustaining a broader Fernandeño community. The community was knit together through ties among the Tujubit, Siutcabit, Cabuepet, and Chaguayabit traditional village lineages. The marriage of Maria Rita Alipaz to Benigno brought members of the Encino (Siutcabit) and Cahuenga (Cabuepet) lineages together and reinforced long-standing social and kinship relations. At the time of the 1850 census, Jose Miguel Triunfo's family (Cabuepet) was living at Encino on the jointly owned land grant of Maria Rita Alipaz. Marriage relations between ancestral lineage members of Tujubit established ties between the Garcias and Rogerio Rocha, who was an influential captain among the mission Indians at San Fernando between 1852 and 1904.

In a grand illustration of this continued network, the marriages of siblings Isidora and Isidoro Garcia to Antonio Maria Ortega (son of Maria Rita Alipaz) and Josefa Leyva (daughter of Leandra, Tujubit), respectively, resulted in in-law relations and godparenting exchanges between those two families, reinforcing ties among the traditional lineages of Siutcabit, Chaguayabit, and Tujubit. San Fernando Mission ceased functioning as a church where children could be baptized in 1855, so Petra Garcia was baptized at La Plaza Church in downtown Los Angeles on May 23, 1882, together with her first cousin, Christina Ortega.[172] The Ortega and Garcia families arranged to meet at La Plaza Church and baptize their two children together. Church records show the two cousins baptized consecutively, with certificate numbers 462 and 463. Isidoro Garcia served as godfather to Christina Ortega. This pattern of Garcia and Ortega families exchanging godparenting among their children became a tradition in the 1880s and 1890s.

The regional network of lineages retained contacts and recognized family relations, but generally each lineage, composed of an extended family or families, remained local and politically autonomous.[173] As in precontact times, decision-making was consensual within and among lineages, usually occurring during family gatherings or informal meetings. By agreement within the Fernandeño community, no lineage would think to interfere in another's decision to stay in San Fernando or to leave. Under conditions not entirely within their control, the Ortegas remained, the Ortizes went to Tejon, and the Garcias eventually left for Newhall. Rogerio Rocha was recognized as an influential captain among the Fernandeño by consensus among lineages, based on his influential kinship ties, sharing of resources, and status as an elder with both traditional and Catholic knowledge. Yet even as he was regarded as a captain, members of each lineage also looked to their own blood lineage leaders for decision-making. Tejon, San Fernando, and, at least into the 1880s, Escorpion had recognized chiefs or captains.[174] Other prominent figures, including Maria Rita Alipaz and Jose Miguel Triunfo, were respected and honored as leaders.

The mission friars had tried to suppress lineage-based political power and authority in favor of their own system of "elected" alcaldes and other offices to be controlled by the friars themselves.[175] Even though the Fernandeños had accommodated to the alcalde system by negotiating the selection of officers, the formation of a more inclusive Fernandeño political identity did not erase the lineage system. Lineage leaders continued to be recognized for ownership of land, control of economic resources, and possession of cultural knowledge. Widespread recognition among the lineages of Rocha's guidance, coexisting with their own lineage leadership, likely reflected new sets of demands on the Fernandeño community, brought about by dispossession and other consequences of colonialism. It was a multilayered social and political arrangement.

Among the lineages, ceremonies and language reinforced a sense of community. Although at least nominally Catholic and still practicing Catholic baptisms, godparenting, and weddings, the Fernandeños were no longer tied to a single parish at the mission. That arrangement ended in the 1840s with secularization. Even after the Catholic Church won the return of 170 acres of land and buildings from the mission in the early 1860s,[176] the buildings were used primarily for administrative purposes. Local Indians were not invited to restore a Catholic community at the San Fernando Mission Church and the land that the church had once declared it held in trust for them was certainly not restored to them.

While Fernandeños found other Catholic churches to attend, they also maintained traditional spiritual traditions that long predated the mission. Observers at the time remarked that the Fernandeños practiced their annual ceremonies well into the 1870s and most likely retained ceremonial contacts with their regional network, always a part of the principal renewal ceremonies practiced by the western Takic-speaking communities.[177] Local observers say the multilineage commemoration ceremonies were carried on at San Fernando even after the dispossession of land. There were eight days of feasting observed last in 1874 at San Fernando.[178] Similarly, the respected Chumash captain Pomposa invited Rocha and his family to participate in her final ceremony at Saticoy, held in 1869.[179] Dispossession stripped local Indians of the resources they needed to feed guests and transfer gifts and food by fire to the ancestors, as the ceremonies required. The ceremonial tradition became unsustainable.[180]

Most Fernandeños continued to speak their own languages. The mission friars had encouraged the Indians to speak Spanish, but they did not discourage the use of Indian languages. Rogerio Rocha, for example, spoke an Indian language, probably Fernandeño, and spoke Spanish and some Latin. After 1850, many Indians took up English as well. The children, including Antonio Maria Ortega and Joseph Ortiz, learned to read and write in English at American-style schools, such as the one that operated at Lopez Station from the early 1860s to 1885.

SUMMARY

By 1885, the lineages we now identify as Ortega, Ortiz, and Garcia were accommodating, more or less successfully, to a new reality without land rights or meaningful political rights. The American political and legal systems had chosen to ignore the unjust dispossession perpetrated by Mexican law and then refused to apply American law that would have protected aboriginal land rights as a matter of common law, international treaty with Mexico, and federal statutes. Even as they adapted, the San Fernando lineages were not blind to the legal, economic, and social discrimination affecting them and other Indians in Los Angeles County. The absence of legal rights and the suppression of Mexican American and Indian workers, as well as the possible threat of murder without legal recourse, weighed heavy on many individuals and families. Weakened in numbers and resources, they were in no position to succeed, as Kroeber observed, "in a sufficiently effective resistance against the incoming white to make themselves felt and their just claims respected."[181] Moreover, there was a real threat that they might be forcibly removed to reservations far from their ancestral territory. Federal agents actively pressed the Fernandeños to move to reservations at Tejon, Pechanga, Morongo, and elsewhere.[182] Some took the agents' advice, although they soon learned how difficult it would be to fit in if they had no lineage relations in those communities. Further, some Fernandeño lineages left the San Fernando Valley to live in nearby Indian communities such as those at Saticoy and Rancho Tejon. Mostly, however, the several lineage groups preferred to function within the regional Fernandeño tribal network of lineages and relations that enabled them to remain in their homelands, although now without any ownership of land.

The loss of lineage land ownership further forced differentiation of lineage from homeland or place and encouraged lineage members to enter local labor and consumer markets. Most lineage males found work as ranch hands or farmhands.

Lineage leaders learned and used healing methods and traditional knowledge. Rogerio Rocha was a widely recognized captain who had considerable lineage and Catholic ceremonial knowledge. Rocha participated in regional commemoration ceremonies, made decisions with Ventureño and Fernandeño captains, and officiated at burial ceremonies. He was a steady participant in Catholic Church masses, a member of the church choir, and had considerable multicultural skills.

Rita was a healer and became a captain at Rancho Encino (Siutcanga) after her father died. She used the surname Ortega, the name of her second husband. The surname became the commonly used lineage name for Rita's descendants. After the epidemics of the 1860s, Antonio Maria Ortega, the son of Rita, was one of three lineage members to survive the plague. He assumed leadership as eldest person remaining within the Chaguayabit lineage. Antonio Ortega passed to his children a considerable amount of ethnographic and cultural information about the lineages and cultures during the post–San Fernando Mission period.

Kinship and leadership remained nondifferentiated. Among the surviving lineages of San Fernando Mission, captains were chosen along kinship lines. Generally, the oldest willing lineage male member became captain. Chumash-related lineages could choose females as captains.

Multilineage tribal commemoration ceremonies were last carried on in the San Fernando Valley in 1874. After the evictions, the commemoration ceremonies soon ended at San Fernando. Thereafter, ceremonial and social activities were carried on within each lineage according to its own way. The lineages were impoverished, having lost use of the land. The commemoration ceremony had been a way for lineage members to pass gifts to honor and support the spirits of their ancestors. The lineages held beliefs of this-worldly rebirth, while Catholic beliefs focused on other-worldly spiritual resurrection. Until the middle 1870s, captains and temporarily designated captains supplied necessities and carried out the tasks needed to support the multiple lineages that attended the commemoration ceremonies.

Engagement of ceremony, spiritual beliefs, and polity remained primarily focused on lineage communities as the regional ceremonies were discontinued. Catholic beliefs and lineage spiritual ceremonies were coexistent, and often Fernandeño lineage members and leaders maintained bicultural skills in both religions.

By the mid-1860s, in the postmission period, partnerships were made between Americans, including Mexican Americans, and Indians outside the system of Fernandeño lineage relations. The children belonged to the lineage partner and were therefore lineage members. Outsiders who married a lineage partner were not granted political or kinship membership in their spouse's lineage. By the 1880s, many, if not most, people who married a lineage member were not descended from a Fernandeño Indian lineage. In-law relations, common political and land interests, and godparenting relations among the Ortega, Ortiz, and Garcia lineages helped create friendly bonds and a common identity as Fernandeño.

Within the bounds of a common Fernandeño historical experience and identity, the lineages remained politically autonomous and each had its own captains. Cooperation among the lineages was voluntaristic and in practice often occurred through joint endeavors such as resistance to evictions and recognition of Rogerio's leadership. The strong traditional moral imperative of the lineages was to remain, as much as possible, politically, economically, spiritually, and socially independent. Work and economy became decreasingly organized by lineage activity and increasingly organized by market relations. Economic relations were increasingly differentiated from lineage control and management. Political leadership remained nondifferentiated from kinship, and leaders were expected to be knowledgeable of lineage ceremonies and cultural history and increasingly expected to be skilled at negotiating with American institutions. The surviving lineages shared a common Fernandeño political identity, based mainly on the collective experience of government within San Fernando Mission. In the 1880s and 1890s, elder captains, such as Rogerio Rocha, exercised influence among Fernandeños through kinship relations, common cultural knowledge, and mutual land and political interests.

The Fernandeño lineages kept a low social and political profile, devoting their energies to maintaining their family relations and sustaining their distinct and tribal identities. The Indian community at San Fernando was reluctant to openly lobby for their rights because they lacked money to do so and were discouraged by the inability of their leader, Rogerio Rocha, to protect his property. These conditions also inhibited the lineages from expressing their identities and community interests in public. But although they did not seek public attention, that attention would soon find them.

CHAPTER 5

Federal Recognition (1885–1904)

Although tribal existence does not depend on it, "federal recognition" of a tribe of Indians means there is a government-to-government relationship between that Native nation and the United States. Under federal law, a "federally recognized tribe" is entitled to federal trust obligations, federal services, authority over tribal territory that is respected in federal and state courts, and many other benefits. In the earliest years of contact between the United States and Indigenous tribes, federal recognition took the form of treaty-making, which Congress banned in 1871. Over time, recognition also occurred via statute, federal executive order, and even administrative action by federal agencies such as the Bureau of Indian Affairs. Beginning in 1978, regulations of the U.S. Department of the Interior[1] formalized the recognition process, setting out criteria and procedures for petitioning tribes. Those regulations emphasize continuity of tribal political and social organization over time, as well as occasions where external actors (newspapers, government bureaus, scholars, religious orders, for example) have noted tribal existence. Official dealings with the group by agents of the federal government weigh especially heavily in favor of recognition.

Lacking a treaty, federal executive order, or federal statute recognizing them as a tribe, the Fernandeños nevertheless can point to official efforts of federal agents, acting as guardians of the tribe, to establish federal recognition. Most of this activity took the form of legal representation when the Fernandeños resisted eviction from their ancestral territories. The case that federally appointed lawyers took up, Rogerio Rocha's, was sensationalized in the Los Angeles press. As portrayed on the pages of the *Los Angeles Herald* and the *Los Angeles Times*, it had all the stock characters of a melodrama: pathetic, upstanding victims and morally unredeemable villains. In fact, the case involved far more than one elderly Indian and his ailing spouse, the victims named in the overheated press reports. Rocha was a leader among the interconnected Fernandeño lineages, and those representing him understood they were carrying out federal obligations to recover land and protect a group of Indian "wards."

RECOGNITION THROUGH REPRESENTATION

Except for those who returned home to Tejon after secularization, the Fernandeños never became parties to a treaty. Federal treaty negotiators had been diverted from their operation in the Los Angeles area in 1851.[2] Yet even those tribes included in California treaty-making saw their eighteen treaties rejected by the U.S. Senate in July 1852. For the next several decades, the Civil War, Indian wars of the Great Plains, and other matters left California Indian affairs relatively unattended by federal officials. It was during that period that state militias massacred Indians in Northern and Central California, and courts throughout Southern California evicted Indians, like the Fernandeños, from their ancestral lands.

As early as the 1870s, specially appointed federal commissioners conducted investigations and delivered scathing reports to the commissioner of Indian affairs on the condition of former mission Indians, including those in Los Angeles County.[3] The 1875 report of special commissioner Charles Wetmore, produced in response to instructions from his superiors in Washington, DC, pronounced that

> the Mission Indians have become practically outcasts, notwithstanding their love for their homes and their willingness to work. Circumstances have made them public nuisances, and serious conflicts between them and the whites are constantly arising. Their condition is wretched in the extreme, and is each year becoming worse.[4]

Prefiguring federal legislation passed sixteen years later, Wetmore urged the federal government to acquire small tracts of land in trust for the benefit of mission Indians.[5]

By 1880, Indian reform organizations, driven by women's and religious groups, began pressing federal officials to rectify the widespread mistreatment of Native peoples.[6] These reformers thought they knew what was best for the Indians—a more humane path to "civilization." Even though they did not respect or support tribes' interests in retaining their cultures and sovereignty, they knew that prevailing federal policies of Indian removal and dispossession were proceeding at too rapid a pace. Animated by the Protestant ethic, the reformers' ultimate goal was to inculcate values of individualism, independence, and salvation through hard work. They campaigned to provide land and education for Indian groups but only in the service of more gradual and successful assimilation. Land, in particular, was not viewed as the territorial basis for tribal government but as a resource that could function as a training ground for farming life, to be followed by dividing and distributing the land as private property to individual Indians, once they were sufficiently "civilized." In language offensive to today's ears, John S. Ward, who was Mission Indian agent for the Department of the Interior from 1885 to 1887, served up the purpose of this reform philosophy in his final report to the commissioner of Indian affairs:

> Clothe the Indian with the insignia of citizenship, and invest him with title to land, in fee simple, and still it does not make him a man, without he has been taught the arts of industry and has solved the problem of self-support. This transition period, from the lounging, loitering, lazy, lousey Son of the Forest, to the full stature of self-supporting citizenship, is one which demands the highest order of practical statesmanship for its solution.[7]

Ward advocated compulsory "apprenticeship on the farm or in the shop in order to make [the Indian] self-supporting and qualify him for the battle of life."[8] Federal recognition of a long-term government-to-government relationship with Indigenous tribes living on their own territory did not figure into this world view,[9] but the reformers' immediate objectives of enforcing rights, fulfilling federal obligations, securing land, and protecting the Indians were consistent with recognition.

Through the writings of Helen Hunt Jackson, a celebrated author and activist reformer, these efforts achieved national visibility for Southern California Indians. In early 1881, before her encounters with California tribes, Jackson published an unflinching critique of broader federal Indian policy titled *A Century of Dishonor*.[10] Jackson's tract drew attention to case after case of treaty violations, unprovoked slaughters, and land grabs. Later that year, she embarked on a trip to California, commissioned by the *Century Magazine* to write a series of illustrated articles about the state. Her visit took her to several Indian communities in Southern California as well as to San Fernando Mission, where she received a cordial welcome from the custodian.[11] In a fateful visit of several days with Antonio Coronel, the former inspector of the southern Indian missions for the Mexican government, she heard him recount tales of the past, some of which found their way into her popular novel *Ramona*.[12] Coronel, an early mayor of

FIGURE 25 Helen Hunt Jackson (1830–1885). Photograph from Flkr.

American Los Angeles, lived amid orchards and vineyards in a western suburb of the city, an area that was ancestral home to some of the Fernandeños.

What Helen Hunt Jackson saw during her encounters with Southern California tribal communities was a "monstrous injustice"[13]—trespassers brazenly settling on lands set aside for the Indians and Indian communities displaced and made homeless because of Mexican land grants confirmed by the U.S. Land Commission. With emotionally powerful prose and insistent prodding of federal authorities, Jackson worked to publicize and remedy the wrongs she had witnessed. By mid-1882, she had written to Secretary of the Interior Henry Teller requesting a federal commission to investigate and report on the conditions of the mission Indians, assuring him that she was "capable of writing judiciously and with exactness, even when I feel intensely."[14] Secretary Teller directed Commissioner of Indian Affairs, Hiram Price, to grant her the assignment, and over the next several months, Jackson and Price worked out the details. Jackson would work jointly with Abbot Kinney, whom she had met in Los Angeles—a wealthy young man with an interest in Indians, an acquaintance with California land laws, and fluency in Spanish. Her duties were to examine the number and location of mission Indians, to identify any government lands available for reservations and any other lands available for purchase for that purpose, and to ascertain how the Indians felt about moving onto reservations.[15]

The report that Jackson and Kinney presented in 1883 made eleven specific recommendations, including "the appointment of a lawyer, or a law firm in Los Angeles, to act as special attorneys in all cases affecting the interests of these [mission] Indians."[16] This recommendation reflected Jackson and Kinney's frustration over the inability of local Indian agents to respond firmly when Indians were driven off lands they had long occupied and to which they had legitimate claims. "He [the local Indian agent] is in the embarrassing position of a guardian of wards with property, and property rights; for the defence of which he is unable to call in legal assistance." The report's description of these Indians as "wards" and the United States as their "guardian" makes it clear that Jackson and Kinney, acting as agents of the United States, were referencing tribal groups to which the United States recognized ongoing obligations. If a tribe has been terminated from federal recognition, or has never been federally recognized, its individual members are not considered federal "wards."[17]

Jackson and Kinney did not recommend just any Los Angeles law firm for the assignment. They mentioned a specific law firm, Brunson and Wells, known to them "to be of high standing at the bar, and to have a humane sympathy for Indians."[18] Beyond that, the firm had already provided a legal opinion, which was appendix A to Jackson and Kinney's *Report on the Condition and Needs of the Mission Indians of California*, presented to the commissioner of Indian affairs. In that opinion, Brunson and Wells concluded that Mexican law protected the rights of Indians to their lands; therefore, any land grants made by the Mexican governor could not confer good title on the grantee as against Indians then in possession of the lands. In his 1883 annual report, the commissioner of Indian affairs stated that he had already carried out Jackson and Kinney's recommendation by arranging for the appointment of Brunson and Wells as "assistants to the United States district attorney in such cases [affecting Indians' interests]."

As specially appointed assistant U.S. attorneys, Brunson and Wells, especially partner G. Wiley Wells,[19] embarked on a vigorous program of asserting

FIGURE 26 G. Wiley Wells (1840–1909), special U.S. attorney for San Fernando Indians. Courtesy of Library of Congress.

and defending Indian land rights. To their credit, they persisted in representing the Indians despite considerable difficulties securing payment for their own expenses and services.[20] Tribal groups at Capitan Grande in San Diego County and Soboba in Riverside County were among their clients.[21] When Porter and Maclay began carrying out Indian evictions from Rancho Ex-Mission San Fernando lands, Wells joined the fray. The case against Rogerio Rocha and several other defendants provided his opening. In many Maclay-Porter eviction actions, the Indian defendants lost because they had no counsel and never responded. In Rocha's case, however, topflight local attorneys filed an answer.[22] The Los Angeles County Superior Court nonetheless ruled against Rocha on what seemed like a meaningless technicality—his attorneys had filed the answer in the name of Rodrigo rather than Rogerio. At the eleventh hour, when the court had already ordered the sheriff to toss Rocha, his belongings, and the other occupants of the tract onto the road, Wells asked the court to stay the proceedings and reopen the default judgment against Rocha and the other defendants.

For purposes of determining federal recognition, the very fact of this representation is at least as important as the outcome of the suit. It reflects a federal relationship with the Fernandeño defendants claiming the land. Repeatedly, Wells, the federal agent involved with this work, refers to a group of "Indians," not merely individuals.

The circumstances that brought Wells into the case are documented in a letter of introduction from E. F. de Celis, son and administrator of the estate of his father, Eulogio de Celis, to Wells.[23] On July 7, 1885, a little over a month after the court directed the sheriff to evict Rocha, Rocha paid a call on Wells, handing him the letter written that day.

FIGURE 27 Rogerio Rocha (1824–1904), lineage captain. Courtesy of Fernandeño Tataviam Band of Mission Indians.

> The bearer Rogerio, an Indian from San Fernando, is one of those who, by my father's title had to be kept and provided by the owners of San Fernando in possession of their lands. Maclay and Widney want to oust them, which I know they have no right to do. Will you please look the case up? You can safely make arrangements with him. He is a good man. I cannot leave the office today or I would go with him.[24]

On December 11, 1883, the superior court entered a default judgment in favor of Maclay and Porter for possession of the Ex-Mission lands that Rocha and several others occupied, as well as for a monetary award.[25] With that judgment in hand, Maclay and Porter were a short step away from seeking a court order directing the sheriff to evict Rocha and the entire group. The two developers waited nearly a year and a half, however, to make their next move, asking the court for a writ of possession. On May 23, 1885, Los Angeles Superior Court judge A. Brunson issued the writ, ordering the sheriff to evict Rocha and the others and to seize any personal or other property that could be used to satisfy the money owed to Porter and Maclay.[26] The sheriff made his way to the disputed property on June 25, 1885, and gave the defendants fifty days to vacate. Disaster for Rocha and the other defendants was therefore imminent at the time Rocha made his way to Wells's office.

Wells had every reason to want to jump into this case, despite its advanced state. The situation confronting the community of Fernandeños was exactly what he had addressed in the legal opinion he had given several years earlier to Helen Hunt Jackson. Rocha's community claimed aboriginal title to the land and continuous possession, and Porter and Maclay were deriving their competing claims from a Mexican land grant. Within a week of his first meeting with Rocha, Wells, acting as a representative of the federal government, formally entered the litigation as counsel for Rocha and the other defendants. He asked the court to set aside the default judgment and to rescind the order to the sheriff to carry out the eviction, known as a writ of possession, arguing that there was "no valid judgment rendered . . . upon which to issue said writ of possession and the said judgment in said entitled cause is void." He pointed out that Rocha had in fact filed a formal answer (response) to the original 1878 complaint and had never abandoned his defense, yet he had never received a hearing or trial on the matter and had never even received notice of the default judgment until the sheriff came to carry out the writ. Wells also asked the court to stay the eviction pending resolution of his motion to "quash and recall" the writ of possession. On July 13, 1885, superior court judge W. A. Cheney granted the stay, forestalling the eviction while the court reviewed the motion.

Nonetheless, two months later, on September 28, 1885, the superior court entered a terse order: "Motion to set aside default denied," a decision that Wells did not appeal. Upon application by Maclay and Porter's attorney, without any new court order, the clerk of the court issued another writ of possession, ordering the sheriff to proceed with the eviction. Wells raced back to court, reminding the court that there had been no ruling on the motion to quash and recall the original writ of possession and requesting a stay until the matter could be properly resolved. In support of his request, Wells provided a sworn affidavit, identifying himself as "special assistant U.S. Attorney in Mission Indian cases for Southern California." The affidavit also refers to the defendants in the case as "Mission Indians of the San Fernando Mission" and points out several errors in the proceedings leading to the default judgment. Some are relatively minor—for example, there was a change of counsel for Maclay and Porter after the complaint was filed but no document requesting or sustaining this substitution. Other claims of error are more serious—for example, an absence of evidence that either the amended complaint, substituting real names for fictitious ones, or the default judgment had ever been served to the defendants. The most important challenge, however, was to the fact that the default was entered despite there being a responsive pleading—an answer—on file for the defendants. Default judgments can be entered only when the defendant fails to file a response.

On October 10, 1885, Judge Cheney gave Maclay and Porter nine days to respond with opposing arguments. Although the record of the proceeding has not survived, Wells was unsuccessful in persuading Cheney to withdraw the writ, doubtless because the default judgment on which it rested had been upheld. On November 2, 1885, Judge Cheney denied the motion. Because Wells again failed to appeal, the stage was set anew for the sheriff to execute the writ of possession and remove Rocha and others from the disputed property.

Wells was not the only federal official monitoring and showing concern for the situation of the Fernandeños. On November 9, 1885, three days before Rocha was tossed onto the rain-soaked road along with others occupying the land, H. N. Rust, future Mission Indian agent and then secretary of the Los Angeles chapter of the Indian Rights Association,[27] wrote to C. C. Painter, national head of the organization.

> I hope to see Mr. Wells tomorrow he tells me . . . that the San Fernando Indians 20 miles north of Los Angeles have been ordered off and twice an officer has attempted to remove them. That Wells has delayed the effort and that last Saturday was set to remove them. That he still hoped to prevent it in some way.

> He is looking up a little which he hopes will protect them even if driven off. He will do all he can he says.[28]

When no help was forthcoming from the court, Wells wrote directly to Maclay and Porter:

> When Mr. DeCeles called on me with this Indian, and informed us that in the grant from the Government to his father there was a provision made that these Indians were to be maintained in possession of the lands which they occupied during their lifetime, I asked him whether this clause had been continued in the deed between the administrator and those purchasing. He informed me, that while it might not be in the deed, yet there was a distinct understanding and pledge between the parties purchasing and the parties selling. . . . Mr. DeCeles informs me that at the time the ranch was sold you and the other purchasers distinctly understood the matter. If that is so, while it may not be a legal obligation, yet the matter rests with you as to whether they are to remain.[29]

Maclay and Porter were not about to relent. The actual circumstances of the eviction were the subject of some controversy. When the Indian Rights Association and the Lake Mohonk Conference publicized the eviction as an injustice perpetrated by heartless land developers, Maclay and Porter, along with their attorney (now judge), R. M. Widney, protested, claiming they had generously offered Rocha housing, provisions, and even compensation to ease the pain of dispossession.[30] But there was eyewitness testimony to the contrary from H. N. Rust himself, who rushed to the scene at the time of eviction. Furthermore, C. C. Painter, national head of the Indian Rights Association, responded with affidavits from Rocha as well as from the deputy sheriffs who had carried out the evictions, testifying to the absence of any such offers.

The facts that land in the San Fernando Valley had become extraordinarily valuable and that the local state courts were arrayed against the Fernandeños' claims made it impossible for the defendants to succeed at affirming rights to land that could have formed the foundation for a reservation. Nonetheless, Wells's efforts to assert and protect the Fernandeños' claims to their ancestral lands demonstrate that the federal government was treating the Fernandeños as a group for which it recognized responsibility.

For the next forty-five years, evicted Fernandeños lived in makeshift shelters on federal public land that in 1908 became known as the Angeles National Forest. Others made shelters on the ranches where they worked.[31] Rocha, being of advanced years, built a rough hut for himself in a wild, inaccessible ravine known as Lopez Canyon, living "in daily fear lest some Christian man shall drive him away."[32] Lopez Canyon is about four miles from downtown San Fernando. Rocha survived on the little he could cultivate and on charity from sympathetic federal Indian agents. In 1903, H. N. Rust, who had served as head of the Mission Agency from 1889 to 1893, received a visit from Rocha at his home in Pasadena. Rust's notes from the occasion reveal the following:

> As an old man to come 25 miles to ask for food to sustain life. He is apparently well and strong considering his age. He speaks Spanish only, is tidy in his habits and took dinner with us conducting himself modestly and well.[33]

Rust did his best to help Rocha survive, knowing that Rocha had a leadership role and would be influential among the Fernandeños. In those same notes from the 1903 visit, he wrote that

> I was appointed Indian agent I visited him and helped him all I could with the miserable pittance allowed the agent for the sick and indigent of three thousand Indians about two hundred dollars per annum. Since then I have twice requested the Agent to send him rations which I think has been done, about five dollars in value. I have requested the present Agent Dr. Wright to send him rations which he will do if he can.[34]

Although such financial assistance alone probably does not establish federal recognition of the Fernandeños, it is consistent with recognition. The United States generally does not dispense federal funds to Indians who have no affiliation with a recognized tribe, simply because of their ancestry.[35] And the fact that aid was given to an acknowledged captain suggests that officials of the United States understood that Fernandeño leaders took care of others in their lineage and network of lineages.

Apart from the efforts of Wells and Rust, another demonstration of federal recognition occurred from 1892 to 1897 when attorney Frank D. Lewis, acting on behalf of the United States, endeavored to reopen Fernandeño land claims.[36] Lewis's introduction to Indian affairs came in 1887, when he was a young lawyer employed by the U.S. War Department.[37] One year earlier, the Lake Mohonk Conference of Friends of the Indian, since 1883 a forum for government officials, academics, clergy, philanthropists, and newspaper editors to discuss and agitate for improvements in federal Indian policy, had established the Committee on

Legal Assistance to the Mission Indians. Legal encroachments on mission Indian lands, well documented in the Jackson-Kinney report of 1883,[38] were continuing and even intensifying as "the great land boom of the 1880s"[39] overtook Southern California. In its report back to the conference in 1887, the Committee on Legal Assistance to the Mission Indians reported the following:

> As the province of this committee (as far as [litigation] was concerned) could not extend beyond *offering* aid to the Government counsel, the committee then sought for a person with legal training to act as field-agent, to prepare for the contingency of other suits already threatened, and to engage in the immediate defense of numerous small bands and individual families, who were too ignorant or too discouraged to apply to Government for protection, and in the invasion of whose rights there had been little or no check, and no regard for the decisions of courts.
>
> The voluntary and frequent visits of a recognized legal adviser to all parts of the field, ready to respond promptly in case of need, restoring long-lost courage in the Indians and checking their timid surrender of rights, was, in the opinion of the committee, a vital step. . . . After a prolonged search the services of Mr. Frank D. Lewis were secured, and he entered upon the work February 23d of this year.[40]

The Soboba Indians of Riverside County had recently achieved a partial legal victory when the California Supreme Court affirmed their rights to occupy land covered by Mexican land grants.[41] The Lake Mohonk committee directed Lewis to work for extension of the benefit of this ruling to other mission Indian tribes and "earnestly acknowledge[ed] . . . the zeal and thoroughness of [his] work."[42]

Lewis emigrated to California in 1888, and a year later, when Rust became Mission Indian agent, Lewis was appointed a U.S. special agent of the Office of Indian Affairs to the mission Indians,[43] a traveling position that included inspection duties. After two years, Lewis moved to Los Angeles, where he resumed his law practice and was also appointed by the Department of Justice as the U.S. special attorney for mission Indians. As special attorney, Lewis was instructed by the U.S. attorney general to take "such action as the Department of the Interior or Commissioner of Indian Affairs might direct, *or as in [his] judgment should be necessary*" (emphasis added).[44] This direction from the attorney general shows that Lewis had discretion to identify and take action on behalf of appropriate Indian entities. His work is documented in annual reports he submitted to the attorney general between 1892 and 1897, reports included, in turn, in each *Annual*

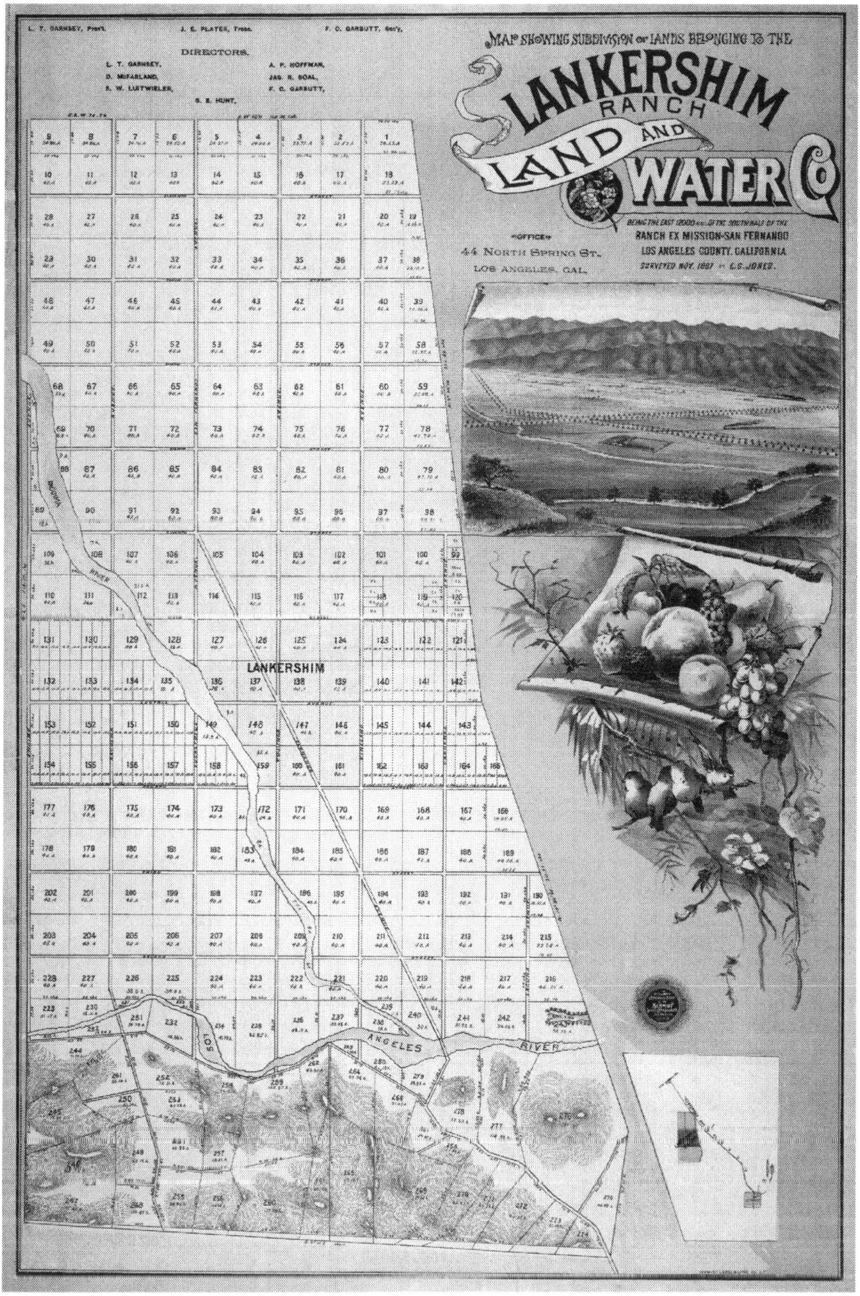

FIGURE 28 Map (1887) showing subdivision of lands belonging to the Lankershim Ranch Land and Water Co., being the east 1,200 acres of the south half of Rancho Ex-Mission San Fernando, Los Angeles County, California. Created by Schmidt Label and Lithographic Co., Lithographer. Courtesy of UCLA, Library Special Collections, Charles E. Young Research Library.

Report of the Attorney General of the United States.[45] Correspondence between Lewis and the commissioner of Indian affairs makes clear that the latter was his client, as he provided accounts of his plans and activities and solicited "further instructions."[46]

While Lewis was operating as a federal official, the committee of the Lake Mohonk Conference that had originally drawn him into Indian affairs work supported him and kept abreast of his activities. The entwining of private reformist and public endeavors in the Indian policy of the late nineteenth century, illustrated sharply in the work of Frank Lewis, was prompted largely by the dearth of government funds to support investigations and legal actions. The first act of the committee was to raise $5,000 for anticipated legal assistance in local tribal matters.[47] In 1892, the U.S. attorney general wrote to Lewis that the Department of Justice had no funds allocated for litigation on behalf of Indians. "If the government is to undertake the whole expense of the litigation such recommendation should come from the officer (secretary of the interior) inasmuch as he is in charge of the Indians."[48] Unfortunately for Lewis, the Interior did not step up. In its 1891 report to the Lake Mohonk Conference, the Committee on Legal Assistance to the Mission Indians observed that during his work on the committee's behalf,

> Lewis . . . was everywhere known among the Indians as the Abogado (the lawyer) who worked for them without pay, and thus acquired their unlimited confidence and regard.
>
> . . . The work of your committee for supply of legal assistance was intended to be supplemental to the limited legal help that could at first be secured from the Government; and during the past year, with such a Government commission at work in the field [the Smiley Commission, charged with implementing the 1891 Mission Indian Act] and Mr. Lewis in the office of special United States attorney caring for the work in the courts, the attitude of your committee has been one of simple waiting for the developments from this enlarged government effort.[49]

One of those "enlarged" government efforts emerged when Lewis took up the cause of the Fernandeños. On October 17, 1892, Lewis wrote the following to the commissioner of Indian affairs:

> Some time ago my attention was called to the condition of company of Indians living on the edge of the San Fernando Grant in Los Angeles County, Califor-

nia, and I was asked to take such steps as I might find possible and advisable in order to secure to them lands of which they had been unjustly deprived.[50]

Lewis's use of the passive voice makes it difficult to identify the source of his concern. It's fair to believe, however, that during Lewis's years working as special assistant to H. N. Rust, from 1889 to 1891, Rust had alerted Lewis to the Fernandeños' situation. In late 1885, at the time of the San Fernando evictions, and while Rust was still a local officer of the Indian Rights Association, Rust had rushed to the aid of the evicted Indians, forsaken and left exposed to the elements. Later, as Mission Indian agent, Rust remained in periodic contact with one of their captains, Rogerio Rocha, supplying pittances of relief and provisions.[51] It seems reasonable that Rust would have briefed Lewis on the injustices surrounding the Fernandeños' dispossession.[52] A few months before writing to the commissioner, Lewis also visited the U.S. General Land Office, where he was given access to the "complete record in the case" of the Ex-Mission San Fernando confirmation and patent and "was informed that this office could not do anything in the matter."[53]

To support his request to engage with this matter, Lewis reported the following to the commissioner:

> Upon examining into the case, I found that these people were the remaining members and descendants of the Band or Village to whom Manuel Micheltorena, governor of California, granted one league of land May 3, 1843. . . .
>
> Further investigation shows that these people had lived in quiet and undisturbed possession of the land called for in the grant, for many years,—that in 1846 Governor Pio Pico made a grant of the Ex Mission of San Fernando to Eulogio de Celis . . .—and that when, after confirmation of the claim was filed with the Commission to settle the private land claims in California of thirteen or fourteen leagues—a survey of the San Fernando Ranch was made, not only was the one league belonging to these Indians included, but about 50,000 acres of adjoining lands, to which other Indians, as well as whites and Mexicans, had valid claims under then existing grants.[54]

Lewis related that on further investigation, he found "not only had these Indians lived quietly and peaceably on the tract granted them by Micheltorena, but that Rojerio, the chief or captain had, up to 1884, paid state and county taxes regularly upon the land—that in 1886 under color of legal process they were removed entirely from the land and have ever since been kept out of possession."[55]

Seeking support from the commissioner for legal intervention, Lewis underscored the need for his services. "These Indians," he wrote, "are extremely poor and are unable to stand the expense of an action in the courts to maintain their legal rights."[56] He argued that the failure of the Board of Land Commissioners to address the interests of the Indians in the land as required by the 1851 Act to Ascertain and Settle the Private Land Claims in the State of California[57] "should not be allowed to in any way militate against the interests and rights of the Indians, but their case is at the present time in such condition that it seems to be impossible to re-establish them in their lands within the outside boundaries of the San Fernando Ranch as long as the grant owners remain in their present position."[58]

Lewis pointed out that if the 1873 land patent confirming that the grant could be canceled and annulled, "the Indians will be put upon in equality with the grant owners before the courts, provided the sixteenth section of the Act of Congress created in the California Board of Land Commissioners is held to exempt the Indians from the necessity of presenting their claims to the Commission, and there seems to be no reason for placing any other construction upon it."[59] Not only failure to comply with the 1851 act but also the absence of markers designating the vast land covered by the patent opened the possibility of successful challenge, Lewis argued.[60]

Concluding his plea for support, Lewis appealed to the commissioner for authorization to bring suit in the federal courts "to cancel the patent for the Rancho Ex Mission of San Fernando . . . on the grounds of fraud, mistake, uncertainty, and that it conflicts with and includes lands of the Indians."[61] For Lewis, the obligations of the United States as trustee compelled such action: "It is clear that by reason of the palpable neglect of its officers, the United States owes to these people the duty of using every means within its power to right the wrong under which they have suffered for so long a time."[62] He enclosed with his letter a translation of the deed to the property and the petition made by the forty Fernandeños for a square league of land.[63]

At the time, Lewis did not receive authorization from the commissioner of Indian affairs for a lawsuit to annul the de Celis patent. What he did obtain, in August of that year, was a quitclaim deed to all of Rocha's rights and title to the square league of Ex-Mission San Fernando lands that Governor Micheltorena had granted to the forty, paying Rocha $10 in exchange.[64] His purpose, he later said, was to acquire standing so he could bring suit as a trustee for the Fernandeños' interests. He had been approached by a "league or association of settlers or squatters"[65] who saw advantage in reviving the Indians' rights and disrupting existing titles. They had raised funds to support litigation to that end, securing an agreement from Lewis that he would deed to them two-thirds of the land awarded to him in the event of success, so long as he retained at least four hundred acres. No such suit was brought at that time, however. He moved to Riverside in 1892, continuing his work as special assistant U.S. attorney but also pursuing his own interests: practicing law and tending to his orange groves.

The legal needs of the Fernandeños do not seem to have claimed much of Lewis's further attention until late 1895, when Los Angeles attorney L. H. Valentine, representing the "league or association," wrote to him: "The parties who are agitating the Indian land question called this morning and paid $50.00 on account of fees, of which I send you, by enclosed draft $25.00."[66] Lewis seemed poised to launch the suit on behalf of the forty Fernandeño grantees and their descendants, including Rogerio Rocha.

What occurred next whipped up a hurricane of controversy. Accounts can be found in the Los Angeles newspapers, in litigation that erupted in the local courts, and in correspondence between Lewis and his superiors. The *Los Angeles Herald* evidently learned of Lewis's quitclaim deed from Rocha, and it broadcast the story as a tale of betrayal and avarice.

> Helen Hunt Jackson were she alive today could write a true story which would rival *Ramona* as a tale of the terrible injustice and wrong which has been done the Mission Indians. All that it would be necessary for her to do would be to detail the history of Rogerio Rocha and his long and futile struggle with the rapacious land grabbers who have despoiled him of his possessions and left him and his posterity beggars, in a comparatively barren mountain canyon, when if the records have been read aright, he and they are the real owners of thousands of the most fertile acres in the San Fernando valley of this county.[67]

After recounting the legal proceedings that resulted in Rocha's eviction, the story portrayed Rocha in the most pitiful terms: "The victim [Rocha] is ekeing out a precarious existence far up in the Soledad canon, a pauper in his old age, when if he were granted his rights, as they seem to be, he would be entitled to an estate worth thousands and thousands of dollars."[68] Setting out, word-for-word, the terms of the quitclaim deed that Rocha made to Lewis, the *Los Angeles Herald* proceeded to decry Lewis's abuse of his trusteeship role.

> Now it is understood that a syndicate is being formed in this city to purchase the right of Lewis, which he acquired from Rocha, and to press the matter in the courts. Lewis' position in the case is very singular. While acting as an

attorney to protect the rights of the Indians he secures for $10 a quit claim deed which is worth thousands and thousands. The matter has been taken in hand by a number of citizens, and it will be presented to the Indian Rights Association. A strong endeavor will be made to compel Lewis to disgorge, and it is believed that this can be done without any very great difficulty, as attorneys assert that he had no right to take advantage of his position as the legal adviser appointed to protect the Indians in their rights to secure for himself for a nominal sum the very rights he had been engaged to defend for them.[69]

A follow-up story in the *Herald,* dated January 24, 1896, reiterated Rocha's pitiful state as "a pauper, without a place to lay his head, while whatever rights he may have had in the broad, rich acres of San Fernando have been lost to him by the treachery of his attorney."[70] This depiction prompted Lewis to file a libel action against the *Herald* for $50,000 in damages.[71] In a scathingly sarcastic report on the filing of the suit, the *Herald* defended its motivation in covering the story: "The Herald has been moved by no desire to persecute Mr. Lewis or to wantonly reflect on his professional ability or motives. But conscious of the rank injustice with which *a ward of the government* has been treated it has given the facts for the good that may result" (emphasis added).[72]

Ten days after its initial report, likely in response to the libel suit, the *Herald* ran a sensationalist, full-page follow-up feature on Rocha's eviction and its aftermath, complete with sketches of him and his "little mud house" in Lopez Canyon.[73] For this story, the *Herald* sent a translator, Pedro Lopez, and a reporter to Rocha's home, where they interviewed him for two hours and obtained a sworn statement. Perhaps to drum up sympathy for Rocha (and also the *Herald* itself), the story was heavy on details about Rocha's devout adherence to the Catholic faith and the pathos of his conditions, as well as the questionable legal circumstances of his eviction and the suffering it caused. The portrayal of R. M. Widney, then attorney for Maclay and Porter in the eviction case, and by the time of the feature on Rocha, a judge, was particularly unflattering, emphasizing the

A STORY OF THE TERRIBLE WRONGS THAT HAVE BEEN PUT UPON ROGERIO ROCHA

Turned Out of His Home With His Bedridden Wife in a Blinding Rainstorm to Die

FIGURE 29 Headline from the *Los Angeles Herald*, February 2, 1896. California Digital Newspaper Collection, University of California, Riverside, Center for Bibliographic Studies and Research.

technical basis for the default judgment against Rocha and the others and doubting Widney's claim that Rocha had no claims to the land to begin with.

Attempting to provide some balance, the *Herald* also quoted Lewis, who explained that his purpose in securing the quitclaim deed was "to protect [Rocha] from the wiles of rapacious land schemers who were endeavoring to secure the same character of a deed." Lewis also pointed out that he had given Rocha back a trust deed, "which would fully and amply protect him." However, the *Herald* reported it could find no recording of such a trust deed. Friends of Lewis argued that failure to record the trust deed was deliberate, designed to discourage predatory speculators who were hoping to take advantage of a naïve and untutored Indian.[74]

Rocha's sworn statement described a visit to his home in Lopez Canyon several years earlier by Lewis and Antonio Coronel, a long-time advocate for the mission Indians and one of the sources for Helen Hunt Jackson. Having introduced Lewis to Rocha, Coronel left the two of them to communicate via sign language, as Lewis spoke no Spanish and Rocha no English. According to Rocha, Lewis asked him to help locate two other surviving Fernandeños, Gregorio Camilo

FIGURE 30 Drawing of Rogerio Rocha's home in 1896, included in an article in the *Los Angeles Herald*, February 2, 1896. California Digital Newspaper Collection, University of California, Riverside, Center for Bibliographic Studies and Research.

and Felicita Buendia (de Capistrano), which Rocha did. (These were individuals who Valentine had identified as descendants of the 1843 grantees from Governor Micheltorena.)[75] However, Felicita Buendia was the daughter of Pastor Cano, and she was the leader of the Cano lineage. The Canos were not among the forty petitioners of 1843. Gregorio Camilo was the son of the captain named Camilo, who was one of the forty petitioners. He was also the grandson of Rafael, captain of the Jotativit lineage. Most likely Gregorio was a captain. The meeting then was between three captains of different lineages.[76]

At Gregorio Camilo's residence on the Geronimo Lopez Ranch, where Camilo worked, Lewis directed both Rocha and Camilo to put their marks on a paper. Felicita Buendia refused to sign. Rocha denied that Lewis paid him $10 for the quitclaim deed or provided a trust deed in return, either to him or to Camilo. He also claimed that he had no understanding of what he was signing but trusted the fact that Lewis was his lawyer. A joint affidavit from Gregorio Camilo and Felicita Buendia confirmed Rocha's account.

Lewis was not about to let such a harsh assessment of his conduct stand unanswered, and the *Herald*'s story included his very different account of the same events. He claimed that Rocha had signed the quitclaim deed and received the trust deed in the law office of Edwin A. Meserve in downtown Los Angeles, and Rocha's mark had been witnessed by a notary. To the reporter from the *Herald*, the notary in question could provide no record or recollection of the transaction. Meserve, however, emphatically corroborated Lewis's version of the story. In the meantime, Rocha made yet another deed, conveying his interests in the disputed lands to Pedro Lopez, who threatened to sue Lewis over his transactions with Rocha.

A few days later, the *Herald* again followed up on the story.[77] Lewis had traveled from Riverside to Los Angeles to meet with a representative of the *Herald*, and the paper surmised from that conversation that Lewis had no belief in Rocha's ability to make a successful legal claim at this point. Lewis also recounted a dispute that had erupted between C. C. Painter, the head of the Indian Rights Association, and Judge Widney regarding Widney's role in perpetrating the injustice against Rocha. Now Widney was threatening to sue Painter for libel, and Lewis relayed that Painter was so eager for the engagement that he had traveled to California so he could be served. An anonymous correspondent for the *Herald*, known only as "Justice," challenged Judge Widney over the technical default entered against Rocha and proposed that he agree to litigate the merits of Rocha's title and acquiesce to the result should it be to annul the de Celis patent.

This was too exciting a story for the *Herald* to let it go. In a few more days, the paper reported its finding that Lewis was simultaneously working for the federal government as special assistant U.S. attorney and for a local organization called the Indian Lands Association, which was formed to obtain Indian property interests, assert those interests in the courts, and then acquire the lands for themselves.[78] That association had paid Lewis over $500 for his services but, according to the *Herald*, fell out with him over further fees and the quitclaim deed. Then Judge Widney felt obliged to weigh in, explaining he had arrived at an agreement with the Indian Rights Association that would obviate any need for a libel action and, in a diversionary move, attacking the anonymous "Justice" for refusing to disclose his true identity. Until that identity was disclosed, Widney would not take the proposal seriously. Adding further conditions, Widney insisted that "Justice" first respond to three other "preliminary" questions:

> Do you now claim that Rogerio Rocha has a title to any lands. . . .—Or do you claim that he ever had a title and lost it? . . . If you claim that he ever had a title, then was it under the De Celis grant? If so, print the clause from the grant. If not under that grant, then name the grant, and state whether it was ever presented to the board of land commissioners for approval and what final action was had upon it.[79]

By insisting that Rocha's claim be founded on a grant that was presented to the Board of Land Commissioners under the 1851 act of Congress, Widney was loading the dice against Rocha and his allies. Of course, the whole point of Wells's legal opinion and Lewis's efforts was to demonstrate that the Indians were *not* required to submit their claims to that very board.

Lewis never followed up with a legal action on behalf of Rocha. And none of the several libel actions developed any momentum in the courts. A month later, at the request of the local U.S. attorney, Lewis wrote a letter to the attorney general in Washington, DC, explaining his actions and insisting that he was at all times true to his role as trustee for the Indians. As he put it, his financial backers "have been given to understand unequivocally that I was acting solely as trustee for the Indians."[80]

Although authorization for Lewis to bring suit on behalf of the Fernandeños would have been strong evidence of federal recognition, recognition was evident even without a lawsuit. Legal and economic obstacles, not the failure to identify a body of Indian "wards," militated against the litigation. Recall that G. Wiley Wells, acting on behalf of the United States, had earlier received permission to represent the Fernandeños in the same matter, at a time, 1885, when the judgment of eviction had not yet reached finality.[81] Once that judgment became final, the chances of successfully attacking the patent weakened considerably. It also did not help that seven years had elapsed between the eviction and Lewis's interest in reopening the issue. As the commissioner of the General Land Office wrote in a related matter where non-Indians challenged the same de Celis patent,

> The patent has been outstanding, in full force and effect, for nineteen years; the land is possessed by a corporation engaged in agriculture, with large interests involved, as appears by papers filed by present petitioners.[82]

What should matter for purposes of federal recognition is the way Lewis characterized the claim he wished to pursue, a characterization he made in his capacity as a federal official. If he was acting on behalf of a collective tribe of Indians, then his actions amount to federal recognition. Indeed, it would only make sense for him to act on behalf of an Indian entity, as it was not the federal government's responsibility to represent (and spend federal resources on) individual Indians who had severed tribal relations or were not part of a recognized Indian group.

Throughout his tenure, which lasted until 1897, Lewis equated the Fernandeños he represented with federally recognized tribes, including them in references without distinction. The same month of October 1892, when Lewis wrote to the commissioner of Indian affairs about his proposed litigation to cancel the de Celis patent, he also made an address to the Lake Mohonk Conference, reporting on the work of the Smiley Commission, which was charged with carrying out the terms of the Mission Indian Act of 1891. In that presentation, Lewis acknowledged that despite the commission's good work, "the Indians living on Mexican land grants—particularly those on the Warner's Ranch, the Santa Ysabel Ranch, the San Felipe Ranch, and the San Fernando Ranch—still faced the possibility of forced removal."[83] Federal recognition was forthcoming or already in place for the Indians occupying all the other lands that Lewis mentioned apart from San Fernando, either through federal executive orders or purchase allowed under the Mission Indian Relief Act of 1891. Of all the tracts mentioned, however, only the "San Fernando Ranch" was in the heart of a major land boom, making acquisition of land for a reservation prohibitive.[84] And it was already clear, through the observations of Helen Hunt Jackson, that the Indians living on their ancestral lands "would almost rather die than be removed" to reservations purchased or established on public lands elsewhere.[85]

Moreover, throughout his tenure, Lewis referred to a community of Indians that shared the land and the land claim, not to an individual or individuals. Lewis's October 1892 letter to the commissioner of Indian affairs referred to "a company of Indians" and noted that "these people were the remaining *members* and descendants of the *band or village* to whom Manuel Micheltorena, Governor of California, granted one league of land May 3rd, 1843" (emphasis added).[86] The record of the names of the grantees from the 1843 grant shows that they are all lineage heads and Fernandeños.[87]

For example, the deed was "instituted by Joaquin an Indian of the Mission of San Fernando soliciting a tract of land together with several neophytes of the same Establishment."[88] In his letter petitioning for the grant, Joaquin identifies himself as alcalde, an elected leadership title within the mission, and he is speaking on behalf of what ultimately amounted to forty Indian petitioners, many of whom are tied to the lineages forming the present-day Fernandeño Tataviam Band of Mission Indians.[89] In fact, Joaquin was a former brother-in-law to Francisco Papabubaba, the direct male ancestor of the Ortega lineage, having married Francisco's sister, Felipa. Furthermore, Rogerio (Rojerio) Rocha was identified in the list of petitioners. Cosme, future father-in-law to Maria Rita Alipaz, the daughter of Francisco Papabubaba, is also identified. Cornelio, a direct male progenitor of the present-day Garcia lineage, is also identified among the forty petitioners. Others are identified in the text of the petition, including Vicente, who was alcalde and primary legal witness at the wedding of Benigno and Maria Rita (a progenitor of the present-day Ortega lineage) in 1845.

The land granted by Governor Micheltorena was collectively owned by all forty petitioners, and the land was held in trust by the Mexican government. The deed forbids the joint owners to sell the land, "that all of them be mentioned without the(m) being able to sell the land."[90] Micheltorena, in a letter of May 3, 1843, wrote, "Joaquin and his partners mentioned in the amended list are entitled to the tract of land they solicit to sow their grain."[91]

By invoking this Mexican grant, Lewis, acting as special assistant U.S. attorney for mission Indians, identified a company of Indians and tied their identities to the Fernandeños, who in collective action won for themselves a square league of land for their self-support in 1843. Members of this "company of Indians" are related to many members and lineages of the present-day Fernandeño Tataviam Band of Mission Indians.

As noted above, and in appendix B, "List and Analysis of the Forty Petitioners," there are many connections between the lineages of the forty petitioners and the lineages constituting or eligible for enrollment in the present-day tribe.[92] Rita and Triunfo had attachments to Cahuenga. Rita, a progenitor of the Ortega lineage, married Cosme's son, Benigno. Cosme was one of the forty petitioners, and he was a descendant of the lineage at Cahuenga. Triunfo's mother was born at Cahuenga, and Triunfo is a progenitor of the Ortiz lineage. Ramon, who was one of the forty petitioners, and his spouse, Eugenia, are both progenitors of the Garcia lineage.

Repeated, melodramatic portrayals of the eviction of the noble and pious Rogerio Rocha do not mean that the efforts of Lewis (and Wells before him) were only for an individual, or at most an individual and his immediate family, rather than for a tribal community. We know there was a group of Indians living in multiple dwellings on Rancho Cienega from which Rocha was evicted.[93] Only one of those people, Rogerio's wife, Manuela, was related to him.[94] Rocha's leadership role[95] also confirms the existence of a tribal community of Indians, for without an entity there can be no leader. At the time of Rocha's eviction, the sheriff who carried it out referred to Rocha as "the old Captain."[96] Ten years later, in an interview with the *Los Angeles Herald*, Rocha himself explained his role: "My father was a captain of my people. . . . Then after my father died I became the captain, as all my people recognized me as such."[97] Rocha's lineages were Ventureño speakers from Quimishag on his father's side and Fernandeño speakers from Tujunga on his mother's side.

A contrary argument, that Lewis was helping only one individual Indian, might focus on an affidavit that Rocha made in 1887 addressing the earlier court proceeding to set aside the ejectment.[98] In that affidavit, Rocha says the land is "mine" and identifies himself as the only Indian paying taxes on the land. There are several reasons to question this reading of the affidavit, however. First, we know that Rocha did not speak English. Hence, the translation may not have captured his full meaning and may have been filtered through non-Native notions of property ownership, which privilege individual, private claims rather than collective rights.

Second, and more important, there is every reason to believe that Rocha's words, even as captured in an imperfect translation, referred to collective rather than individual rights. Rocha swears that "my antecedents from time immemorial" lived in the area of the Rancho Cienega. But he could not have been referring to his father's biological ancestors, who were from a Chumash village many miles away to the northwest. Rocha's ten-acre farm was just northeast of the mission, directly to the east of the mission village. Rocha's mother's lineage was Tujubit, whose central village, Tujunga, was nearly fifteen miles to the east of his farm. Thus, when Rocha referred to "antecedents" (assuming correct translation), he meant the Tujubit lineage or the lineage living in the Tujunga area. Villages need water, and so lineages form settlements near drinkable water within their joint lineage territory. Rocha, referring to his antecedents, was speaking about thousands of years of land and water legacy experienced by the Tujubit people.[99] Water was shared among lineage members and members of friendly lineages. Mission Indians expected that the water at Rancho Cienega would be shared. Even the reference to paying property taxes can be understood within the context of traditional leadership. As a captain, Rocha was obliged to provide for his community and to share resources.[100] Given his earning capacity based on the value of his metalworking skills in the local economy, he would have been expected to support the community by paying the property taxes.

Third, unlike other Fernandeños, such as Samuel and Odon, Rocha and his father never received a grant or deed to Rancho Cienega. As noted above, this land was also outside the square league that had been granted to forty Fernandeño petitioners, including Rocha and his father, by California governor Micheltorena in 1843. Thus, there is no record of individual title having been conferred on Rocha or his father. On the advice of Eulogio de Celis, Rocha had paid taxes on the land. Nonetheless, any rights that Rocha had to the land were necessarily embedded in rights of the Tujubit (Tujunga) lineage through the doctrine of aboriginal title and the terms of the Ex-Mission grant to de Celis. Hence, any efforts to prevent the evictions invoked these broader claims and were not for the benefit of a single individual.

When federal agent Frank Lewis later took up the cause of the Fernandeños, Rocha and others had already been evicted from Rancho Cienega. In his October 1892 letter to the commissioner of Indian affairs, Lewis's attention was drawn to the beneficiaries of the separate grant of one square league. Rocha was included in this account not because he had been living on (or been evicted from) that square league but because he was one of the original grantees and an acknowledged leader among the small group of surviving Fernandeños. Indeed, in his letter to the commissioner, Lewis describes Rocha as a "Chief or Capitan" of the group of Indians who "lived quietly and peacefully on the tract of land granted to them by Micheltorena."[101]

Both Wells and Lewis were pursuing a program launched by the federally sponsored Jackson-Kinney report, which was intended to establish protected land bases for Southern California Indian tribes. For example, Lewis's letter to the commissioner of Indian affairs in 1892 uses the plural form when he refers to taking steps to "secure to them land of which they had been justly deprived." Their charge was not to help isolated private-land claimants who happened to be Indian. Establishing Indian rights to Rancho Cienega would have provided a foundation for just such a land base and reservation for the Fernandeños. Establishing Indian rights to the square league granted by Mexican governor

Micheltorena would have provided an even larger land base. Thus, treating Wells's and Lewis's legal representation of Rocha as action on behalf of a tribal group is consistent with their full range of activities. Unfortunately, land in the San Fernando Valley was far more valuable and coveted for development than land that was sought for other tribal groups. Furthermore, the legal theories that Lewis wished to propound would have upset a great many established land titles, making government officials, such as those in the U.S. Land Office, unwilling to lend support. Had Wells and Lewis succeeded in establishing Rocha's and other Fernandeño Indians' rights to the ten-acre farm or the square league, the federal government would have been spared the considerable expense and political difficulty of purchasing the land. Unfortunately, the Indians' legal rights were given little consideration or respect in the courts, so there was no realistic prospect at the time of a land base for the Fernandeño lineages.

SUMMARY

When the work of G. Wiley Wells, H. N. Rust, and Frank D. Lewis on behalf of the Fernandeños (meaning members of interconnected lineages born at the mission and their descendants) is put together, the elements of federal recognition come into focus: official federal activity on behalf of a community of Fernandeños, including pursuit of legal actions to recover land originally granted to that community in 1843. From Lewis, as well as other sources, there is also evidence that this tribal community had a political leadership or captains, such as Rogerio Rocha, who managed land and took action to preserve the community's last remaining collective assets. From a more contemporary perspective, it is particularly important that the members of this community include lineage ancestors of the present-day Fernandeño Tataviam Band of Mission Indians.

CHAPTER 6

Lying Low but Laying Groundwork (1900–1950)

Over the first half of the twentieth century, the Ortega, Garcia, Ortiz, and other Fernandeño families—English-named versions of precontact lineages—struggled to sustain their communities and ties with one another while also seeking to escape the notice of hostile government and private actors. Although they kept a low profile to the outside, they simultaneously found new frameworks to carry out their traditional lineage organization, cultural forms, and decision-making processes, acting collectively and interacting meaningfully as Fernandeño lineage groups and with external communities. They were, in effect, laying the groundwork for more formal political and social relationships to emerge in the second half of the century.

FERNANDEÑOS AT THE TURN OF THE TWENTIETH CENTURY

As of 1900, the population of the entire San Fernando Valley was less than three thousand,[1] and in 1913 a visitor to the San Fernando Valley could still observe "league on league of grain, waving ready for harvest, a crop to be measured by the thousands of tons."[2] Even without the massive population influx that everyone anticipated soon, land losses and evictions had already dispossessed all the Fernandeños. To survive, they found work as artisans, laborers, and farmhands and ranch hands, living on the margins of a Southern California economy that would soon be transformed by massive infrastructure investments in water and transportation.[3] While adapting as low-wage workers in the changing economy and stratified society of Southern California, they never lost sight of their Indigenous identities and lineage relations.

Espiritu Leonis, daughter of the Chumash leader Odon, was able to hold on to her family's Rancho El Escorpione (Escorpion) through her common-law marriage to Miguel Leonis, who had bought out her relatives in 1871. When Leonis died in 1889, Espiritu spent years in court defending her claim, ultimately succeeding in 1905. Following her death the next year, her son from a prior marriage, Juan Jose Menendez, inherited the land, which was sold after his death in the 1920s. Menendez had no children, and there are no longer any descendants from that lineage.

Other lineages fared even worse. Rogerio Rocha, the highly visible symbol of mistreatment of the Fernandeños, succumbed to death at a very old age in 1904, a year after making the trek to Pasadena to seek support from H. N. Rust. At the time of his death, Rocha was still living in his “little mud house” in undeveloped Lopez Canyon, just a few miles northeast of the mission. No children or grandchildren survived him either, though through his marriage to Manuela he was related to Josefa Leyva, a progenitor of what was later called the Garcia lineage.

A few other lineages did escape the direst fate and became more fruitful. Josefa Leyva, the Garcia lineage progenitor, had left her husband, Isidoro Garcia, by the late 1880s, and married William Gardner. With two of her three children by Isidoro, Petra and James, Josefa and William Gardner headed for Tejon, where her maternal relatives lived.[4] After Josefa separated from Gardner around 1907, she and Petra moved southwest, near the present-day cities of Oxnard and Ventura, an area associated with Josefa’s Chumash ancestors.[5] Through all of this, Josefa’s second daughter by Isidoro, Frances, remained with her father in Newhall, just ten miles northwest of San Fernando.[6] In 1901, Frances gave birth to Mary, the first of her eleven children. Like her mother, Mary would become a Garcia lineage captain. Petra stayed in Ventura County, where she married a man of Mexican ancestry, Jesus Valenzuela, and lived with her family until her death in 1930. Josefa remarried about 1908 to Antonio Gutierrez, and they had one male child in 1909. After the passing of her husband, Josefa reconciled with her first partner, Isidoro. She returned to San Fernando to live with him from the mid-1930s until his death in 1943.[7] The center of gravity for the Garcia lineage, however, was Newhall, at least until Frances and her family moved back to San Fernando in the late 1930s.

In the early decades of the twentieth century, life in Newhall revolved around ranching and farming. The Newhall family had assembled over one hundred thousand acres around the former Rancho San Francisco, earlier the site of a Tataviam village, an estancia or rural outpost for San Fernando Mission, and then a Mexican land grant.[8] With the help of irrigation, citrus groves and fields of wheat, alfalfa, corn, and sugarcane generated work into the 1920s.[9] Emblematic of the ranching life at Newhall was the life and career of Frances Garcia Cooke’s

FIGURE 31 Josefa (1865–1952), lineage captain, and Isidoro (1860–1943), reunited in San Fernando ca. 1940. Courtesy of Fernandeño Tataviam Band of Mission Indians.

son, Cy Cooke, born in 1909. Cy was a quintessential cowboy, who broke his first horse when he was eight years old and showed horses by the age of fourteen. A dashing figure of renowned horsemanship, he married the daughter of the ranch owner who employed him and so impressed the owner of Newhall Ranch that he was brought to Northern California to train the owner's polo ponies.[10]

Sadly for that way of life, tragedy struck in 1928, when the St. Francis Dam, situated about ten miles above the Newhalls' ranch in San Francisquito Canyon, suddenly collapsed.[11] The dam had been constructed by the Los Angeles Department of Water and Power just a few years earlier to hold water brought to the city by the recently completed California Aqueduct. The dam fell apart suddenly and completely, sending more than twelve billion gallons of water and waves higher than ten stories flooding down the canyon and into the Santa Clara riverbed at speeds exceeding ten miles per hour. An estimated four hundred people were killed in what is considered the second most severe natural disaster in the history of California.[12] Many of the livestock, orchards, and buildings on the Newhall properties were destroyed.[13] Because the Garcia ancestors were buried on a hillside near the dam and relatives on the Yaqui Garcia side continued to live nearby, Mary Garcia and her husband were among those who went to identify the casualties.[14]

Among the Ortiz lineage, progenitor Rosaria Arriola, her son, Joseph Ortiz, and his wife and two children were living in Bakersfield as the twentieth century opened. Located on the Kern River at the base of the San Joaquin Valley, the agricultural lands of Bakersfield provided work for farmhands such as Joseph. The family's ancestral territory was much closer to San Fernando, in Cahuenga, however.[15] A few years after Rosaria's death in 1911, Joseph Ortiz and his extended family returned to San Fernando, living in a home that was next door to members of the Ortega lineage.[16] Angie Campero, Joseph Ortiz's granddaughter through his daughter Helen, recalls life in San Fernando in the early 1930s. Grandpa Joseph was largely bedridden, and mother Helen worked in a local toy factory. Roads were still unpaved[17] and largely free of vehicle traffic, so children could ride their horses and enjoy hay rides up and down the streets of the town.

The two sons of Rita Alipaz, Antonio Maria Ortega and Luis Ortega, had many children during this time span who survived to adulthood, perpetuating what is now called the Ortega lineage. Rita had lost the Los Encinos land grant early in the American period when non-Indians took advantage of her difficulty managing the sudden burden of property taxation.[18] She and her husband died shortly thereafter. Orphaned as small children, Antonio Maria and Luis were taken in by the Lopez family and found employment and marriage partners of ethnic Mexican (or Yaqui Indian) descent in San Fernando. By 1900, Antonio Maria and his wife, Isidora Garcia, were completing their large family of nine children, one of whom died in childhood. Their eldest child, Christina, had been born in 1881, and their youngest, Sally, entered the world in 1900. Between 1899 and 1912, Luis and his wife had five children, before moving to Bakersfield in the early 1920s in search of jobs in farming and ranching. Only one of their children, Clarence Pete Ortega, had surviving children of his own.

Antonio Maria's descendants have strong recollections of the early decades of the twentieth century. Since 1889 Antonio Maria and his family had been living in a small house on still-unpaved Coronel Street in San Fernando, where the sidewalks were made of raised wooden slats and most of the lots were still empty.[19] Blessed with its own distinct supply of groundwater, two-mile-square San Fernando had held out for municipal independence when the rest of the valley joined the city of Los Angeles in 1915 to share water from the Los Angeles Aqueduct.[20] Beneath a broad, shaggy tree that occupied the dirt-filled front yard, Antonio Maria set up a stand where he sold candy to neighborhood children and their families. In a time before zoning, the store reached nearly to the street, eventually forcing cars to drive around it. For supplemental income during Prohibition, Antonio Maria and his sons turned a garage at the back of the house into a makeshift winery,[21] stomping barefoot to crush the grapes they picked from the arbor that shaded their small rear yard. When Antonio Maria's wife, Isidora, died in 1932, they brought the coffin back to the house for her wake. Soon thereafter, Antonio Maria moved in with his youngest daughter, Sally Ortega Verdugo, across the street. Sally had married a Cahuilla Indian, and after her husband died from tuberculosis contracted during World War I, she married his brother.

As Antonio's children reached adulthood, they also remained nearby. The two youngest of three sons, Eulogio and Luis, were draft age during World War I, and when they returned from the trenches of Europe, they both showed the effects of what would now be labeled post-traumatic stress disorder.[22] Some family members took Eulogio to the West Los Angeles Veterans Hospital for

FIGURE 32 Eulogio Ortega (1887–1966) in military uniform, ca. 1917. Courtesy of Fernandeño Tataviam Band of Mission Indians.

mental health treatment,[23] an arrangement he resisted until the eldest brother, Estanislao (a.k.a. Jimmy or James), secured his release. Eulogio then took up work picking grapes and olives in local vineyards, living in a little house with Luis in the adjacent town of Sylmar until he died on the streets in 1931. On occasion Eulogio would escape to the sparsely settled hills of Castaic, bunking temporarily in local trailers he knew of.[24]

Estanislao, who worked mainly as a caretaker for a clothing factory in Tujunga, also earned money as a gardener and from packing fruits and vegetables.[25] He and his family never lived farther than easy walking distance from Antonio Maria and Sally. Neither did Antonio Maria's daughter Vera Ortega Salazar, whose nearby home was a welcoming gathering place. Eldest daughter Christina Ortega Rodriguez, who had no children of her own, likewise stayed within the San Fernando orbit, as did Refugia Ortega Tapia, who resided in the adjacent town of Pacoima. Daughter Kathryn Ortega Newman, a petite woman who loved to cook and regularly opened her home for get-togethers with other lineage and community members, lived just down the street from father Antonio Maria's

FIGURE 33 Vera Ortega Salazar (1898–1981) with husband, Manuel, and child, Vivian, ca. 1923. Courtesy of Beverly Folkes.

house, near a local slaughterhouse and lots of grazing cows.[26] As Antonio Maria Ortega's children reached maturity and started families of their own, they began to form into several sublineages consisting of the Tapia, Estanislao Ortega, Verdugo, Newman, and Salazar families. Over time, the several sublineages grew with more children, grandchildren, and great-grandchildren and formed relatively autonomous family lineages that compose a good number of the present-day Fernandeño Tataviam Band of Mission Indians.

HIDING FROM PREJUDICE AND DISCRIMINATION

Both formal discrimination and informal prejudice burdened the Fernandeños in the early twentieth century. With some justification, they believed themselves at risk of banishment from their ancestral territories and homes to reservations or other parts unknown. And even though the government never took such action against the Fernandeños during that period, prospects of adverse treatment in housing, education, employment, and otherwise were a fact of life in the San Fernando Valley. Understandably, the response within the Fernandeño community was to downplay their identities, protect their children, and drive cultural practices below the radar.

The Fernandeños' fear of removal to reservations can be traced to policies dating from the earliest days of the state of California, when the state successfully prevented ratification of eighteen treaties. A resolution of the state's senate, adopted February 11, 1852, instructed representatives in both houses of the U.S. Congress "to use their best endeavors to induce the Federal Government to remove the Indians of this State beyond its jurisdiction."[27] When that proposal failed, many citizens of California began murdering Indians, mainly in Northern California, through widespread killings that have been documented as genocide.[28] For purposes of assimilation and out of concern for the California Indians' homeless condition, the federal government established four reservations, including one in the south at Tejon, and tried to round up Indians into those locations. Although some of the Fernandeños had lineage ties to Tejon, many did not, and they preferred to remain closer to their ancestral territories in the greater San Fernando Valley. For Indian groups farther to the south and east of Los Angeles County, the United States acted during the late nineteenth and early twentieth centuries to establish small, relatively unproductive reservations, primarily through executive orders and the Mission Indian Act of 1891.[29] It was evident, however, that the high value of the land in the San Fernando Valley, apparent as early as the 1870s, precluded the creation of reservations there.[30] Thus it would have made sense to the former Fernandeños that if the government was going to acknowledge any responsibility to them or deal with them at all, a part of the plan would be their removal to Indian reservations far away from their home territories.

Underscoring this fear was a general antagonism toward Indians in the city of San Fernando, primarily among the Anglo-white population.[31] Perhaps based on negative stereotypes, perhaps based on fear that the Indians would try to reclaim their ancestral lands, this hostility took extreme forms. Rudy Ortega Jr., grandchild of Estanislao Ortega and great-grandchild of Antonio Maria Ortega, relates that Charles Maclay, who had evicted the Fernandeños in the final decades of the nineteenth century, also ordered county sheriffs to remove all the Indians in the city of San Fernando, an order that remained on the city's books until 2008.[32] Dave Salazar Jr., another great-grandchild of Antonio Maria, recounts that in the 1920s, "You had to say that you were Mexican American because if you were to say that you were Native American here in San Fernando then they would ask you to leave the city."[33] Tribal members recall that their elders expressed deep concern that revealing their Indian identities would bring negative consequences, ranging from banishment to ridicule. Tribal member Shirley Newman Traba, granddaughter of Antonio Maria Ortega, recounts that in family conversations with her grandmother, Antonio Maria's wife, Isidora, they "used to say things until we'd be afraid of saying things or putting our self into any situation that they could send her back to the reservation."[34] According to a story passed down through generations of the Ortega family, when California Indians were asked to register for potential benefits from land claims litigation in the late 1920s, Estanislao Ortega, son of Antonio Maria Ortega, "was afraid if he registered as a Native American he would be sent to a reservation. He loved his culture, his language, but he feared being put on a reservation, taken from his family."[35]

Another child of Antonio Maria Ortega, Vera Ortega Salazar, recalled being told by her father that when the two of them "used to walk, the laborers used to go into town from the mission into town, San Fernando, people would ridicule them and say, 'Oh, look, there's the Indians, look.' And then they'd make fun of them and everything."[36] Charlie Cooke, grandson of Frances Garcia Cooke, explained that "it was detrimental to the family if they even mentioned something like that [the traditional bear dance], you know, because they'd get ridiculed and everything else."[37] He remembers that he "got razzed about it [being Indian] quite a bit. . . . They called us derogatory names. . . . They called me Piute."[38] One of the sons of Estanislao Ortega recalls that when he and his brother attended school in San Fernando, "everyone called them Apaches."[39]

These policies and practices in San Fernando echoed broader patterns of discrimination statewide. The state's supreme court steadfastly refused to recognize the land rights of California Indians.[40] The 1848 Treaty of Guadalupe Hidalgo between the United States and Mexico offered Indians who were Mexican citizens the right of U.S. citizenship. Indians, however, were denied voting rights in California, and litigation all the way to the state's supreme court was required for nonreservation Indians to secure the right to vote in 1917.[41] Discrimination against Indians in California's public schools was pervasive. A 1906 report to the commissioner of Indian affairs about California Indians stated the following: "For many years all Indian children were refused admission to public schools, and today, in a majority of school districts where Indians live, public sentiment is against their admission."[42] Discrimination against Indians in public education was not outlawed until another decision by the California Supreme Court in 1924.[43] Even with these rulings, practices did not change immediately.[44] Employment discrimination against Indians was also widespread.[45]

The large Mexican American population in the city of San Fernando and throughout the San Fernando Valley suffered prejudice and discrimination as well, which typically swept in the Indian community because of the Indians' darker skin color.[46] Mexican Americans had to live on one side of the railroad tracks that crossed the city of San Fernando, in a barrio that came to be known as Sonoratown.[47] Angie Campero, granddaughter of Joseph Ortiz, explained about growing up in San Fernando: "The Mexican Americans could not cross the railroad tracks . . . going east. . . . All the white people lived on [the other] side. . . . You couldn't go any further than San Fernando Road. You couldn't cross on the other side of San Fernando. The Mexican American, you had to be on this side."[48] All the Fernandeños could be found on that side of the tracks as well. That didn't change until the 1940s, after World War II. There was also school segregation against Mexican Americans in various parts of the valley, at least until the practice was outlawed by a federal lawsuit decided by the U.S. Court of Appeals for the Ninth Circuit in 1947.[49] Jessie Murphy, who became part of the privileged white community in San Fernando when she and her husband moved there in 1911, recalled in an oral history interview how the prejudices of the white townspeople led to the founding of a separate elementary school to segregate the whites from the Mexicans.[50] According to Mary Garcia's grandson, Ted Garcia Jr., his father, Ted Garcia Sr., born in 1920 and living at that time in Newhall, had to go to a "brown school and learn Spanish" because of "the darkness of his skin. . . . My dad up until the time he went to junior high he had to learn Spanish and go to the brown school. He was discriminated against, basically."[51] The Ku Klux Klan demonstrated openly in San Fernando at least during the 1930s, and likely a decade earlier.[52]

Even within this segregated regime, the Fernandeños believed they would be better off characterized as Mexican American than as Indian. Speaking of the time of his grandmother, Vera Ortega Salazar, Stanley Salazar relates, "If you were a Native and said that you were Native in that time you were a second class citizen. If you were Indian, the Indian was the lowest, even lower than being Spanish. If you were Spanish you were treated differently. They treated Indians really badly. . . . So people even denied that they were Natives."[53] It was difficult for the Indians to "pass" as Mexican American, however, because many of them did not speak Spanish. Indians intermarried as often with whites as with Mexican

FIGURE 34 Admission of a member by the "Great Dragon" of the organization at a meeting of the Ku Klux Klan in the San Fernando Mountains near Sun Valley, California, 1939. Photograph from Alamy.

Americans.[54] Furthermore, because most Indians had not abandoned their Native languages for Spanish during the mission period, they took up English when the Americans seized control and learned only enough Spanish to get by in the barrio of San Fernando.[55] Antonio, for example, knew only limited Spanish and spoke that with an accent that family members describe as Indian.[56]

The cumulative impact of this adverse treatment on the Fernandeños was predictable. They chose to take their identities and cultural practices underground, sharing them only in "safe spaces." Sometimes they went even further, hiding them from their own children and grandchildren in hopes of protecting them from prejudice and harm. The oral history makes that plain. Rudy Ortega Sr. said of his grandfather, Antonio Maria Ortega,

> No Tataviam people here ever talk about the past of their families or what they did. I don't know. Maybe because they were afraid that the white people will punish them if they did something. And they didn't want nobody to do anything. . . . He had a lot of knowledge, but he never gave it up to us at all. I think that's maybe because they were afraid that we'd get punished when we talked their language and all.[57]

Charlie Cooke has made the same point:

> People back in the forties particularly, and they were still downgraded as low class, and everything else. Nobody wanted to have anything to do with them. So it was safer not to say anything. . . . They would never claim they were Indian because they would be persecuted that way.[58]

Verne Newman Jr., grandson of Kathryn Ortega Newman (and great-grandson of Antonio Maria) shared the same experience of silencing because of fear:

> And I do remember comments that were made and it was kind of making fun about being a Native American or being an Indian. And part of the reason I think that was, from what I remember from some of the stories was because there was such a negative connotation to say you were Indian at that time. It's not something you want to be proud of or speak loudly about. And talk about what happened San Fernando and how they were booting people out and upsets around the country. . . . It wasn't something you just went around and said, "I am." Because it was too negative. It had all that stereotypical stuff that went along with it. So they would kind of talk about that, but it was done

> quietly and it's not something you just go out and start, "Hey, you know what I am?" You didn't do that. So it kind of always—that always stuck with me, is you are, but you don't talk about it much.[59]

Some family members even use the language of closeted sexual-orientation identities to describe the strategies deployed by the Fernandeño community. Stanley Salazar, grandson to Vera Ortega Salazar (and another great-grandchild of Antonio Maria), points out that his grandmother and great-grandfather, Antonio Maria, were "some of the last elders to really know the culture, and you know from the time of my grandma it was, like, it was almost better to keep it hidden."[60] For his grandma, "the government was so brutal on us that our formal government was, kind of, in the closet. . . . When a family is so annihilated, so beaten up on, the only thing they can do is put it in the closet. And that's how we . . . we, kind of, hid everything."[61] Even their identities as Indians had to be hidden.[62] Rudy Ortega Sr. recalls that he first discovered his Indian identity when a teacher at his elementary school demanded that he bang on an Indian drum at a school performance. When he complained about this assignment to his mother, she referred him to his father, Estanislao, who finally traced family history to San Fernando Mission and before then.[63] Yet even then his father would not go in depth. "They just wouldn't like to talk about their heritage on the Indian side. I don't know for what reason."[64]

SUSTAINING IDENTITIES AND CULTURE

Despite keeping their identities and cultural practices hidden from public view, the Fernandeños managed to sustain both, although sometimes in new ways. Traditional language, healing, community structures and leadership, and interlineage and interethnic relations all found expression during the first decades of the twentieth century.

Indigenous languages were a serious casualty of the community's fears and self-protective caution, but they were not entirely lost. Antonio Maria Ortega's children and grandchildren knew that he spoke the Tataviam language fluently[65] and observed that he spoke Spanish and English with a strange accent,[66] but most of the children rarely heard him speak his Indian language. According to his grandson, Rudy Ortega Sr., "they were afraid that we'd get punished when we talked their language and all. Because then the government they wanted no languages but English."[67] Estanislao Ortega, Antonio Maria's son, apparently never told his children that he knew the Tataviam language, even though he loved it.[68] Even so, some of his grandchildren heard him speak it and picked up a few words that were forgotten over time.[69] According to Vera Ortega Salazar's grandson, she was bolder in her willingness to speak the language, conversing in it openly and teaching select words to the younger generation.[70] Vera was an important source of cultural continuity within the lineage and tribe in many other ways as well. She taught bird songs, burial chants, and other traditional songs to her son, Dave Salazar Sr., and her nephew, Rudy Ortega Sr., who passed that knowledge along to subsequent generations within all the Fernandeño lineages.[71] Rudy Ortega Sr. also reports that although his father (Estanislao) and grandfather (Antonio Maria) didn't discuss their family background much, they danced, dressed with their regalias, and sang bird songs.[72]

When Charlie Cooke, grandson of Frances Garcia, was asked whether the elders in his family taught him their Indian language, he said "no," explaining, "It was detrimental to the family if they even mentioned something like that, you know, because they'd get ridiculed and everything else."[73] Charlie's cousin, Victoria Stokes, descended from Petra Garcia and growing up in Oxnard rather than in Newhall, had a somewhat different experience in the 1950s:

> My grandfather [Petra's son] spoke his mother's language and he taught us before we ever learned English or Spanish. As very small children, my cousins and I spoke—and I think it was whatever language was spoken, you know, like Native American languages. And it was a first language, and of course we lost it as we got older, interacting with children in the neighborhood or going to school or whatever.[74]

> So we knew we were different because we spoke different words than other people. And it wasn't until we started going out into the neighborhood, which wasn't very often because I grew up with a set of grandparents of either side of an alleyway, so our world was very small. And it wasn't until we started going into school or in the streets or whatever that, you know, we spoke English. We spoke a little bit of Spanish, and then we spoke a lot of words that our grandfather and grandma taught us. And so I didn't feel any kind of identity with anybody else because I didn't realize that there were other different people.[75]

Not only language but also knowledge of healing practices survived into the twentieth century. Beverly Folkes, daughter of Antonio Maria's second-youngest child, Vera Ortega Salazar, learned from Vera how Antonio Maria practiced and

FIGURE 35 Beverly Folkes (1938–), tribal activist, at Rancho Encino, 2016. Courtesy of Fernandeño Tataviam Band of Mission Indians.

passed on his medicinal ingredients and techniques. "People used to come to him and then she used to say that they'd always say to him, 'Papa, why do you have those bag of weeds. . . .' Because he'd carry it on his side. He'd say, 'They're not weeds.'"[76] Antonio Maria also taught Vera which plants to gather for their healing properties, such as leaves that could be made into tea for relief from menstrual cramps or difficulties in pregnancy. He also aided people who suffered from gonorrhea.[77] One of Vera's grandsons was born with severe eczema, which Vera treated with a plant she remembered Antonio Maria gathering. Vera took Beverly to the undeveloped spot in Sylmar where the plants could be found, pulled them up, and made them into a tea that they dabbed with cotton on the grandson's rash. "Overnight, it cleared up his eczema, like a miracle."[78] Vera "just knew things," according to Beverly, and community members came to her for all sorts of help: "to rub or snap their back, and to rub the stomachs of pregnant women when something was 'stuck.'"[79] Vera also made use of aloe vera plants in their yard to relieve sufferers from painful burns. Another of Vera's children, David Salazar Sr., confirms that when someone was ill, Vera would seek out plants that she knew held healing powers. "Go to the mountain and pick out different, not all kinds of herbs, but there was things up there that it would heal you. Take it and boil it, whatever you needed to do with."[80] And Vera was not the only Fernandeño in the community who held this knowledge. "If somebody else told you, 'Look, there's other little tea or herbs up around the mountain up there, or something,' then you'd go up there. Then you would find some that somebody else knew."[81]

Charlie Cooke, of the Garcia lineage, also recounted that his father, Cy Cooke, taught him and his brother about using native plants for food and medicine. Charlie's father had gained that knowledge from Grandma Frances Garcia Cooke, who had been taught by her own mother.[82]

This oral history accords nicely with the broader observations of anthropologist Alfred Kroeber. Writing early in the twentieth century, Kroeber observed that Americans had come to California only sixty years earlier, which is not a long period of time "as men live." For those whose lives bridged the Mexican and American periods, "These old people have never lost the belief in the efficacy

FIGURE 36 Joseph Ortiz (1861–ca. 1938), lineage captain (*right*), with stepbrother, Miguel Raphael. Courtesy of Fernandeño Tataviam Band of Mission Indians.

of the native medicine-man, and have imparted most of their conviction, often secretly but yet tenaciously, to their children and grandchildren, who form the majority of the fifteen thousand Indians today in California."[83]

Lineage community and leadership likewise remained active during the first half of the twentieth century, even as they adapted to new conditions, continued to affirm a broader Fernandeño identity, and maintained a low profile to outsiders. Physical proximity helped and was driven by strong lineage ties. The farthest anyone in the Fernandeño lineages moved from San Fernando Mission was to Bakersfield or Tejon Ranch, and even the lineage families that settled there, Joseph Ortiz and his family, returned to San Fernando by the 1920s.[84] Josefa Leyva Garcia traveled to Tejon and to the Oxnard-Ventura area in the early twentieth century, ultimately returning to her first husband, Isidoro, and her extended family in San Fernando. By the 1940s, many other members of the Garcia lineage had also congregated back in San Fernando.[85] The family of Luis Ortega, Antonio's brother, moved to Fresno in the 1920s, and some members returned to San Fernando in the first decades of the twenty-first century.

Within each of the lineages, leadership and community gatherings remained powerful cohesive forces, reinforcing collective values and actions. As in times past, a combination of lineage seniority, cultural knowledge, and willingness to serve mattered in the community's selection of a leader or captain.[86] Wide consultation invariably preceded leadership transitions so that these qualities could be identified.[87]

For the Ortega lineage, Antonio Maria maintained the traditional leadership role as captain until his health began to decline following the death of his wife, Isidora, in 1932.[88] His respected position derived at least in part from his knowledge of the Tataviam language, knowledge possessed by only a handful of others.[89] Antonio Maria was also the oldest living member of the lineage. Antonio Maria's eldest son, Estanislao, who worked as a caretaker in Tujunga and packed fruit in Pacoima,[90] became the agreed-upon captain thereafter, "to bring the people, keep the people together," serving in that capacity until his death in 1951. On the weekends, accompanied by son, Rudy, Estanislao visited families within the lineage, talking and joking.[91] While these gatherings were undoubtedly enjoyable social occasions, they also fulfilled Estanislao's duty and mission as captain to hold the lineage together. Oral tradition attests that the Ortega lineage also convened regularly during the tenure of both Antonio Maria and Estanislao at festivals and special meetings to discuss community issues and problems in order to reach agreement on solutions whenever possible—a process consistent with older ways.[92]

FIGURE 37 Estanislao (James) Ortega (1885–1951), lineage captain, with one of his sons. Courtesy of Fernandeño Tataviam Band of Mission Indians.

In keeping with longtime practice, captains not only had responsibilities to care for the lineage but also to carry on relations with the broader multitribal and, in the American period, multiethnic communities.[93] Rudy Ortega Sr. recalls that when he was a child, in the 1930s, the community organized car washes to raise funds for families that were "hard up for a burial."[94] Estanislao would also spread the word to local community members, both within and outside the tribe, asking them to contribute funds, no matter how small, to help with funerals within the community.[95] In addition, he collected food and vouchers from local stores and other organizations for elderly people, both Indian and non-Indian.[96]

Estanislao's sister, Vera Ortega Salazar, who also functioned as a leader in the lineage, held this sense of responsibility as well. Known as a "backbone for a lot of families," she was "not only an ear, but she was there to help people and I think it was, kind of, an unspoken because all her elders, her grandfather and her great grandfather were the Ortegas."[97] As Vera's grandson, Stanley Salazar, observed, "My grandma kept everything together by keeping the families together, and extended families, too. There was other Garcias and other families. Like my dad said, whoever came, but they knew they were Indian and they didn't have a tribal office. They were, I think, in a way, they were ancestors and they knew it. They were living ancestors."[98] Part of Vera's claim to leadership was her knowledge of the tribe's culture and history.[99] As her daughter, Beverly Folkes, remembered, "She was such a great, strong lady. And one thing about her, she knew history."[100]

Estanislao's son, Rudy Ortega Sr., began assuming a vigorous role early in the 1940s, first conducting genealogy research at the request of his aunt Vera. Born in 1926, Rudy Sr. left high school at fifteen and attended classes on Saturdays while working at Lockheed Aircraft as one of their top riveters, making the XB-38 Flying Fortress bomber.[101] Aunt Vera spurred Rudy to organize the community. She needed, he recounts, "something to where [she could] go out and enjoy and talk to people,"[102] so that's what he did. Rudy had been working as a community liaison for a nonprofit social group formed by Mexican American women. That group met at night at a local San Fernando meeting hall, and Rudy's job was to secure the facility and ensure the women's safety.[103] Having observed their meetings, he realized his own community could gather there as well. Their meetings began before World War II but became more regular and organized after Rudy returned from the service, a time when his father, Estanislao, was increasingly ill and bedridden.[104] Members of the Fernandeño community met twice a month, once at the local meeting hall and once at an extended family member's home.[105]

This group was the nucleus of the San Fernando Mission Band, a Fernandeño tribal organization that adopted that name in the late 1940s. All Indians or lineages who were descended from San Fernando Mission were invited to join as tribal members. Only direct San Fernando Mission descendants could vote and participate in discussion of tribal issues. As in traditional times, married-in spouses were not members of the patrilineal lineages. The Garcia, Ortega, and Ortiz lineages formed the core of the San Fernando Mission Band membership. Each lineage retained its own identity and leadership patterns of elders or captains. Married-in spouses, interested individuals, and Indians not descended from San Fernando Mission were invited to participate in a nontribal organization, or club, in which the Fernandeños participated. The two organizations typically met on the same days, though at separate times. Although the band's bylaws were not committed to writing until the 1970s, discussions about bylaws began early, continuing in the traditional way until the community reached consensus. If no agreement could be reached among band members, the matter was deferred until the next discussion.[106] Culture and heritage were a central focus of these gatherings, and Rudy Sr. was proud that the participants began to pepper him with questions about their own ancestry and tribal history.[107] When strictly tribal matters came up, decisions were made at family gatherings or only those within one of the recognized Fernandeño lineages were allowed to vote as participants in the San Fernando Mission Band.[108]

Among the Garcia lineage, leadership fell first during this era to Josefa Leyva Garcia's daughter, Frances Garcia Cooke.[109] Born in 1880, Frances was particularly active in family matters in the late 1920s and 1930s, when questions surfaced about participation in federal claims processes.[110] She had a large extended family, which gathered regularly, sometimes in Tejon or Saugus, as well as in Newhall.[111] But Frances also maintained strong ties with her cousins among the Ortegas.[112] When Frances moved her family from Newhall to San Fernando during the late 1940s, she took in one of Vera Ortega Salazar's children, a son then in his teens.[113] One day in 1946, Frances was riding in the passenger seat of the family's Ford Model A, traveling back to San Fernando along old Foothill Boulevard from a visit in Newhall, and a drunk driver sped across the highway, colliding head-on with their vehicle. Frances soon died from her injuries, and leadership passed in traditional fashion to her eldest child, Mary.[114] By this time Mary was nearly fifty years old and did not drive. But she organized many gatherings to discuss family and Fernandeño issues and looked after the welfare of lineage members. Photos of her around this time reveal a warm smile, her hair pulled tightly back into a tiara of tight curls that framed her broad forehead. She was, however, formidable. Her powerful voice, echoing Frances's, conveyed that perpetuating heritage was the most important thing in life for lineage members, more important even than making a living. "Don't forget," she would repeat. "Don't forget."[115]

In addition to the efforts of leaders, community social events also maintained traditional connections within and across lineages, reinforcing tribal identity. Lineage members came together regularly for holidays and life cycle events, such as baby showers, baptisms, weddings, and funerals.[116] Some gatherings were at nearby Santa Rosa Catholic Church,[117] and others were at homes. These gatherings resembled lineage meetings but often conformed to American Christian holidays, such as the Fourth of July. Fiestas at the church tended to be more pan-Indian in nature, reflecting longtime lineage participation in interethnic communities, both before and during the mission era. As a child in the 1930s, Rudy Ortega Sr. often went to these fiestas, which occurred monthly. "And they

FIGURE 38 Mary Cooke Garcia (1901–1975), lineage captain. Courtesy of Geraldine Perez.

always [had] a group of Indians come from out of town to do some dancing and so forth,"[118] teaming up with the local Tataviam. The church phased out its fiestas in the 1940s, during which time Rudy Sr. began researching Fernandeño genealogies and bringing lineage members together in other ways.

Events at homes were more exclusive, limited to extended lineage members and relatives from other Fernandeño lineages. As Rudy Sr. recollected, "And then we had our own fiestas. Like we had the weddings. We had showers. We had birthday parties and we had big birthday parties that we invited a lot of our people to come down to the party. We had music and dancing, food. It was just a big blowup with our families."[119] When Dorothy Moran was dating a son of Antonio Maria's daughter, Kathryn Ortega Newman, she attended many such gatherings of extended family at Kathryn's house and recalls that there was always Indian fry bread.[120] Because members of the Garcia lineage were cousins, they participated in many of the festivities as well.[121] Indeed, the travel went both ways. Throughout the early 1900s, the Ortega family made regular social calls on their close relatives in Newhall, as Isidora Ortega was Isidoro Garcia's sister.[122]

The strength and interconnectedness of the Fernandeño Tribe during the first half of the twentieth century was fully on display in 1951 at Estanislao Ortega's funeral, held at the Noble Funeral Chapel in San Fernando. The guest book shows that progenitors, tribal members, and family all paid their respects to Estanislao. Among those attending were Estanislao's sisters and their families, as well as members of the Garcia lineage: Della Cooke Martinez (granddaughter of Josefa Leyva Garcia and active in her lineage community in Newhall) and Ted Garcia Sr. (great-grandson of Josefa).[123] Ted's mother, Mary Garcia, then the Garcia lineage head, sent flowers on behalf of her family.[124] Both Ted Garcia Sr. and Mary Garcia became active participants in the Fernandeño community during the 1950s and remained active for most of the rest of their lives. Mary Garcia became a close confidant of Rudy Ortega Sr., and Ted Garcia Sr. participated as a tribal officer during the 1940s and later. The Ortiz lineage was also represented at the funeral through the presence of the widow of Miguel Raphael Ortiz and her family, all longtime residents of San Fernando.[125] The participation of different families at Estanislao Ortega's funeral indicates continuing contacts and relations among the lineages and between the Newhall and San Fernando lineages, reaffirming the interrelated tribal identities and obligations.

POLITICAL CONTINUITY REFLECTED IN DECISION-MAKING ABOUT THE 1928 ROLL

The greatest political challenge presented to the Fernandeño community during the first half of the twentieth century concerned compensation for lands and other benefits promised in the eighteen unratified treaties of the 1850s.[126] The fact that each lineage convened collectively and looked to lineage leaders to guide their response to the treaty claims process demonstrates that traditional forms of social and political organization persisted well into this period. The fact that the three lineages conducted these deliberations separately and made these decisions differently underscores the political distinctness of each of the lineages within the broader Fernandeño tribal community.

In 1928, after nearly a decade of false starts, Congress enacted legislation[127] acknowledging the tremendous harm done to California Indians when those treaties were defeated in the Senate because of opposition from the California delegation. Those treaties had promised the Indians 7.5 million acres of land as well as money and other benefits in return for lands that would be ceded by the Indians to the United States. Soon after the treaties were rejected, Congress proclaimed nearly all the land of California to be "public lands of the United States," leaving the California Indians homeless. Even worse, they were left vulnerable to the genocidal impulses of non-Indian settlers in the state.[128] Congress's reasons for affording compensation were not entirely bighearted or driven by a sense of injustice. As a 1922 editorial in the *Fresno Republican* observed, "There can be no atonement for the degradation to which the Indians have been subjected during more than two generations. [But if compensation is provided] it will make the rest of us feel better for having their land."[129]

The 1928 federal law, known as the California Indians Jurisdictional Act, took a distinctive form, authorizing the attorney general of California to sue in the Court of Claims on behalf of "the Indians of California," defined as all Indians residing in California on June 1, 1852, plus their living descendants within the state. There was no requirement that Indians trace their ancestry to particular Indians who had signed the treaties. The secretary of the interior was directed to compile a roll of all eligible Indians, and individuals were given two years from the date of enactment of the law to petition for inclusion, a provision soon amended to afford them four years.[130] One year following the close of the petition process, the secretary was required to finalize the roll.[131] The statute also affirmed that loss of promised treaty lands and other benefits[132] could serve as an equitable basis for relief and set the value of those lands at a pitifully low $1.25 per acre.[133] Moreover, no interest was allowed from the time of the taking, and the Court of Claims was directed to decide the amount that should be subtracted from the judgment for offsets in the form of gratuitous funds and material goods—whether desired or useful—supplied in past decades to California Indians. Any resulting judgment was to be put into a U.S. Treasury account for the benefit of the California Indians, to be subject "to appropriation by Congress for educational, health, industrial, and other purposes . . . including the purchase of lands and building of homes."[134] Per capita payment to the Indians was specifically prohibited, though that ban was lifted via amendment in 1950.[135]

The 1928 act was the culmination of decades of agitation by California Indians and their supporters. The surveys and reports that Helen Hunt Jackson and Abbott Kinney had carried out in the 1880s produced limited results in the form of the Mission Indian Act of 1891 and the establishment of several executive order reservations in Southern California.[136] Not one of these reservations was adequate in size or quality of lands, however, and Indians who had been evicted in the Los Angeles area, including the Fernandeños, did not benefit at all. The situation in Northern California was at least as bad, as there were only three reservations for a vast area[137] and an off-reservation Indian population in the thousands known to be in desperate need.[138] In 1905, following a major petition campaign, a large coalition of advocacy organizations finally persuaded Congress to remove the injunction of secrecy that the Senate had attached to the eighteen unratified treaties with California Indians and to authorize the Department of the Interior to "investigate through an inspector or otherwise existing conditions of the California Indians and to report to Congress."[139] That report, known as the Kelsey report after its author, Northern California Indian Rights Association leader C. E. Kelsey, emphasized the responsibility of the U.S. government for the dire condition—including near starvation—of nonreservation California Indians:

> Had the Government given these Indians the same treatment as it did other Indians in the United States [meaning treaties, annuities, possibly reservations], their condition today would be very different. . . . It should be remembered that the Government still owes these people considerable sums of money, morally at least, but the Government owes more than money. No amount of money can repay these Indians for the years of misery, despair, and death which the Governmental policy has inflicted upon them. No reason suggests itself to your special agent why these Indians should not be placed in the same situation as all other Indians in the United States; why they should not receive a minute portion of the lands which they have not as yet ceded to the United States.[140]

Kelsey did not recommend claims legislation, nor did he favor establishment of reservations, which he believed were too costly to administer and, at least in the past, not very well administered.[141] As he put it rather obliquely, "Some of the past reservation experiences in California have been so harrowing that the Indians fear reservations above all things."[142] What he proposed, instead, was that the federal government acquire or allocate from the public domain small plots of land, which he called *allotments*, that would be just large enough for the Indians to survive, without making them rich.[143] He also emphasized the importance that

California Indians continued to attach to remaining close to the burial places of their ancestors, which meant that they would only settle on lands on or close to their aboriginal territories.[144] Kelsey envisioned that these allotments would be in lieu of any claims the California Indians might have against the United States, "moral or otherwise."[145]

Kelsey's report led to an appropriation of $100,000 to purchase the first of what are now known as California's Indian rancherias in Northern California. Another $50,000 followed in 1908.[146] Nearly all the attention went to Northern California tribes, even though Kelsey had reported that only "substantially" all the Southern California tribes had been aided by earlier legislation and executive orders.[147] Even with the focus on Northern California, however, these appropriations were grossly insufficient to address the needs of nonreservation California Indians. Another survey and report on "landless" California Indians, carried out by the commissioner of Indian affairs in 1919, showed that conditions had improved very little. After pointing out that "landless Indians (nonreservation Indians who do not live on Rancherias and who have no allotments) are found in almost every county of the State,"[148] the report recommended "permanent home sites for landless Indians, grouped in colonies on tracts of land in every way suitable for villages, to be bought and, for a time, held by the Government."[149] It did not recommend a claims process.

Nonetheless, support for federal claims legislation had been growing within the state since revelation of the unratified treaties. The first bill proposing compensation for the unratified treaties was presented in the final Congress of the Woodrow Wilson administration, but even with the administration's support and extensive hearings, the bill failed to advance in the House after passing the Senate.[150] Meanwhile, fierce lobbying by Indian advocates prompted the California legislature to adopt a joint resolution in 1921 that urged the federal government to provide services for California Indians and "allotments" for the "homeless" among them, as well as "enactment by Congress of a bill conferring jurisdiction upon the Court of Claims . . . to hear and to adjudicate all claims, both legal and equitable which the several tribes or bands of Indians of California may have against the United States government for lands taken from them without compensation therefor."[151] Apart from the agitation of pro-Indian groups, California's leaders may have been motivated by a 1917 state supreme court decision affirming that California Indians were citizens of the state,[152] a decision that prompted federal officials to view the Indians as the state's responsibility. Significantly, the state legislature's resolution was encompassing, as it did not differentiate between compensation for lands promised in the unratified treaties and the other remaining lands (far more extensive) from which California Indians had also been dispossessed. By this time, however, the new administration of Warren Harding, through Secretary of the Interior Albert Fall, no longer supported a claims bill and favored targeted appropriations for identified needy California Indians instead.[153] A particular point of opposition for Secretary Fall was that the pending bill provided for per capita distribution of any claims judgment, without regard "to whether such persons are in need of assistance and without any regard as to their qualifications to wisely use the money that they might receive."[154] The Indian Board of Cooperation, a well-organized advocacy group led by Methodist minister Fredrick Collett,[155] responded to Fall, contending that targeted appropriations for California Indians had long been wholly inadequate and touting the claims bill as "a just and final disposal of the California Indian problem." This last assertion implied that the federal government would be relieved of any future responsibilities after paying out the claims judgment.[156] The California congressional delegation made the same pitch on behalf of the claims bill, arguing that the claims bill would provide "a satisfactory and final and early settlement of the California Indian question."[157]

Bills continued to be introduced in various forms throughout the 1920s, and one even passed both houses of Congress in 1925, only to be thwarted by President Coolidge's pocket veto.[158] Whether the claims legislation would shift responsibility off the shoulders of the federal government onto the state of California was a persistent question. In 1922, Northern California congressmember John Raker, a prominent supporter of the claims bills, firmly believed that settlement of claims should not relieve the United States of responsibility for the California Indians, who were not yet ready for "emancipation," and the Indian Service should not be removed from California following payment of any judgment.[159] John Collier, testifying on behalf of the Indian Defense Association in 1926, also stressed that federal guardianship and appropriations for the benefit of California Indians would need to continue even after any land claims settlement.[160] Other vexing issues addressed in various iterations of the proposed land claims legislation included (1) who should be entitled to claim—only those descended from treaty-making tribes or all California Indians, and if the former, how those would be ascertained;[161] (2) whether the settlement should be achieved by a direct appropriation or through litigation in the Court of Claims, given that the acreage and value of lands taken were likely to be fixed by Congress, and if via litigation, how attorneys would be compensated;[162] (3) what the fixed value of the land should be;[163] (4) whether the settlement should be limited to treaty-promised lands and benefits or extended to all the lands of California from which California Indians had been dispossessed;[164] (5) whether interest should be paid from the time of taking;[165] and (6) how any settlement should be disposed of—via a commission that could acquire land and direct other benefits for California Indians, through per capita payments to them, or otherwise.[166] Non-Indian-led advocacy groups disagreed about the form the legislation should take, though the majority of them favored litigation in the Court of Claims.

In 1928, administration opposition to claims legislation finally weakened, and the plan to use the attorney general of California to represent all California Indians before the Court of Claims, limiting the recovery to treaty lands and benefits and arbitrarily valuing the land at $1.25 per acre without interest from the time of taking, with offsets allowed, got the legislation finally enacted. Earlier in that same year the Institute for Government Research (later known as the Brookings Institution) submitted its now-classic 847-page report titled *The Problem of Indian Administration* to Secretary of the Interior Hubert Work.[167] This well-researched critique of federal Indian policy later provided support and impetus for enactment of President Franklin Roosevelt's "Indian New Deal," primarily manifest in the Indian Reorganization Act of 1934.[168] But the Meriam Report, as it came to be known after its lead author, Lewis Meriam, also had some bearing on what was then a nearly decade-long struggle for a land claims bill for California Indians.[169] The report pointed out that dissatisfaction over unresolved claims kept Indians from cooperating with U.S. policy initiatives and even apart from such practical considerations, "simple canons of justice and morality demand that no Indian tribe should be denied an opportunity to present for adjustment before an appropriate tribunal the rights which the tribe claims under recognized principles of law and government."[170] Interestingly, in light of the choice Congress made in the California land claims bill, the Meriam Report argued persuasively against allowance of offsets against land claims awards: "It is difficult to see why a particular group of Indians who have been treated with injustice by the government should have deductions made for gratuities already given them, when other Indians who have suffered no wrongs are permitted to keep their gratuities in full. Such, however, is frequently the case."[171]

The attorney general of California, charged with prosecuting the case on behalf of the Indians, found serious fault with the legislative scheme. He pointed out, for example, that the offsets encompassed disbursements made to *all* California Indians, while the compensation was paid for breach-of-treaty promises to only one-third to one-half of those Indians. His overall conclusion was that "the rigid formula of recovery . . . is purely arbitrary and artificial, making it impossible for the Court of Claims to do complete justice and equity."[172]

It fell to the Roosevelt administration to carry out the terms of the 1928 California Indians Jurisdictional Act in the midst of the Depression. As the law dictated, the secretary of the interior completed the roll of eligible California Indians in 1933. But the case filed by the California attorney general, numbered K-344, lumbered along in the Court of Claims much longer.[173] Finally, on December 4, 1944, the Court of Claims awarded the Indians of California $17,053,941.98 for the eighteen reservations the Indians were promised but never received and then promptly subtracted $12,029.099.64 for the amount the United States had spent since then for the "benefit" of California Indians, including approximately 610,000 acres in reservations. The net award was $5,024,842.34.[174] Following further amendments to the process, the secretary approved a roll bearing 36,095 names.[175] In 1950, with interest having increased the award since entry of the judgment, Congress authorized payment of $150.00 to every person on the roll and their descendants.[176]

The judgment amount glaringly shortchanged California Indians. Even apart from the questionable offsets and the lack of interest paid from the time of taking, the valuation of treaty lands at $1.25 per acre vastly understated what the Indians could have gained from the establishment of reservations through the treaties. During a 1926 hearing in the House of Representatives on a predecessor of the 1928 act, Representative Clarence Lea of California pointed out that $1.25 per acre was the lowest amount that public lands of the United States in California—lands the government had seized from the Indians—had been opened for sale; other public lands had been sold at $2.50 or $5.00 per acre.[177] Furthermore, completely left out of the $1.25-per-acre valuation was the value of timber and gold on the land. Lea quoted from the chair of the California Assembly in February 1852, who had urged senators to reject the treaties because the land set aside for reservations was too valuable: "'Your committee are of opinion that . . . the aggregate value of those reservations is not less than $100,000,000. If they are set apart for the exclusive occupation and use of the Indians, the loss to the State and National Governments could not be less than $100,000,000—at a fair computation of the mineral and agricultural lands.'"[178] If he had taken inflation into account, the amount in 1944 dollars would have been closer to $220,000,000. Furthermore, as Representative Lea noted in 1926, compensating the Indians solely for the loss of treaty-promised lands ignored all of the remaining lands in the state, amounting to nearly 92,000,000 acres, from which they had also been dispossessed.[179] Finally, the calculation of offsets took account of benefits provided to *all* California Indians, even though the legislation limited compensation to loss of treaty lands and benefits only. As California attorney general Robert Kenny complained, "*All* the Indians of California are suing on promises made to from *one-third* to *one-half* of the Indians of California [those who participated in the treaty process], while the offsets representing expenditures for *all* the Indians of California are to be pleaded and deducted from a recovery"[180] (emphasis in original).

The Fernandeños definitely knew about the California Indians Jurisdictional Act of 1928, although it is unclear how they first learned of it. Reports did appear in local newspapers,[181] but it is unclear how many tribal members read them.[182] In addition, between 1928 and 1933, several federal Indian agents traveled throughout California enrolling Indians who could establish they were descended from a California Indian living in the state in 1852.[183] The managing agent, Fred Baker, created a questionnaire for applicants to complete and required sworn affidavits from two individuals who could confirm that the applicant was who he or she claimed to be. Committees of elders, relatives, friends, and local non-Indians familiar with the applicant all participated in supporting the applications.[184] The questionnaire asked for information about the applicant as well as his or her parents and grandparents, including where they may have been living in 1852. Also on the application were questions that addressed tribal affiliation, including the following:

- What is your degree of Indian blood and to what Tribe or Band of Indians of the State of California do you belong?
- Give the names of your California Indian ancestors living on June 1, 1852, through whom you claim, who were parties to any Treaty or Treaties with the United States.
- Give the names of the Chiefs, Captains and headmen of the Tribe or Band to which your ancestors belonged on June 1, 1852, who executed the Treaty or Treaties herein referred to, if you know them.

A final section of the application asked for any additional "remarks," which afforded the applicant an opportunity to explain why the application was being submitted.

Members of two Fernandeño lineages—the Garcias and Ortizes—were willing to enroll under the 1928 California Indians Jurisdictional Act. Members of the Ortega lineage held back. Looking back at the history and terms of the 1928 act, it is not difficult to see why opinions about enrollment may have differed. It was not until 1950 that per capita distributions were possible. Up until then the most tribal members could hope for was congressional appropriation of judgment funds for federal services such as health care or for acquisition of lands for reservations or allotments. Given that the roll was being prepared in the early years of the Depression, the prospect of any benefits at all must have had some appeal. Yet appropriations for land acquisition would likely come at a price for the Fernandeños. Knowing that land would never be acquired in their homelands because of its high cost, they could anticipate being required to move some distance to secure any land rights. There was certainly a history of non-Indians seeking to banish the Indians from the city of San Fernando, as well as from the state,[185] and Fernandeños still remembered the policy of relocation to the Tejon Reservation.[186] Thus, there were considerations to be weighed on both sides, and each lineage had to evaluate those considerations for itself, looking to leadership from their respective captains.

FIGURE 39 Frances Garcia Cooke (1883–1946), lineage captain, and Fred Cooke (1881–1958). Courtesy of Fernandeño Tataviam Band of Mission Indians.

Interviews with San Fernando elders, conducted decades later, independently mention these discussions and provide relatively similar and consistent points, even where the ultimate choices of the lineages differed. Among the Garcias, active efforts by lineage captain Frances Garcia Cooke and her non-Indian husband, Fred, overcame concerns about displacement. There was apparently some genuine fear that those who signed up would be forced off their traditional territory onto a distant reservation.[187] Indeed, Rudy Ortega Sr. later recalled that there was a general rumor in the valley at the time "that said don't register because the government wants to put you all in the reservation and keep you there and take you away from the town."[188] The strong leadership of Frances Garcia Cooke prevailed, however. As grandson Charlie Cooke noted, "In the twenties she [Grandma Frances] was one of the people that was instrumental in the California Indian rolls. And she got all my aunts and uncles and everything else enrolled."[189] The economic struggles of the Depression era seem to have pushed people toward enrolling. According to Ted Garcia Jr., his great-grandmother and her husband argued to the family that there were dollars owed to them because of the unratified treaties. As Ted Jr. recounted, "Well, it could've been, you know, more benefit because that was a pretty hard time. It was a hard time in 1928, you know, that was just before the year of the crash. There was a lot of hard times. . . . By the time people enrolling in '32 and '33 it's, yes, it's the Depression."[190]

FIGURE 40 Jose Juan Olivas. Taken from papers of linguist John Harrington, Harrington Papers, National Anthropological Archives, Smithsonian.

Descendants of Josefa Leyva are amply represented on the 1928 act roll, their ancestry and tribal affiliations supported by a noted informant to linguist John Harrington, Jose Juan Olivas.[191] Children of Josefa's daughters with Isidoro Garcia—Frances Garcia Cooke and Petra Garcia Rivera—can be found on the roll. Frances herself enrolled, including all six of her unmarried children on the application.[192] To the question asking, "To what Tribe or Band of Indians of the State of California do you belong," she answered, "San Fernando Mission," and she named Rogerio Rocha as the captain as of 1852. Her married children, Della Cooke Martinez, Lida Cooke Manriquez, Manuel Cooke, and Mary Cooke Garcia, provided very similar information on their applications.[193] Petra's children, Margaret Ward, John Valenzuela, Louis Valenzuela, and Paul Valenzuela, signed up, listing their affiliation as "San Fernando Mission Tribe" and also naming Rogerio Rocha as the captain in 1852.[194] Finally, Josefa's daughter by William Gardner, Clara Maude Callis, applied, describing her affiliation as "Mission Indian, San Fernando Mission" and failing to identify a captain as of 1852.[195] The fact that the form identifies the mission, equivalent to Fernandeño, as the tribal affiliation and designates Rogerio Rocha as captain suggests a tribal identification and connection. He had connections by marriage

FIGURE 41 Antonio Maria Ortega (1857–1941), lineage captain, with some of his grandchildren, San Fernando, ca. 1932. Courtesy of Fernandeño Tataviam Band of Mission Indians.

to the Garcia lineage through his wife, Manuela. His leadership role thus could be associated with a particular lineage, as in the traditional manner. But he also had a broader base of connections to other lineages, including the Canos, originally from Pimu (Catalina Island), the Ortegas, originally from Chaguayabit, and the Odons, originally from Escorpion—connections that sustained his leadership position for many decades beyond the mission.[196] San Fernando Mission is the place where all these lineages lived and shared experience after they were displaced from their traditional villages. It was the location of a collection of politically autonomous lineages, long interconnected socially and culturally. After the mission period, these lineages were open to maintaining their connections as a Fernandeño Tribe while sustaining distinct kinship and political identities.[197]

Among the Ortegas, the debate was actively engaged, discussions taking place at family events, casual meetings, and meetings arranged to discuss the issue. Christina Ortega Rodriguez and her husband, Ed, advocated that families sign on to the judgment roll. As Rudy Ortega Sr. recalled, from overhearing family conversations, "I remember that Ed Rodriguez, my brother-in-law, . . . he was trying to get people to register. But they didn't want to do it because they were going to the reservation. They didn't want to sign."[198] Vera Ortega Salazar was influential in leading family members away from enrolling,[199] espousing a view that accorded with the position taken by her parents, Antonio Maria and Isidora Ortega. When the enrollment agent from the Bureau of Indian Affairs knocked on Isidora and Antonio's door, Isidora evidently told Vera that they weren't interested, "'Because nothing's going to come of it and they don't need to be getting in our business.'"[200] Despite active lobbying by some families, the general discussion gravitated toward the view that signing on to the 1928 judgment roll might lead to removal to reservations.[201] Antonio Maria Ortega, lineage captain at that time, expressed caution about enrolling in the judgment program, fearing possible removal to a reservation and suggesting that the community would be better off managing its own affairs in their accustomed manner.[202] The story passed down by Antonio's son, Estanislao, was, "At that time the world was not friendly to people of color especially in this area to Native Americans. He [Antonio] was afraid if he registered as a Native American he would be sent to a reservation. He loved his culture, his language, but he feared being put on a reservation, taken from his family."[203] Rudy Ortega Sr. remembered hearing from family members: "All I heard was that they didn't want to register because they were going to send them to a reservation. They didn't want to go there."[204] Antonio Maria was then in his early seventies and his wife, Isidora, was ill and bedridden. He made some cash selling candy outside his house along Coronel Street, but financial need was

FIGURE 42 Antonio Maria Ortega, lineage captain, with daughter, Sally Verdugo, and her children at the beach, ca. 1932. Courtesy of Fernandeño Tataviam Band of Mission Indians.

definitely present. So the community decided to allow any one or any family to enroll if they wished. The entire Ortega extended lineage, however, held rank, and no one applied for the 1928 judgment roll. Antonio Maria Ortega's opposition was enough to deter younger and relatively independent family members[205] from pursuing the land claims and securing federal recognition as individual California Indians.

The best evidence of how the Ortiz family responded to the offer of enrollment under the 1928 act comes from the application of family elder and leader Joseph Ortiz, who included his children and grandchildren on his application in May 1932.[206] Joseph was sixty-seven at the time. He listed his tribe as "Fernandeño" and could not identify who the captain was as of 1852. Asked to explain whether he was claiming any particular lands that were taken from his ancestors, he replied, "I am not making any land claim in particular but wish to benefit with other California Indians if settlement is made." Elaborating later in the application, he noted, "I am making this application because on account of my age I can no longer obtain work, and need the help which, as an Indian, I think I am entitled to, and any benefits which may belong to me as a California Indian." Thus, the economic hardship of the Depression, as well as his relatively advanced age, drove Joseph Ortiz to seek whatever benefits—at this point still unknown—the federal government might choose to allocate with judgment funds. One of the affidavits supporting the application was from J. J. Lopez, grandson of a former mayordomo of San Fernando Mission and longtime foreman at Tejon Ranch, stating that Joseph had worked for him for fifteen years and that Joseph's mother, grandmother, and grandfather were all "pure blood" Indians from San Fernando Mission.

SUMMARY

Despite widespread discrimination during the first half of the twentieth century, the lineages now participating in the Fernandeño Tataviam Band of Mission Indians maintained their distinct identities, leadership patterns, political autonomy, and connections to one another. The fact that each Fernandeño lineage made its own choice to register or not to register for the 1928 act roll, acting as a unified entity, underscores the political independence of each lineage as well as the ongoing political influence of lineage leaders. Functioning in that manner, the Fernandeños continued longstanding cultural practices. Kinship, political leadership, and traditional knowledge remained strongly interrelated or nondifferentiated. Cultural practices, identity, and Indian languages became more private during this period and were deliberately hidden from outsiders. Most, at the same time, remained nominal Christians. Men and some women worked as wage laborers subject to the ebb and flow of the market. The tribal Fernandeño identity was defined as membership within one of the collection of autonomous lineages, whose ancestors were moved to and baptized at San Fernando Mission. The U.S. census of 1940 recorded that all leaders of the three lineages were living in close proximity to one another and to old town San Fernando.

FIGURE 43 J. J. Lopez (1853–1939), foreman at Rancho Tejon for many years, ca. 1880. From the cover of *Saga of Rancho El Tejón*.

By the time the federal government got around to establishing a settlement amount and authorizing per capita distribution, it was already mid-century. By then, leadership transition was underway, at least within the Garcia and Ortega lineages, as the older generation was passing or becoming infirm. Fears of discrimination and removal to reservations were becoming less important than learning about and reasserting their Native heritage. Antonio Maria Ortega's grandson, Rudy Ortega Sr., and Frances Garcia Cooke's grandson, Charlie Cooke, would take on major roles in the next half-century, carrying on, revitalizing, and—where appropriate—adapting tribal identities, cultures, ceremonies, and political traditions.

CHAPTER 7

Captions, Tribal Government, and Community (1950–2019)

After Estanislao (James) Ortega's death in 1951, Rudy Ortega followed his father and became captain of the Ortega lineage, one of several lineages still living in the San Fernando Mission area.[1] Born in 1926, Rudy was young to be a captain. His aunts, however, saw that even as a high school student, in the early 1940s, Rudy was dedicated and possessed leadership qualities. His leadership qualities remained apparent when he returned to San Fernando following military service in the Pacific theater during World War II.[2] When Estanislao was captain, he kept the lineage together by making regular visits to families, holding and attending family gatherings, and organizing and raising funds for giveaways. He gathered donations for both needy tribal members and needy local families.[3]

Vera Ortega Salazar, who was Rudy Ortega's aunt, wanted to sustain lineage and tribal relations, teach culture, and maintain community history, but she preferred meetings, cultural events, and the formation of a cultural-social club. Rudy Ortega was appointed captain, or lineage leader, by his aunts and family elders. Vera Ortega Salazar and her Ortega sisters played a leading role in supporting and mentoring Rudy, helping him to gain acceptance as captain. Antonio Maria Ortega's other daughters, Cristina Ortega Rodriguez, Kathryn Newman, and Rufugia (Erolinda) Tapia, all were active in helping organize family, tribal, and local community activities. Katie Newman exemplified traditional manners of self-effacing, quiet leadership.[4] Most of the aunts eventually accepted Rudy Ortega's leadership based on his political acumen and fruitful efforts to research family and tribal history and genealogy.[5] At the time he was appointed captain and chief of the tribe, he also received the name of Chief Little Bear, the tribal name he carried for the rest of his life.[6]

Captains, or lineage leaders, and tribal chiefs were appointed by consent among the elders and general community. There were no elections. Captains usually were selected from a central family in the lineage. Rudy belonged to the central family—his father was the eldest son of Antonio Maria Ortega. Rudy, however, was not the eldest son in his immediate family. A candidate for captain needed to demonstrate willingness to assume collective responsibility for the affairs of the lineage and tribe. The issues confronting a Fernandeño captain in the 1950s were increasingly demanding. A captain needed to take on projects such as recovering land, gaining membership within one of the California Indian rolls, creating government-to-government recognition with city, county, state, and federal governments, updating and verifying lineage genealogies, reclaiming Fernandeño history and culture, and maintaining lineage and tribal community and political goals, values, and social activities.[7] Lineage elders appointed captains based on their observations, understanding, and agreement. They sought to find the member who was most suited to keep the lineage and tribe together and address contemporary challenges to identity, self-government, land recovery, lineage culture, and other goals.[8]

MISSION INDIAN CLUB AND THE (SAN FERNANDO) MISSION BAND

While there was more than one candidate for political leadership, most of the community came to recognize Rudy Ortega as the tribal (or band) captain (or chief):[9]

> They had different perspectives about who was going to run the tribe. It was like you got presidency here. You got people fighting over who wants to be in the White House. It was the same thing as being president or the chief of the Tataviam tribe. Then we were Mission Band Indians. We found out we were from that part of Indian. . . . They called (Rudy Ortega) up and told him that they wanted him to be the leader. So my father started putting things together, projects and all of that, and the next thing you know the organization just started growing with the family, and then we started getting people say they were Indian.[10]

Around 1948, Rudy Ortega introduced a proposal to create bylaws for a mission Indian club, eventually known as the San Fernando Mission Indians of San Fernando, which included the Mission Indian Band but was also open to persons who were not tribal members.[11] Those in the Mission Indian Band were descendants of the lineages who were baptized at San Fernando Mission. The mission Indian club was geared to non–mission Indians but mainly aimed at inviting the spouses of Mission Indian Band members. Although draft bylaws were presented, the mission Indian club did not immediately adopt them. The process of adoption took many years and was the focus of extended discussion on numerous occasions. Nevertheless, the draft bylaws provided a guideline for meetings and decision-making from the late 1940s through the 1970s.[12]

Meetings of the club were held every other week and decisions were made by discussion and consensus. Members often met at Catholic churches, family homes, and public parks. St. Ferdinand's Catholic Church on Coronel Street in San Fernando had its roots in the parish of Mission San Fernando Rey.[13] St. Ferdinand was built in 1902, adding to a chapel that had been constructed about 1875, but it did not have steady attention from a parish priest. The parish community at St. Ferdinand originally covered the entire San Fernando Valley. San Fernando and Pacoima parishes sponsored Catholic feast days and San Fernando Mission restoration events and provided rooms for Fernandeños to meet. After World War I, St. Ferdinand's was increasingly populated by European immigrants and tended to give less attention to Indian parishioners.[14]

In some ways, the parish churches in San Fernando and Pacoima echoed the completion of centuries-old colonial secularization goals from the Mexican and Spanish periods. Secularization laws aimed to transfer mission Indians to parish churches and parish spiritual administration. However, colonial laws calling for the distribution of protected farmland to Indian families and collective land to self-governing Indian pueblos were not realized.

In the late 1940s and early 1950s, Rudy Ortega took on the task of recovering Fernandeño lineage histories and genealogies by researching the San Fernando Mission baptismal records that contained information on births, deaths, parents, godparents, witnesses, baptisms, and marriages. The records contained names of lineages and villages, indicating where Mission Indian Band ancestors were born and lived before the mission and during the mission period. Rudy found San Fernando Mission records for each tribal member. His research verified that the Ortega, Garcia, and Ortiz lineage ancestors lived and worked at San Fernando Mission. Because Rudy Ortega conducted the needed genealogy research and clarified the history of the Fernandeños, he became a knowledgeable cultural and historical resource, always a key feature of traditional leadership.

Until Rudy's genealogy studies were complete, the Mission Indian Band name was treated as temporary or provisional. Participants remained organized as extended families, with membership available to any person who could trace lineage to San Fernando Mission and to an associated ancestral village-lineage. The term mission Indians in local usage usually meant Indians whose descendants lived and worked at San Fernando Mission[15] because Indians from other California missions descended from different lineages. However, all non-Indians and Indians could join the openly inclusive mission Indian club.

Mary Cooke Garcia was registered in the California Indian Roll of 1933 as a mission Indian of San Fernando, another way of saying Fernandeño. Mary became captain of the Garcia lineage after her mother, Frances Garcia Cooke, died in a car accident in 1946.[16] During the late 1940s, Mary Garcia's eldest son, Theodore Cornelius (Ted) Garcia, joined the multilineage tribal Mission Indian Band and served as treasurer and in other offices. Over time, from the 1940s until his death in 2008, Ted Garcia served in many capacities for the club and Mission Indian Band government.[17] In 1950, Mary Garcia assisted Rudy Ortega in his attempt to enroll in the 1933 California Indian Roll. The Bureau of Indian Affairs denied his request, however, because they could not locate a blood relative already on the roll. After the roll closed in 1933, only direct blood relatives could be added to the judgment roll. Since none of the Ortega family members signed on to the California Indian Roll of 1933, there were no blood relatives to claim on the existing roll.[18] Mary Garcia's assistance demonstrated the ongoing tribal connections among Ortega and Garcia lineages.

During the 1950s, many of Mary and Frances's sons and daughters, the Garcia lineage, gave their cultural identity as Chumash. The Garcias had lineage connections to the Ventureño Chumash village of Escorpion through their ancestor Jose Juan Leyva, father of Josefa Garcia. In the same way, the Ortega lineage had connections to the Ventureño Chumash village of Tapuu through their ancestor Tiburcio Cayo.[19] In the American period, ancestors were honored and recognized bilaterally through multiple past generations.

Over time, the San Fernando Indians came to be known by a variety of names. By the 1950s, few, if any, spoke traditional Indian languages. The names of ancestral lineages and villages embedded in Indian language grammar were not well-known or used.[20] Those names were recovered by the research that tribal members conducted during the late 1940s and early 1950s. Typically, San Fernando Mission lineages were named after the eldest known ancestor and, in colonial times, given Spanish or English surnames. Hence, the surnames Ortega, Ortiz, and Garcia are used to identify separate lineages. The tradition of a close identification between the lineage name and the captain's name was recorded by Hugo Reid.[21] Locals, however, often used the expression mission Indians to signify Indians from San Fernando Mission, or Fernandeños, rather than California mission Indians as a whole.[22]

Before the mid-1950s, the mission Indian club invited everyone who was willing to support local Indian issues and socialize with the Indian members. Since persons who married into the tribe could not become tribal members, many people who had married in joined the club. Indians whose tribal territories were outside the San Fernando area and who were members of other tribes participated and voted in the club as well. In close association with the tribal government, the club held events, potluck dinners, and dances, celebrated holidays, visited regional powwows, raised money and resources, distributed food and aid to the needy, and engaged in the legal and political issues of concern to local Indian people.

The separate group, the Mission Indian Band, was a coalition of the Fernandeño lineages. All members of the mission Indian club participated in and voted on nontribal issues. Only tribal members of the Mission Indian Band voted and made decisions on matters of tribal interest. Descendants of Fernandeño lineages were welcome to join and enjoy voting rights on tribal issues as members of the Mission Band.

SAN FERNANDO MISSION INDIANS AND SAN FERNANDO MISSION BAND

By the mid-1950s there was enough confidence in the research about tribal history and genealogy that the club members renamed the club San Fernando Mission Indians (SFMI), sometimes referred to as the San Fernando Mission Indian Council.[23] The tribe, led by Rudy Ortega Sr., was renamed the San Fernando Mission Band (SFMB). Tribal membership in the SFMB was restricted to persons who traced their ancestry to the San Fernando Mission records and to associated lineages named in mission baptismal registries.[24] The SFMI formed a voluntary association for social and club activities and for engagement with Indian issues, including education, land recovery, land compensation, Bureau of Indian Affairs (BIA) enrollment, and state and federal recognition.

The SFMI club was a multitribal, multiethnic, multiracial, multilineal alliance of Indians and friends from the San Fernando area. It was envisioned as a voluntary association with regular meetings and bylaws. Though an outline of a set of bylaws guided activities for many years, discussion of numerous fine points inhibited a positive vote to accept formal bylaws. The SFMI and tribal SFMB discussed and used, but did not accept, written bylaws until 1973.[25]

The SFMB lineages remained attached to their own leadership of elders and captains even as they recognized Rudy Ortega, the Ortega captain, as a Fernandeño chief. During much of the 1950s, the Garcia lineage was led by Mary Cooke Garcia. And after the death of Joseph Ortiz in the late 1930s, the Ortiz lineage was led by several elders, mainly Joseph Ortiz's daughters, Helen Ortiz and Juanita Ortiz de Montez. Perhaps because captains were traditionally male, neither Helen nor Juanita claimed to be captain. Other lineages who traced their ancestry from San Fernando Mission and associated villages were invited to join, as they might choose.

Captains and elders remained appointed by their lineages, while leaders of the SFMI club were elected. Rudy Ortega was the first person elected president of the SFMI, but others could be and subsequently were elected to offices of president, vice president, and treasurer. Both Rudy Ortega and Ted Garcia, son of Mary Cooke Garcia, provided leadership and continuous community service to the SFMI as a social club and a community-activities organization. At the same time, they worked toward maintaining and building friendly and working relations among culturally and politically active Fernandeño lineages in the local area. Their goal was to recover their history and culture and "carry on where their ancestors left off."[26] Many elders were passing on, and there was a concerted effort to recover as much information and traditional knowledge as possible.[27]

Mary Cooke Garcia moved to the San Fernando area by 1940, living in Pacoima, only a few miles from the Ortega residences in San Fernando. In the late 1940s and early 1950s, Rudy Ortega and family were also living in Pacoima. Mary Garcia was a close political confidant of Rudy Ortega and an active participant in the community of San Fernando Indians through the 1950s, '60s, and '70s. Mary's eldest son, Ted Garcia, held offices with the SFMI club and was active in developing the tribal version of the San Fernando Mission Indians, the SFMB.[28] Mary Garcia identified as Chumash and was an in-law relative to the Ortega family. She regularly organized gatherings of the Garcia lineage, where Indian issues confronting their relations and other tribal lineages were discussed. Sometimes Rudy Ortega and Ortega lineage members joined those meetings and gatherings.

Anthropologist Alfred Kroeber commented on meetings within lineages: "They acted together in times of emergency. They were likely to act together in times of visits, festivals, and dances."[29] Lineage gatherings took place during holidays and special events, partly because American and Christian holidays dominated the calendar but also because the demands of wage labor organized people's schedules around five-day workweeks, weekends, and holidays. Holidays

FIGURE 44 Helen Ortiz (1907–1995), holding child, Angie, at San Fernando Mission garden (1930–). Courtesy of Fernandeño Tataviam Band of Mission Indians.

were times when large extended families could get together. Certain lineage-tribal members, often elderly persons, took on the obligation to organize these family gatherings.

Vera Ortega Salazar organized such family events until the late 1970s. Gatherings for holidays, life cycle events, and crisis situations were opportunities to meet and socialize but also a time for significant discussion and decision-making that affected individuals, families, and the lineage communities.[30] David Salazar Sr., Vera Salazar's son, commented that

> Christmas, New Years. It was for everybody. . . . All the relatives, and if they brought somebody they could come too. Because I had my aunts' kids and my uncles' kids. Everybody would come over. They'd come in groups. They liked my mom's cooking. She loved to have them by.[31]

David's son, Stanley Salazar, also emphasized the role of gatherings in maintaining tribal cohesion.

> And it was through weddings, funerals and holidays. And all of them were very important. I think my dad was even at Rudy's wedding, and those kind of things . . . what kept our tribe together was the people.[32]

THE GARCIA CAPTAIN

About the same time that Rudy Ortega was researching and organizing the club and band, leaders of the Garcia lineage were grappling with similar challenges. In 1959, Mary Cooke Garcia decided to step down as captain of the Garcia lineage because she did not feel she could meet the need for increasingly activist, mobile, and knowledgeable leadership. Neither she nor her husband, Luis, had a driver's license, and the country was filled with roads and automobiles. She called some family members and leaders together at her home in Pacoima, explaining that although she would step down as captain, she would continue organizing the Garcia lineage social gatherings, something she loved to do. In fact, she continued hosting them until her death in 1975. Among those present for Mary's announcement were her son, Ted Garcia Sr., his son, Ted Garcia Jr., and her two paternal nephews, brothers Alvin and Charlie Cooke.

According to tradition, Mary's son, Ted Garcia Sr., then about twenty-nine years old, was first in line for consideration for political leadership. The group agreed, however, that Charlie Cooke showed the most interest, dedication, and understanding regarding preservation of their Indian heritage. Charlie Cooke was appointed captain of the Garcia lineage, often subsequently called the Cooke-Garcia lineage. Ted Garcia Sr. was wholeheartedly in favor of Charlie Cooke's leadership. For the next several decades, he aided and assisted Charlie Cooke on many tribal issues, cultural resource management projects, and other activities. Over the same period, Ted Garcia Sr. and family were actively engaged with the San Fernando Mission Indian club and the San Fernando Mission Band. Ted Sr. remained a regular participant in tribal affairs and loyal assistant to both lineage captains, Rudy Ortega and Charlie Cooke.

Charlie Cooke served as captain of the Cooke-Garcia lineage for fifty-four years, from 1959 until his death in 2013. Similarly, Rudy Ortega served the Ortega lineage as captain, as well as the tribe as chief, from at least 1951 until his death in 2009, a period of fifty-eight years. The relative stability of political leadership among the Fernandeños was one reason for their ability to build and maintain social, political, and economic growth over many decades. Rudy Ortega and Charlie Cooke were distant cousins through their common ancestor, who was father to both Isidora Garcia, Rudy's grandmother, and Isidoro Garcia, Charlie's great-grandfather.

Ted Garcia Jr. was a future captain in the Garcia line. As a boy he attended the meeting at Pacoima in 1959, later commenting that

> if you think about the past, you know it is related to the present and future. Charlie was a hero to me when I was a child. I remember Charlie visiting our house about fifty years ago after he came home from the service. I was about ten then, but right then I knew he would represent our family in Indian affairs. I was in awe of that. I looked up to him. Growing up in Pacoima with a Latin name, people assumed we were Mexican; but my Grandmother Mary made sure we were Indian. She got that from her mother, Charlie's grandmother Frances. . . . Charlie went on to represent us in an intelligent way. He does research. He knows what he is talking about. I always knew he would become our chief.[33]

Charlie Cooke went on to an outstanding and eventful career as captain of the Cooke-Garcia lineage and as a leader in Southern California Indigenous cultural resources protection.[34]

In the late 1950s, Charlie Cooke and his brother, Alvin, attended meetings to gain more knowledge about Indian rights and issues. The two brothers attended meetings in Compton, California, on weekends. Sam Kolb, an Indian activist and descendant of the nonfederally recognized San Luis Rey Mission Indian community, knew about unrecognized Indians and Indian cultures. Over the years he had advocated for federal legislation on tribal issues, worked for the Bureau of Indian Affairs, and helped many Indians arriving in the Los Angeles metropolitan area as they adjusted to life in the city. By 1971, Kolb joined the San Fernando Mission Indians as a nontribal member and worked and socialized with both Charlie Cooke and Rudy Ortega. For several years, for all who would come to listen to him, Kolb held meetings and discussed Indian land issues, federal Indian law, tribal enrollment for unrecognized Indians, and other related matters.

At a meeting in 1958, Sam asked Alvin and Charlie whether their ancestors lived at San Fernando Mission. They answered that their grandmother, Frances Garcia, was born at the mission, although many years after San Fernando

Mission was deserted by the Franciscan friars. Sam's response was: "We need to organize a San Fernando Mission Band for anyone with Indian ancestors from that mission. You two guys get the people together and I'll come talk with them."[35] This suggestion strongly echoed the endeavor already underway by Rudy Ortega for the Fernandeño community. Many Indians at San Fernando Mission originally lived in lineages in the Santa Clarita Valley. Josefa Garcia and family had left San Fernando in 1882 and moved to work and live at Newhall Ranch, near the site of the ancient village of Tochonanga. The land around San Fernando was taken up by real estate companies, and the remaining San Fernando Indians were evicted from the former mission lands in the 1870s and 1880s.[36] Many Indians living in the Santa Clarita Valley were members of the expanding Garcia lineage. So Kolb visited Newhall, calling on people who lived near the Cooke brothers and their Garcia lineage relatives. The brothers started searching for Indians whose ancestors could be traced back to San Fernando Mission.[37] Most of those they found were members of the Garcia lineage. Josefa Leyva, Charlie's great-great-grandmother, had been one of very few Fernandeños with surviving children.

Kolb, whose own community was not federally recognized, understood federal recognition issues and kinship organization within California Indian communities. Kolb's suggestion of the name San Fernando Mission Band indicates that the Indians were still organized into communities and kinship groups that at the same time were political entities with leaders and government. Although each lineage had its own captain, Rudy Ortega was, by consensus, leader of all three lineage components of the San Fernando Mission Band. The expression "Band" recognized that the San Fernando Mission Band was a political entity composed of a voluntary coalition of politically active lineages.[38]

In late 1961, Alvin and Charlie Cooke started the San Fernando Mission Association.[39] The thirty members of the San Fernando Mission Association were all members of Charlie Cooke's extended family or lineage.[40] As captain of the Cooke-Garcia lineage, Charlie Cooke maintained relations with and obligations to the entire lineage. Most Garcia lineage members may have been satisfied with the regular family gatherings and warm kinship ties and identity. Others, however, were beginning to ponder whether regaining recognition, recovering land, protecting sacred spaces, and generally defining and defending Indian rights would require new forms of social and political organization. In 1967, Charlie Cooke was reelected president of the San Fernando Mission Association by thirty voting members, all from the Garcia lineage. Their action reaffirmed the strong support he had from the Garcias.

PAN-INDIAN DANCING (1960–1998)

During the early 1960s, Rudy Ortega and some other Fernandeños began attending pan-Indian powwows. Because Rudy's second wife was a member of the federally recognized Chumash Tribe, from the Santa Ynez Reservation, he attended powwows there, often setting up a booth and making friends and greeting relations.[41] Then Rudy and others began visiting powwows elsewhere in Southern California, with stops at Southern California Indian reservations and in the Los Angeles metropolitan area.

The pan-Indian powwow forms of dancing and social traditions are not those of California Indians. However, during the 1950s and 1960s, many Indians migrated to urban areas through a federal relocation program that promised (but did not always deliver) financial rewards for reservation Indians who moved. Members of over one hundred different tribes came to the Los Angeles metropolitan area, which the federal government designated as a central destination.[42] Many Indians who came were from the powwow traditions of the Great Plains and southeast, which many non-Indian Americans viewed as the primary form of Indian culture. For the general public, the prevailing stereotype of Indian dances,

FIGURE 45 San Fernando Mission Indians (club), powwow booth selling refreshments, 1960s. Courtesy of Fernandeño Tataviam Band of Mission Indians.

ceremonies, and music left no room for the very different California Indian cultures. The stereotype was equally inappropriate for many other Indian nations as well. The Navajo and Apaches, for example, practiced Indian dance, music, and religious traditions that were different and distinct from the Plains Indians.

Powwows became increasingly popular among many Indian groups, both within and outside of California. Even if they were not part of a tribe's historical and cultural tradition, the powwows were colorful and dramatic, even sacred for those who understood them. Dancers from many tribes began asking their tribal elders whether it was possible to participate in the powwow, even if powwow dancing was not part of their own culture. Tribal elders often granted their consent, with the caveat that powwow dancing and their own traditional tribal dancing should not be mixed. Consequently, many Indians who did not have a powwow tradition began to attend and participate in powwows throughout Southern California.[43] From the 1960s to the 1990s in Los Angeles, one could attend a powwow almost every weekend. There was sometimes competition among powwow leaders for openings on the community powwow calendar.

FIGURE 46 Parade of San Fernando Inter-Tribal Indian dancers, with Rudy Ortega Sr. (1926–2009), lineage captain, and sons. Courtesy of Fernandeño Tataviam Band of Mission Indians.

FIGURE 47 Rudy Ortega Sr. (1926–2009), lineage captain (*left*), in regalia with San Fernando Inter-Tribal Indian dancers, ca. 1982. Courtesy of Fernandeño Tataviam Band of Mission Indians.

Many young people among the Fernandeños wanted to join the powwows. Rudy Ortega agreed to help the young dancers attend powwows and receive instruction in proper powwow dancing styles.[44] The dancers and many Fernandeño leaders dressed in Plains outfits and over the next several decades, until the late 1990s, attended and appeared in powwows, school presentations, parades, giveaways, and ceremonies and maintained an annual powwow at San Fernando.[45] The San Fernando powwow was a tribal event with both Fernandeño/Tataviam and Chumash dancers, held in the San Fernando Valley during the month of June each year, starting in the 1960s.[46] Chumash dancers from Santa Barbara instructed many of the Fernandeño dancers.[47] Although the pan-Indian performances of the Fernandeños were witnessed widely, the Fernandeños did not generally display their own traditions and specific dancing, singing, and religious styles. The Chumash dancers were an exception.

The powwows were one avenue of engagement in an emergent pan-Indian culture in the Los Angeles area. With the migration of Mexican and Latin American Indians into the region, the cultural complexity of Indian identity and politics increased but also offered more opportunities. The early 1960s saw the winding down of federal Indian termination policy and the slowing down of urbanizing relocation programs.

CULTURAL RESOURCES AND LAND

By the early 1970s, Fernandeños were actively engaged in protecting cultural sites and gaining federally recognized land.[48] Rocketdyne was a place for testing moon engines and defense weapons. However, there were ancient rock paintings discovered on the Rocketdyne property. The artwork, usually considered to have sacred significance, became a point of concern for the San Fernando Mission Indian club. As tribal coordinator, Rudy Ortega secured protection of several ancient Indian wall inscriptions at the Rocketdyne site by getting the wall inscriptions listed as a California historical site.[49] Protection of ancient Indian village and sacred sites from construction, defacing, and destruction became major tribal activities.[50]

FIGURE 48 Rudy Ortega Sr. at Burro Flats rock art site with Boeing consultant, 1971. Courtesy of Fernandeño Tataviam Band of Mission Indians.

INDIAN POLICY

Termination policy of the late 1940s and 1950s was promoted, both domestically and internationally, as an effort to relieve Indians of second-class citizenship. Federal officials characterized the collective nature of tribal lands, as well as federal controls over those lands, as oppressive. Termination meant the federal government would eliminate Indian reservations, turning nontaxable, nontransferable reservation trust land into parcels of marketable fee simple land that could be taxed and bought up by non-Indian buyers. Termination also aimed to block federal recognition of tribes as governments, dismantling Indian self-government and subjecting Indians to state jurisdiction extended over reservations. Services, such as health care and education, that the federal government provided on reservations were discontinued with termination.[51] For many tribes, termination meant the full extinguishment of their treaty rights. Most American Indians were willing to embrace full citizenship, but not at the cost of losing tribal land and treaty rights, the power to maintain their cultures, and tradition-based tribal governments. Termination was imposed on the tribes, over their opposition, because it was more about gaining access to tribal resources than it was about empowering Indians. The actual consequences for terminated tribes were disastrous.[52]

Through the 1950s, many Southern California Indian tribes struggled against the termination bills presented in Congress. The termination policy was implemented through a series of individual termination enactments, which identified specific tribes, rather than through a nationwide law. By gaining support of local county and state governments, national Indian coalitions cooperated to stop termination. Organizational and tribal leaders convinced local, county, and state governments that the extensive burden of Indian support would be shifted to them.[53] Nevertheless, about forty-three reservations, mainly in Northern California, were terminated by the early 1960s. Since 1975, most terminated California Indian reservations have been restored to federal recognition through litigation or federal statute.[54] Federal Indian policy evolved in this period toward accepting Indians as dual citizens, simultaneously citizens of the United States and tribal citizens able to exercise self-government within reservations.

The Kennedy-Johnson administrations championed antipoverty programs and provided funding and opportunities for disadvantaged people. Urban Indian centers and Indian antipoverty programs emerged in the Los Angeles area and were very active until the early 1980s. The Nixon administration opened some doors for tribes by advancing a policy of self-determination, which focused on the development and action of tribal government and the recognition of treaties as the foundation of Indian policy. Responding to a congressional mandate, the American Indian Policy Review Commission issued a sweeping report in 1977 that addressed, among other topics, ways in which the federal government could grant recognition to nonfederally recognized tribes. About 130 Indian communities had petitioned the U.S. government for federal recognition. Another 100 tribes were terminated and were looking for restoration of self-government and opportunities for economic development.[55] Shortly thereafter, the Bureau of Indian Affairs adopted its first-ever regulations with procedures and criteria that nonfederally recognized tribes could use to establish their government-to-government relationship with the United States.[56] Over time, several hundred Indian communities have written letters of intent to the U.S. government seeking to gain federal recognition, among them the Fernandeño Tataviam Band of Mission Indians.

THE 1968 CALIFORNIA LAND CLAIMS ACT AND THE 1972 ROLL

In a broad effort to settle Indian land claims for loss of aboriginal territories, Congress enacted the Indian Claims Commission Act in 1946.[57] For California Indians, this new law opened the door to claims for ancestral lands that had not been included in reservations for which the 1928 California Indians Jurisdictional Act had purported to provide compensation.[58] By 1951, scores of petitions had been presented to the newly formed Indian Claims Commission on behalf of individual California tribes and all the "Indians of California." After considerable wrangling and complex litigating, most of these cases were consolidated into a single proceeding, known as Dockets 31 and 37, designed to resolve nearly all the claims statewide.[59] Following an initial ruling by the Indian Claims Commission and an arduously negotiated settlement between the Indians' many representatives and the United States, the commission entered a final judgment in 1964 in favor of the "Indians of California" in the amount of $29.1 million.[60] Four years later, Congress passed Public Law 90–507, "to provide for preparation of a roll of persons of California Indian descent and the distribution of certain judgement funds."[61] The law required the creation of a new California Indian Roll and the distribution of about $29.5 million.

The 1968 enrollment and payment legislation required all California Indians to prove descent from persons on the 1933 California Indian Roll or, alternatively, prove lineal descent from Indian ancestors born on or before June 1, 1852. The Ortegas supplied baptismal and birth records to support their applications and qualified under the requirement of California Indian ancestry before June 1, 1852. The Garcia and Ortiz lineages qualified by proving their ties to ancestors already on the 1933 California Indian Roll.[62]

In 1968, brothers Charlie and Alvin Cooke started calling meetings for people of Indian descent to inform them of their rights and to enlist them in the California Indian Land Settlement roll. Enrollment would make them eligible for land settlement payments and give them state recognition of their Indian ancestry. The deadline for application to the judgment roll was September 22, 1969.[63] That early deadline was eventually moved to June 30, 1972. The roll was finalized in December 1972.[64]

Rudy Ortega had become a knowledgeable source of cultural and bureaucratic information. For decades he had been active in securing historical genealogical information, and he worked to gain California Indian enrollment with the Bureau of Indian Affairs. The Fernandeños distributed over five hundred applications and provided help to Indians collecting their genealogy documents. Rudy Ortega had begun contacting BIA officials as early at the 1940s. He and Ortega lineage members had long sought official state and federal tribal recognition, admission to the California Indian Roll based on the 1928 California Indian Jurisdictional Act, and reservation land for the San Fernando Mission Indians.[65] Fears of being sent to a remote reservation, which had kept the Ortegas from participating in the 1928 act,[66] were no longer dominant.

The 1972 judgment roll resulted in success for the Ortega lineage. Rudy Ortega presented federal officials with a list of lineage-member applications for the California Indian Roll. These individual applications often used the expressions Fernandeño or San Fernando Mission Indians in response to questions seeking statement of a tribal name. Among Ortega lineage members, when the application asked for a tribal name, the expression Fernandeño often was used. However, for the same applicant, when the genealogy charts asked for the name of the applicant's tribal entity on or before June 1, 1852, the answer often given was San Fernando Mission Indian.[67]

On the 1933 California Indian Roll, in response to the inquiry for a tribal name, the Ortiz lineage responded with Fernandeño, while the Garcia lineage responded primarily with San Fernando Mission Indian.[68] The Ortega lineage used both Fernandeño and San Fernando Mission Indian as tribal names in 1969 applications for the 1972 roll. All three lineages were speaking about the same tribal entity when they interchangeably used the expressions Fernandeño and San Fernando Mission Indians. A voluntary, friendly, and consensual coalition of the Indian lineages at San Fernando Mission formed a tribal political entity through sustained cooperative agreement among the lineages. Each lineage, however, traditionally and continuously retained considerable autonomy. Rudy Ortega, as tribal coordinator, reported that in January 31, 1971, there were sixty-two adults in the Fernandeño Tribe, also known as the San Fernando Mission Band.[69]

On August 27, 1971, Rudy Ortega sent a letter to the BIA area director in Sacramento requesting reservation land for the San Fernando Mission Band.[70] Ortega had been talking with BIA officials about tribal recognition and tribal land since the late 1940s.[71] The acting BIA area director sent a letter to the SFMB suggesting they identify land, obtain a legal description, and explore with the California congressional delegation the possibility of introducing a bill to Congress.[72] The acting area director attached federal regulations pointing out that new reservations could no longer be created by executive order and were possible only through acts of Congress.

While eligible Fernandeños submitted their applications relatively early in 1968, they grew impatient when verification of applications took longer than expected. They invited BIA officials to visit at Mary Immaculate Catholic Church in Pacoima on November 7, 1971. "A big effort was made to sign up Indians having claim to the money, but nothing has happened in the way of allocating it to us," Rudy Ortega said. Norman Sahmaunt, an official from the Sacramento office of the Bureau of Indian Affairs, was invited to attend. At the same meeting, ceremonies were scheduled to install new officers of the San Fernando Mission Indians club, which included non–Fernandeño Indians.[73] The *Los Angeles Times* reported that Rudy Ortega was president of the San Fernando Mission Indians, and he "said local Indians are wondering about the status of the allocations."[74] Ortega, however, preferred the title of tribal coordinator. As he later recalled, the meeting took an unexpected turn:

> And so we had that meeting in Pacoima at the church and Ed Diaz came down. I don't know who invited him. And he came over. . . . He threw his weight around like a politician. And after I introduced him to us, a gentleman to a gentleman, you know. And told them who he was and everything. So they clapped their hands. But then, he started . . . he started talking politics and this and that. He said how about me running for president . . . we weren't working with the politicians to support us or anything like that. We were going on our own as individual natural people. That's what I wanted to do. Not feel that we're up there. We have nothing to prove. So he still started talking to the people. So I got mad and I got up. I says, "You know what? You can have this group. You can have everybody that's in it, the chairs that belong to the church. I'm leaving." So

> I got up and I started walking out. Before I knew it, Vera [Salazar] was behind me. She says, "Come on, Rudy. Let's go." And she didn't like it either the way he was talking. So the rest of the people started getting up. The relatives started walking out. I think they left about five or eight people in there that weren't from our tribe. They stayed there with him.[75]

In early February 1972, Diaz and others were written up in a local newspaper introducing the San Fernando Mission Indian Council. "The San Fernando Mission Indian Council . . . is the same formerly known as San Fernando Mission Indians but has added 'council' to its name."[76] Rudy Ortega explained, "He [Diaz] had invented . . . The San Fernando Mission Indian Council. . . . Because it was already Mission Indians with me."[77] The San Fernando Mission Council originated in late 1971 as a pan-Indian activist organization, but without San Fernando Mission Indian tribal member participation.[78] San Fernando Mission Indian tribal members wanted nothing to do with it, and it was never active after 1973.

SAN FERNANDO VALLEY INTER-TRIBAL INCORPORATED (1972–1994)

Two months after the tumultuous November 7, 1971, meeting, Vera Salazar telephoned Rudy Ortega and urged him to gather the tribal community together.[79] There were about eighty tribal adults active in late 1971.[80] Vera already had contacted them, and they all wanted to restart the tribal and club meetings again. Vera made arrangements for a potluck dinner. In February 1972, Rudy Ortega wrote to a Sacramento-based BIA official, "I am making a new club called the San Fernando Valley Inter-Tribal Indian Club. Can you help us get some kind of hall or Indian center for the Mission Indians here—San Fernando Valley. My people could use something like this."[81]

Both the *Los Angeles Times* and the *Valley News and Green Sheet* carried news of the new club and tribal gathering. "Rudy Ortega, who has been the tribal coordinator for the San Fernando Mission Band Indians, has announced the meeting for Sunday Feb. 27, 1971." "All Valley Indians are invited to a meeting Sunday, Feb. 27 at the San Fernando Mission Park to form a new San Fernando Valley Inter-Tribal Club. Mission Band members are only those who are descendants of San Fernando Mission Indians." The gathering included a potluck dinner, the election of officers, and "a small powwow of our own."[82] The call went out to tribal members of the San Fernando Mission Band, which was the name of the tribal entity, a coalition of Fernandeño lineages. Tribal members and lineages living in the San Fernando Valley, Santa Clarita Valley, and Simi Valley were asked to gather and discuss the formation of an Indian center and an intertribal club. The meeting resulted in agreement to adopt a tribally managed nonprofit named the San Fernando Valley Inter-Tribal Incorporated (SFVII). Meanwhile the San Fernando Mission Band, after the February 27, 1972, meeting, started using the SFVII name for its numerous projects, such as social gatherings, entertainment, meetings, preservation of sacred sites, charities, cultural events, and other activities.[83]

Late in 1972, the California Settlement Act paid out $661.51, more or less, to enrolled California Indians. The payment depended on whether the enrollee qualified for one or more judgment funds.[84] For the San Fernando Mission Band, the settlement accomplished the goal of recognition as American Indians by the state of California. Band members now were added to the California Indian Roll. Acquiring reservation land and federal recognition continued as major tribal goals.[85]

In California, nonprofits are registered as business corporations. The San Fernando Mission Band adopted bylaws and on October 30, 1973, the San Fernando Valley Inter-Tribal Incorporated was registered as a nonprofit in the state of California.[86] State senator Alan Robbins helped move the application for nonprofit incorporation though California government processes.

In the mid- to late 1970s, the SFVII was engaged in Los Angeles metropolitan pan-Indian cultural and organizational activities.[87] Rudy Ortega served as a board member of the Los Angeles Native American Commission.[88] The SFVII tried to secure funding for an Indian medical clinic in the San Fernando Valley, and Rudy Ortega served as chairperson of the Los Angeles Urban Indian Health Center, Inc., from 1978 to April 1981.[89]

San Fernando Valley Inter-Tribal Incorporated was led by Rudy Ortega and elected members of the board. Ortega stood for election as well, and he always won the vote and maintained the confidence of his community. On a regular multiannual basis, the SFVII offered assistance to tribal members and other Indians to find housing, gave employment referrals, sponsored summer youth-employment programs, made welfare and social service referrals, organized cultural events,[90] supported annual powwows and an Indian dance troupe,[91] gathered funds for and awarded college scholarships, engaged in monitoring Encino excavations and ancestral reburials,[92] sponsored giveaways to needy people and children, and supported other activities.

Tribal members now added the 1972 California Indian Roll numbers as markers for broader Indian identity, but tribal and lineage identities remained the

FIGURE 49 Rudy Ortega Sr. (*left*) giving college scholarships to community members, 1970s. Courtesy of Fernandeño Tataviam Band of Mission Indians.

same as before. Rudy Ortega wrote in a 1986 letter, "We are from the Fernandino (Fernandeño) which is the San Fernando Mission Indians."[93]

THE FERNANDEÑO TATAVIAM TRIBAL COUNCIL (1995–2002)

In 1995, the tribe decided to make some changes in tribal government. Boards for the nonprofit and tribal organizations were merged in 2000. The tribal name became the Fernandeño Tataviam Tribe, or the Fernandeno Tataviam Tribal Council (FTTC).[94] Fernandeño continued to mean a person who could prove ancestral ties to one of the lineages that was moved to San Fernando Mission. For example, the identity of Tataviam was given to individuals who could trace ancestry to a Tataviam-speaking lineage that was removed to San Fernando Mission. Over the years, the tribe used a nonprofit that managed contracts, fundraising, social relations, and cultural-identity issues. Primary FTTC interests were state and federal recognition as a tribal government. Tribal government meetings were held on the first Saturday of each month, and the meeting took place in the homes of the council members because there were no tribal offices throughout the 1990s.[95] The meetings were open to everyone interested in politics, education, grants, cultural resources, cultural exhibitions, and medical, social, and employment referrals, but tribal decisions were made only by tribal members.

Enrollment

The Fernandeño Tataviam Tribe called on community members to formally register as members of a tribal organization. Members were asked to file genealogy charts, provide documentation, describe family relations, and account for new children. The tribal roll, reopened for applications every four years, provided more accurate and extensive data on tribal members.

FIGURE 50 Ted Garcia Sr. (1920–2008), oldest son of captain Mary Cooke Garcia, with sisters, 1997. Courtesy of Geraldine Perez.

Tribal members were always members of a lineage or clan, but now enrollment processes caused some elders to demur. Some elders understood they were blood kin within lineages, and consequently they did not need to apply for membership in the tribe. Highly regarded elder Ted Garcia Sr. refused to enroll, although he continued to take part in tribal issues and affairs. Out of respect for him, the Garcia lineage members in San Fernando did not enroll either. Many Garcias only enrolled after Ted Garcia Sr. passed at a very old age in 2008. After his father's passing, Ted Garcia Jr. and family members enrolled in the tribe. Among the Ortiz family, Helen Ortiz in 1995 encouraged her children and grandchildren to enroll. By the early 2000s, the Fernandeño Tataviam gave their enrolled membership at about 450 people.[96]

CULTURAL AND POLITICAL ACTIVITIES

In 1995–96, the tribe actively supported the Advisory Council on California Indian Policy (AICCP), which Congress established to address current and past policies affecting federally recognized and unrecognized Indians in California.[97] In 1997, the tribe cooperated with the city of San Fernando and local Catholic Church parishes in the bicentennial commemoration of the 1797 founding of San Fernando Mission. State parks and local high schools asked for cultural demonstrations, and in 1999, tribal members constructed a traditional Tataviam village for study by students at North Hollywood High School. The Fernandeño Tataviam Tribe shared ceremonial activities such as blessings for the Day of the Dead family festival, an annual bear ceremony, a spring equinox or new year ceremony, and activities supporting local museums and cultural groups.[98]

The Fernandeño Tataviam Tribe, however, held their last public pan-Indian powwow in 2000.[99] Thereafter, the tribal leadership preferred to pursue songs, dances, and spiritual knowledge by sharing teachings with nearby culturally related tribes, including the Serrano, Vanyume, Kitanemuk, and Chumash. The Garcias, including Charlie Cooke and the Ted Garcia family, followed Chumash dancing, songs, and ceremonies. Charlie Cooke participated in Chumash community organizations and cultural resource management along the coast from Malibu to Ventura. Charlie Cooke was considered a Chumash chief as well as captain of the Garcias. Among the Ortegas, Beverly Folkes, daughter of Vera Ortega Salazar, honored Tapuu Chumash ancestor Tiburcio Cayo and was a board member of the Santa Barbara Museum of Natural History.[100] Beverly Folkes, Charlie

FIGURE 51 Charlie Cooke (1935–2013), lineage captain, performing ceremony at Sherman Oaks, California, in 2002. Photo by Phil Bedel.

Cooke, and other Garcia family members developed and opened the Chumash Indian Museum at Thousand Oaks, California, in 1994.

Rudy Ortega Sr. was elected tribal coordinator in 1972, and he was reelected continuously through the 1980s, 1990s, and 2000s.[101] As noted above, in the early 1970s he and other tribal leaders organized a nonprofit entity, named San Fernando Valley Inter-Tribal Inc., that could work with local federal, state, county, and city legislatures and commissions to acquire funds allocated for American Indian tribes and nonprofit organizations.[102] Meetings were often held at Christmas, Easter, summer, and, sometimes, spring gatherings. Food and entertainment for children in the form of games, dancing, and stories by elders were always present at meetings.

At these meetings, older tribal members convened to discuss the business of the day. Nontribal board members were elected and invited to all events but could not vote on issues before the general tribal assembly and were not allowed to express their viewpoints on tribal matters in the general meetings. Some nontribal board members, who often had children or spouses who were tribal members, were upset that they were not allowed to engage in the discussions of issues that affected their family members who were tribal members. Elections were conducted during the general meetings during the early 1970s through the 2000s. "As I remember how I got on the council was during a general council meeting. I was nominated by Rita (Newman) Rivera and my uncle Ernie (James) Ortega. The tribe always got together during Christmas, Summer and Easter and conducted tribal meetings."[103] "In general meetings, [candidates for all positions] were nominated by any tribal member in attendance and voted by all tribal members in attendance."[104]

In 1997, Rudy Ortega Jr. went through ceremonies confirming his role as designated future captain of the Ortega lineage and Fernandeño tribal leader. Rudy Ortega Sr. served as Ortega lineage captain and tribal chief until his death in 2009. In preparation to become captain designate, Rudy Ortega Jr. was tasked with fasting for four days and approaching the spirit of the bear who killed Ortega and Garcia lineage ancestor Santiago Garcia in 1873. The ceremony was attended by tribal elders. Rudy Ortega Jr. made peace with the bear and reported that lineage ancestors appeared and were glad they were not forgotten.[105] Lineage captains and tribal leaders were expected to be knowledgeable about ceremonies and to understand traditional beliefs.

Since childhood, Rudy Jr. had taken an interest in tribal activities, cultural events, administration, and community participation. He became an assistant to his father, Rudy Ortega Sr., and traveled with him and learned about the tribe and the issues that confronted the tribal community. By 1999, at age twenty-four, he was elected vice chair of the Fernandeño Tataviam Tribal Council. He became the tribal administrator, taking care of day-to-day management activities and planning and coordinating events. As the youngest son of Rudy Ortega Sr., he was not necessarily in line to become captain (and therefore candidate for tribal leadership) by order or timing of birth. The role of captain usually was offered to the oldest willing son. However, Rudy Ortega Jr.'s enthusiasm, capabilities, cultural knowledge, and dedication to the tribal community singled him out as a natural captain.

In 2000, leaders of the tribal council, who were also directing the nonprofit, decided that they needed a distinct 501(c)(3) nonprofit organization for financial reasons and to allow for greater participation by affiliated nontribal members.[106] Discussion also emerged favoring the formation of a tribal constitution that would revise and separate the organization of government and nonprofit activities.[107] Late in the year, the Fernandeno Tataviam Tribe called for volunteers to form a committee and, with the aid of UCLA School of Law's Tribal Legal Development Clinic, began work on a formal constitutional document.[108]

THE FERNANDEÑO TATAVIAM BAND OF MISSION INDIANS

On November 15, 2002, the Fernandeño Tataviam Band of Mission Indians (FTBMI), with its new official name, adopted a constitution.[109] The tribe also wrote a set of codes to govern tribal members.[110] The code titles included education and cultural learning, government administration, rules for officers, rules governing the senate, election and campaign guidelines, finance and taxation enforcement, and tribal history and cultural preservation. The senate was the primary body for addressing tribal issues.[111]

Membership in the FTBMI was defined in Article I of the constitution. "The Fernandeño Tataviam Band of Mission Indians and cited as the Fernandeño Tataviam Tribe, Fernandeño Tribe, Tataviam Tribe, and San Fernando Mission Indians, is a participatory union of clans, families, and persons descended from the original people of the Fernandeño Tataviam traditional villages, rancherias, and of Mission San Fernando." The constitutional definition of membership is rooted

FIGURE 52 *From left, front row,* Angie Berns, Rudy Ortega Sr., state legislator Sheila Kuehl, and Charlie Cooke; *back row,* Ted Garcia Jr. and unknown person, at grand reopening of Los Encinos Park, 2002. Courtesy of Fernandeño Tataviam Band of Mission Indians.

in and depends on descent from one or more of the villages or clans that are recorded by the San Fernando Mission baptismal records. The villages or clans originally were politically autonomous and often gathered together, willingly, in friendly and ceremonial unions.[112] The constitution provides a list of names by which past and current tribal entities are known. A person or lineage joins the tribe voluntarily, by choice. Inclusion of the term "Band" in the FTBMI name implies that the San Fernando Mission Band and the (San Fernando) Mission Band are included as former tribal names.

The new constitution formally split the tribal and nontribal members into two distinct boards rather than the combined board that had served the community since 1972. The tribal senate was composed of elected tribal members only, while nontribal members could serve on the board of the Nonprofit Council.[113] The tribal council was now formed into a president and standing senate committee, which managed the issues and affairs of the band, or tribal members.[114]

In many ways, nevertheless, political leadership remains similar to traditional patterns. Political leadership and community values follow patterns of

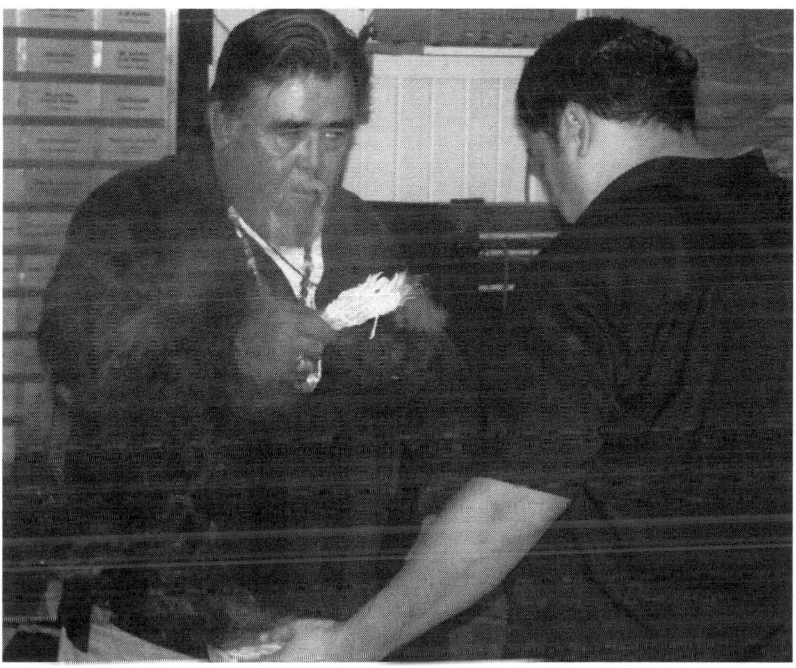

FIGURE 53 Charlie Cooke (*left*) performs a blessing for Rudy Ortega Jr. at the 2007 conveyance of artifacts from Newhall Land's River Village development site. From SCVhistory.com.

community self-help, as well as provide aid and support to other Indian and non-Indians families living in the surrounding and regional community.[115] While leaders are elected under the constitution, traditional lineage and family ties continue to influence leadership and management positions. Contemporary political leaders must be concerned about individual and family issues and be ready to provide leadership for the entire tribal community. Early in 2004, Rudy Ortega Jr. resigned his elected post as vice-president and took on the full-time job of tribal administrator. The nonprofit and tribal governments were growing and needed more administrative attention.[116]

In December 2008, Charlie Cooke, captain of the Garcia lineage, passed the captain's staff to Ted Garcia Jr.[117] The new captain was the eldest son of recently deceased Ted Garcia Sr., son of former captain Mary Cooke Garcia. The right to name a captain returned to the hereditary guardianship of the Frances Cooke and Mary Cooke Garcia family. Like Charlie Cooke, Ted Garcia Jr. and family had strong ties to Chumash dance, art, and culture and were concerned about preserving burial and village sites in Southern California. The Garcias have ancestral ties to traditional Chumash and Kitanemuk villages, as well as other villages.[118] As captain, Ted Garcia Jr. does not automatically have an official post with the FTBMI but has the privilege to directly discuss issues with the tribal senate.

As in traditional times, leaders of the FTBMI lead by example, by accumulating and sharing cultural knowledge, and by willingness to put aside personal interests in favor of family and community interests. Each of the constituent lineages retains considerable political and social autonomy, and the leaders must respect the autonomy of individuals, families, and lineages in their exercise of governance. Contemporary persons gain political influence by showing leadership within the community and tribal government. Politically active individuals gain broader respect and acknowledgment within the community and tribe. Individuals from the several lineages are incorporated into the senate or legislative branch, and families express their views in the senate meetings, during regular committee meetings, and at community events. Leaders are expected to listen to the views and positions of the families and members. The constitution allows for the development of a culturally informed court system that will uphold the tribal constitution and laws.[119]

The Fernandeño Tataviam Band of Mission Indians is a growing tribe, both in numbers and in activities. In 2015, there were 692 enrolled tribal members, 40 percent of whom lived in the San Fernando Valley. Of all tribal members, 69 percent lived either in the San Fernando Valley, Simi Valley, Santa Clarita Valley, or Lancaster-Palmdale-Rosamond area, all of which may be considered

FIGURE 54 Ted Garcia Jr. (1948–), lineage captain, conducting a blessing ceremony, 2014. Photo by Leon Worden. From SCVhistory.com.

traditional land. After the 2020 enrollment period, there were 800 enrolled tribal members. Expanding its reach, the Fernandeño Tataviam Band of Mission Indians solicits external grants, organizes monthly meetings and community events, invests in business enterprises, engages in cultural-resources preservation, and carries on relations with federal, state, local, and tribal governments.[120] The tribal government has built many contacts with local businesses, tribal governments, and local community leaders and carries on friendly and cooperative relations with city, county, and state governments and officials.[121]

THE NONPROFIT AND PUKÚU

The FTBMI senate approved bylaws for a Nonprofit Council in August 2005. The Nonprofit Council was created to address the tribe's interests in developing public and Native social awareness. It was separated from the tribal government and expanded and refocused on cultural and social awareness within the tribal community.[122]

Over the years, Fernandeño nonprofits have changed names. In September 2006, the Nonprofit Council was renamed Pukúu, which means *one*, an expres-

FIGURE 55 Rudy Ortega Jr. (*left*) confers 2007 Pukúu award on James Ramos, San Manuel tribal leader and California legislator. Courtesy of Fernandeño Tataviam Band of Mission Indians.

FIGURE 56 Rudy Ortega Jr. (1975–), lineage captain, at dedication of Camulos village, 2019. Courtesy of Fernandeño Tataviam Band of Mission Indians.

sion of community unity. The new name was considered better for fundraising and other purposes. One reason for maintaining the nonprofit was that it has more inclusive membership than is allowed under the lineage out-marriage kinship rules that prevail in the tribal government. Many people who married into the tribe wanted to have a more active role in the future of their children and the Fernandeño community. Lineage community rules do not allow those who have married in to vote on tribal issues or hold elected tribal office.

Some major goals of the nonprofit have been to raise funds, create a cultural center, and deliver social services to the greater Los Angeles Indian community. The nonprofit is a platform for fundraising, grant writing, and pan-Indian identity and presence. Pukúu grants include aid to low-income American Indian families, the Chief Little Bear Scholarship Fund, fire disaster aid, aid to strengthen father and family relations, job training, learning cultural songs and dances, elders' aid, an Indian culture center, and other community-building activities.[123]

SUMMARY

The contemporary Fernandeño Tataviam government operates in a drastically changed economic, political, and cultural environment from premission times. Nevertheless, the contemporary tribal government and community remain built on a voluntaristic coalition of lineages. Over the past seventy years, the tribal government has adopted bylaws, nonprofits, and a constitution that make the Fernandeño Tataviam government more compatible with contemporary American government, culture, and institutions. The lineages retain traditional leadership patterns of captains and elders. The rules of voluntary political leadership and lineage relations continue to prevail and are compatible with American democratic ideals. The union and relative stability of the lineage alliances created a platform for institutional change manifested by the development of nonprofits, government, constitutions, and recovery and continuity of lineage traditions. The coalition of lineages respects and honors multiple cultural traditions, such as dance, ceremony, and knowledge derived from Tataviam-, Chumash-, and Fernandeño-speaking lineages.

The Fernandeño Tataviam Band of Mission Indians was formed and is maintained by several lineages that have multiple cultural and linguistic identities. It is composed of lineages that have bound together and have social relations that are rooted in diverse identities from the premission period. A single Fernandeño political and cultural identity coexists with multiple identities originating in the cultural uniqueness of each ancestral lineage-village. Tribal membership requires showing lineal blood connection to premission villages such as Chaguayanga, Cahuenga, Siutcanga, Tujunga, Tochonanga, Pimunga, Piru, or others. The present Fernandeño Tataviam community is culturally mixed, as were the culturally distinct and politically autonomous lineages and villages of the premission period.

All three participating lineage communities retain their lineage identities and operate through lineage elders or captains as well as through the tribe. The rules for acknowledging captains and lineage elders have not changed substantially over time. Lineage elders make the choices about appointing lineage captains, and the lineage members affirm the decisions through consensus, respect, and deference to the leadership. Captains are appointed, not elected. Presidents, officers, and boards of nonprofits and multilineal Indian governments are elected.

The sustained unity of the lineages over time, solidified by their common history at San Fernando Mission, has supported an expanding and consensual tribal government and constitution. The political and social community of the Fernandeño Tataviam Band of Mission Indians is not a collectivity of individuals but rather a consensual union among three lineages. The three lineages remain autonomous socially and politically and act within a coalition as voluntary political partners.

This voluntaristic multilineal community parallels the multilineal communities of most federally recognized Southern California Indian reservation governments and communities. Most Southern California Indian tribes form general councils composed of members of lineage communities. In Southern California, tribes have generally rejected American constitutional forms in favor of governments that preserve the voluntarism of lineage or multilineal communities.

In its own way, the Fernandeño Tataviam Band of Mission Indians supports a constitution, nonprofit association, and cultural diversity and has been constructed with consensus and voluntarism. In the competitive Los Angeles social, political, and economic environment, the Fernandeño nonprofits and constitutional government have supported tribal businesses, community service, tribal self-government, and preservation and empowerment of cultural diversity and lineage identity.

Several nonprofits or clubs of varying names have been sustained by the Fernandeños for seventy or more years. Similarly, the nonprofits and the tribal governments have been closely related and mutually interdependent. Varying names were given to the tribal government over the last seventy years, starting with the San Fernando Mission Band. Forms of tribal government also varied during this period, as they had before the mission and since.

Today, the Fernandeño Tataviam Tribe and community are more economically, politically, culturally, and socially self-sufficient than at any time in their recent history. At the same time, the age-old lineages remain distinct social, cultural, and political forms. A voluntary coalition of lineages upholds the unity of contemporary Fernandeño Tataviam constitutional government and nonprofits while sustaining consensual cultural diversity, both within and outside the tribe.

The adoption of an American-style constitution in 2002 reflected new specializations in political process, courts, and bureaucracy and increased differentiation between lineage and government. Government officers are now elected. Political power is vested in the elected leadership of president and senate and court officials. The constitution and senate are separated from the leadership of the nonprofit now named Pukúu. The nonprofit organization is a bridge to socially integrating nontribal members, who often, but not always, are married to tribal members. The nonprofit raises money and carries on projects that benefit tribal members and local nontribal community members.

Political decision-making is more differentiated from kinship, economy, and cultural knowledge. Captains and elders no longer make day-to-day political decisions for the tribal community, unless there is a crisis. Then captains and elders may be consulted for advice. Elders and captains retain leadership over cultural knowledge, ceremonial activities, and lineage affairs.

The coalition of lineages is a voluntary alliance, formalized in a constitution. A participating lineage is one that descended from a traditional lineage community that was present at San Fernando Mission and now is willing to accept the constitution of the Fernandeño Tataviam Band of Mission Indians.

Most adult tribal members work as individuals within the local market economy. Many lineage families now have long histories of labor employment. Increasingly more tribal members have college educations. The tribal government and Pukúu invest and participate in business ventures. Tribal members and tribal government are actively engaged in the U.S. market.

The tradition continues that all persons must marry outside their lineage. Although the nonlineage person who marries a lineage member cannot become a tribal member, the children of any marriage are considered tribal members. In other words, lineage membership is possible only for those persons who share a common blood ancestor with the rest of the lineage. The children of a lineage member, male or female, are considered lineage members and can become tribal members after application and acceptance.

Participation in markets and adoption of constitutional forms are not seen as surrendering tribal identity. Rather, the more differentiated political, cultural, community, and economic relations are deemed useful for promoting and protecting tribal political sovereignty, community, culture, and economic well-being. Tribal persistence within an environment of transformative colonial inclusion can be fruitfully examined through a lens of multidimensional processes of cultural, political, economic, and community institutions and relations.

Conclusion

A Recognizable Tribe

For centuries, ancestors of the present-day Fernandeño Tataviam Band of Mission Indians belonged to self-governing lineages—*ministates* or *tribes*—situated in villages and settlements across the landscape of the valleys we now call San Fernando and Santa Clarita and the surrounding areas. Although the lineages spoke different languages and dialects, and some were matrilineal while others patrilineal, they joined together for ceremonies, marriage relations, and trade. Their descendants today live in a very different material world, the product of three unjust dispossessions depicted in this book: by Spain, then Mexico, and finally the United States. Spain unilaterally claimed their territories and relocated them to San Fernando Mission. Mexican governor Pio Pico deprived them of their limited rights to portions of the San Fernando Mission lands in trust and the formation of a self-governing pueblo by unlawfully granting the mission land to non-Indian Eulogio de Celis. And the United States repeatedly refused to recognize their aboriginal rights to land and their rights under the Treaty of Guadalupe Hildalgo through the rejection of treaties, a flawed federal land commission process that disregarded the legislative mandate to investigate mission Indian rights, the failure to establish a reservation, and two rounds of inadequate federal claims legislation that look more like efforts to "close the books" than to achieve fair compensation.

Geography, in a sense, was destiny. As shown in chapter 4, the early American treaty negotiators got diverted on their trip to Los Angeles. Had those federal agents entered into treaty negotiations with Los Angeles–area Indian groups, later federal recognition would have likely followed, despite the fact that the Senate never ratified those treaties. Reservations were set aside by statute and executive order for most of the tribes in present-day San Diego and Riverside Counties because they were known to have participated in treaty negotiations. The most recent manifestation of this pattern is federal recognition for the Tejon

Indian Tribe, a community with close ties to Fernandeño lineages and the closest group to Los Angeles to have participated in treaty negotiations in the 1850s. Even so, it is more than sixty miles from San Fernando Mission and seventy-five miles from the early settlement of Los Angeles.

Geography was destiny in another way. As shown in chapters 5 and 6, even when the concerns of Fernandeños came to the attention of federal authorities in the late nineteenth century, the ancestral territories of these lineages were just too close to the future metropolis of Los Angeles to be set aside for reservations. The United States wouldn't pay the price to acquire such coveted land for Indians.

Despite the dispossessions and the missionaries' concerted campaign of conversion and assimilation, the lineages brought to San Fernando Mission never forgot who they were, their patterns of leadership, and their interwoven connections to other lineage groups. Chapter 7 explains in detail how these understandings produced new forms of governance and cooperation over time, and it also demonstrates that the threads of continuity with earlier ways remain strong.

Formal federal recognition of the Fernandeño Tataviam Band of Mission Indians through the Office of Federal Acknowledgment would be an affirmation of that continuity and a correction of past injustices. It would not, however, be the first act of federal recognition directed toward this tribe. Chapter 5 shows how official representatives of the United States, especially U.S. assistant attorney G. Wiley Wells and U.S. special Indian agent and special attorney for mission Indians Frank D. Lewis, acted under direction to pursue the land rights of the Indians evicted from San Fernando Mission lands. These efforts were directed not at individuals but at a Fernandeño tribal group that included the lineages of the present-day Fernandeño Tataviam Band of Mission Indians.

Demonstrating continuity of tribal existence to the Office of Federal Acknowledgment requires, at the outset, defining what constitutes the "historical Indian tribe." As ethnographers such as Alfred Kroeber and linguists such as John Harrington have insisted, large centralized tribes never existed in precontact California. Kroeber preferred the term *tribelets*, groups composed of several friendly lineages. This book understands the basic units of organization to be the lineages themselves, as historical kinship communities and individuals who sustained, adapted, and engaged consensual social, political, and ceremonial relations through time. Each one of the lineages is properly characterized as a "tribe" for purposes of federal law. Starting with the precontact presence of autonomous, consensually linked lineages, we have shown how several lineages maintained their distinct identities and kinship communities but also their relationships to one another. As a consequence of shared experience at San Fernando Mission and collective efforts to protect their land and self-government rights as the mission era ended and thereafter, a more unified tribal identity and arrangements arose, building on the precontact networks of cooperation among autonomous lineages. The present-day Fernandeño Tataviam Band of Mission Indians, with its nonprofit arm, carries on constitutional government and promotes community welfare supported by a coalition of lineages that is distinctive among Southern California Indian tribes. The physical displacement of lineages to San Fernando Mission did not displace their cooperative norms of political, social, cultural, and economic relations. Postmission dispossession and discrimination may have forced this network of related lineages to lie low and adapt but did not prevent them from maintaining identities and organizing, as they always did, for their mutual welfare. That is the ongoing mission of the Fernandeño Tataviam Band of Mission Indians, whether or not the federal government understands the tribe sufficiently to again provide formal recognition.

APPENDIX A

Captains and Lineage Leaders at San Fernando Mission

1. Jose Maria (?–1840) was captain of rancheria Tochonabit and had the Native name Seuyeuyeminasu (SFR Baptism #00223). His birthday was not recorded, but he died in 1840. He had several children who had chiefly names: son Elias (1798–1831), whose Native name was Nu (SFR Baptism #00151); daughter Eusebio (1793–1825), born at rancheria de Tochonanga and whose Native name was Mu (SFR Baptism #00149); and son Estanislao (1796–1836), also born at rancheria Tochonanga, whose Native name was Cabuti and who was recognized as a chief at the Sebastian Reservation and Tejon Ranch during the early 1850s (SFR Baptism #00150). Another daughter, Eudoxia (1790–?), did not have a recorded Native name and survived the San Fernando Mission period past 1845 (SFR Baptism #00152). There may have been about 50 people from Tochonabit/Tochonanga who moved to San Fernando Mission by 1810.
2. Vito (1793–1845) was captain of Mujubit, but his Native name was not recorded (SFR Baptism #00186). See also Timoteo and Policario, *infra*. There seem to have been 3 captains at the village of Mujubit.
3. Francisco Xavier (1752–1821) was captain of Chaguayabit and had the Native name Chachaguayuba (SFR Baptism #00702). There were about 45 people who moved from Chaguayabit to San Fernando Mission.
4. Rafael (1769–1841) was captain of Jotativit, but his Native name was not recorded (SFR Baptism #01440). Rafael's son was Camilo (SFR Baptism #01597), and Rafael's grandson was Gregorio Camilo, the latter a confidant to Rogerio Rocha. At least 8 people moved from Jotativit to San Fernando Mission.

5. Faustino (1775–?) was a captain of Najavait, but his Native name was not recorded (SFR Baptism #01354). Faustino lived through the San Fernando Mission period past 1845.
6. Mateo (1786–?) was a captain of the rancheria Najayabit (Najavait, Najbatabit, Najay). His Native name was not recorded (SFR Baptism #02220). There were about 10 members of Najayabit who moved to the mission, and three captains are recognized, including Mateo.
7. Jose Vicente (1766–1818) was captain of Achoycomiabit, but his Native name was not recorded (SFR Baptism #00459). About 15 members of Achoycomiabit moved to San Fernando Mission.
8. Ponciano (1758–1811) was captain of Ajuavit and his Native name was Eenacu (SFR Baptism #01139). Ponciano may have been the only migrant to San Fernando Mission from the village of Ajuavit.
9. Desiderio (1746–1809) was captain of Apebit, but his Native name was not recorded (SFR Baptism #00409).
10. Urbano (1745–1812) was captain of Apevit, but his Native name was not recorded (SFR Baptism #01366). Five people appear to have moved to San Fernando Mission from Apevit.
11. Domingo (1773–?) was captain of Apuvit, but his Native name was not recorded (SFR Baptism #01368). Domingo lived through the entire San Fernando Mission period past 1845. There were at least 4 migrants from Apuvit to San Fernando Mission. The similarity of the names and phonetic likeness of Ajuavit, Apevit, and Apuvit/Apubit suggest they were from the same village. If that is true, then 4 captains and a total of 12 people migrated from the same village to San Fernando Mission.
12. Simon (1744–?) was captain of Atamovit, and his Native name was Puussa (SFR Baptism #01277). Simon appears to be the only migrant to San Fernando Mission from Atamovit.
13. Juan Jose (1761–1815) was captain of Cacuycuyjavit, and his Native name was Tubacumanicua (SFR Baptism #01147). The lineage Cacuycuyjavit had 10 migrants to San Fernando Mission. Juan Jose's son was Maria Reyes (1803–?), and he lived past the San Fernando Mission period (SFR Baptism #00757).
14. Pedro Jose (1770–?) was captain of Coaybet or Coaybit, and his Native name was Quiya (SFR Baptism #01149). There were at least 5 migrants to San Fernando Mission from Coaybet. Pedro Jose lived through the San Fernando Mission period past 1845.
15. Miguel (1764–1812) was captain of Escorpion, and his Native name was Semenia (SFR Baptism #01167). Miguel's daughter was Eulogia, and on

Eulogia's baptismal record her father was listed as "Capitan de Jucjauybit" (SFR Baptism #00831). With a group of at least 52 persons from Escorpion moving to San Fernando Mission, Escorpion was a significant Chumash-speaking village. The combination of Jucjauybit and Escorpion yields 69 persons who entered San Fernando Mission. Jucjauybit was the same place as Escorpion but named in a different language. Jucjauybit may have been the Fernandeño language, while Escorpion is a Spanish translation of a Chumash word.

16. Pio (1772–before 1850) was captain of Humaliu, and his Native name was Chapray (SFR Baptism #01379). With the various spellings Humaliu, Humaligo, and Humalibo, they were probably the same location. About 66 persons moved from what is known today as Malibu to San Fernando Mission. Humaliu, or in English, Malibu, would have been a well-represented village of Chumash speakers.
17. Tranquilo (1775–1850) was a captain of Jajamovit, and his Native name was Chauva (SFR Baptism #01025, SFR Burial #02409). See also SFR Baptism #0677, SFR Burial #0256. The lineage of Jajamovit contributed at least 15 people to San Fernando Mission.
18. Atanasio (1775–1840) was captain of Jotojomvit, and his Native name was Suynuit (SFR Baptism #01273). The lineage of Jotojomvit contributed about 10 people to San Fernando Mission.
19. Miguel (1764–1812) was captain of Escorpion, and his Native name was not recorded (SFR Baptism #01167). See also Jucjauyabit, as it appears to be another name for the lineage that lived at Escorpion. The lineage of Jucjauyabit contributed at least 17 members to San Fernando Mission.
20. The captain of Juuvit did not have either his Native or a Spanish name recorded. Teodosia (1779–1807) was the daughter of the captain of Juuvit (SFR Baptism #01357). The lineage Juuvit gave 7 members to San Fernando Mission.
21. The captain of Ypuc (Triunfo) did not have either his Native or a Spanish name recorded. Maria Dolores (1779–1812) was a daughter of the captain of Ypuc (SFR Baptism #00561, SBV Burial #01614a). Ypuc, or in Spanish, Triunfo, contributed 10 persons to San Fernando Mission. Ypuc was a Chumash-speaking village. Maria Antonia (SFR Baptism #01045) was also daughter of the captain of Triunfo in 1815, and she survived the San Fernando Mission period past 1845.
22. The captain of Triunfo (Ypuc-Ipuc-Hipuc) did not have his Native or a Spanish name recorded. Maria Antonia (1791–?) was the daughter of the captain

of Triunfo (SFR Baptism #01045). Maria Antonia lived through the San Fernando Mission period past 1845.

23. Eduardo (1733–1817) was captain of Ongoberet, and his Native name was not recorded (SFR Baptism #01036). Ongoberet contributed at least 4 persons to San Fernando Mission.
24. Juan Manuel (1765–1835) was captain of the rancheria Cabuepet, and his Native name was not recorded (SFR Baptism #00573). See Vitorio, also a captain among the Cabuepet.
25. Vitorio (1745–1825) was a captain of Cabuepet, and his Native name was not recorded (SFR Baptism #01364). The people of Cabuepet numbered 66, including those recorded as Cahuenga (4) and those recorded as Cahuenga and Cabuepet (62). Cabuepet/Cahuenga was a significant and relatively large group at San Fernando Mission.
26. Apolonio (1776–?) was captain of Chibuna, and his Native name was Yataguopia (SFR Baptism #01852). Chibuna contributed at least 33 people to San Fernando Mission. Apolonio survived through the San Fernando Mission period ending in 1845.
27. Odorico (1744–1806) was the captain of the rancheria Giribit, and his Native name was Tubaampaguinassum (SFR Baptism #01233). The Giribit lineage contributed at least 32 people to San Fernando Mission.
28. Tiburcio (1760–1806) was captain of the rancheria Japsivit, and his Native name was not recorded (SFR Baptism #01472). Japsivit contributed 13 people to San Fernando Mission.
29. Epimaquoi (1771–1821) was captain of the rancheria Sujuiyojos, and his Native name was Jotoio (SFR Baptism #01946). Sujuiyojos was a Chumash-speaking village that contributed at least 10 people to San Fernando Mission.
30. Rogerio (1743–1818) was captain of Mapabit, and his Native name was not recorded (SFR Baptism #00929). From Mapabit, 19 persons went to San Fernando Mission.
31. Timoteo (1741–1805) was captain of Mujubit, and his Native name was not recorded (SFR Baptism #00396). The Mujubit lineage contributed 14 persons to San Fernando Mission. See Vito, also a leader of the Mujubit lineage.
32. Primo (1712–1804) was captain of Piibit, a Tataviam-speaking community, and his Native name was not recorded (SFR Baptism #00703). At least 10 persons from the lineage Piibit went to San Fernando Mission.
33. Emeterio (1771–1813) was the captain of Quecchao (Cuecchao), and his Native name was Alaguo (SFR Baptism #01861). Quecchao was a Tataviam-speaking community and contributed 32 persons to San Fernando Mission.

34. Benvenuto (1777–1816) was captain of Quissaubit, and his Native name was not recorded (SFR Baptism #00923). Quissaubit and similarly spelled lineages contributed 17 persons to San Fernando Mission.
35. Ygnacio (1751–1825) was captain of Siutcabit, and his Native name was not recorded (SFR Baptism #00363). Siuticabit contributed about 35 persons to San Fernando Mission.
36. Salvador (1758–1813) was captain of Taapu, and his Native name was Yalasuit (SFR Baptism #01166). See also SFR Baptism #01313 of Salvadora, another wife of Salvador Yalasuit, captain of Taapu. If Taapu, Tapuu, and Tapu are considered the same village, then Taapu/Tapuu/Tapu contributed 61 persons to San Fernando Mission.
37. Matias (1759–1832) was captain of Tochaburubit, and his Native name was Tubiguaiguisum (SFR Baptism #01142). The Tochaburubit lineage contributed 19 persons to San Fernando Mission.
38. Juan de Mata (1772–1811) was captain of Tubimobit, and his Native name was not recorded (SFR Baptism #00740). If Tubimobit is accepted as the same lineage village as Tibimonga, then Tubimobit/Tibimonga contributed 14 people to San Fernando Mission.
39. Bruno (1743–1812) was captain of Tubimobit, and his Native name was not recorded (SFR Baptism #00930). Bruno was father to Juan de Mata. Both were captains of Tubimobit/Tibimonga.
40. Julian (1751–1806) was captain of Tujubit, and his Native name was not recorded (SFR Baptism #00391). Tujubit contributed 86 people to San Fernando Mission and was one of the largest lineages at the mission. Julian worked actively to marry his children and relatives to the leadership of Siutcabit and Cabuepet. These marriages combined three large lineages in alliance during the early San Fernando Mission period.
41. Candido (1776–1803) was captain of Uijabit, and his Native name was not recorded (SFR Baptism #00392). The Uijabit lineage contributed 2 persons to San Fernando Mission.
42. Eleuterio (1775–1822) was captain of Uijavit, and his Native name was Yuncar (SFR Baptism #01372). It appears the lineage Uijavit/Uijabit contributed 2 persons, both captains, to San Fernando Mission.
43. One of three captains at Piiru did not have his Native or Spanish name recorded in the San Fernando Mission record. He was the father of Eudoxia from rancheria Piiru (SFR Baptism #00753). Eudoxia's godmother was the daughter of the captain of Tochonanga. If Piiru and Piru are the same village-lineage, then Piiru/Piru contributed 82 persons to San Fernando Mission. Piiru/Piru was a Tataviam-speaking village.

44. "Uno de los tres Capitanes" at Piiru, whose Native name went unrecorded. His daughter, Ynes (SFR Baptism #00752), was born in 1795 and died in 1816. Ynes's godmother, Eudoxia, was the daughter of the "Capitan de Tochonanga."
45. Santiago (1744–1806) was a captain of Piirubit, and his Native name was Aczayu (SFR Baptism #01121). If Piiru and Piru are the same lineage, then Piiru/Piru contributed 82 persons to San Fernando Mission. Piiru/Piru was one of the largest lineages at San Fernando Mission.
46. The Spanish and Native names of the captain of Atumobit were not recorded. The "Mother of Captain of Atumobit" was Cypriana (SFR Baptism #00670). Atumobit contributed 2 persons to San Fernando Mission.
47. Benigno (1766–1818) was captain at Payuchibi, and his Native name was Suguepit (SFR Baptism #01854). His son was Manuel (SFR Baptism #01835), who died in 1835.
48. At Santa Catalina Island (Pimunga), Pastor Cano (SFR Baptism #02608) has the leader name of Cano, and his wife, Maria del Carmen (SFR Baptism #02606), has the leadership name of Caroni. Cano did not accept being a Christian, or was an adult non-Christian, before or after he was baptized.[1] Cano (ca. 1794–ca. 1869) was a leader of Pimubit, a village on present-day Catalina Island (SFR Baptism #02608; SFR Baptism #02029; SG Baptism #07306). Cano's baptismal name was Pastor, but on the 1850 census he gives his name as Josefo and age as forty-five.[2] Cano was a recognized captain and ceremonial leader who lived beyond the San Fernando Mission period and was noted by Reid in 1852.[3]
49. Francisco (1774–1807) held the name Sicsaquiquaguit, within which the name Quiqua (Kika) was embedded (SFR Baptism #01557). Among the Serrano, Kitanemuk, and related speakers such as the Tataviam, Kikas were primary ceremonial and community leaders. Francisco's burial information suggests he was from the village of Zumo (SFR Burial #00691).[4]
50. Puyoquicay (1773–1801), also with the leadership term embedded, was born to the village and community of Tochaboronga. His baptismal name was Deogracias (SFR Baptism #00098). His Native name has the Kika leader's label.[5]
51. Quijaycuiric was born about 1768 at the Tataviam-speaking rancheria Piru. He died in 1806, after taking Basilio as his baptismal name (SFR Baptism #01194). Basilio's Native name contains the leadership title of Kika.[6]
52. The name given the leader second in influence was eyacque or caca.[7] Among the San Fernando recruitment villages, the expression *eyacque* is found

among at least three Tataviam-speaking villages. The eyacque or caca was a hereditary office that required singing and knowing the songs and creation stories of the village-lineage. The name *eenacu* was the Native name for the captain of Ajuavit, as mentioned above. The Native name of Cacachena was given to Bernardino, who was baptized in 1798 (SFR Baptism #00106). His name contains the leadership title. Bernardino was born about 1770, and he survived past the end of San Fernando Mission in 1845. Bernardino-Cacachena was born to the rancho of Piitnga or Piibit village-lineage.[8]

53. Cacaguama (1774–?) was baptized in 1811 and was born in the Tataviam-speaking village of Cuecchao (SFR Baptism #01881). His Native name bears the leadership title of caca. He would have conducted songs and ceremonies and been a keeper of tribal knowledge for the Cuecchao village-lineage community. Cacaguama was given the baptismal name of Ysac. He was born about 1774 and lived past the end of San Fernando Mission period in 1845.[9]

54. Taari was the father of Teofila (SFR Baptism #01848) and grandfather to Eugenia, a progenitor of the contemporary Garcia lineage. Taari was also the leader of the Topipabit (Toquipabit) people. He died before 1811. The descendants of Taari (a variation on the chief name Chari) make up the main leadership line of the present-day Tejon Indian Tribe. Taari and his son, Kawana, later Vicente, did not join the mission.[10] In the early 1850s, Vicente Francisco (born before 1819 and died about 1880 at Tejon Ranch), whose Native name was Tinoqui, returned to Tejon, and Tinoqui served as chief of the Tejon after his brother Vicente's death about 1873. "The title Chari designated important Gabrielino, Serrano and Tataviam political leaders and their sons. Many Gabrielino men with the name of Chari were said to be chiefs. It appears that the title Chari passed from fathers to sons. The title like Nu, the next described, was found at some of the same settlements, including Seobit, that also have Kiki. It appears that men with different titles only inherited their father's title."[11]

55. Chari (1755–1806) was captain of Siutcabit, and his baptismal name was Rafael (SFR Baptism #00233). See Ygnacio, same place, Siutcabit. Rafael held the chief name of Chari, while Ygnacio, also a captain at Siutcabit, did not have a Native name in the mission record. Urbano, given below, also had the leader name Chari, and his patrilineal line ties him to Siutcabit. About 35 people were contributed to San Fernando Mission from Siutcabit.

56. Cheri or Chori (1792–?) was born at rancheria Tochonabit. He was baptized in 1797, the first year of San Fernando Mission, and was given the baptismal name of Santiago Miguel (SFR Baptism #00016). Cheri's father was not a

Christian, and his father held the leadership name Nu. Santiago Miguel held the title of Cheri at the same time his father held the title of Nu. Jose Maria was recognized as captain at rancheria Tochonabit. Jose Maria's two children held titles of Mu and Nu at rancheria Tochonabit.[12]

57. Chari (1786–1825) was born at San Pedro, and his baptismal name was Jose Antonio (SFR Baptism #02234). Jose Antonio was baptized at San Fernando Mission, probably following his wife, Josefa Antonia, who was born at one of the Channel Islands. They were baptized on the same day in 1816.[13]
58. Chari (1760–1832) was born to Cabuepet, and his baptismal name was Ygnacio (SFR Baptism #00277).[14] See also SFR Baptism #00200. His name suggests he was a recognized leader among the Cabuepet.
59. Chari, the father of Jose Luis (SFR Baptism #00591) was not a Christian. Most likely Chari, the father of Jose Luis, was born and was recognized as a leader at Cabuepet. Jose Luis was born in 1799 at Cabuepet and baptized in 1801. He survived the San Fernando Mission period past 1845.[15]
60. Chari (1771–1838) was born to Cabuepet and was given the name Celestino when baptized in 1805 (SFR Baptism #01370). Celestino was brother to Juan Manuel (1765–1835), one of the captains at Cabuepet. Celestino's son, Angel, was born in 1807 and survived the San Fernando Mission period to 1845 (SFR Baptism #01637). Vitoria (SFR Baptism #01364) was also a captain of Cabuepet, and he was baptized on the same day in 1805 as Celestino, who was Chari.
61. Chari Chupin (1755–1823) was baptized in 1803. He was given the baptismal name of Ugólino and was born to Cabuepet (SFR Baptisms #00615, #00944, and #00927; SFR Burial #00385).
62. Urbano (1799–1860) may not have been born with the name Chari at Siutcabit. His Native name was not written into his baptismal record (SFR Baptism #00358). The San Fernando Mission baptism registry recorded that Urbano's father, Eduardo, was born at Siutcabit, and Urbano would have followed the line of his father.[16] Urbano was listed in the 1850 and 1860 U.S. censuses with the traditional leadership name of Chari.[17] He began to use the name as a surname, and in the 1860 census he gave his children the Chari name as surname. Urbano probably acquired the title and a leadership position later in life. He, with his son, Manuel, and Odon, a chief and Urbano's father-in-law, negotiated with Governor Pico for the Escorpion land grant in 1845. Urbano was witness for three weddings between 1843 and 1845 (SFR Marriages #00910 and #00911). He held the position of llabero, literally "keeper of the keys," at San Fernando Mission. Llabero was a significant

mission administrative position, something like a quartermaster. In 1839, Urbano asked William Hartnell, inspector of the missions for the Mexican government, to intercede with the town council of Los Angeles to grant to him the right to use a cattle brand. The council declined Urbano's request, saying he must leave the mission and accept emancipation before the city council would give him permission to hold a brand. Urbano was ready and willing to take up ranching, but he was reluctant to leave the administrative work he had long performed for the Indian people at San Fernando Mission. Ultimately, Urbano served as llabero from 1826 to the end of the mission in 1845, a total of nineteen years.[18]

63. Chari of rancheria San Vicente did not become a Christian. However, his Native name, Chari, was recorded on his daughter Maria Francesca's baptismal record in 1803 (SFR Baptism #00961). The land known as San Vicente was a Spanish name for an Indian rancheria or rancherias in the area of the present-day streets of Bundy and Wilshire Boulevards in West Los Angeles, near University High School.[19] The present-day local Indians call this place Kuruvungna and consider themselves direct descendants of the village.[20] Chari of San Vicente (Kuruvungna) had a second daughter, Teopista (1797–1830). On Teopista's baptismal record (SFR Baptism #00974), her father's name is partially illegible, recorded as Ch[. . .]ré.[21] Maria Francesca, daughter of the Chari of San Vicente, was born in 1800 and lived past the mission period ending by 1845.

64. Nú was the Native name of the father of Santiago Miguel (SFR Baptism #00016), who was born to rancheria Tochonabit. Nú and his wife, named Tocó, did not become Christians and therefore do not have Christian names in the mission record. Nú was a name equivalent to Net among the Cahuilla and Nota among the Luiseño and similar to the position of Kika, discussed above.[22] Nú was used by the Serrano and western Gabrieleño and at Nú's Tataviam-speaking village-lineage of Tochonabit. Tocó may have been an honorary name of the wife of the Nu.

65. Nu of Tujunga (SFR Baptism #00176) was given the baptismal name of Felipe Neri (1769–1808). Nu was born at rancheria Tujunga.[23]

66. Nuuri was born at Atongayna (Atongaina) in 1811 and lived through the Mission San Fernando period past 1845. His baptismal name was Aquilino (SFR Baptism #01847).[24]

67. Canu (1754–1800) was born to Tujubit and was baptized at rancheria Tujubit (SFR Baptism #00222). His baptismal name was Andres.[25] The captain's title of Nu is incorporated into his name.

68. Cunu was the Native name for the father of Pedro Pablo of Tujunga (SFR Baptism #00230). The father's name incorporates the captain's title of Nu. No Native name was recorded for Pedro Pablo. Cunu, the father, did not become a Christian.
69. Mu (1793–1825) of rancheria Tochonanga was the daughter of Jose Maria, who was captain of Tochonabit (SFR Baptisms #00149 and #00223). Her baptismal name was Eusebio.[26]
70. Nu (1799–1831) was born at rancheria Tochonanga, and his father was Jose Maria, the captain of rancheria Tochonanga (SFR Baptisms #00151 and #00223).[27]
71. Nuquit (1773–1839) was born at rancheria Tochonabit and was also baptized there in 1801 (SFR Baptism #00383.[28] See also SFR Baptism #0092.
72. Genu (1768–1803) was baptized at rancheria Chaguayabit in 1802 and was a member of Chaguayabit (SFR Baptism #00687). His baptism name was Jacob, and his Native name incorporated the leadership term Nu.[29]
73. Genuminaban (1777–after 1845) of Pabassapet was a relative to the captain of Giribit, Idirico. Her baptismal name was Fortunata (SFR Baptism #01515), and she survived through to the closing of San Fernando Mission in 1845. The leadership term Nu is incorporated in her name.
74. Genunchinugasu (1799–1824) was born at rancheria Cuecchao, a Tataviam-speaking village. The leadership term Nu is incorporated into his Native name. He was baptized in 1811 and given the name German (SFR Baptism #01875).
75. Genuariguinasu (1772–1819) was the captain of Pabutan, and the leadership term Nu is incorporated in his name. Julio was his baptismal name (SFR Baptism #01867). He was married before the San Fernando Mission period to Faustina (SFR Baptism #01890), born at Piru.
76. Nuchqui (1762–1834) was born at rancheria Passenga and was given the baptismal name of Laureano (SFR Baptism #00022). His mother, Faviana (1740–1808), was born at Pasecubit (SFR Baptism #00234). This village was located near the site of San Fernando Mission.[30]
77. Nu (1781–1803) was born in a village that was left unstated in the San Fernando Mission record (SFR Baptism #00440).[31]
78. Nuu was born in 1798 and lived past the closing of San Fernando Mission in 1845 (SFR Baptism #00196). He was born at Rancho del Encino and baptized at age one. Nuu's father, (1757–1812), had the Native name Piar and was born to the Siutcabit (SFR Baptism #01371).[32]

79. Caroni (ca. 1794–1829) was married to Cano of Pimubit, although she was born at San Fernando Mission according to her burial record (SFR Burial #01181; SFR Baptism #02606). Her baptismal name was Maria del Carmen. Caroni, at some villages, was the mother of the sun, Tamet. Caroni was an important women's ceremonial and leadership name and often the first wife of a chief but was only recorded once at San Fernando Mission. It is not clear whether Cano or Caroni ever accepted Christian teachings, as they are listed as gentiles.[33]
80. Tomear, Tomiar, or variations are names recognized as chiefs among several Serrano- and Gabrieleño-language dialects.[34] Tomearsaxabia was born in 1761 to the Navayabit, where people spoke a dialect of Serrano. He was baptized in 1811 and took the baptismal name of Eulogio (SFR Baptism #01862). There is no mission record for his death. He survived the mission but would have been about eighty-five years old in 1846. Tomearsaxabia was a leader of the Navayabit village-lineage.[35]
81. Tomearunasjum (1767–1798) was born at rancheria Tochonanga and baptized in 1797 (SFR Baptism #0023). He was the first person buried at San Fernando Mission (SFR Burial #00001).
82. Tomapiyunachet (1792–1806) was the son of Chari (Rafael), one of the captains of rancheria Siutcabit. Tomapiyunachet was baptized in 1798 and given the baptismal name of Matheo de la Cruz (SFR Baptism #00105). From an early age, based on his Native name, Tomapiyunachet would have been targeted to follow his father, Chari, as a leader among the Siutcabit. Given Tomapiyuachet's early death, while he would have been in training and preparation, he may have had limited influence within the Siutcabit lineage.[36]
83. Camilo (1806–ca. 1875), baptized in 1806, was the son of Rafael, captain of Jotativit (SFR Baptisms #01440 and #01597). Camilo was a member of the forty petitioners for a square league of farming land. Governor Micheltorena agreed to the grant on May 3, 1843.[37] In 1892, Camilo's son, Gregorio Camilo (1838–after 1892?), along with Felicitas (Cano) and Rogerio Rocha, met with special U.S. attorney for mission Indians Frank Lewis.[38] Gregorio, son of Camilo, was a descendant of one of the forty joint owners of the May 3, 1843, land grant. Gregorio Camilo signed an agreement to enable special attorney Frank Lewis to present a proposal to the U.S. government to recover the one square league of land from the 1843 grant.[39] Camilo appears to have moved to Tejon Ranch. J. J. Lopez reminisced about him: "I had this from some of the old Indians including Francisco Cota and the old chief, Camilo."[40]

84. Tinoqui was baptized as Vicente Francisco in 1819 (SFR Baptism #02385). His father was Taari and after his death his brother, Kawana, became leader, and both were signers of the 1851 Treaty of Tejon. Kawana did not become a Christian and was not a member of San Fernando Mission, although his brother, Tinoqui, and sister, Teofila, and mother were baptized at the mission. Vicente Francisco was a member of the group of forty petitioners who received the May 3, 1843, grant from Governor Micheltorena.[41] In 1845, Vicente Francisco served as alcalde at San Fernando Mission (SFR Marriages #00910, #00911, #00912, #00913, and #00914). When Tinoqui signed the January 1851 Treaty of Tejon, his brother, Kawana, took the name Vicente, while Tinoqui remained with the name Francisco. Francisco took the surname Cota, and after the death of his brother in 1873 served as chief for some years thereafter. Francisco, Eugenia, and others returned to their village-lineages in Tejon and reclaimed their old identities or took on new identities after following spouses to Tejon.[42] In 1854, Vicente (Kawana) was chief of the Tejon Indian Tribe, or Vicente's tribe, with about 400 persons. Francisco (Tinoqui) probably was one of Vicente's captains.[43]

85. Raphael Maria was among the first baptisms at San Fernando Mission in September 1797 (SFR Baptism #00005). His Native name was Aquinamogihuason. As John Johnson has noted, Raphael Maria was alcalde at San Fernando Mission for the year 1836, and he signed the Tejon treaty of January 1851, representing the Castaike Tribe. He was documented as a cochief in 1862 with a community of 162 people at the Sebastian Reservation.[44]

86. Jose Zapatero was a chief who signed the 1851 Tejon treaty and led a tribal group of 300 persons at the Sebastian Reservation in the 1850s.[45] In 1839, and probably in prior years, "Jose el Zapatero" had a connection to the prefecture's office in Los Angeles, as noted by William Hartnell in a report to the governor. Hartnell wrote, "The Neophyte of this Mission, Jose el Zapatero sorely missed at this establishment; therefore I will be grateful if you will kindly send him here as soon as possible."[46] J. J. Lopez said Zapatero's name was Pablo.[47] Zapatero means *shoemaker*, which was the occupation he took up and was trained for at San Fernando Mission. John Johnson claims that Lopez was mistaken and the first name for Zapatero was Antonio or Jose.[48] Documents in 1854 give Zapatero the first name of Jose,[49] but his name could have been Jose Antonio. Johnson has suggested that Antonio was born at Ranchera Unupea (SFR Baptism #02812), but this Antonio died in 1838 (SFR Burial #02198).[50] There is no person in the San Fernando Mission record with the name Jose Antonio who fits the age range for Zapatero. There are numer-

ous persons with the name Antonio, Jose, or Pablo but no way to determine which was Jose Zapatero or Jose el Zapatero. With current data, it is not possible to match Jose Zapatero to a specific individual in the San Fernando Mission records. Jose Zapatero was the leader of a tribal group, "Zapatero's Tribe," at the Sebastian Reservation in the 1850s and most likely was still a chief later at Tejon Ranch. "Captain Jose Zapatero, leader of the Tulareño Yokuts, made a special visit to Los Angeles in December 1851 to assure the citizens of his peaceful intent."[51]

87. Estanislao (1792–?) was baptized in 1817, and his Native name was Quimatobit (SFR Baptism #02271). He was also a member of the forty petitioners who secured a grant of a square league near San Fernando Mission granted by Governor Micheltorena. Also known as "Stanislao, in 1854 he led a group of 100 people known at Sebastian Reservation as Stanislao's Tribe."[52] He married a woman from Tejon and retired from politics before 1873. Estanislao was acquainted at San Fernando Mission with Vicente Francisco, before the latter returned to Tejon about 1850.[53] Stanislao was recorded as a laborer working for owner Dolores Ochoa in the 1850 census.[54] His home village-lineage was Totipabit.

88. Odon Chihuya (1795–ca. 1882) most likely was among the forty petitioners receiving the May 3, 1843, grant from Governor Micheltorena (SFR Baptism #00780).[55] Jose Odon petitioned for emancipation, which was granted in 1839 by interim governor Manuel Jimeno. After the land grant of the forty petitioners was not preserved by Governor Pico, Odon, Urbano, and Manuel, the son of Urbano, negotiated joint ownership of a land grant for one square league at Escorpion in July 1845. Odon was recognized as a leader, chief, or captain of the San Fernando Indians living on the western portion of the San Fernando Valley after the closing of San Fernando Mission. The land was sold or lost by the end of the 1860s. Both Urbano and Manuel died about 1860. Odon's daughter, Maria del Espiritu Santo, partnered with Miguel Leonis in 1859, and he took possession of Odon's remaining share of the land by 1871. Leonis herded cattle and sheep. After Leonis's death in 1889, Espiritu, after many court cases ending in 1905, was awarded one-half of Leonis's land. Juan Melendez, Espiritu's only surviving child, sold the remaining property in 1912. Melendez left no descendants.[56]

89. Mateo (1836–?) and Melchor (1824–1892?) were grandsons of Jose Maria, captain of Tochonabit (SFR Baptisms #02877, #02552, and #00223). Paula was married to Francisco, and they are both progenitors of the present-day Ortega line. Paula was also Mateo's godmother. Mateo's father was Estanislao,

who had the Native name of Cabuti. Estanislao was the son of Jose Maria, captain of Tochonabit (SFR Baptism #00150). Mateo, Melchor, and their mother, Epifania, are listed with Clemente and Stanislao (Estanislao from Nangivit) on the 1850 U.S. census, working on the farm of Dolores Ochoa.[57] Mateo and Melchor were brothers, and both were recognized as chiefs at the Sebastian Reservation and Tejon Ranch. As recounted by J. J. Lopez, "The old chief, Mateo Martin, was an Indian doctor, and an important man who had been at the Sebastian Reservation under General Beale. He was a cripple and quite a character, being a typical fakir or Indian Medicine Man. He did no work, but his brother, Melchor, who lived with him and also was a leader in Mateo's tribe, with another brother, Camilo, herded sheep for me for about thirty years."[58]

90. Melchor represented the Tochonabit lineage among the forty petitioners for one square league of land, which was ultimately granted by Governor Micheltorena on May 3, 1843. Melchor's grandfather, Jose Maria, a captain, died in 1840, and Estanislao, the father of Melchor and Mateo, died in 1836. The oldest son of Jose Maria, Elias Nu, was most likely the heir apparent, but he died in 1831 (SFR Burial #01913). Elias Nu's four children also passed by 1832 (SFR Burials #01556, #01665, #01855, and #01962). As eldest surviving son, Melchor, represented the Tochonabit in the claim to the land grant requested by Pedro Joaquin, first alcalde, and thirty-nine others. Vicente Francisco, San Fernando Mission alcalde in 1845 and a participant in the forty petitioners for the land grant in 1843[59] and later a chief of the Tejon Indian Tribe, was godfather to Melchor (SFR Baptism #02552). Many of the Tochonabit lineage moved to the Sebastian Reservation and then to Tejon Ranch after dissolution of first the San Fernando Mission and then the Sebastian Reservation. At Tejon Ranch, the tribe-lineage settled on a piece of land, as J. J. Lopez explained: "Their rancheria was on the south side of Rancho Creek, just above the present (1933) ranch house and the commissary, about one half mile east of them."[60] See also #89, *supra*.

91. Emeterio (1799–?) was baptized in 1804 (SFR Baptism #01226; SFR Marriage #00675). His Native name was not recorded, and his godfather was Vicente, possibly Vicente Francisco, who was San Fernando Mission alcalde in 1845, and after 1873, chief of the Tejon Indian Tribe. If Vicente Francisco was the godparent, then Emeterio would have had support and assistance while he was living at the Sebastian Reservation during the 1850s. In January 1851, Emeterio was a signatory for the Senahow Tribe to the Tejon treaty. Emeterio was regarded as one of the leading tribal leaders in 1854 at the Sebastian

Reservation. He was chief of over 300 persons there in 1854.[61] Emeterio's followers were Yokuts, and they selected him partly because of his mission experience, as a useful leader to manage relations with the Americans. Emeterio may have been born in a Yokut village, and hence he returned after the mission to a Yokut-speaking community.[62]

92. Clemente (1823–?) was a captain allied to Stanislao, who was chief of 100 people at the Sebastian Reservation in 1854. Clemente's father was born at Siutaasegena, while his mother was born at Tochaborunga. Subchiefs, or allied captains loyal to a chief or principal captain, had their own followings, usually composed of kin. Many captains at the Sebastian Reservation managed approximately five to six men and their families, while other captains led about ten men and their families. A principal chief at the Sebastian Reservation managed his own lineage and worked together with his allied captains, all of whom composed a separate tribe, ranging from 100 to 500 persons. There were at least seven tribal communities led by principal chiefs and allied captains during the mid-1850s at the Sebastian Reservation.[63] Following Stanislao (Estanislao), Clemente helped establish the rancheria of Chipowhi at the Sebastian Reservation and later Tejon Ranch.[64] Clemente was baptized at San Fernando Mission on his birthday in 1823; however, his Native name was not recorded (SFR Baptism #02544).

93. German (1796–ca. 1849) was born at Quimisac, a Chumash-speaking village near present-day Santa Paula, California (SFR Baptism #00817). He was one of the forty petitioners for joint ownership and use of the land grant of May 3, 1843, given by Governor Micheltorena. German's son, Rogerio, identified German as a captain and stated that after German's death, Rogerio succeeded him as a captain of the same group.[65]

94. Rogerio Rocha (1824–1904) became a captain from the time of his father German's death until his own death in 1904 (SFR Baptism #02565). There was no Native name recorded for Rogerio. Rogerio did not have any children who survived to adulthood. Rocha testified that "my antecedents from time immemorial" lived in the area of the Rancho Cienega, a place with sweet water. But he could not have been referring to his father's biological ancestors who were from Chumash villages miles away to the northwest. Rocha's ten-acre farm was just northeast of the mission, directly to the east of the mission village. Rocha's mother's lineage was from Tujunga, whose central village was nearly fifteen miles to the east of the farm. Thus, when Rocha referred to "antecedents" (assuming the translation is correct), he meant the Tujubit lineage or the lineage living in the Tujunga area. Villages need

water, and so lineages formed settlements near drinkable water within their joint lineage territory. Rogerio, referring to his antecedents, was speaking about thousands of years of land and water legacy experienced by the Tujubit people.[66] Water was shared among lineage members and members of friendly lineages. Mission Indians expected that the water at Rancho Cienega would be shared. Even a reference to paying property taxes can be understood within the context of traditional leadership. As a captain, Rocha was obliged to provide for his lineage community and to share resources.[67] Given his earning capacity because of the value of his metalworking skills in the local economy, he would have been expected to support the community by paying the property taxes. There are numerous references to Rogerio's leadership as a captain.[68] Rogerio was a member of the forty petitioners to the one square league of land granted by Governor Micheltorena on May 3, 1843. In the 1860s, Rogerio was active in regional ceremonial events, such as the commemoration ceremony. As a Chumash ceremonial leader, Rogerio had two ceremonial assistants. He had relatives and chiefly obligations at several villages. Fernando Librado referred to "Captain Rogerio of San Fernando, who as himself tied to the village of Humaliwo." Rogerio was a captain among a group of Chumash captains who helped select a captain for the village of Muwu, about 1862. In 1869, Rogerio attended the leader Pomposa's first and last fiesta at Saticoy. "And from San Fernando came Captain Rogerio with his family."[69] Rogerio Rocha himself stated: "My father was a captain of my people. His name was Jerman. He never went away. . . . Then after my father died I became the captain, as all my people recognized me as such. I do not remember how long this was when I became captain of my people."[70]

95. Pedro Joaquin (1813–?) was born at San Fernando Mission and elected or appointed first alcalde of the mission in 1843 (SFR Baptism #02080). No Native name was recorded for Pedro Joaquin. His father, Mariano, was born at "rancheria de la Sanja" and died very young, during the same year as Pedro Joaquin's birth (SFR Baptism #00963; SFR Burial #01028). Pedro Joaquin led the forty petitioners who secured the land grant of May 3, 1843, from Governor Micheltorena. Pedro Joaquin first was married to Felipa, sister of Francisco Papabubaba, the latter a progenitor of the Ortega line (SFR Baptism #02286; SFR Marriage #00819) and father to Rita. After Felipa's death in 1842, Pedro Joaquin married Maria del Carmen on May 21, 1843 (SFR Marriage #00898). Maria del Carmen was the daughter of Petra (SFR Baptism #02062), who married Emeterio on November 16, 1835 (SFR Marriage #00853). Emeterio was a chief at the Sebastian Reservation and at Tejon Ranch (see #91,

supra). Petra's father, Zenon, was born at the Tataviam-speaking village of Cuecchao (SFR Baptism #01879), and his Native name was Chaamel. Zenon's father, Dioniso (SFR Baptism #01925), with the Native name Napcos, was also born at "rancheria de Cuecchao."

96. Jose Miguel (1814–1859?) held the honorary title in Spanish of Triunfo. He was born at San Fernando Mission, although his mother was born at Cahuenga. Jose Miguel's father was a mixed-blood who had ties to San Gabriel Mission. The padres did not record a Native name for Jose Miguel (SFR Baptism #02140). Triunfo was used as a surname later by his family, but Jose Miguel did not use Triunfo as a surname, as shown in the 1850 census.[71] For his service to San Fernando Mission, Jose Miguel was granted land near Cahuenga, which in 1843 was confirmed by Governor Micheltorena.[72] Jose Miguel is a progenitor of the Ortiz lineage.

97. Tiburcio Cayo (1793–1844) was born in the Chumash village of Tapuu and negotiated a square league of land at Encino from San Fernando Mission about 1840 and then affirmed the same grant from Governor Micheltorena in 1843 (SFR Baptism #00849).[73] In 1810, Tiburcio Cayo married Teresa, who was born at Encino. Tiburcio was leader at Encino of a group consisting of Francisco Papabubaba and Roque, both of whom married daughters of Tiburcio and lived at Encino. Also living at Encino and granted joint ownership with Tiburcio, Francisco, and Roque was Ramon, whose father was born at Sanja.

98. Rita (1830–1866?) was the daughter of Francisco Papabubaba and granddaughter of Tiburcio Cayo (SFR Baptisms #00849, #01617, and #02742). Both Tiburcio Cayo and Francisco Papabubaba were among the joint holders of a deed to one square league at Encino, first granted by the mission about 1840 and later affirmed in 1843 and 1845 by Mexican governors Micheltorena and Pico. Rita is a progenitor of the Ortega lineage. At her marriage to Fernando Ortega in 1862, the apparent surname Alipaz was recorded. However, since she doesn't use Alipaz as a surname in any other record, the name Alipaz may have been an effort to write a Chumash name for a healer or doctor in Spanish letters. The name or title used by some Chumash healers was "alagicpsh" and would have been pronounced by Rita as *al-eye-psh*. Following her grandfather Tiburcio's Chumash tradition, young boys and girls who were trained for leadership were taught the arts of medicine, ceremony, and healing.[74] Rita and her aunt Agueda, daughter of Tiburcio, inherited joint ownership of two-thirds of the Encino square league but sold or lost the land by 1857.[75]

99. Antonio Maria Ortega (1857–1941) was lineage headman, captain, or spokesman of the Ortega lineage. Antonio Maria and his younger brother, Luis Ortega (1862–1948), are the progenitors of the contemporary Ortega lineage. As eldest surviving sibling, Antonio led the surviving remnants of the Ortega family, descendants of Rita (SFR Baptism #02742). Antonio Maria was a defendant in the *Porter v. Cota* case of 1878 in a dispute over land rights to Rancho Ex-Mission San Fernando. Most likely following in his mother Rita's footsteps, Antonio served as a healer for members of the Indian community at San Fernando.[76]
100. Joseph Ortiz (1859–1938?) is progenitor and was leader of the Ortiz lineage. He was the grandson of Jose Miguel Triunfo and the son of Rose Arriola (Triunfo) (LPC Baptism Book 3:218).[77] In 1877, when Indian evictions were evident from Rancho-Ex Mission San Fernando, Joseph, his mother, and grandmother, Perfecta, moved to join the Indian community at Tejon Ranch. Joseph attended school and worked for Tejon Ranch under the management of J. J. Lopez, son of Geronimo Lopez, the ranch owner and Indian community benefactor living at San Fernando. After the death of General Beale in 1893, many Indians, including the Joseph Ortiz family, were forced to move from Tejon Ranch. Joseph Ortiz, mother, and children moved to live in the Indian community at Bakersfield and continued to work as farmhands. In the early 1920s, Joseph Ortiz and many of his family members returned to live at San Fernando. He and family moved into the neighborhoods of the Ortega and Garcia families in old town San Fernando. In the 1930s, Joseph Ortiz and family petitioned and were accepted onto the 1933 California Indian Roll generated under the auspices of the act of 1928.
101. Josefa Leyva (1865–1952) is a progenitor of the Garcia lineage (LPC Register Vol. 4, p. 9, #53).[78] Her baptismal godparents were Felicitas Cano and Estanislao, both prominent persons in the San Fernando Indian community and both having strong political ties to Rogerio Rocha.[79] Josefa's mother, Leandra, had ties through Leandra's mother, Eugenia, to the leadership of the Tejon Indian Tribe.[80] Josefa's father, Jose Juan Leyva (Lieba), was the brother-in-law of Rogerio Rocha. In the 1928 act rolls, the Garcia family recognized Rogerio Rocha as captain at San Fernando.[81] Josefa had three children with Isidoro Garcia: Petra, Frances, and Jim. Jim Garcia eventually married into the Tejon Indian Tribe, and his descendants are not members of the Fernandeño Tataviam Band of Mission Indians. Petra and Frances both created families and lineages, and many are members of the present-day tribe. Josefa found a new partner, William Gardner, in the early 1890s and had four

children with him. It appears that only one of the Gardner children, Maude, has been active in seeking California Indian enrollment. After about 1905, Josefa took up a new partnership with Antonio Gutierrez and had one child. At least two Gutierrez grandchildren of Josefa have been accepted to the California Indian Roll.

102. Captain or lineage leader Frances Garcia Cooke (1884–1946) remained in Newhall with her father, Isidoro Garcia, after her mother, Josefa, left for a new partnership with William Gardner, about 1890. Frances Garcia is the direct progenitor of a leadership line and descendants who are known as the Garcia lineage. Frances encouraged and organized her family members to apply for inclusion in the California Indian Roll created by the act of May 18, 1928, in which Congress authorized compensation to California Indians for the lands promised in the unratified treaties of 1851–52. Frances married Alfred Cooke and became known as Frances Garcia Cooke. In 1940 she moved from Newhall back to San Fernando and took up residence in the old town where other tribal members lived. In 1946, she was killed in a car accident.[82]

103. Captain or lineage headman was the position assumed by Estanislao (James) Ortega (1885–1951), as oldest son, after the death of his father, Antonio Maria Ortega, in 1941. In his later years, in the 1940s, on account of illness, James Ortega deferred active leadership to his son, Rudy Ortega Sr.[83]

104. Margaret Rivera Ward (1899–1975) was the granddaughter of Josefa Leyva and daughter of Petra Garcia.[84] She is a progenitor and leader of the Ward family line. She lived much of her life in the farming areas around Santa Paula and Piru, where many San Fernando Indians once had villages and tribal members came to work as laborers in the orchards and farms. Margaret Ward is progenitor of a large family, many of whom are active in the Fernandeño tribe.

105. Captain Mary Cooke Garcia (1901–1975) was the daughter of Frances Cooke Garcia and granddaughter of Josefa Leyva. After her mother's death in 1946, she assumed leadership of the lineage, organizing family gatherings and related discussions of family concerns and issues. She was the host and head of the family. About 1940, Mary Cooke Garcia and family moved to Pacoima, a township near old town San Fernando, where many tribal members still lived. While she gathered the family around during most of her life, she turned the active political leadership over to nephew Charlie Cooke in 1957. Mary Garcia thought that other persons could lead the lineage in addressing Indian issues affecting the lineage and Indians in general. She held a meet-

ing in 1957 at her home with family and lineage elders. After some discussion, the gathering decided that Charlie Cooke would be best suited to take leadership or become captain of the Garcia family line. Mary's son, Theodore Garcia Sr., would normally be next in line for captain, but he also agreed with the decision in favor of Charlie Cooke. Theodore Garcia and Charlie's brother, Alvin Cooke, for many years were strong supporters and partners in the many activities that Charlie would engage in on behalf of Indian issues and rights.[85]

106. Tomiear was the name or title assumed by Rudy Ortega Sr. (1926–2009), who was the son of Estanislao Ortega and grandson of Antonio Maria Ortega. Tomiear was translated roughly as *chief*. His Native name was Little Bear, or Tsinju Hunar. During his lifetime he held many leadership positions in the community and with the Fernandeño Tataviam Band of Mission Indians and its variously named predecessors and community nonprofit organizations.[86] He assumed a leadership role while a high school student in the early 1940s, after getting the attention and approval of his five aunts, the daughters of Antonio Maria Ortega. Captains are chosen for their lineage lines and their leadership ability and through agreement within the lineage. Rudy Sr. was honored with the captain's hat ceremony in 1998.[87]
107. Captain Charlie Cooke (1935–2013) was the nephew of Captain Mary Cooke Garcia and assumed leadership after his appointment in 1957 by a group of Garcia family leaders. Charlie had an illustrious career engaged in Indian and tribal issues throughout the area where the Fernandeños lived and continue to live.[88]
108. Captain John Valenzuela (1938–2017) was the grandson of Petra Garcia, who married Jose Jesus Valenzuela. John Valenzuela was active in Newhall and engaged in cultural and community events, including environmental preservation, Indigenous cultural-resource protection, and organization around his lineage group. He was the chairman of the San Fernando Band of Mission Indians, an organization that represents Indians in the Santa Clarita Valley. They have organized a nonprofit organization called Seven Feathers, Inc.[89]
109. Captain Theodore Cornelius Garcia Jr. (1948–) was designated captain of the Garcia lineage with support and blessings from Charlie Cooke in December 2009. Theodore and his father, Theodore Sr., were strong supporters of Charlie Cooke and took part in many of his activities. Theodore Jr. worked and apprenticed with Charlie Cooke for many years. The passing of leadership to Theodore Garcia Jr. brought the leadership back into the direct line of Frances Cooke Garcia and Mary Cooke Garcia.[90] Theodore Garcia Jr. is a ceremo-

nial leader and Indigenous artist. Like his father, Theodore Garcia Sr., and his grandmother and great-grandmother, Ted Jr. has been active in upholding and participating in tribal relations with the Ortega and Ortiz lineages that currently compose the Fernandeño Tataviam Band of Mission Indians and also nonprofit community activities through the present-day organization Pukúu.

110. Tomiear or captain is a position held by Rudy Ortega Jr. (1974–). Rudy Ortega Jr.'s Native name is Standing Bear. He went through the bear dance ceremony in 1997. Standing Bear was tasked with making peace with the bear who had killed the lineage ancestor Santiago Garcia in 1873. Rudy Jr. fasted for four days and saw a vision of ancestral lineage members who welcomed his ceremonial efforts.[91] Over the years, Rudy Ortega Jr. has held many positions with the tribe, including tribal administrator, president of the tribe, vice president of the senate, as well as serving as ceremonial and community leader for the Ortega lineage and for the administration of the community nonprofit, most recently known as Pukúu. He was designated as future captain of the Ortega lineage in the late 1990s and assumed the role of captain after the passing of his father in 2009.[92]

111. Tomiear Benicio Ortega was born in 2005 and is a designated hereditary captain or lineage leader of the Ortega lineage. He is being groomed for future leadership within the Ortega line.

APPENDIX B

List and Analysis of the Forty Petitioners

LAND GRANT OF ONE SQUARE LEAGUE

Governor Manuel Micheltorena

May 3, 1843

1. **Pedro Joaquin** (1813–?) was born at San Fernando Mission and elected or appointed first alcalde of San Fernando Mission in the year 1843 (SFR Baptism #02080). No Native name was recorded for Pedro Joaquin. His father, Mariano, was born at "rancheria de la Sanja" and died very young, during the same year as Pedro Joaquin's birth (SFR Baptism #00963; SFR Burial #01028). Pedro Joaquin led the forty petitioners who secured the land grant of one square league on May 3, 1843, from Mexican governor Micheltorena.[1] Pedro Joaquin first was married to Felipa, sister of Francisco Papabubaba, a progenitor of the Ortega line (SFR Baptism #02286; SFR Marriage #00819) and father of Rita. After Felipa's death in 1842, Pedro Joaquin married Maria del Carmen on May 21, 1843 (SFR Marriage #00898). Maria del Carmen was the daughter of Petra (SFR Baptism #02062), who married Emeterio on November 16, 1835 (SFR Marriage #00853). Emeterio was a chief at the Sebastian Reservation and at Tejon Ranch. Petra's father, Zenon, was born at the Tataviam-speaking village of Cuecchao (SFR Baptism # 01879), and his Native name was Chaamel. Zenon's father, Dioniso, with the Native name Napcos, was also born at "rancheria de Cuecchao" (SFR Baptism #01925).
2. **Jaunado** (?) was an officer at San Fernando Mission, serving in that capacity with alcalde Pedro Joaquin in the year 1843. John Johnson suggests Conrado (listed as Inerado) (SFR Baptism #00553) was born at Cahuenga and lived

through the San Fernando Mission period.[2] Then there is a second Conrado (SFR Baptism #02253) who was born at rancheria Nacaya. The latter Conrado was born in 1812 and lived through the San Fernando Mission period.

3. **Jacinto.** There are three individuals with the name Jacinto who fit the age window of petitioners to the May 3, 1843, land grant from Mexican governor Micheltorena. (SFR Baptisms #02695, #02133, and #02480). Jacinto held the post of corporal during the year 1843.
4. **Emeterio** is missing on the document and translation of the May 3, 1843, land grant that the Office of Federal Acknowledgment provided to the Fernandeño Tataviam Band of Mission Indians. There are forty petitioners rather than thirty-nine, as OFA suggested. Emeterio (1799–?) was baptized in 1804 (SFR Baptism #01226; SFR Marriage #00675). His Native name was not recorded, and his godfather was Vicente, possibly Vicente Francisco, who was San Fernando Mission alcalde in 1845 and chief of the Tejon Indian Tribe after 1873. If Vicente Francisco was the godparent, then Emeterio would have had support and assistance while he was living at the Sebastian Reservation during the 1850s. In January 1851, Emeterio was a signatory for the Senahow Tribe to the Tejon treaty. Emeterio was regarded as one of the most prominent tribal leaders in 1854 at Sebastian Reservation, serving as chief for over three hundred persons.[3] Emeterio's followers were Yokuts, and they selected him partly because of his mission experience, as a useful leader to manage relations with the Americans. Emeterio may have been born in a Yokut village, and hence he returned after the mission to a Yokut-speaking community.[4] A possible alternative is Hemeterio, born to the Tujubit (SFR Baptism #00398), who was about eighteen years old and alive in 1843. Hemeterio, however, was very young and had no direct ties to Pedro Joaquin.
5. **Camilo** (1806–ca.1875), baptized in 1806, was the son of Rafael, captain of Jotativit (SFR Baptisms #01440 and #01597). For additional information, see appendix A, number 83. A possible alternative is Camilo born to Juubit in 1794 (SFR Baptism # 00893), but there is no further information on the latter other than that he survived the San Fernando Mission period past 1845.
6. **Odon Chihuya** (1795–ca. 1882) most likely was among the forty petitioners (SFR Baptism #00780). For additional information, see appendix A, number 88.
7. **Calistro** or Calisto or Calixto (1807–?) was born in Chibuno (SFR Baptism #01834). He was married with children. There is another person with the name Calixto who matches the age window for participating in the 1843 land grant of the forty petitioners. The second candidate Calixto would have been

age seventy-five in 1843 and was born to the Piirucbit, a Tataviam-speaking group. Calixto's age may rule him out.

8. **Tanislado**, a Spanish variation on Estanislado or Estanislao (1792–?), was baptized in 1817 and his Native name was Quimatobit (SFR Baptism #02271). He was also known as Stanislao, a name anglicized into Stanislaw. For additional information, see appendix A, number 87.
9. **Lanislado.** As with Estanislao, this name is a variation of Ladislao or the Spanish version Ladislado. There are two possible candidates at San Fernando Mission. Ladislao, who was born at Tapuu in 1794 and survived the mission period (SFR Baptism #00820). There is little information about Ladislao from Tapuu. The second candidate is Ladislao of Nauqivit (SFR Baptism #01242), who was born to the Punivit in 1789 and was active in community affairs at the mission and most likely a confidant of Rogerio Rocha. Punivit was one of the lineages within which Rogerio Rocha exercised some influence, according to Eugenia.[5]
10. **Patricio**. There are three possible candidates with the name Patricio. They were all alive in 1843 and already relatively aged. Patricio with the Native name Jumus (SFR Baptism #00084) was born at rancheria Sibunga in 1778 and would have been sixty-five years old in 1843. Patricio Jumus did not have any children in the mission record. Patricio with the Native name Aguacates was born at rancheria Escorpion in 1784. He was fifty-nine years old in 1843. Patricio Aguacates had five children, and three survived past the mission period. Patricio with the Native name Sicsaytset (SFR Baptism #01493) was born at the Chumash village of Ypuc. Sicsaytset was born in 1788 and died in 1844, not quite a year after the May 3, 1843, land grant. Patricio Sicsaytest had six children, but only one survived the San Fernando Mission period past 1845.
11. **Norberto [No. 1]**. There are four persons with the name Norberto and one with Norverto among the forty petitioners, all of whom fit the age window for the 1843 land grant petition. They are presented here in order of age, since it is not possible to determine which Norberto is correct without additional information. All four Norbertos and Norverto should be considered equal candidates until additional information can be obtained. Norberto [No. 1] (SFR Baptism #01212) was sixty-four years old in 1843, and his Native name was Ayeymuinassun. He was born in 1779 to the Tochavuruvit (Tochaburubit) and survived the San Fernando Mission period, ending in 1845. Norberto Ayeymuinassun had eight children with two wives, but only one child survived the mission period. The captain of Tochaburubit died in 1832, and possibly Norberto Ayeymuinassun took leadership, at least for this occasion.

12. **Meliton** was born to the people of Giribit in 1794 and died in 1847 (SFR Baptism #01282; SFR Burial #02391). Meliton fathered one child, who died in 1821. His partner, Eulalia, was born at rancheria Tujunga (SFR Baptism #00181). There is no record for a captain at Giribit. It is likely that Meliton, at age fifty, was representing Giribit, his kinship group among the forty petitioners.
13. **Jose Flores.** There is no person in the San Fernando Mission record who has the name Jose Flores. The closest name is Florencio, who was born in the Chumash-speaking village of Taeepop in 1802 (SFR Baptism #00813). Florencio would have been forty years old in 1843. There is no record of a Native name for Florencio. He had two girls, Maria Antonia and Maria del Espiritu Santo, who were born about 1831 (SFR Baptisms #02903 and #02901), and they both survived the San Fernando Mission period.
14. **German** or Jerman (1796–ca. 1849) was born at Quimisac, a Chumash-speaking village near present-day Santa Paula, California (SFR Baptism #00817). German's son, Rogerio, identified German as a captain and said that after his father's death, he succeeded German as a captain of the same group.[6] German was married to Maria Guadalupe, born to the Tujubit or at Tujunga. They had at least six children, although only the son Rojerio (Rogerio) lived to maturity.[7]
15. **Rojerio.** Rogerio (Rojerio) Rocha (1824–1904) was a captain from the time of his father German's death until his own death in 1904 (SFR Baptism #02565). There was no Native name recorded for Rogerio. Rogerio did not have any children who survived to adulthood. He was married to Maria Manuela, whose mother, Maria Ygnacio Nerea, was from Piiru and whose father, Efren, was born at Jucjauybit, or Escorpion, a Chumash-speaking village (SFR Baptisms #00803, #00898, and #02639). Maria Manuela had twin brothers who lived with them at Escorpion in 1850.[8] One of the brothers, Jose Juan Leyva, married Leandra, and they are progenitors of the Garcia line (SFR Baptism #02908).[9] For additional information about Rogerio, see appendix A, number 94.
16. **Martiniano** was born in 1812 at San Fernando Mission (SFR Baptism #02023). No Native name was recorded for him. His godfather was Tomas, perhaps one of the forty petitioners. Martiniano and his wife, Pastora, were well connected among the leaders and petitioners. They had five children, but only one, Antonino, survived to the postmission period, starting in 1845 (SFR Baptism #03009). Antonino's godfather was Vicente Francisco, who served as San Fernando Mission alcalde for 1845 and was also one of the

forty petitioners. Vicente Francisco returned to his Tejon Indian Tribe in the 1850s, and after the death of his brother the chief, Francisco became chief. Urbano Chari and his wife, Marcelina, daughter of Odon, were godparents to Jose Canuto, child of Martiniano and Pastora (SFR Baptism #02061a). However, Canuto died after living for about fourteen months. Pastora, wife of Martiniano, was the daughter of Jose Francisco, another one of the forty petitioners. Martiniano and family were well connected to the leadership of the forty petitioners.

17. **Jose Francisco** was born at rancheria Tujunga in 1796 (SFR Baptism #00113). His Native name was Ginunchiguinasum. He married Odorica, an Indian woman from San Buenaventura Mission (SBV Baptism #01681). They had six children, and four lived past the end of the San Fernando Mission period. Jose Francisco and Odorica are progenitors of the present-day Addington line. In particular, Basilio was born to Jose Francisco and Odorica in 1818 (SFR Baptism #2318). Basilio and his partner, Petra, gave birth to Jacinta in 1841 (SFR Baptism #03015). Jacinta married Cerval Sepulveda and had a daughter, Valentina Sepulveda, who married James Addington in 1887.[10]
18. **Narciso or Narcizo** was born to Pinibit in 1798, and his Native name was Yamiguit (SFR Baptism #01096). He married Crisanta (Chrisanta), who was born at rancheria Te(st)uguaguiya in 1797 (SFR Marriage #00704; SFR Baptism #02465). Ladislao, also one of the forty petitioners, was her uncle (SFR Baptism #02465). Narciso and Crisanta had ten children, and four survived the San Fernando Mission period.
19. **Guido** was born at Piiru in 1788. No Native name is recorded for Guido (SFR Baptism #00915). He married Guida (SFR Baptism #00932) and together they had nine children, only one of whom, Genaro (1807–?), lived past the San Fernando Mission period (SFR Baptism #01675). Guida (1788–1827) was the daughter of Pedro Jose (1770–?), captain of Coaybet or Coaybit.
20. **Pedro.** There are forty-six people who use the name Pedro in some form. It is not possible to determine which Pedro is intended without more information.
21. **Bruno** was born at the mission in 1820. No Native name was recorded for him (SFR Baptism #02431). His father was born at Tujunga and his mother was born to Pasecuhit. Bruno married Bruna, who was born at Liam (Liyam) among the Channel Islands (SFR Baptism #02233). Together they had two children, only one of whom lived past the San Fernando Mission period.
22. **Odon [No. 2]** or Odilon was born at Oumaliu near present-day Malibu in 1797 (SFR Baptism #00824). He appears not to have married.

23. **Pascacio** was born at Juubit in 1799 (SFR Baptism #00894). There is no Native name recorded for him. Pascacio appears not to have married and did not have children. He survived the San Fernando Mission period.
24. **Tomas [No. 1].** Tomas is a relatively common name and five individuals with that name were alive on May 3, 1843. There are three eligible individuals named Tomas, and two named Thomas. More information is needed. Tomas No. 1 considers all the Tomases, and Tomas No. 2 considers all the Thomases. Tomas (SFR Baptism #01838) was born at Atongaina, a Serrano village, and his Native name was Tucuparguinaray. His father was born in the same village. Tucuparguinaray appears not to have married or had children at San Fernando Mission. He survived the San Fernando Mission period. Tomas (SFR Baptism #02230) was born in 1791 with the Native name Naguguay. He was born at one of the Channel Islands. Naguguay married Tomasa and had five children, one of whom, Jose, survived the San Fernando mission period. Naguguay also survived the San Fernando Mission period. A third candidate is Tomas de Cora (1807–1843), who died later in the same year as the land grant. He did not have a recorded Native name. De Cora's grandfather was born to the Siutcabit.
25. **Vicente**. There are three individuals named Vicente who could have been among the forty petitioners. Jose Vicente (SFR Baptism #02010) was born at Tapuu in 1782. Jose Vicente was the older brother of Tiburcio (SFR Baptism #00849), who is a progenitor of the Ortega lineage. Jose Vicente did not have a wife or children in the mission record. A second Vicente was born to the Cabuepet (SFR Baptisms #00350 and #00349) in 1793. He married Maria from San Gabriel Mission, and they had six children, two of whom, Jacoba and Estefana, survived the San Fernando Mission period. The third candidate is Vicente Francisco, whose Native name was Tinoqui (SFR Baptism #02385). Tinoqui was San Fernando Mission alcalde in 1845 and a chief among the Tejon Indian Tribe in the 1870s. He appears to have had leadership capabilities and was dedicated to upholding the mission as long as it was operational. For additional information about Vicente Francisco, see appendix A, number 84.
26. **Mejias** or **Metias** was born in 1755 at Tubimovit, and he survived the San Fernando Mission period (SFR Baptism #01359). There is no Native name recorded for Metias. Juan de Mata was Metias's nephew; however this Juan de Mata was not among the forty petitioners (SFR Baptism #00074). Metias partnered with Nazaria, and they had one child, who did not live past the San Fernando Mission period.

27. **Romaldo or Romualdo.** There are three candidates for Romualdo. First, Romualdo (SFR Baptism #00729) was born in 1802 at Mapabit. A Native name was not recorded for him. This Romualdo appears not to have married and did not have children. The second Ramualdo was born at Giribit and his Native name was Erayaminassum. He was born in 1770 (SFR Baptism #01237). Erayaminassum married Romualda and they had one child, who did not survive the San Fernando Mission period. The son, Juan Francisco, however, had a daughter, Juana, who is recorded in the 1860 census (Juana Martir, SFR Baptism #02795). The third possible Romualdo was born at rancheria Nacaya in 1815 (SFR Baptism #02257). His Native name was Garurgly. Garurgly married Maria of rancheria Tuucinga, and they had three children, two of whom survived the San Fernando Mission period.
28. **Juan de Mata** was born at San Fernando Mission in 1807, and there was no Native name recorded for him (SFR Baptism #01633). His father, Geronimo, was born at Tujunga, and his mother, Francisa, was born at Jochanabit (possibly, Tochanabit) (SFR Baptism #01377). Juan de Mata married Angela, and they had one child, who did not survive the San Fernando Mission period.
29. **Melchor** represented the Tochonabit lineage among the forty petitioners. Melchor partnered with Angela, and they had two children, who did not survive the San Fernando Mission period (SFR Baptisms #02058a and #03011). For additional information, see appendix A, number 90.
30. **Norb(v)erto [No. 2].** The second oldest Norberto (SFR Baptism #01648) given in the record sometimes is spelled Norverto. No. 2's mother, Francisca, and father, Pasqual, were born at Humaliu, present-day Malibu. His mother's birth village is unstated, although she, Maria Manuela, was baptized at Calabasas, which indicates she was probably a Chumash speaker. Noverto had at least three children, Silvestre, Pascuala, and Baltasar, who survived the San Fernando Mission period. Silvestre appears on the 1850 census, living on the ranch of Urbano Chari. Baltasar had godparents, which indicates a close attachment to leadership and the forty petitioners. Baltasar's godmother was Eugenia, who was at that time married to Ramon, one of the forty petitioners. Baltasar's godfather was Vicente Francisco, alcalde and chief, who was married to Serafina and likely also one of the forty petitioners (SFR Baptism #02073a). Baltasar is found on the 1850 census, living at Escorpion under the leadership of Urbano Chari.[11] Pascuala was born in 1834 or 1835, and she was listed in the 1860 census.[12] A possible fourth child, Mauricio, is listed on the 1850 census with Silverstre and Baltasar,[13] but being born in 1849, he was not listed in the mission record.

31. **Norberto [No. 3]** The third oldest Norberto was age thirty-three in May 1843, when the land grant was made. His Native name was Siusiguaba, and he was born at rancheria Tochaborunga (SFR Baptism #01836). Norberto No. 3 and Noberto No. 1 were born at the same village of Tochavuruvit (Tochaburubit) or Tochaborunga, following Fernandeño language rules. Norberto No. 3's mother, Georgia (SFR Baptism #01905), was born at rancheria Tochborunga, but his father, Romulo, was born at Suitaasegena. Norbertos No. 1 and No. 3 were related through marriage, having been born in the same village. Norberto Siusiguaba appears not to have had any children during the San Fernando Mission period. There are two younger Norbertos [3A and 3B] yet to consider. Norberto 3A (SFR Baptism #02158) was born at San Fernando Mission, while his father, Francisco Xavier (SFR Baptism #00088), was born at Cahuenga. The mother of Norberto 3A, Anastasia, was born to the Passecubit, a rancheria very near San Fernando Mission (SFR Baptism #00018). There was no Native name recorded for Norberto 3A. He was twenty-seven years old when the land grant to the forty petitioners was given in 1843. Norberto 3A did not have any children recorded in the mission record. Norberto 3B, who was born at San Fernando Mission, was twenty-three years old in 1843 (SFR Baptism #02317). His father, Emerando, was born at Jucjauybit, or Escorpion, while his mother's father was born at Cahuenga (SFR Burial #00105; SFR Baptisms #00556 and #00805). Norberto 3B had one child, who died in 1837 (SFR Burial #02123).
32. **Ramon Sotelo or Ramon**. The name Ramon Sotelo is not found in the San Fernando Mission record. Ramon (SFR Baptism #01712) was born in 1808 at San Fernando Mission. The mission record does not provide a Native name. His father was Cornelio (SFR Baptism #00765), one of the forty petitioners, and both are progenitors of the Garcia lineage. Ramon married Eugenia in 1832, and they had four children, including Leandra (SFR Baptism #02987), who is also a progenitor of the Garcia lineage. Ramon died in 1845.
33. **Cornelio** was born in 1778 at an unstated place. He died in 1846 (SFR Baptism #00765; SFR Burial #02372). Cornelio was the father to Ramon, one of the forty petitioners, and both are progenitors of the Garcia lineage. He married Maria Antonio, and they had ten children, two of whom lived past the San Fernando Mission period.
34. **Basilio** was born at the Serrano-speaking village of Atongaina in 1807. His Native name was Amau (SFR Baptism #01833). Basilio partnered with Ysabel (SFR Baptism #01694) and they had six children, two of whom survived the San Fernando Mission period.

35. **Cosme** was born in 1805 at San Fernando Mission and no Native name was recorded (SFR Baptism #01519). His father, Marcelo, was born to Cabuepet (SFR Baptism #00558). Cosme married Esperanza and together they had six children. Three children, including Benigno, survived past the end of the San Fernando Mission period. In 1845, Benigno married Rita, who is a progenitor of the Ortega lineage. Benigno's children with Rita appear not to have survived past 1870.
36. **Martin.** No eligible persons named Martin.
37. **Juan.** Too many possible candidates.
38. **Olorico.** No eligible persons named Olorico.
39. **Tomas [No. 2].** There were two persons with the name Thomas alive at the time of the May 3, 1843, land grant. The first Thomas (SFR Baptism #00037) had the Native name Guiris and was born in 1787 at Momonga. Guiris had seven children with three wives. All seven children did not survive the San Fernando Mission period. The second Thomas (SFR Baptism #02550) was born at San Fernando Mission in 1823. His grandfather, Martin (SFR Baptism #00338), was born to Siutcabit. The grandson Thomas did not have a recorded Native name. Thomas, grandson of Martin, married Luisa, but they appear not to have had any children.
40. **Manuel.** Too many possible candidates.

APPENDIX C

Genealogies of Progenitors

PROGENITORS OF PRESENT-DAY GARCIA LINEAGE[1]

Primary Progenitor: Josefa Leyva Garcia

Primary Progenitor's Maternal Grandparents
Eugenia (1817–1928, Topipabit and Tujubit)
Ramon (1808–1845, ? and Chaguayabit)

Primary Progenitor's Paternal Grandparents
Efren (1796–1850s, Jucjauybit)
Maria Ygnacia Nerea (1799–1850s, Piiru)

Primary Progenitor's Parents
Jose Juan Leyva (1838–ca. 1869, Huwam/Jucjauybit and Piiru)
Leandra (1840–ca. 1869, Chaguayabit, Tujubit, Topipabit)

Primary Progenitor

Josefa Leyva (1865–1952), partnered ca. 1880 with Isidoro Garcia (1860–1943)[2]

Primary Progenitor's Surviving Children with Isidoro Garcia
Frances Garcia (1881–1946), married Fred Cooke
Petra Garcia (1882–1930), married Pedro Rivera and Jose Jesus Valenzuela
James Garcia (1888–ca. 1949)[3]

Primary Progenitor's Surviving Children with William Gardner

Clara Maude Callis (1902–1984), married John Joseph Callis (San Buena Ventura Mission)

Primary Progenitor's Surviving Grandchildren

By Petra Garcia Rivera/Valenzuela

- Margaret Rivera Ward (1899–1975)
- Louis Valenzuela (1902–1978)
- Ola Valenzuela (1904–?)
- John Valenzuela (1907–1965)
- Paul Valenzuela (1909–?)

By Frances Garcia Cooke

- Mary Cooke Garcia (1901–1975)
- Adela/Della Cooke Martinez (1903–1982)
- Lida Cooke Manriquez (1905–2003)
- Manuel Cooke (1909–?)
- Cy Cooke (1912–1985)

Primary Progenitor's Great-Grandchildren

By Mary Cooke Garcia

- Ted Garcia Sr. (1920–2008)

By Cy Cooke

- Charlie Cooke (1935–2013)
- Alvin Cooke (1938–?)

By Louis Valenzuela

- Victoria Stokes (1955–)

By John Valenzuela

- John W. Valenzuela (1938–2017)

PROGENITORS OF PRESENT-DAY ORTEGA LINEAGE[4]

Primary Progenitor: Maria Rita Alipaz

Primary Progenitor's Maternal Grandparents

Tiburcio Cayo (1793–1844, Tapuu)

Teresa (1797–1850s, Siutcabit)

Primary Progenitor's Paternal Grandparents
Juan Maria (1778–1831, Chaguayabit)
Francisca Xaviera (1784–1822, Tochonabit)

Primary Progenitor's Parents
Francisco Papabubaba (1806–1847, Chaguayabit)
Paula Cayo (1813–1849?, Siutcabit)

Primary Progenitor

Maria Rita Alipaz (1830–1869?), married Fernando Ortega in 1862[5]

Primary Progenitor's Surviving Children
Antonio Maria Ortega (1857–1941), married Isidora Garcia
Luis Ortega (1862–1948), married Refugia Moreno

Primary Progenitor's Surviving Grandchildren
By Antonio Maria Ortega
  Christina Ortega (Rodriguez) (1881–1972)
  Refugia Ortega (Tapia) (1883–1955)
  Estanislao (James) Ortega (1885–1951)
  Eulogio Ortega (1887–1966)
  Luis Ortega (1890–1931)
  Kathryn Ortega (Newman) (1896–1958)
  Vera Ortega (Salazar) (1898–1981)
  Sally Ortega (Verdugo) (1900–1995)
By Luis Ortega
  Clarence Pete Ortega (1911–1977)

Primary Progenitor's Great-Grandchildren
By Estanislao (James) Ortega
  Ernest Ortega (1919–2002)
  Rudy (James) Ortega Sr. (1926–2009)
  Richard Ortega (1929–2008)
By Vera Ortega (Salazar)
  David Salazar Sr. (1932–2014)
  Beverly Salazar (Folkes) (1938–)

By Kathryn Ortega (Newman)
- Verne Newman Sr. (1922–1985)
- Catherine Newman (Traba) (1928–2010)

By Sally Ortega
- Irene Verdugo (Reyes) (1929–1991)

PROGENITORS OF PRESENT-DAY ORTIZ LINEAGE[6]

Primary Progenitor: Joseph Ortiz

Primary Progenitor's Maternal Grandparents
Jose Miguel Triunfo (1814–ca. 1858, Cabuepet)
Maria Rafaela Perfecta (1822–after 1877, Yabit[7])

Primary Progenitor's Parents
Alexander Godey (1818–1871, non-Native)
Rosaria Arriola (1840–1911, Cabuepet)

Primary Progenitor

Joseph Ortiz (1861–ca. 1938), married Remegia Miranda in 1893

Primary Progenitor's Surviving Children
Fortino V. Ortiz (1899–1951)
Juanita Ortiz de Montez (1903–2001)
Elena/Helen Ortiz (1907–1995)

Primary Progenitor's Surviving Grandchildren

By Helen Ortiz
- Eduardo/Edward Sierra (1928–2018)
- Angie Molina Campero (1930–)

By Fortino V. Ortiz
- Antonio Ortiz (1917–?)
- Francisco Ortiz (1919–?)

APPENDIX D

Names of Tribe and Nonprofit

Years	Tribe Name(s)	Nonprofit/Club Name(s)
1930s and earlier	San Fernando Mission San Fernando Mission Tribe Mission Indian, San Fernando Mission San Fernando Mission Indians Fernandeño (all in applications for 1928 act roll)[1]	NA
1940–1971	San Fernando Mission Band[2] San Fernando Mission Indian Fernandeño	San Fernando Mission Indians of San Fernando (Club)
1972–1995	Fernandeño[3]	San Fernando Valley Inter-Tribal Inc.
1995–2002	Fernandeño Tataviam Tribal Council Fernandeño Tataviam Tribe Tataviam Tribe	the nonprofit (unincorporated)
2002–	Fernandeño Tataviam Band of Mission Indians[4]	nonprofit council (until 2006)
2006–		Pukúu[5]

GLOSSARY

ALCALDE: At California missions, an elected official for the resident Indians, to prepare them for assuming management of a town or pueblo. The first alcalde worked directly under mission authorities. For most of California mission history, the elected alcaldes were under the authority of the missionaries. Numerous town or pueblo offices were also elected and managed by mission and Indian alcalde authorities. Elections took place on January 1 of every year. At San Fernando Mission there are very few surviving reports about election procedures or activities. From Spanish, "alcalde" translates as *judge*, a person with some local authority.

BAND: An expression used by Indians of San Fernando during the twentieth century to identify political tribal membership and to distinguish the non-membership of married-in relatives. For example, the San Fernando Mission Indian Band consisted of members who were descendants of baptized Indians at San Fernando Mission. Band members could trace their lineage to San Fernando Mission records and identify the name of the village where their ancestors were born.

CALIFORNIOS: Spanish-speaking residents of California who were born there during the periods of Spanish and Mexican colonization. The first Californios were children of the early Spanish military expeditions.

CAPTAIN, OR CAPITAN: The expression *capitan* in Spanish or *captain* translated into English describes a person in command. In the California Indian mission records, the missionaries recorded the leader or sometimes several leaders of Indian lineages or villages as captains. However, the Spanish usage of captain is more hierarchical, individualistic, and authoritarian than the usage among Southern California Indians. Indians in California had their own words and meanings for leadership, such as Chari or Tomiear. Indian leaders were knowledgeable about community history, ceremonies, and beliefs. Indian leadership was embedded in kinship groups such as lineages or villages and were egalitarian while dependent on sustained consensual recognition from supporting kin. For detailed information about individual captains associated with San Fernando Mission, see appendix A.

CHUMASH: Name given by linguists for the language spoken by Indians in lineages along the California coastal regions from present-day Malibu to present-day San Luis Obispo. The Chumash-speaking lineages and the villages they occupied did not form a single, unified political entity. Chumash is more accurately a language family associated with numerous lineage-villages.

FERNANDEÑO: A Spanish term referring to the Indigenous people brought to San Fernando Mission, regardless of their diverse village, lineage, sociopolitical, linguistic, or cultural attributes, as well as the Indians living in the general area near the mission. Another way we sometimes refer to the same people who lived at San Fernando Mission and their descendants is "Indians of San Fernando." Anthropologists and linguists have also used the term Fernandeño to refer to a specific linguistic group whose villages stretched from Malibu through the western end of the San Fernando Valley, sometimes describing it as a subdivision of Gabrieleño,[1] the language spoken by most Indians who were brought to San Gabriel Mission, near present-day Los Angeles. Since the postmission period, Indians descended from those brought to and baptized at San Fernando Mission began referring to themselves as Fernandeño. This usage is much broader than the linguists' use and is not concerned with language so much as descent, lineage affiliation, and location. Descendants of all the Indians at San Fernando Mission are called Fernandeño, regardless of the languages their ancestors spoke. By the late nineteenth century, a Fernandeño tribal entity came to coexist with constituent lineage identities and organization. For further discussion of the contemporary tribal use of this term, see chapter 7.

FRIAR: In California, during the colonial period, a member of the Franciscan Catholic religious order. The Franciscans were mendicants who, like the first apostles, begged for daily support or otherwise sought to gain support from a host community. In California, the Franciscans sponsored the construction of mission estates and relied for their own support on the Indian mission communities.

GABRIELEÑO: A Spanish term referring to the Indigenous people brought to San Gabriel Mission in the present-day Los Angeles Basin, regardless of their diverse village, lineage, sociopolitical, linguistic, or cultural attributes, as well as the Indians living in the general area near that mission. Linguists and anthropologists have used the term Gabrieleño to refer to a group of villages where a common dialect was spoken, closely related to the Fernandeño dialect. The Gabrieleño-speaking lineages and the villages they occupied did not form a single, unified political entity. Gabrieleño is not an Indigenous expression.

GENTE DE RAZÓN: One of two classes of people at San Fernando Mission and the other California missions. The other class of people were Indians. "All that were not Indians went by the designation of *Gente de Razon.*" "People who reasoned, or used their reason or Intelligence." "People with reason." "The Indians followed their instincts or appetites more generally, it was said." "People who speak Spanish." Some gente de razón migrated from Lower California and others came from Sonora.[2]

INDIANS (INDIOS): The colony of Upper California was divided into two social classes: Indians and gente de razón. Few Indians at San Fernando Mission spoke or read Spanish, one requirement for being gente de razón, while more eventually understood Spanish to some degree. Throughout the mission period, most Indians preferred their own languages, place and group names, ceremonies, and kinship relations. Indians were the lowest class of people in the California colonial caste system. Since Indians usually were not strong Catholics, did not talk, read, or write Spanish, and preferred to live in their kin-based communities, most were not considered citizens and were without interest or knowledge to live in Spanish or Mexican society. The word Indians is derived from a Spanish expression (Indios) and is not an Indigenous expression.

KITANEMUK: A dialect of the Serrano language. Anthropologists and linguists have also used the term Kitanemuk to refer to speakers of this dialect whose independent villages were located in the present-day Tejon area. These villages and the Kitanemuk-speaking lineages who occupied them did not form a single, unified political entity.

LINEAGE: A kinship group composed of related families with patrilineal or matrilineal leaders and elders. All lineage members share a common ancestor. In California, several consenting extended families form a lineage. Lineages held territory and were and are the primary political, ceremonial, and economic entities. The overlapping relations of kinship, government, land, ceremonies, and economy make the lineage an internally focused and enduring social community. In precontact and postcontact California, the independent lineage was and is the primary form of Indigenous social and political organization and would be characterized today as a tribe.

LLABERO: The keeper of the keys. Often a mission Indian who was charged with keeping the supplies and goods of the mission store. Something like a quartermaster.

MAYORDOMO: A paid manager at San Fernando Mission and other missions. The mayordomo and assistants helped organize Indian work groups for herding, agriculture, construction, and other activities.

MEXICAN LAND GRANT: Under the Mexican constitution of 1824, the Mexican Congress passed a law in 1828 that authorized the permanent granting of land in territories such as California to Mexican citizens and other residents. Lands occupied by missions were excluded from grants until it could be determined whether particular tracts were to be allocated to the Indians. Numerous grants to individual Californios and some Indians followed passage of this law.

NATIVE, NATIVE AMERICAN, INDIAN, AND AMERICAN INDIAN: These terms refer to the diverse Indigenous peoples of North America. All these terms suffer from overgeneralization, treating people of different languages, cultures, and sociopolitical organization as if they were one. The preferred usage is the particular tribe or cultural group with which individuals identify. In discussion of the Spanish and Mexican periods, we use the term Indian (translated into English) because that is the term found in their documents, such as mission records. See above. The term "Native American" was introduced in the middle of the twentieth century.

NEOPHYTE: The earliest and lowest religious status for a beginner in the Catholic religion. The friars called the Indian people neophytes after they came to the mission and were baptized. Most Indians did not advance past the neophyte stage.

PAN-INDIAN: American Indians in multitribal coalitions or organizations promoting the well-being of tribal communities and individuals and the protection of mother earth. Some examples are multitribal powwows, National Congress of American Indians, the American Indian movement, and sacred walks.

SERRANO: A linguistic term referring to a language within the Takic language family, spoken by Indigenous people in parts of Southern California near the present-day San Bernardino Mountains and Mojave Desert. Serrano is not an Indigenous expression.

SPANISH LAND GRANT: When Spanish subjects reached California, they took hold of the land, protecting the ownership of the land from any other European king or nation. According to Spanish law, the land was immediately taken from Indian control. Spanish subjects could be granted land from the king, but during the period of Spanish domination, between 1769 and 1822, the Spanish king or his representatives did not make permanent grants of land to subjects. Some grants were made and lasted until the grantee died and the land was returned to the management of the government.

TAKIC: A linguistic term referring to a branch within the larger Uto-Aztecan language family, consisting of languages spoken in coastal Southern California and the Mojave and Colorado Deserts.

TATAVIAM: A linguistic term that refers to a dialect of the Serrano language, spoken by members of the lineages whose independent villages were located in the upper Santa Clara River basin of Southern California, including Santa Clarita, Newhall, Castaic, Piru, and nearby parts of the northern San Fernando Valley. The term has been loosely translated into English as *people of the sun*, or *people who sun themselves*. Linguists and anthropologists of the early twentieth century learned of this term from speakers of the language and individuals from neighboring territories.[3]

TONGVA/GABRIELEÑO/KISH: Tongva is a place-name term first recorded by ethnographer C. Hart Merriam in 1903, referring to parts of present-day Southern California, mainly the Los Angeles Basin and southern Channel Islands, where lineage members spoke a specific dialect of the Takic language family. The terms often used for that language today, as well as for descendants of those who spoke it, are Tongva, Gabrieleño, or Kish.

TRIBELET: A term coined by anthropologist Alfred Kroeber referring to a substantially sized lineage or a consensual coalition of several autonomous lineages.

VENTUREÑO: A Spanish term linguists have applied to a dialect of Chumash, spoken by lineage members from present-day Ventura to as far south as present-day Malibu and into the Simi Hills of California. Some of the Ventureño speakers were brought to San Buenaventura Mission and others went to San Fernando Mission. The Ventureño-speaking lineages and the villages they occupied did not form a single, unified political entity. Ventureño is not an Indigenous expression.

NOTES

INTRODUCTION

1. These names are used to refer to languages, not political entities. The language groups do not form political entities, although they may be the basis for affinities among lineages. See *infra* in this chapter. Note that the term Fernandeño is also used in this book to refer to the Indians at a particular place, namely San Fernando Mission. We observe the usage by linguists as well as the Spanish understanding of the word as a place name. As we explain later in this chapter and in chapter 7, these usages are not the same. For further explanation of this term, see the glossary.
2. See chapter 3.
3. This calculation comes from data provided in Engelhardt, *San Fernando Rey*, 92–93.
4. Among those present was Manuel, who served as the first testimonial witness. Though Manuel was born at the mission, his father was Cabuepet from Cahuenga, and his father's father was from Siutcanga, or Encino. The second testimonial witness, Vicente Francisco, was alcalde of the mission and a prominent member of a Kitanemuk lineage. Later, Francisco would return to his village, high in the mountains, where his brother was the leader, and sign the 1851 Tejon treaty with the United States, a treaty the U.S. Senate would refuse to ratify. See chapter 4. The third testimonial witness was Secundino, who was born in the Serrano village of Chibuna. Secundino's mother and maternal grandmother were members of the lineage at Cuecchao, a Tataviam-speaking community. Other witnesses were Thomas, the sacristan who looked after the sacred objects at the mission, and Pedro Joaquin, first alcalde at the mission in

1843. The elderly Thomas came from Momonga, a village located due west of the mission, en route to the Chumash villages of Simi and Tapuu. Because it was on the border between the territories of Tataviam and Chumash lineages, it probably had speakers of both languages. Pedro Joaquin's father came from Sanja, a village adjacent to the mission, and his mother was from Tapuu, the Chumash village that was home to Tiburcio Cayo, the bride's influential grandfather on her mother's side. In fact, Pedro Joaquin was the bride's uncle, the widower of her father's sister. Thomas, Pedro Joaquin, and Cosme, the groom's father, were among the owners of the square league of mission land granted to the Indians in 1843, the same land that Pio Pico wrenched away from them less than three years later.

5. See chapter 3.
6. See chapters 3 and 4.
7. See chapter 4.
8. Note that the term Fernandeño is also used in this book to refer to a language dialect spoken among some of the lineages that were brought to San Fernando Mission. We observe the usage by linguists as well as the Spanish understanding of the word as a place-name. As we explain later in this chapter and in chapter 7, these usages are not the same. For further explanation of this term, see the glossary.
9. 25 U.S.C. §§ 2701–21.
10. See chapter 5.
11. See chapter 1.
12. See chapter 2.
13. See chapters 5–7. As historian James Sandos has observed, the mission experience was not uniform throughout California. Most Indian societies in the San Francisco Bay Area, he contends, "were overwhelmed by the mission experience and lost touch with their old culture quickly. . . . In southern California, the home of the Toloache Cults, Indians proved more resilient. Southern California Indians continued as much of their pre-contact religion and culture as they could throughout the life of the missions and beyond, just outside of the view of missionaries and other outsiders." Sandos, *Converting California*, 181. See also Haas, *Conquests and Historical Identities*, 26: "Although the Spaniards went far toward regulating outward behavior by imposing regimented time in the workplace and spatial confinement, in the end they were unable to eradicate all preconquest traditions, material culture, and historical, religious, and practical knowledge."
14. See appendix C for charts showing ancestors and descendants of these progenitors.

15. An intellectual history of social action theory includes: Alexander, *Theoretical Logic*; Parsons, *Societies*; Weber, *Protestant Ethic*; Hegel, *Philosophy of History*.
16. See Parsons, *Societies*.
17. See, e.g., Jackson and Castillo, *Indians, Franciscans, and Spanish Colonization*; Sandos, "Between Crucifix and Lance," 196–213.
18. E.g., Panich and Schniede, *Indigenous Landscapes*, 5–24; Lee M. Panich, *Narratives of Persistence*, 9, 11, 177–78.
19. See Panich, "Mission Archaeology in North America," 4955–60 (pointing to continuities among Mission Indians in use of ceramic and stone tool technologies and habitation in traditional structures). Archaeologists sometimes try to infer changes in social and political organization from burials or other material culture indicators. See, e.g., Panich, "Indigenous Vaqueros," 196.
20. See, e.g., Lightfoot, *Indians, Missionaries, and Merchants*, 72–73; Hackel, "Staff of Leadership," 366, 376. Lightfoot only goes so far as to say that in some cases "the traditional and the new social hierarchies operated side-by-side." Hackel, 372.
21. See, e.g., Johnson, "Indians of Mission San Fernando," 252, 260 (characterizing mission as a melting pot); Monroy, *Thrown Among Strangers*, 128: "Once the missions were gone, they had little left of either their original cultural ways or the new discipline that made them social beings." See also R. L. Hoover, "Spanish-Native Interaction," 395–406 (arguing that Indians acting as mission officials eventually supplanted traditional lineage leaders). Lisbeth Haas presents a somewhat contradictory account regarding the persistence of distinct and autonomous lineages. She suggests, on the one hand, that Indian alcaldes, appointed by Mexican authorities, displaced traditional captains as legitimate leaders among the Indians (p. 41), but she also acknowledges that "after their emancipation," many Indians from San Juan Capistrano Mission "returned to their former villages near San Juan" (p. 43) in *Conquests and Historical Identities*. Haas refers to the Indians subsequently by the collective term Juaneños and does not differentiate them by lineage or village affiliation. San Juan Capistrano is the only California mission from which a Mexican pueblo was created (p. 54). The existence of the pueblo political formation seems to be (contrary to our view) equated with the loss of separate lineage political identities and loyalties. See, e.g., *Conquests and Historical Identities*, 63. For a contrasting view, see chapters 2 and 3.
22. Sandos, "Between Crucifix and Lance," 204.
23. Governor Gavin Newsom, Executive Order N-15–19 (June 18, 2019).

CHAPTER 1

1. Kroeber, *Nature of Land-Holding Groups,* A. L. Kroeber Papers, 1869–1972, BANC 2049, 5, 9, Reel 152; Kroeber, "Statement of Native Land Use," A. L. Kroeber Papers, 1869–1972, BANC 2049, 1951, 1–24, Reel 151. That label has not achieved wide usage, however.
2. Kroeber, *Nature of Land-Holding Groups,* 1; Kroeber, "Minutes and Report Given by A. L. Kroeber to Commonwealth Club of California," A. L. Kroeber Papers, 1869–1972, BANC 2049, 436–37, Reel 70.
3. Hyslop, *Contest for California*, 43–44.
4. Kroeber, *Nature of Land-Holding Groups,* 1; Kroeber, "Minutes and Report Given by A. L. Kroeber to Commonwealth Club of California," 436–37; Kroeber, "Statement of Native Land Use," 9–11, 14–15, 22, 36; Driver, *Excerpts from the Writings of A. L. Kroeber on Land Use and Political Organization of California Indians*, A. L. Kroeber Papers, 1869–1972, BANC 2049, 1953, 35, 82; Pauley and Pauley, *San Fernando Rey De Espana*, 25–27.
5. See also Bean, "Social Organization in Native California," 99–124; Bean, "Introduction," xiv–ix; Phillips, *Chiefs and Challengers*, 8–10, 348–49n22.
6. Thus, for example, the village called Cahuenga was the home of the lineage called Cabuepet. See text at notes 16–18, *infra*.
7. Engelhardt, *Missions*, 2:623.
8. Heizer, *Hugo Reid's Letters*, 9.
9. Heizer, 9; Preston, "Serpent in Eden," 2–37; Preston, "Portents of Plague," 69–121.
10. Librado, *Eye of the Flute*, 90, 117.
11. Bean, *Mukat's People*, 89–97.
12. Heizer, *Hugo Reid's Letters*, 15–17.
13. Heizer, 7–9; Kroeber, *Nature of Land-Holding Groups*, 8–9.
14. Heizer, *Hugo Reid's Letters*, 7–9.
15. "Tribes do not exist in California in the sense in which the word is properly applicable to the greater part of the North American Continent." Driver, *Excerpts from the Writings of A. L. Kroeber*, 11, 18. A. L. Kroeber states the following:

> The proposition is herewith submitted that more often than not in native North America the land-owning and sovereign political society was not what we usually call "the tribe," but smaller units. . . . What was generally denominated tribes really are small nationalities, possessing essentially uniform speech and customs and therefore an accompanying sense of likeness and like-mindedness,

which in turn tend to prevent serious dissensions or internal conflicts. The genuinely political units were smaller units—corresponding rather to what is customary to loosely called "bands" or "villages." These were de facto self-governing and it was they that each owned a particular territory, rather that the nationality owned the overall territory. Ordinarily, the nationality, miscalled tribe, was only an aggregate of miniature sovereign states normally friendly to one another.

Kroeber, *Nature of Land-Holding Groups*, 1–5, 13–14.

16. Heizer, *Hugo Reid's Letters*, 7–9, 108n7. See also J. P. Harrington's Field Notes Fernandeño, 2, 7–8, 14, 18, 21, 29, 32, 44, Reel 106 (Davis, CA: UC Davis Native American Language Center).
17. Heizer, *Hugo Reid's Letters*, 7–8, 15; Strong, *Aboriginal Society in Southern California*, 14.
18. Richard Reyes, as told by Sally Ortega, "Customs" (collected 1962), Fernandeño Tataviam Tribal Offices, San Fernando, CA, 9; Munro, "Topanga, Cahuenga and Tujunga—sounds from a rediscovered local language," available at http://newsroom.ucla.edu/stories/topanga-cahuenga-and-tujunga-sounds-from-a-rediscovered-local-language (visited October 15, 2019).
19. Heizer, *Hugo Reid's Letters*, 9.
20. Engelhardt, *Missions*, 2:236.
21. Heizer, *Hugo Reid's Letters*, 16–17. See also Hudson, "Rare Account," 356–61; Librado, *Breath of the Sun*, 38.
22. "Los Angeles County Indians: Letter No. IV," *Los Angeles Star*; "Los Angeles County Indians: Letter No. V2I, Births and Burials," *Los Angeles Star*; Bean and Smith, "Gabrielino," 544.
23. Weber, "Politics as a Vocation," 77–128.
24. Heizer, *Hugo Reid's Letters*, 15–17.
25. Merriam, *Studies of California Indians*, 78–80.
26. King, "Japchibit Ethnohistory," 26–31; King, "Ethnographic Overview," 46–47.
27. King, "Ethnographic Overview," 46–47.
28. King, 47. Nu was a name equivalent to Net among the Cahuilla, Nota among the Luiseño, and similar to Kika among the Serrano. Nu was used by the Serrano, Tataviam, and western Gabrieleño speakers.
29. King, 47.
30. SFR Baptisms #00223, #00151, #0149, #0016. See also SFR Baptism #00383 and SFR Baptism #0092.
31. SFR Burial #0023 and SFR Burial #0001.

32. King, "Japchibit Ethnohistory," 28–38.
33. SFR Baptism #00702.
34. SFR Baptism #00687; King, "Japchibit Ethnohistory," 47.
35. Kroeber, "Statement of Native Land Use," 36; Driver, *Excerpts From the Writings of A. L. Kroeber*, 13–14.
36. Kroeber, "Statement of Native Land Use," 33–36; Gunther, *Ambiguous Justice*, 69. See also Heizer, *Hugo Reid's Letters*, 15–17.
37. See SFR Baptisms #00573, #00277, #00200, #00591, #01370, #01637, #01364, #00615, #00944, #00927, revealing how chiefs of Cabuepet, Tujubit, and Siutcabit were engaged in arranging marriages to foster mutual ties and relations among the leading families within several independent Fernandeño-speaking villages.
38. Weber, "Politics as a Vocation," 77–128.
39. Richard Reyes, as told by Sally Ortega, "Customs," FTBMI Archive Doc. 91007. FTO, at 1.
40. Heizer, *Hugo Reid's Letters*, 15–17.
41. Gunther, *Ambiguous Justice*, 69. See also Heizer, *Hugo Reid's Letters*, 15–17.
42. Heizer, *Hugo Reid's Letters*, 15–17.
43. Heizer, 37–38, 126n82.
44. Kroeber, *Nature of Land-Holding Groups*, 15.
45. Kroeber, *Nature of Land-Holding Groups*, 44–46.
46. Driver, *Excerpts from the Writings of A. L. Kroeber*, 112; Kroeber, *Nature of Land-Holding Groups*, 3–8, 13. Kroeber says the following at page 13:

> The total drift is this. The more we review aboriginal America, the less certain does any consistently recurring phenomenon become that matches with our usual conventional concept of tribe; and the more largely does this concept appear to be a white man's creation of convenience for talking about Indians, negotiating with them, administering them—and finally impressed upon their own thinking by our sheer weight. It cannot yet be fairly affirmed that the current concept of tribe is wholly that. But it is certainly is that in great part; and the time may have to come to examine whether it is not overwhelmingly such construct. The larger nationalities, ethnic but non-political, are sure. So are smaller units, whether they are called villages, bands, towns, tribelets, lineages, or something else—and they no doubt varied regionally in kind and function. On the whole, it was these smaller communities that were independent, sovereign, and held and used a territory. The tribe is the least defined and the least certain in the chain of native socio-political units.

See also Kroeber, "Statement to Indian Board of Co-Operation," University of California, Berkeley, Department of Anthropology, CU-23, Box 76, Folder: Indian Board of Co-Operation, July 13, 1920.

47. Smith, *This Land Was Ours*, 22. Strong, *Aboriginal Society in Southern California*, 56–57.
48. Kroeber, "Statement of Native Land Use," 14–15.
49. Phillips, *Chiefs and Challengers*, 9.
50. Chester King has done extensive empirical work on regional ties and intermarriages in the San Fernando Mission area. For a map, see King, "Ethnographic Overview," 58. For a discussion of marriage and other ties within the San Fernando Mission area according to the mission record, see King, 58–94.
51. Heizer, *Hugo Reid's Letters*, 7–10, 15–17.
52. Heizer, 101.
53. Librado, *Breath of the Sun*, 38.
54. Trafzer, *People of San Manuel*, 20–22; Librado, *Breath of the Sun*, 37–39 (Jose Sebastian *Naiyait*).
55. Richard Reyes, as told by Sally Ortega, "Customs," FTBMI Archive Doc. 9, 2.
56. Reyes, 3–4, 13; Carpenter, "Rancho Encino," 2.
57. Heizer, *Hugo Reid's Letters*, 43–44; Richard Reyes, as told by Sally Ortega, "Customs," 91007.FTO, 2.
58. Driver, *Excerpts from the Writings of A. L. Kroeber*, 11. A. L. Kroeber explains the following:

> In 1929 Strong published a large volume on aboriginal society in southern California. This intensive and large-scale work confirmed and extended Gifford's observations. It established that where the clans had been little disturbed by removal to the Missions or by American settlement, as among the Desert Cahuilla, they were what are now called patrilineages, that is to say, groups of people who were related by descent in the male line and lived together. Strong established also that these groups were land owning in the sense they had first rights to food products in certain territories which were theirs by tradition and heredity. He further showed that the chief was the religious head of this group in virtue of guarding an inherited package or bundle of ceremonial paraphenalia. Where Caucasian influence had been delayed or remote, as in the desert, these religious lineage heads were the only chiefs: there was no evidence in native times of subordination of several lineages under one chief or into any larger controlling group. Nearer the coast, in more fertile land, but where the Indians had been missionized, several lineages might inhabit the same settle-

ment or village, although the lineages tended to retain, as lineages, food gathering rights over certain tracts. (Strong, *Aboriginal Society*, 26.)

59. Driver, *Excerpts from the Writings of A. L. Kroeber*, 11; Strong, *Aboriginal Society*, 342–43.
60. See, e.g., Champagne, "Cultural and Institutional Foundations," 25–65; Trafzer, *People of San Manuel*, 16–23.
61. See, e.g., Johnston, *California's Gabrielino Indians*, 26, 40, 43–50, 55, 140.
62. Father Pedro Muñoz and Joaquin Pasqual Nuez, *Respuesta*, Mission San Fernando Rey, February 3, 1814, Number 31, translated in Engelhardt, *San Fernando Rey*, 26–33.
63. McCawley, *First Angelinos*, 95. See also Bean, *Mukat's People*, 113–14; Hudson and Underhay, *Crystals in the Sky*, 29; Hudson and Blackburn, "Integration of Myth," 231, 238, 242–43.
64. McCawley, *First Angelinos*, 96.
65. McCawley, 95–96.
66. McCawley, 94.
67. Librado, *Breath of the Sun*, 37–39 (Jose Sebastian *Naiyait*).
68. Harrington, Kitanemuk Notes, informant Eugenia (Javar-Dead Anniversary at Piru, Saticoy, and SFR) 2, 7–8; Heizer, *Hugo Reid's Letters*, 21, 41.
69. Heizer, *Hugo Reid's Letters*, 16; Strong, *Aboriginal Society*, 37–39.
70. Richard Reyes, as told by Sally Ortega, "Customs," FTBMI Archive Doc. 91007. FTO, 1.
71. A drink made from chia seeds was also prepared in a similar way. Reyes, 3–4, 13.
72. Dubois, "Religious Ceremonies," 620–29; Blackburn, "Ethnohistoric Descriptions," 34; Blackburn and Bean, "Kitanemuk," 565–66.
73. Danchevskaya, "Concept of Soul," 90–91; Anderson, *Kuta Teachings*, 7–8, 12–13.
74. Blackburn, *December's Child*, 34, 97.
75. For the different creation stories see: RayBourn, "'The People' in the Beginning," 61–68; Kroeber, "Two Myths," 309–21.
76. Milles and Slobodin, *Amerindian Rebirth*.
77. Anderson, *Kuta Teachings*, 9.
78. Blackburn, *December's Child*, 98–100; Anderson, *Kuta Teachings*, 13–32.
79. Anderson, *Kuta Teachings*, 9, 12.
80. Anderson, 12.
81. Anderson, *Fox Jumps*, 9–11.
82. Blackburn, *December's Child*, 97–101; Anderson, *Fox Jumps*, 9.
83. Anderson, *Kuta Teachings*, 45; Blackburn, *December's Child*, 31, 95–96.

84. Anderson, *Fox Jumps*, 9–11.
85. Librado, *Breath of the Sun*, 38 (Jose Sebastian *Naiyait*); Anderson, *Kuta Teachings*, 13.
86. Anderson, *Kuta Teachings*, 13; Anderson, *Circle Within the Abyss*, 34.
87. Heizer, "Mythology," 656–57.
88. Anderson, *Kuta Teachings*, 9.
89. See Sanger, *When the Animals Were People*, 16.
90. Eugenia, "Five Brothers and One Sister," John Harrington Collection, National Museum of Natural History, National Anthropological Archives, MF No. 3, Reel 99, Frames 669–72; Reel 100, Frames 274–75, 300–301.
91. Trafzer, *People of San Manuel*, 18–19.
92. Trafzer, 34.
93. Richard Reyes, as told by Sally Ortega, "Customs," FTBMI Archive Doc. 91007. FTO, 10.
94. Reyes, 10.
95. Engelhardt, *San Fernando Rey*, 32.
96. Eugenia, "Five Brothers and One Sister," Frames 274–75; Eugenia, "Five Levels to the World," John Harrington Collection, National Museum of Natural History, National Anthropological Archives, MF No. 3, Reel 100, Frame 287.
97. Eugenia, "Two Worlds: Dead and Living," John Harrington Collection, National Museum of Natural History, National Anthropological Archives, MF No. 3, Reel 100, Frames 275–76; Eugenia, "Five Levels," Frame 276.
98. Eugenia, "Two Worlds," Frame 287.
99. Eugenia, "Two Worlds," Frame 287.
100. Eugenia, "Fiesta for the Dead," John Harrington Collection, National Museum of Natural History, National Anthropological Archives, MF No. 3, Reel 100, Frames 269–73, 307–12.
101. Bean and Vane, "Cults and Their Transformation," 668; Strong, *Aboriginal Society*, 30–31, 81–83, 116–17, 172–77, 297.
102. "The people of Mission San Gabriel, Gabrieleño referred to the Fernandeño as *Pavasikwar*, which exemplifies the separate native identities association with the two post-mission era names. Additionally, the Fernandeño referred to the Gabrieleño inhabiting the areas further east of the Los Angeles Basin as *Komivitam*, or the people in the eastern portion San Gabriel Valley, which further established a line between the two mission associated regional terminologies." SCVHistory, available at https://scvhistory.com/scvhistory/ftbmi_ethnohistory 2016.pdf (visited July 30, 2019).
103. Heizer, *Hugo Reid's Letters*, 19.

104. Heizer, 19.
105. Heizer, 19.
106. Heizer, 19–20.
107. Heizer, 53.
108. Heizer, 52–54.
109. Heizer, 36; see also Librado, *Breath of the Sun*, 37–39 (Jose Sebastian *Naiyait*).
110. Heizer, *Hugo Reid's Letters*, 51.
111. Heizer, 64–65.
112. Heizer, 64–68.
113. Bean and Vane, "Cults and Their Transformation," 668.
114. Engelhardt, *Missions*, 2:237.
115. Engelhardt, 237.
116. Blackburn, *December's Child*, 72.
117. Blackburn, 72.
118. Engelhardt, *Missions and Missionaries*, 2:237–39. See also comments by A. L. Kroeber in Heizer, *Hugo Reid's Letters*, 130–31.
119. Blackburn, *December's Child*, 103.
120. See SFR Baptism #1320. Tiburcia's birth year is given in the mission record as 1744, but her son, Tiburcio, was born in 1793, which would have made Tiburcia forty-nine years old when she had him, which seems biologically doubtful. For adult baptisms, the neophytes did not have exact ages but rather the age of a new member of the mission was estimated. Consequently, we estimate Tiburcia's age a decade younger.
121. See chapter 2.
122. SFR Baptism #0320.
123. SFR Baptism #00226.
124. SFR Baptism #00235, SFR Burial #00080, SFR Baptisms #00317, #00070, #00217. See also Family Chart for Antonio Maria Ortega, on file at Fernandeño Tataviam Band of Mission Indians Tribal Offices, San Fernando, CA.
125. See chapter 2.
126. See chapter 2.
127. See notes 15–16 and accompanying text in the introduction.

CHAPTER 2

1. Spanish theologians such as Franciscus de Victoria, who denied the pope's temporal authority, still acknowledged that the pope could allocate to specific nations the power to carry out his spiritual responsibility of conversion and

salvation and the exercise of any necessarily associated temporal powers. De Vitoria, "First Relectio," 284.

2. De Vitoria, 285.
3. See generally Banner, *How the Indians Lost Their Land.*
4. Decree of King Phillip V, September 15, 1713, quoted in Engelhardt, *Missions,* 2:517–18.
5. Engelhardt, *Missions,* 3:38, appendix G.
6. Engelhardt, 38, appendix G.
7. Temple, "Toypurina," 136–52; Hackel, "Sources of Rebellion," 649.
8. Frith, "Rebellion," 14.
9. Hackel, *Children of Coyote,* 262–63.
10. Sandos, "Social Control," 262–64. See San Gabriel Mission Baptism #1408, San Carlos Mission Marriage Register #387, and Mission San Juan Bautisto Burial Record #27.
11. Guest, *Fermin Francisco Lasuén,* 65, 67, 121, 207.
12. Engelhardt, *Missions,* 2:541.
13. Branciforte to Lasuén on election of alcaldes, Santa Bárbara Mission Archive-Library. Orizaba. 12/20/1797. Spanish. 4 pp. Lasuén's reply, San Buenaventura, April 3, 1798. CMD (California Mission Documents) 348; Engelhardt, *Missions,* 2:540–42.
14. Hyslop, *Contest for California,* 100–101.
15. Some of those records, including records for San Fernando Mission, have not survived or never existed.
16. Phillips, *Chiefs and Challengers,* 47. See also Phillips, 54–77; Engelhardt, *Missions,* 3:113–15; Hyslop, *Contest for California,* 117.
17. Hackel, *Children of Coyote,* 229–52.
18. Fr. Lasuén, "Circular Letter of Lasuén to the missionaries from Soledad to San Diego and alcaldes and regidores," November 2, 1796, CMD 285, Santa Bárbara Mission Archive-Library (Spanish); Engelhardt, *Missions,* 2:540–41.
19. Fr. Lasuén to Fr. Guardian Gasol, June 16, 1802, CMD 532, Santa Bárbara Mission Archive-Library; Viceroy Jose de Iturrigaray to Governor, Arrillaga, April 30, 1803, CMD 575, Santa Bárbara Mission Archive-Library; Engelhardt, *Missions,* 2:584–90.
20. Fr. Lasuén to Lull, "Respuesta," June 16, 1801, CMD 510, Santa Bárbara Mission Archive-Library; Engelhardt, *Missions,* 2:567.
21. Engelhardt, *Missions,* 2:586–87; Fr. Lasuén to Fr. Guardian Gasol, June 16, 1802 in Santa Clara, CMD 532, Santa Bárbara Mission Archive-Library.

22. Fr. Lasuén, "Informe Bienal," February 21, 1803, quoted in Engelhardt, *Missions*, 2:595.
23. The terms for *village* and *lineage* or *clan* are largely interchangeable. See chapter 1, text at notes 2–6.
24. Johnson, "Indians of Mission San Fernando," 252.
25. Harrington writes, "In the text the term [Fernandeño] refers to a linguistic and cultural subdivision of the Gabrieleño occupying the coast from Malibu to just north of Santa Monica and inland San Fernando Valley." Librado, *Eye of the Flute*, 90, 117. See also Kroeber's 1925 linguistic map of California Indian languages, which is not to be confused with tribal territories or tribal political entities. Available at http://cla.berkeley.edu/language-maps.php (visited July 3, 2019). The linguistic names of Gabrieleño and Fernandeño were introduced by anthropologist John Harrington in the early twentieth century. We use the linguistic group names adopted by Harrington, for simplicity and clarity. However, the Indians themselves did not until the twentieth century use anthropological linguistic names, and they did not use such names to designate collective political or cultural entities throughout the region.
26. Librado, *Eye of the Flute*, appendix C, 142–43; Johnson, "Indians of Mission San Fernando," 251–55; Kroeber, "Mission Record"; Pauley and Pauley, *San Fernando Rey De Espana*, 27.
27. Fr. Pedro Muñoz and Fr. Joaquin Pasqual Nuez, *Respuesta* (Alta California, San Fernando Mission, 1814), Item 31; Engelhardt, *San Fernando Rey*, 33.
28. Schuetz-Miller, "Biofile of Building Artisans," 1–107.
29. For descriptions of life at the missions and the organization of production, see Costo and Costo, *Missions of California*; Lightfoot, *Indians, Missionaries, and Merchants*; Fray Juan Cortés and Fray Tapis to Fr. Lasuén, Santa Barbara, October 10, 1800, CMD 497, Santa Bárbara Mission Archive-Library; Fr. Lasuén to Lull, "answering the charges of Horra" San Carlos, June 19, 1801, CMD 510, Santa Bárbara Mission Archive-Library; Engelhardt, *Missions*, 2:552–98.
30. Engelhardt, *San Fernando Rey*, 30–32.
31. See, e.g., Tochonabit recorded in SFR Baptisms #00223, #00149, and #00151. See also appendix A.
32. Translated in Engelhardt, *Missions*, 3:95–97: "Two Decrees of the Spanish Cortés concerning Indians and Secularization: 1/5/1811–9/13/1813," CMD 959, Santa Bárbara Mission Archive-Library.
33. Engelhardt, 95–97.
34. Engelhardt, *San Fernando Rey*, 33.
35. Engelhardt, 33.

36. Engelhardt, 30
37. Engelhardt, 32.
38. Engelhardt, 33.
39. Engelhardt, 28–29.
40. Muñoz and Nuez, *Respuesta*; Engelhardt, *San Fernando Rey*, 30–33.
41. Hackel, "The Staff of Leadership," 366, 376; Hackel, *Children of Coyote*, 229–52. Historian Steven Hackel has observed that another historian (referencing Phillips, *Chiefs and Challengers*) "has downplayed the role of the missionaries in appointing alcaldes, claiming instead their legitimacy came from kinship and lineage networks." Hackel, "Staff of Leadership," 347n115.
42. Costo and Costo, *Missions of California*; Lightfoot, *Indians, Missionaries, and Merchants*; Engelhardt, *San Fernando Rey*, 30.
43. Engelhardt, *Missions*, 3:119.
44. Fr. Payéras, "Memorial," June 18, 1821, CMD 2161, Santa Bárbara Mission Archive-Library; Engelhardt, *Missions*, 3:120.
45. Solá to Fr. Payéras, July 10, 1821, translated and quoted in Engelhardt, *Missions*, 3:104.
46. See SFR Baptism #01320.
47. SFR Baptism #00342.
48. SFR Baptism #00226.
49. SFR Baptism #01916.
50. SFR Baptisms #01848 and #02385; Johnson, "Indians of Mission San Fernando," 262.
51. SFR Baptisms #01848, #00171.
52. An obituary for Eugenia described her age as well over one hundred. "Century-Old Native of Kern County Is Called," *Bakersfield Californian*, May 15, 1928, 1, FTBMI Archive Doc. 80947.BC.
53. SFR Baptisms #02987, #00898, #00803, and U.S. Census, San Buenaventura Township (Saticoy), Santa Barbara, California, United States, 1860, M653, 14.
54. Fr. Pedro Muñoz and Fr. Joaquin Pasqual Nucz, *Respuesta* (Alta California, San Fernando Mission, 1814), Item 31; Engelhardt, *San Fernando Rey*, 33.

CHAPTER 3

1. Mexican policies regarding the pace and manner of secularization so often wavered that there was little incentive for Alta Californians to carry out decrees that could soon be annulled. The Mexican government and Catholic Church also had no resources to carry out secularization. Because Spain did not recognize Mexico's declaration of independence, mounting four separate

invasions of Mexican territory in the early years, the Mexican government was occupied with national defense. Later, the war in Texas presented further distraction.

2. Engelhardt, *Missions*, 3:312, 315, 338–44; Fr. Narciso Durán to Mexican president Anastasio Bustamante, Mission San Jose, September 23, 1830, CMD 3294, Santa Bárbara Mission Archive-Library; Beechey, *Narrative of a Voyage*, 12–13.
3. Beechey, *Narrative of a Voyage*, 13.
4. Pio Pico to Mariano Vallejo and others, Port of San Diego, May 15, 1832, CMD 3366, Santa Bárbara Mission Archive-Library.
5. Emancipation Decree of Figueroa, July 15, 1833, Monterey, CMD 3438, Santa Bárbara Mission Archive-Library; Engelhardt, *Missions*, 3:473–76.
6. Few, if any, California Indians became Mexican citizens under the 1834 emancipation proclamation.
7. Jackson and Castillo, *Indians, Franciscans, and Spanish Colonization*, 89–91.
8. Decree of the Mexican congress secularizing the missions, Aug. 17, 1833. A translation of the act can be found in Bancroft, *History of California*, 3:336–37. The law installed parish priests in lieu of the missionaries and allocated a relatively small amount of mission property to church functions.
9. Engelhardt, *Missions*, 3:523–30.
10. Engelhardt, 480–81, 478; Fr. Durán to Governor Figueroa, July 3, 1833, "destitute state of the emancipated Indians," CMD 3436, Santa Bárbara Mission Archive-Library; Fr. Durán to Governor Figueroa, San Gabriel, August 6, 1833, CMD 3443, Santa Bárbara Mission Archive-Library.
11. Bancroft, *History of California*, 3:331–32.
12. Engelhardt, *Missions*, 3:351, 483–84, 491–92, 496–500, 535–36 (citing Bancroft, the California Archives, Hittell, and many other sources).
13. Vallejo Papers, Vol. 31, pt. 1, 109, 111, BANC.
14. Haas, "Emancipation," 16–17.
15. Under U.S. law, at least since Congress affirmed Indians' citizenship in 1924, Indians may maintain and participate in tribal government while enjoying U.S. citizenship. See Newton et al., *Cohen's Handbook*, 1401. Mexican law of the nineteenth century did not allow for that possibility.
16. Dana, *Two Years Before the Mast*, 194–95; Engelhardt, *Missions*, 3:535, 540.
17. Miguel Barragan, interim president of Mexico, November 7, 1835, "on the temporary suspension of secularization as decreed by the Congress, August, 1833," CMD 3580, Santa Bárbara Mission Archive-Library. Barragan, a centrist politician, served as interim president from January 28, 1835, to February 27, 1836. Engelhardt, *Missions*, 4:6.

18. Pio Pico to Mariano Vallejo, Santa Barbara, April 7, 1836, CMD 3601, Santa Bárbara Mission Archive-Library; Engelhardt, *Missions*, 4:18.
19. "These are the lawful property of the neophytes, who have created them with their own hands under the guidance of the missionaries." Fr. Durán to Governor Mariano Chico, Santa Barbara, June 15, 1836, CMD 3605, Santa Bárbara Mission Archive-Library; Engelhardt, *Missions*, 4:23.
20. Engelhardt, *Missions*, 4:17.
21. Coronel, *Tales of Mexican California*, 21.
22. Engelhardt, *Missions*, 4:185.
23. Hartnell, *Diary and Copybook*, 46.
24. See land grant map (diseño) Rancho San Francisco, Natural History Museum of Los Angeles County; Smith, *This Land Was Ours*, vi.; Diseño of Rancho San Francisco, available at https://scvhistory.com/scvhistory/lw2570a.htm, (visited, July 20, 2019).
25. Dakin, *Lives of William Hartnell*, 227–28.
26. Smith, *This Land Was Ours*, 13.
27. A previous effort to grant part of Rancho San Francisco to Francisco Avila had been successfully resisted by the missionaries because the land belonged to San Fernando Mission. See Engelhardt, *San Fernando Rey*, 20; Engelhardt, *Missions*, 4:148; Smith, *This Land Was Ours*, 12–13, 16, 245n26.
28. Smith, *This Land Was Ours*, 19–23.
29. Weber, *Mission in the Valley*, 31–32.
30. SFR Baptisms #02298, #00171, #01848, #02987; John P. Harrington, "Eugenia: Javar," 1–8, Kitanemuk Reel Citations, National Museum of Natural History, National Anthropological Archives MF #3, Reel 100, Frames 269–73, 307–9. For further information about Eugenia, see chapter 2, text at notes 51–52.
31. Weber, *Mission in the Valley*, 32.
32. See chapter 1.
33. There are several other descriptions of the commemoration ceremonies in Southern California. Heizer, *Hugo Reid's Letters*, 19–21, 40–42; Kroeber, *Handbook*, 626–27; Merriam, *Studies of California Indians*, 78–86; Harrington, "Eugenia: Javar," 1–8.
34. Merriam, *Studies of California Indians*, 78–80.
35. Merriam, 78–80.
36. Heizer, *Hugo Reid's Letters*, 101–2.
37. Heizer, 102–3.
38. Heizer, 102.

39. Heizer, 126n86.
40. Heizer, 9.
41. Letter from Garcia Diego to the Mexican government on the needs of the California Missions, Mexico, November 17, 1840, CMD 3794, Santa Bárbara Mission Archive-Library; Engelhardt, *Missions*, 4:206–11.
42. Engelhardt, *Missions*, 4:210–11.
43. For information about his ancestry and lineage ties, see appendix A.
44. SFR Baptisms #02071 (Paula), #02649 (Agueda), #02887 (Gertrudis), #03051 (Francisco Xavier); Santa Barbara Baptism #03604 (Roque); SFR Marriage #00785 (Francisco Papabubaba and Paula).
45. The captains identified by other sources listed among the forty petitioners are: Pedro Joaquin, Emeterio, Camilo, Odon Chihuya, Tanislado (Estanislao), Lanislado (Ladislao), German, Rogerio, Vicente Francisco, and Melchor. See appendix A, "Captains and Lineage Leaders," and appendix B, "List and Analysis of the Forty Petitioners." See also attachments to Letter from Frank D. Lewis to U.S. Commissioner of Indian Affairs, October 17, 1892, Letter No. 37571, RG 75, NA, FTBMI Archive Docs. 80856, 80858, 80859.
46. See appendix A, "Captains and Lineage Leaders"; SFR Baptisms #01519 (Cosme) and #02735 (Benigno). The marriage of Rita and Benigno is described in detail in the introduction.
47. See appendix A, "Captains and Lineage Leaders," and appendix B, "List and Analysis of the Forty Petitioners."
48. Letter from Governor Micheltorena, proclamation of land grant, May 3, 1843, FTBMI Archive Doc. 80867, attached to letter from Frank D. Lewis to Commissioner of Indian Affairs, October 17, 1892, Letter No. 37571, RG 75, NA, FTBMI Archive Doc. 80856. When Governor Pico started to make grants several years later, he did not grant Indians the land in government trust as required by the centuries-old colonial laws. He granted Indians land as private property, although Indians wanted and had always held land in collective ownership. See text at note 53, *infra*.
49. See Salomon, *Pío Pico*, 75–76; Hyslop, *Contest for California*, 338–39.
50. Governor Pico to the deputies, A. Carillo and Ignacio de Valle, giving recommendations to be forwarded to the presidents of the missions, Los Angeles, March 18, 1845, CMD 3943, Santa Bárbara Mission Archive-Library; Governor Pico to Fr. Durán on the need to reform the missions and the status of Indians, Los Angeles, March 18, 1845, CMD 3941, Santa Bárbara Mission Archive-Library; Engelhardt, *Missions*, 4:340–42.

51. Fr. Durán to Governor Pico, answering his letter of March 18 and protesting against the contemplated sale and renting of mission land, Santa Barbara, March 26, 1845, CMD 3945, Santa Bárbara Mission Archive-Library; Engelhardt, *Missions*, 4:347.
52. Engelhardt, *Missions*, 4:446.
53. SFR Baptism #01763; Carpenter, "Rancho Encino," 12–13.
54. See the introduction (providing additional description of the wedding and its attendees).
55. See the introduction. The names of the captains and future captains alive in 1843–45 with their number on the list of captains: Vito (2), Faustino (5), Mateo (6), Domingo (11), Simon? (12), Pedro Jose (14), Pio (16), Tranquillo (17), Apolonio (26), Pastor Cano (48), Bernardo (52), Cacaguama (53), Chori or Cheri (56), Chari (59), Nuur (66), Genuminaban (73), Nuu (78), Tomear (80), Raphael Maria (85), Jose Zapatero (86), Mateo (89), Clemente (92), and Rita (98).
56. Engelhardt, *Missions*, 4:448–49.
57. Engelhardt, 4:448–49.
58. Pico, *Historical Narrative*, 121–22.
59. "Terrible Wrongs," *Los Angeles Herald*, 3.
60. Heizer, *Hugo Reid's Letters*, 101–2.
61. Engelhardt, *Missions*, 4:351, 683.
62. Demetrio Montesdeoca to Governor Pico, protesting against the misuse of mission property, Mexico, November 14, 1845, CMD 4007, Santa Bárbara Mission Archive-Library; Engelhardt, *Missions*, 4:455, 502–6, 771.
63. Salomon, *Pío Pico*, 84.
64. United States v. Workman, 68 U.S. (1 Wall.) 745 765 (1864). The case involved San Gabriel Mission.
65. The confirmation of de Celis's title by the American Board of Land Commissioners is discussed in chapter 4.
66. "Interesting Facts Concerning the Mission San Fernando," *Los Angeles Star*.
67. Engelhardt, *Missions*, 4:505–8.
68. See "Wrongs of Rogerio Rocha," *Los Angeles Herald*, 4.
69. Detailed discussion of the forty petitioners is at text at notes 45–48, *supra*. The group of Fernandeños includes progenitors of the present day Garcia lineage of the Fernandeño Tataviam Band of Mission Indians. One of the progenitors, Leandra's father, Ramon, died during the turmoil over dispossession, in June 1845. See SFR Baptism #00765, SFR Burial #02372.
70. Robinson, *Story of the San Fernando Valley*, 10–12.

71. Engelhardt, *San Gabriel Mission*, 218–24; Engelhardt, *Missions*, 4:485, 486n23.
72. Deposition of Pio Pico, transcript of the proceedings in Case No. 378, Eulogio de Celis v. United States, Case No. 343, United States District Court for the Southern District of California, 6–7, BANC.
73. Quoted in *Workman*, 68 U.S. (1 Wall.), 16–17.
74. Decision of the Board of Land Commissioners, transcript of the proceedings in Case No. 378, Eulogio de Celis v. United States, Case No. 343, United States District Court for the Southern District of California, 27, BANC.
75. *Workman*, 68 U.S. (1 Wall.).
76. Hyslop, *Contest for California*, 395–96; Haas, "War in California," 331–55.
77. Bancroft, *History of California*, 5:277, 561–64; Engelhardt, *San Gabriel Mission*, 220–21.
78. But see United States v. Ritchie, 58 U.S. 525, 538 (1854), suggesting they were considered citizens of Mexico. Governor Figueroa's 1833 provisional regulations allowed only those who had participated at least twelve years in a mission, were married, and had mastered an occupation to petition for emancipation. Few petitioned for emancipation under this process. His 1834 rules didn't specify any assimilation conditions but referred to the emancipated as those who had received land distributions.
79. The records for emancipated Indians at San Fernando Mission and elsewhere are nearly nonexistent. At San Fernando Mission, Odon, a leader at Escorpion, was granted emancipation directly by acting governor Juan Alvarado in 1839. Both Roque and his wife, Agueda, living at Encino, may have been emancipated in the early 1840s.
80. Jorgensen, *San Fernando Valley*, 76–77.
81. See Thompson v. United States, 8 Ind. Cl. Comm. 1, 28 (1959); Wilson, "Indians of Southern California," 24.
82. Bean and Smith, "Gabrielino," 541, table 1; Wilson, "Indians of Southern California," 26–27.
83. See, e.g., Brewer, *Up and Down California*, 44; Wilson, "Indians of Southern California," 24.
84. Mariano Vallejo to Governor Mason, "On Indians, their character. Futile efforts to civilize them," Sonoma, CA, October 20, 1847, CMD 4074, Santa Bárbara Mission Archive-Library.
85. Mariano Vallejo to Governor Mason, "On Indians, their character. Futile efforts to civilize them."
86. Thompson v. United States, 8 Ind. Cl. Comm. 1, 28 (1959); Castillo, "Euro-American Exploration," 105; "Report of Hon. B. D. Wilson," *Los Angeles Star*,

August 8, 1868; Pauley and Pauley, *San Fernando Rey De Espana*, 256; Caughey, "Introduction," xxvi; Wilson, "Indians of Southern California," 24–25; Haas, *Conquests and Historical Identities*, 39; Jorgensen, *San Fernando Valley*, 76; "Manner of Their Treatment," *Los Angeles Times*, 2.

87. Thompson v. United States, 8 Ind. Cl. Comm. 1, 28 (1959).
88. Hansen, *Search for Authority*, 87–88. The town councils of Santa Barbara and Los Angeles asked for a territorial government in the south, hoping for some freedom from property taxation, but they did not prevail.
89. See generally Faracher, *Eternity Street*.
90. See notes 78–79 and accompanying text.
91. Hansen, *Search for Authority*, 122.
92. See Madley, *American Genocide*.
93. *California Senate Journal*, February 11, 1852, 105–6, reprinted in "Indian Tribes of California," Hearings before a Subcommittee of the Committee on Indian Affairs, House of Representatives, 67th Congress, 2nd Session, April 28–29, 1922, 268–72.
94. See chapter 4.

CHAPTER 4

1. Wetmore, *Report of Chas A. Wetmore*, 3.
2. Wetmore, 2.
3. See discussion of captains German and Rogerio in appendix A.
4. The Plan of Iguala, adopted by the revolutionary government of Mexico on February 24, 1821, stated that "all the inhabitants of New Spain, without distinction, whether Europeans, Africans, or Indians, are citizens of this monarchy, with a right to be employed in any post according to their merit and virtues." This statement was incorporated into the Treaty of Cordova, August 24, 1821, between Spain and Mexico, establishing Mexico's independence. The Plan of Iguala was further reaffirmed by decrees of the Mexican Congress in 1822 and 1823. See *United States v. Ritchie*, 58 U.S. 525, 538–39 (1854). For discussion of why these aspirational statements likely did not result in citizenship for mission Indians of Alta California, see chapter 3. Nonetheless, delegates to the California constitutional convention apparently assumed that all Indians were Mexican citizens, based on the 1824 Mexican Constitution and then proceeded to disenfranchise them. See Madley, *American Genocide*, 151. Both the Plan of Iguala and the Treaty of Cordova were annulled by the Mexican Congress on April 23, 1823, in favor of forming a constitutional government. The Mexican Constitution of 1824 did not address Indian citizenship,

which was left to the various state and territorial governments. In Mexican and Spanish California, Indians were not considered "people of reason" and could only gain citizenship through secularization, which included land distributions, formation of Indian pueblo governments, and Indian acceptance of Catholicism. The emancipation proclamation and secularization plans of Governor Figueroa in 1833–34 are discussed in chapter 3 at notes 5–11. The Mexican Constitution of 1824 did not provide for Indian citizenship, especially if the Indians were not Roman Catholic. The Plan of Iguala did not have legal validity for more than nine months in 1822. There was no legal basis for using the Plan of Iguala or the Mexican Constitution of 1824 to imply that Indians had rights to citizenship in Mexico or California, or in the United States. Imagining Indians as citizens in the 1850s made them legally vulnerable and contributed to land dispossessions, as well as denial of the modest protections afforded by centuries-old Spanish and Mexican colonial laws of secularization. See Anna, "Rule of Agustin de Iturbide," 79–80, 82, 107–9.

5. See chapter 3.
6. California Constitution of 1849, art. II, § 1 (superseded by Const. of 1879).
7. Excerpt of letter from Helen Hunt Jackson to the Commissioner of Indian affairs, RG 75, NA, Special Cases, SC-31 (Flat Files), Box #24, Folder SC-31 17276 (1883), FTBMI Archive Doc. 00193.DC; "Report of Honorable B. D. Wilson," *Los Angeles Star*.
8. He [B. D. Wilson] recommended "that the Superintendent be authorized and empowered to gather them together, by force of arms if necessary, and convey them to the Reservation, where they will at least be free from the contaminating influences of whiskey, and where, if they can be induced to labor, they will receive some better compensation than imprisonment in jails and watch-houses. The system pursued towards the Los Angeles Indians, is infinitely worse than the peonage of Mexico; it is slavery in the most aggravated form." Report of J. Ross Browne to the Commissioner of Indian Affairs, RG 75, NA, 1824–1880, M-234, Roll #35, CA Superintendency, FTBMI Archive Doc. 40151D.DC; Bell, *Reminiscences of a Ranger*, 34–36.
9. Johnson v. McIntosh, 21 U.S. 543 (1823).
10. 25 U.S.C. § 177 (2012).
11. Chapter 133, Cal. Stats., April 22, 1850.
12. Heizer, *Eighteen Unratified Treaties*, 4–5.
13. Heizer, California Indians vs. the United States of America.
14. Hoopes and Barbour, "Journal of George W. Barbour," 256.

15. See Ellison, "Federal Indian Policy in California," 125–26.
16. "Interesting Facts," *Los Angeles Star.*
17. Kenny, *Claims of California Indians*; DuBois, *Condition of the Missions Indians*; "Indians Again," *Los Angeles Star*; "Finis," *Los Angeles Star.*
18. Heizer, *Eighteen Unratified Treaties.*
19. An Act to Ascertain and Settle the Private Land Claims in the State of California, 9 Stat. 631 (1851).
20. An Act to Ascertain and Settle the Private Land Claims in the State of California, 9 Stat. 631 (1851) § 15.
21. Possible exceptions are Pauma and Santa Ynez. See Wood, "Trajectory of Indian Country," 40.
22. Wood, 40.
23. See chapter 3.
24. A right of preemption is the right to be offered the property first should the owner decide to dispose of it; it is also referred to as the "Right of First Refusal." See also Garner and Black, *Black's Law Dictionary*, s.v. (Right of Preemption).
25. Barker v. Harvey, 181 U.S. 481 (1901).
26. See Thompson v. United States, 8 Ind. Cls. Comm., Interlocutory Order of July 31, 1959, 1 (1959).
27. Wood, "(Non-)Extinguishment." Without nearly as much detailed support, esteemed anthropologist Florence Shipek made a similar point that the 1851 act "specifically required the [Board of Land Commissioners] to determine Indian claims but did not require the Indians to present their claims." Shipek, *Pushed into the Rocks*, 31.
28. Shortly before the grant to de Celis, Andres Pico, Pio's brother, had leased the Ex-Mission for a period of nine years. See chapter 3. Pio and Andres later purchased interests in the land from de Celis. See *infra*, this chapter.
29. A provision in the grant allowed the Mexican government to reclaim the land upon refund to de Celis of that amount. But no such refund occurred. Transcript of the Proceedings in Case No. 378, Eulogio de Celis v. United States, Case No. 343, United States District Court for the Southern District of California, Decision of the Board of Land Commissioners, 27–28, BANC.
30. Transcript of the Proceedings in Case No. 378, Eulogio de Celis v. United States, Case No. 343, United States District Court for the Southern District of California, Deposition of Pio Pico, 9, BANC.
31. Transcript of the Proceedings in Case No. 378, Eulogio de Celis v. United States, Case No. 343, United States District Court for the Southern District of California, Deposition of Pio Pico, 9, BANC, 26.

32. Transcript of the Proceedings in Case No. 378, Eulogio de Celis v. United States, Case No. 343, United States District Court for the Southern District of California, Deposition of Pio Pico, 9, BANC, 27 (Decision of the Board of Land Commissioners).
33. Transcript of the Proceedings in Case No. 378, Eulogio de Celis v. United States, Case No. 343, United States District Court for the Southern District of California, Deposition of Pio Pico, 9, BANC, 40 (Letter from Attorney General Caleb Cushing to Pacificus Ord, U.S. Attorney for Southern District of California, instructing that appeal will not be pursued). The United States did, however, challenge the survey of the land.
34. Workman, 68 U.S. (1 Wall.) 745 (1863).
35. Workman, 765–66. The court also opined that Governor Pico never had authority to grant the mission land in the first place, including under wartime powers.
36. See Thompson v. Los Angeles Farming & Milling Co., 180 U.S. 72 (1901).
37. Jackson and Kinney, Condition and Needs of the Mission Indians, 35.
38. Hyer, *We Are Not Savages*, 59.
39. Cleland, *Cattle on a Thousand Hills*, 117.
40. Caughey, *Indians of Southern California*, 24–27.
41. Castillo, "Euro-American Exploration," 99–127. Violence against Mexicans was common. One author observed that "on July 5, 1851, a mob of miners in Downieville lynched a Mexican woman who was three months pregnant. . . . Juries would convict greasers on very moderate evidence indeed, and the number of lynchings has never been computed. . . . The practice of lynching Mexicans [by the late 1850s] soon became an outdoor sport in Southern California." Jorgensen, *San Fernando Valley*, 80–81. Many Americans could not tell the difference between a mission Indian and a Mexican, especially if, as was common in the region, the mission Indian spoke Spanish and had a Spanish name.
42. Report of J. Ross Browne to the Commissioner of Indian Affairs, 1824–1880 M-234, Roll #35, CA Superintendency, FTBMI Archive Doc. 40151D.DC; Bell, *Reminiscences of a Ranger*, 34–36; Caughey, "Introduction," xxvi–xxviii; "Report of Honorable B. D. Wilson, (No. VII)," *Los Angeles Star*.
43. Cleland, *Cattle on a Thousand Hills*, 138.
44. Cleland, 138.
45. DeBow, *Seventh Census of the United States*.
46. *San Fernando Mission Indians Around 1880s*, photograph, San Fernando Valley Historical Digital Library, California State University, Northridge; *San Fernando Mission Indians Women Around 1880s*, photograph, San Fernando Valley Historical Digital Library, California State University, Northridge.

47. DuBois, *Condition of the Mission Indians*; Wilson "General Observations"; Jorgensen, *San Fernando Valley*, 76–77.
48. Jackson and Kinney, *Condition and Needs of the Mission Indians*, 5; Harrington, review of *The Mission in the Valley*, 313–15; Bean and Smith, "Gabrielino," *Paper for the Handbook of North American Indians*, (Robert Fleming Heizer Papers, BANC Film 2106, Reel 116/ Frame 541); DuBois, *Condition of the Mission Indian*.
49. Cleland, *Cattle on a Thousand Hills*, 174–75 ("Indian and mestizo villages . . . clustered about the ranchos and abandoned missions").
50. Robinson, *Lawyers of Los Angeles*, 58–59; "Back to Rancho," *Los Angeles Times*, 1.
51. Brewer, *Up and Down California*, 44–45.
52. Castillo, "Euro-American Exploration," 99–127; "Report of Honorable B. D. Wilson," *Los Angeles Star*, July 25, 1868; Pauley and Pauley, *San Fernando Rey De Espana*, 256; Caughey, *Indians of Southern California*, 24–27; Haas, *Conquests and Historical Identities*, 36–39; Jorgensen, *San Fernando Valley*, 76–77; "Manner of Their Treatment," *Los Angeles Times*, 2; Before the Indian Claims Commission Decision. A.L. Kroeber Papers, 1869–1972, BANC 2049, July 31, 1959.
53. Bean and Smith, "Gabrielino"; unsigned review of *The Indians of Southern California in 1852*, by John Walton Caughey, ed., *Southern California Quarterly*, 183–84.
54. Johnson, "Indians of Mission San Fernando," 262–63; Johnson and Earle, "Tataviam Geography and Ethnohistory," 191–214.
55. None of the members of the three lineages from the contemporary Fernandeño Tataviam Band of Mission Indians was party to the Fort Tejon treaty.
56. Latta, *Saga of Rancho El Tejón*, 128–29; Johnson, "Indians of Mission San Fernando," 262. His mother, Paulina, whose Indian name was Yucsuiban, and grandmother, Zenona, both were baptized at San Fernando Mission. Vicente Francisco also had an unbaptized brother, who signed the 1851 treaty at Tejon as Chico, the chief of the Tejon Indian Tribe. Francisco later split his name and gave Vicente to his brother and thereafter he used Francisco and later Francisco Cota. Johnson 262, 285–86.
57. Phillips, "Bringing Them Under Subjection," 36.
58. SFR Baptisms #01916 and #01848.
59. Phillips, "Bringing Them Under Subjection," 120.
60. Johnson, "The Indians of Mission San Fernando," 262–64.
61. Phillips, "Bringing Them Under Subjection," 246–56; Johnson, "The Indians of Mission San Fernando," 265.

62. The website for the Tejon Indian Tribe, https://www.tejonindiantribe.com/our-history/.
63. Latta, *Saga of Rancho El Tejón*, 133.
64. Johnson, "Ethnohistory of the Tejon Indian Tribe"; Wilson, "Indians of Southern California," 4–5, 18–19. Federally recognized since 2012 as the Tejon Indian Tribe of California, the members continue to form a related and friendly community for other historical lineages in the area, including those who now constitute the Fernandeño Tataviam Band of Mission Indians.
65. David Salazar Sr., Stanley Salazar, Rudy Ortega Sr., Rudy Ortega Jr., and Dave Salazar, interview by Gelya Frank, February 22, 2008 (part 1), FTBMI Archive Doc. 80323.INT, 19–20 (Stanley Salazar).
66. Wilson, "Indians of Southern California," 24.
67. For example, Jose Miguel Triunfo and his wife, Maria Rafaela Perfecta Cañedo, were godparents to Urbano Chari and Marcelina's son, Jose Rafael Perfecto. SFR Baptism #03000. Urbano Chari and his son, Manuel, were joint owners of the Escorpion grant and had ancestral ties to Siutcabit, the lineage at Encino, where Maria Rita Alipaz's maternal relatives lived. Conrado Leyva, born to Cabuepet, was the godfather, or *padrino*, to Manuel, son of Urbano Chari, and padrino at the marriage of Francisco Papabubaba and Paula Cayo, the parents of Maria Rita Alipaz. SFR Baptism #02494; SFR Marriage #00765. Conrado Leyva was also a father-in-law to Jose Miguel Triunfo and stepfather to Triunfo's wife, Rafaela. Samuel was born to Chaguayabit and so had blood ties to Francisco Papabubaba and Maria Rita Alipaz, who also had ancestral ties to Chaguayabit. Rogerio Rocha lived on a land grant about two miles northeast of San Fernando Mission, and he had ancestral ties to Tujunga and therefore to Leandra's family, who had maternal ancestral ties to Tujunga. SFR Baptisms #00553 (Conrado Leyva), #00439 (Estefana).
68. See this chapter, *supra*.
69. David Salazar Sr., Stanley Salazar, Rudy Ortega Sr., Rudy Ortega Jr., and Dave Salazar interview (part 1), FTBMI Archive Doc. 80323.INT, 22 (Stanley Salazar); Rudy Ortega Sr., interview by Gelya Frank, February 22, 2008, FTBMI Archive Doc. 80318.INT.
70. David Salazar Sr., Stanley Salazar, Rudy Ortega Sr., Rudy Ortega Jr., and Dave Salazar interview (part 1), FTBMI Archive Doc. 80323.INT, 22 (Stanley Salazar).
71. Rudy Ortega Sr. interview, February 22, 2008, FTBMI Archive Doc. 80318.INT, 21–22. The fact that she later took the surname "Alipaz" suggests she was recognized as a healer. See *infra*.
72. SFR Burial #02393, Francisco's Death Record, Feb 17, 1847.

73. "Brief History of Vicente De La Ossa and Family," Los Encinos State Historic Parks, 4, http://historicparks.org/documents/DeLaOssaHistory.pdf (visited September 12, 2019). Apparently, he had sold a parcel near present-day Burbank, granted to him by the Mexican government, for 1,500 pesos. He paid only 100 pesos for his one-third joint interest in Rancho Encino, which gave him access to the entire property.
74. Record of the case of United States v. Vicente de la Osa et al., available at https://www.bia.gov/sites/bia.gov/files/assets/as-ia/ofa/petition/158_ferntv_CA/web_docs/158_PFWD_1858_USSCDelaOsaVUnitedStatesDocs.pdf (visited June 27, 2019).
75. Los Angeles City and County Census, 1850 (Encino), Schedule I, Page 23, Dwelling 293, Family 293, Dwelling 292, Family 292, Dwelling 294, Family 294, July 1, 1850; Jorgensen, *San Fernando Valley*; "Two Accounts of the Battle of Providencia," Wes Clark, available at http://wesclark.com/am/providencia.html (visited May 13, 2019), which includes an excerpt from Jackson Mayers, *Burbank History* (1975).
76. See discussion, *supra*, of ties between the tribes.
77. *Field Notes on the Fernandeno*, Papers of John Peabody Harrington in the Smithsonian Institution, 1907–1957, Fernandeno, Reel 106, Autry Center Braun Library, Los Angeles, California.
78. Miguel Triunfo's name appears as a cosigner of a deed with his stepson, Yldefonso Triunfo, in 1858. Land Record, Los Angeles County, California, Deed, Book 4, no. 189, Triunfo to Burrows, July 28, 1858.
79. Samuel was born into Chaguayabit and had direct ties to Rita and Francisco Papabubaba, of the same lineage, now called Ortega, within the present-day Fernandeño Tataviam Band of Mission Indians.
80. Norton, "My Ancestors."
81. See *supra*.
82. See SFR Burials #00984 and #01632.
83. See 1850 Census, Los Angeles, CA, Roll M432_35, Pages 22A, 22B, and 33A, Images, 49–51, FTBMI Archive Docs. 80803.USC, 80804.USC, 80805.USC.
84. *Field Notes on the Fernandeno*, Papers of John Peabody Harrington.
85. SFR Baptisms #2089a (Pacifico), #03051 (Francisco Xavier), #02406 (Marcelina Chihuya), #00358 (Urbano Chari).
86. Further information about Rogerio Rocha's ancestry and life can be found in appendix A at notes 65–70.
87. Neither he nor his wife appears on the 1850 census.
88. SFR Baptisms #02639 (Maria Manuela), #00803 (Efren), and #00898 (Nerea); Johnson, *Ethnohistoric Overview*.

89. Cleland, *Cattle on a Thousand Hills*, 130–37, 209.
90. Cleland, 80, 132.
91. For a sense of the devastation, see Cleland, *Cattle on a Thousand Hills*, 80–81, 132. For the census data, see FTBMI Archive Docs. 91181.USC (1860) and 91182. USC (1870).
92. Cleland, *Cattle on a Thousand Hills*, 161–62.
93. Cleland, chapter 11. See also Cleland, 160–83.
94. "Manner of Their Treatment," *Los Angeles Times*, 2.
95. See United States v. Vicente de la Osa, U.S. Supreme Court Record, affidavit of Saturnino Reyes, available at https://www.bia.gov/sites/bia.gov/files/assets/as-ia/ofa/petition/158_ferntv_CA/web_docs/158_PFWD_1858_USSCDelaOsaVUnitedStatesDocs.pdf (visited June 27, 2019).
96. Minutes of the U.S. Supreme Court in *United States v. Vicente De La Osa et al.*, Case No. 288, Microcopy Number 215, Volumes, W–Y, Reel 7, Thursday, March 4, 1864 (dismissing appeal by the United States).
97. Stewart, *Los Encino's Past and Present*, 45–46; "A Brief History of Vicente De La Ossa and Family," Los Encinos State Historic Parks, available at http://historicparks.org/documents/DeLaOssaHistory.pdf (visited June 29, 2019); Jacobs, "Indian Points Out Error," *The Valley Green Sheet and News*.
98. Los Angeles City and County Census, 1860, Schedule 1, Page 29, Dwelling 295, Family 287, July 21, 1860.
99. Fernandeño Tataviam Tribe Red Book: Documentary Support of Submission of Letter of Intent to Office of Federal Acknowledgement, Fernandeño Tataviam Band of Mission Indians, FTBMI Archive Doc. 80301.FTO.
100. Alipaz was likely a Spanish rendering of the Chumash word *Alalxiyepsh*, which means a "good healer who used herbs." These healers were probably also participants in the 'antap ceremonies described in chapter 1. Walker and Hudson, *Chumash Healing*, 55. As the oldest surviving child of Francisco Papabubaba and Paula Cayo, she would have been groomed for leadership. Rita's mother, Paula, came from a recognized line of leaders and healers, and Rita may well have succeeded her in leadership after Paula's death in the early 1850s.
101. Most likely the Indian language was the language of preference for Rita Alipaz. Unlike the practice at American mission schools, the friars at San Fernando Mission did not discourage, or were not successful at discouraging, the everyday use of Indian languages. Many San Fernando Indians learned Spanish and some Latin, although the language of the household may well have been the preferred Indian dialect of the parents or mother.
102. See chapter 6.

103. Considerable evidence confirms that Antonio Maria Ortega is the same person as Jose Rosario, son of Maria Rita. There is a 1969 affidavit from respected genealogist Thomas Workman Temple to that effect, filed in connection with the successful claim made by Antonio Maria's descendants for compensation under the Indian Claims Commission, claim of "Indians of California." There is also evidence from 1860 and 1870 census records showing Antonio Maria as a child in the same household with siblings whose baptismal records show they are children of Maria Rita. The 1870 records show Antonio Maria and brothers Luis and Pablo, by then orphaned, in the extended household of the Lopez family. (There is no later record of Pablo after the 1870 census.) In addition, in a 1924 book about Rancho Tejon, J. J. Lopez, whose father was foreman at the property, recalled, "An expert carreta maker worked for my father for many years. . . . This man was a half-blood Indian and Spaniard named Fernando Ortega. He was born on the Yaqui River in Sonora, Mexico, of a Yaqui mother and a Spanish father . . . Ortega was one of my father's most trusted employees. He has a son, Antonio Maria Ortega, living [1924] in San Fernando. Another son, Luis Ortega, lives in Fresno." Latta, *Saga of Rancho Tejón*, 61.
104. Angela was the sister-in-law of Geronimo Lopez and daughter of Pedro Lopez, mayordomo of San Fernando Mission in the 1830s and 1840s. For a photo of Geronimo and Catalina Lopez, taken late in their lives, see page 123, *supra*.
105. Latta, *Saga of Rancho El Tejón*, 61.
106. Baptismal record for Jose Rosario Ortega, Baptism Register 1826–1864, LPC, FHL Microfilm #0002537, entry 1832, FTBMI Archive Doc. 80004.LPC.
107. See discussion, *infra*.
108. LPC Baptism Book 3:218, FTBMI Archive Doc. 91150.PLC.
109. LA Baptism #01022; Los Angeles City and County Census, 1850 (Encino); U.S. Census for Year 1880, Poso Creek, Kern, California, Roll T9, 1, 454, Page 14, June 16, 1880.
110. U.S. Census for Year 1900, Poso Creek, Kern, California; Roll T623 87, Page #A, June 26, 1880; José Ortiz, Application for enrollment with Indians of the state of California under the Act of May 18, 1928, RG 75, NA, 1928 Application #11171, FTBMI Archive Doc. 80126.DC.
111. Lopez Adobe, "Gerónimo and Catalina López."
112. These transactions and the following quote are from the Porter et al. v. Rinaldi et al. lawsuit, of 1878, Case No. 04713, LAACR, HL.
113. Description as a widow comes from "Los Angeles County, CA, Biographies," http://www.rootsweb.ancestry.com/~cagha/biographies/r/rinaldi-c-r.txt (vis-

ited May 13, 2019), which is said to be from Kathy Sedler, trans., *An Illustrated History of Los Angeles County, California* (Chicago: Lewis Publishing, 1889), 611.

114. *Field Notes on the Fernandeno*, The Papers of John Peabody Harrington; Norton, "My Ancestors." Note that in the suit by Porter et al. v. Geronimo Lopez et al., the answer states that the tract is twenty-seven acres and was granted in a deed from Maria de Los Angeles in 1871. Case No. 04278, LAACR, HL.
115. 1880 U.S. Census, San Fernando, CA, Roll 67, Page 440C, Enumeration District, 035, Image 0581, FTBMI Archive Doc. 80889.USC.
116. Lopez Adobe, "George K. Porter and San Fernando."
117. Soon thereafter, Benjamin Porter bought shares in the property from his cousin, George, and Maclay, and then after the property was divided, took the western section, where the community of Porter Ranch is located.
118. Cleland, *Cattle on a Thousand Hills*, 217–18.
119. George Porter et al. v. C. R. Rinaldi et al., Case No. 04762, LAACR, HL, FTBMI Archive Doc. 80833.USSC.
120. Similar detail can be found in the answers filed in the lawsuit by Porter et al. against Geronimo and Catalina Lopez. George Porter et. al v. Geronimo et al., Case No. 04278, LAACR, HL.
121. Link, *Universal City*, 27.
122. That hotel, known as Pico House, still stands at 430 North Main Street in Los Angeles and is a registered historic landmark. "Pico House," https://en.wikipedia.org/wiki/Pico_House (visited May 13, 2019).
123. A huge swath of land that extended from the Simi Hills in the west to the Burbank city limits in the east . . . and from the crest of the Santa Monica Mountains in the south to Roscoe Boulevard in the north. Masters, "A Tale of Two Isaacs." See also photo of indenture from Pio Pico, http://homestead.pastperfectonline.com/photo/13810DAB-1609-412D-842D-110825234521 (visited September 12, 2019).
124. "Afterwards the said Eulogio F. de Celis, administrator, and the other parties in the partition suit . . . filed their written consent and agreement that judgment might be entered in favor of the said Maria de Los Angeles . . . and said judgment was accordingly duly made and entered by the said court." From the answer. Repeated in the answer by Geronimo Lopez in the suit by Porter et al. against him. Case No. 04278, LAACR, HL.
125. In the Lopez lawsuit, the answer states that when the California Land Claims Act was passed in 1851, "the said Ildefonso & Jose Antonio Triunfo applied to the said Andres and Eulogio deceased for advice and counsel as to what they should do about their land, and thereupon the said Andres and the said Eulogio

advised and counselled them that it was unnecessary for them to present their claim to the land Commission of the United States, stating to them that they, the said Andres and Eulogio set up no claim to the land of the said Triunfos, that it was useless for them—the Triunfos—to go to any expense or trouble in reference to their title, and that they, Eulogio and Andres, would do whatever was necessary to make their title good." George Porter et al. v. Geronimo et al., Case No. 04278, LAACR, HL.

126. "Los Angeles County, CA, Biographies."
127. See discussion of Rogerio Rocha, *supra*.
128. See Barker v. Harvey, 181 U.S. 481 (1901).
129. The United States brought an unsuccessful appeal. Transcript of the Proceedings in Case No. 392, Urbano Odon Manuel et al. v. The United States for the Place Named "Escorpion," BANC; Hoffman, *Reports of Land Cases*, 54. The 1860 census shows Odon, his daughter, Marcelina, and her husband, Urbano Chari, all living in close proximity and with a group of at least two dozen Indians. 1860 Census, Los Angeles, CA, Roll M653_59, p. 513, FTBMI Archive Doc. 80831.USC.
130. See "Wrongs of Rogerio Rocha," *Los Angeles Herald*, 4.
131. Jorgensen, *San Fernando Valley*, 102.
132. King, *Ethnographic Overview*.
133. Porter et al. v. Rinaldi et al. lawsuit, Case No. 04713, LAACR, HL. See discussion of Samuel's grant, *supra*.
134. Rogerio's farm was also a short distance from Colonel Street, which became the long-term residence of Antonio Maria Ortega, son of Maria Rita Alipaz, and his family. "Rocha, San Fernando Heritage Park," *Fernando Tataviam Band of Mission Indians Tribal News*, August 2006.
135. "Roger Rocha's History," *Los Angeles Herald*, 8.
136. Weber, *Mission in the Valley*, chapter 42; "Golden Secret in His Grave," *Los Angeles Times*, A7.
137. For more details on Rogerio Rocha's eviction from the land, see Painter, "Visit to the Mission Indians," 6–7.
138. These individuals were identified in the 1885 eviction suit brought against Rogerio by Maclay and Porter. Letter from C. C. Painter, Re: An Indian named Rogerio Rocha from San Fernando, RG 75, NA, Special Cases, 1821–1907, SC-31 (1876–1886) Box #17; Condition of Indian Affairs, Court Transcript Re: San Fernando Indians. Date: 1887. Information about the houses is from Fernandeño Tataviam, "Rogerio Rocha, San Fernando."
139. Librado, *Breath of the Sun*, 31.

140. Although the place of birth of his mother, Benita Maria Guadalupe, is not noted on her baptism, her brother (Rogerio's uncle) Gervasio, was born four years earlier at Tujunga. SFR Baptisms #00124 and #00312.
141. Applications for enrollment with the Indians of the State of California under the Act of May 18, 1928, RG 75, NA, 1928 Applications: Delia Cooke (Martinez) (#11014), Manuel J. Cooke (#11016); Mary Cooke (#11017); John Valenzuela (#11019). He was very popular in the Fernandeño Tribe and was recognized as captain by both Indians and non-Indians. King, "Japchibit Ethnohistory"; Rudy Ortega Jr., *History: Tribal Chronology*, Email, May 8, 2008, FTBMI Archive Doc. 80006.FTO; "Little Interviews: Straws on the Currents of Public Opinion," 4.
142. Painter, "Condition of Indian Affairs," 82–88; Painter, "Visit to the Mission Indians," 6–7. See also "Terrible Wrongs," *Los Angeles Herald*.
143. See "Rogerio Rocha's Rights," *Los Angeles Herald*, 6.
144. "Statement by Judge Widney," *Los Angeles Times*, 1; Rudy Ortega Jr., *History: Tribal Chronology*, Email, May 8, 2008, FTBMI Archive Doc. 80006.FTO; "Little Interviews: The San Fernando Indians," *Los Angeles Times*, 1; De Celis, "Indians' Side of the Controversy," 4; Widney, "San Fernando Indians," 3; De Celis, "Card of Thanks," 5; "Briefs," *Los Angeles Times*, 4.
145. "Terrible Wrongs," *Los Angeles Herald*, 3.
146. Porter et al. v. John Doe Palo et al., Case No. 04280, filed January 2, 1878, LAACR, HL, FTBMI Archive Doc. 80835.USSC.
147. The exact spelling of this name is difficult to discern from the handwriting.
148. There are no matching Teresas in the mission record, which ends in 1846. However, in the 1860, 1870, and 1880 censuses for Los Angeles, there is a Teresa, who is married to Jesus Ramirez in the 1880 census. See FTBMI Archive Docs. 80958.USC, 80959.USC, 80960.USC. This Teresa is recorded as an Indian in the 1860 and 1870 censuses, and she is recorded among the names of other San Fernando Indians. In the 1860 census, at age five, Teresa is living in the household of Maria, who was thirty-eight. In the 1870 census, Teresa is fourteen, and her name is next to Pablo, age thirty-five. It is possible the Teresa is the child of Pablo Cota, or a younger sibling, but there are no clear records providing verification for that position. Pablo Cota is hard to place, but Francisco Pablo is the only Pablo in the San Fernando Mission record young enough to approach the age of the Pablo in the 1870 census data. Francisco Pablo's mother was Mariana, and so fits the Maria of the 1860 census. In this interpretation, Teresa is the grandchild or child of Maria in the 1860 census. Teresa may have been the younger sister to Francisco Pablo who was age twenty-eight/twenty-nine in

1870. While baptized at San Fernando Mission, the parents of Francisco Pablo are given only as Rufino and Mariana, and both are difficult to trace.

149. "One Who Knows the Record," *Los Angeles Herald*, 7.
150. See "Early Practices," *Los Angeles Herald*, 4.
151. "Manner of Their Treatment," *Los Angeles Times*; S. S. Lawson to E. A. Hayl, Honourable Minister of Indian Affairs, "Re: passage of Bill for Relief of Mission Indians," March 1, 1879, RG 75, NA, Special Cases, 1821–1907, SC-31 (1876–1886), Box #17; "8th Recommendation for appointment of lawyers in Los Angeles in all cases affecting the interests of the Indians," RG 75, NA, Special Cases, 1821–1907, SC-31 (1876–1886), Box #17; Petition Before the Indian Court of Claims, No. 80, 1951, A. L. Kroeber Papers, 1869–1972, BANC 2049. The Fernandeño Mission Indians were nominal Catholics and acquired farming, trade, ranching, and other skills, which distinguished them from non-mission Indians.
152. Castillo, "Euro-American Exploration," 99–127.
153. Letters about Indians in Southern California: San Diego, San Bernardino, and Los Angeles, November 3, 1854, RG 75, NA, Letters Received by the Commissioner of Indian Affairs 1824–1880, M-234, Roll #35, CA Superintendency.
154. Cleland, *Cattle on a Thousand Hills*, 160–83; Jorgensen, *San Fernando Valley*; Robinson, *Lawyers of Los Angeles*, 58–59.
155. "Back to Rancho," *Los Angeles Times*, 1.
156. Federal Indian agent B. D. Wilson reported that "even the sober, industrious, and best skilled among them could earn but little; it having become custom of the country to pay an Indian only half the wages of a white man." Excerpt of letter from Helen Hunt Jackson to the Commissioner of Indian Affairs, RG 75, NA, 1821–1907, Special Cases, SC-31 (Flat Files), Box #24, Folder SC-31 17276 1883; "Report of Hon. Wilson," *Los Angeles Star*.
157. Report of J. Ross Browne to the Commissioner of Indian Affairs, RG 75, NA, 1824–1880, M-234, Roll #35, CA Superintendency, FTBMI Archive Doc. 40151D. DC; Bell, *Reminiscences of a Ranger*; Caughey, *Indians of Southern California*, xxvi–xxviii; "Report of Hon. Wilson to the Superintendent of Indian Affairs," *Los Angeles Star*.
158. U. S. Census, 1880, San Fernando, CA, Roll 67, P. 439B, Enumeration District 35, Image 0581, FTBMI Archive Doc. 80893.USC. The Lopez Adobe is located in the old part of San Fernando near the present-day main business areas at 1100 Pico Street, San Fernando, CA 91340. See also Kathryn Shirley Traba and Kathryn Gonzales, interview by Gelya Frank, April 18, 2008, FTBMI Archive Doc. 80321.INT; Rudy Ortega Sr., interview by Gelya Frank, April 3, 2008, FTBMI Archive Doc. 80318.INT.

159. Leandra, SFR Baptism #02987. See appendix C, "Genealogies of Progenitors."
160. SFR Baptism #00803.
161. SFR Baptism #00898. *Ethnological Data From the Ledger of the BIA Sacramento Office Identified by California Missions*, 1955, A. L. Kroeber Papers, 1869–1972, BANC 2049; SFR Baptisms #02987 and #02908; Sally McLendon and John Johnson, *Cultural Affiliation*, 348.
162. Adding to the confusion is the fact that Leandra was previously married. There is a Jose who married Cecelia, who died. The widower Jose then married Leandra in 1853. The documents suggest that this person is Jose Cupertino, the son of Pedro Antonio Chuyuy and Euqeris, who married Leandra. Jose and Leandra, SBV Marriage #1231, FHL 913170, FTBMI Archive Doc. 91157.SBV; J. P. Harrington, Kitanemuk Reel Citations, National Museum of Natural History, National Anthropological Archives MF #3, Reel 100, Frame 19, FTBMI Archive Doc. 91136.Field Notes; Jose Cupertino, SFR Baptism #02763; Jose Jesus, SBV Baptism #01756, FHL 913170, FTBMI Archive Doc. 91154.SBV. Leandra would have been about thirteen years old. They had two children, both of whom died in 1859. Jose Jesus and Jose Manuel, Santa Buenaventura Mission, Burial #01157 and Burial #01161, FHL 913171, FTBMI Archive Doc. 91153.SBV. By early 1860, Leandra left the marriage with Jose Cupertino, as the 1860 census records her with Jose Juan Leyva, listed at an age too young for him to be Jose Cupertino. Jose Cupertino, SFR Baptism #02763.
163. SFR Baptism #02908.
164. U.S. Census, 1860, San Buenaventura Township, Santa Barbara, California, P. 14, household 73, FHL microfilm 803,065, FTBMI Archive Doc. 80809.USC. The brothers were identical twins, but the census agent probably assumed the brothers were one year apart. Jesus was recorded at age twenty-three.
165. The twins Jose Juan and Jose Jesus did not have recorded godparents.
166. Maria Josefa Leyva was born in San Fernando and baptized at the La Plaza Church in downtown Los Angeles. LPC Baptism Vol. 4, P. 9, Number 53 (April 10, 1865); *Ethnological Data From the Ledger of the BIA Sacramento Office Identified by California Missions*, 1955. A. L. Kroeber Papers, 1869–1972, BANC 2049. Through her life, she used several variants on her given or first name, including Josefina and Josephine. Rudy Ortega Sr. interview, May 9, 2008 (part 1), FTBMI Archive Doc. 80312.INT, 33–35; Josephine Levies, Birth, Residence, 1900, Death 1952; Parents, Spouses and Children, http://trees.ancestry.com/pt/person.aspx?tid=7040146&pid=-1176397259.
167. SFR Baptisms #02068a and #01242.

168. Isidoro was living with his mother, Catalina Leyva Garcia, in San Fernando in 1880 as recorded by the census of that year. *Ethnological Data From the Ledger of the BIA Sacramento Office Identified by California Missions, A. L. Kroeber Papers*, BANC.
169. Frances Garcia Cooke, Application for enrollment with the Indians of the State of California under the Act of May 18, 1928, RG 75, NA, 1928 Applications #11022, FTBMI Archive Doc. 40064.DC.
170. José Ortiz family, Application for enrollment with the Indians of the State of California under the Act of May 18, 1928, RG 75, NA, 1928 Applications #11171, FTBMI Archive Doc. 80126.DC.
171. See discussion of intermarriage between lineages or clans, *supra*.
172. La Plaza Church Baptisms #462 (Petra Garcia), #463 (Cristina Ortega), Baptism Registry, 1826–1864 (Our Lady of Queen of Angels), FTBMI Archive Doc. 80128.LPC.
173. Many of the families and relations at Escorpion and the western San Fernando Valley, generally people descended from Chumash and Fernandeño speakers, tended to move into their own communities, some at San Fernando, and others throughout Los Angeles or Ventura County.
174. There is less published information about political leadership among the families in Ventura and Oxnard during the 1847 to 1885 period.
175. After the American takeover of California, the military government continued to recognize the Mexican political system of alcaldes. Thereafter, Californians moved quickly to replace military rule and the Mexican alcalde form of government. By late December 1849, a working state government was established. The last actions of the government by alcaldes were to monitor the polling for the casting of votes on whether to ratify the proposed constitution. *Official History of California Legislation: Chapter 2, Law and Order*, available at http://www.leginfo.ca.gov/pdf/2011/2011_Cal_Legi_Ch_02.pdf (visited September 16, 2019); Greene, "Alcaldes of California," 26–29. Despite these efforts by the state to eradicate the alcalde system, federal Indian agents in Southern California tried to use the alcalde form of government to manage relations with Indian communities. These efforts to create greater centralization over the management of Southern California Indian affairs were unsuccessful, and abandoned by the 1860s. Because the Indians preferred to manage their affairs through lineages or coalitions of lineages, the alcalde system did not entirely supplant leadership and kinship-based government among those groups. See Phillips, *Chiefs and Challengers*.

176. Robinson, *Story of the San Fernando Valley*, 15–16.
177. "Interesting History of Memory Garden Given by Local Woman," as told by Mrs. J. C. Maclay, *San Fernando Sun*, June 21, 1927, FTBMI Archive Doc. 90148. SFS, 7. See discussion of Rogerio Rocha, *supra*.
178. Lewis et al., *Valley of San Fernando*, 57.
179. See page 131, *supra*.
180. Librado, *Breath of the Sun*, 91.
181. A. L. Kroeber, "Report to Indian Board of Co-operation," July 13, 1920, UCB Department of Anthropology, CU 23, Box 76, Indian Box of Co-operation Folder, FTBMI Archive Doc. 30034.BL, 3.
182. McFarland, "Arrival of Lieut. Beale."

CHAPTER 5

1. These regulations, as amended several times since 1978, can be found at 25 C.F.R. Part 83.
2. See chapter 4.
3. Wetmore, *Report of Chas A. Wetmore*, 6.
4. Wetmore, 5.
5. Wetmore, 17. Wetmore did not, however, advocate full rights and privileges of citizenship for these Indians, such as the right to vote. The later legislation is the Mission Indian Relief Act of 1891, 26 Stat. 712.
6. See Mathes, *Helen Hunt Jackson*, 1–37.
7. "Hon. J. Shirley Ward's Final Report," *Los Angeles Herald*, 10.
8. "Hon. J. Shirley Ward's Final Report," *Los Angeles Herald*, 10.
9. As Julius Seelye, president of Amherst College, wrote in his introduction to Jackson's *Century of Dishonor*, "When the Indian, through wise and Christian treatment, becomes invested with all the rights and duties of citizenship, his special tribal relations will become extinct. This will not be easily nor rapidly done; but all our policy should be shaped toward the gradual loosening of the tribal bond, and the gradual absorption of the Indian families among the masses of our people." Jackson, *Century of Dishonor*, 3.
10. Jackson, *Century of Dishonor*.
11. Mathes, *Helen Hunt Jackson*, 45.
12. Jackson, *Ramona*.
13. Mathes, *Helen Hunt Jackson*, 47.
14. Mathes, 50.
15. Mathes, 52–53.

16. Jackson and Kinney, *Condition and Needs of the Mission Indians*, 11. This recommendation is endorsed, almost verbatim, in Office of Indian Affairs, *Annual Report*, 40.
17. Newton et al., *Cohen's Handbook*, 171–72.
18. Jackson and Kinney, *Condition and Needs of the Mission Indians of California*, 12.
19. In the fall of 1884, Brunson was elected a judge of the Los Angeles Superior Court, a position he occupied from January 1885 to 1887. Once he joined the bench, he ceased service as a special assistant United States attorney. Shuck, *Bench and Bar of California*, 671.
20. Mathes, *Helen Hunt Jackson*, 88.
21. Mathes, 78–79, 87–89.
22. See chapter 4.
23. The circumstances are also described in an affidavit from E. F. De Celis, son and administrator of the estate of his father, Eulogio de Celis: "The Indian Rogerio came to me for protection at the time Maclay et al. were trying to eject him. After hearing his statement, I took him to Col. G. Wiley Wells, who investigated the state of affairs." Painter, "Condition of Indian Affairs," 82.
24. E. F. de Celis to G. Wiley Wells, July 7, 1885, in C. C. Painter Papers, "Refers Letters Regarding an Indian Rogerio Rocha from San Fernando," No. 28392, Case No. 31, HL, FTBMI Archive Doc. 00168.DC.
25. The following proceedings are from *George K. Porter et al. v. John Doe Rogerio et al.*, Case No. 04279, LAACR, HL. The affidavit of G. Wiley Wells in the case can be found at FTBMI Archive Doc. 80834.USSC.
26. The complaint asked for $500 plus $50/month for every month that Rocha and the others occupied the land since Maclay and Porter became owners.
27. Apostol, "Horatio Nelson Rust," 309. At the time of his appointment as Mission Indian agent in 1889, Rust was "secretary of the Los Angeles branch of the Indian Rights Association." Frank and Goldberg, *Defying the Odds*, 335n11.
28. Letter from H. N. Rust to C. C. Painter, Nov. 9, 1885, in C. C. Painter Papers, "Refers Letters Regarding an Indian Rogerio Rocha from San Fernando," No. 28392, Case No. 31, HL, FTBMI Archive Doc. 00168.DC.
29. Quoted by Painter, "Condition of Indian Affairs," 83.
30. "Judge R. M. Widney's Say," *Los Angeles Herald*, 7. Widney also contended that Rogerio had no rights to the land, either from occupation or by virtue of the grant by Governor Micheltorena to the forty petitioners.
31. Horatio Nelson Rust, Notes, "Rugerego of San Fernando," undated, Horatio Nelson Rust Papers, RU 500, HL (reference to 20 or so Indians "scattered").

32. Horatio Nelson Rust, "Indian Affairs, South Pasadena, Notes on the Mission Indians," ca. 1890, RU 497, HL.
33. "The Last of the Mission Indians of San Fernando, a Sad Page of American Pioneer History," 1, Horatio Nelson Rust Papers, manuscript dated October 28, 1903, RU 500, HL.
34. "The Last of the Mission Indians of San Fernando, a Sad Page of American Pioneer History," 5.
35. Newton et al., *Cohen's Handbook*, 135. Such distributions might well run afoul of equal protection guarantees in the U.S. Constitution.
36. From 1886 to 1889, attorney Shirley C. Ward served as the special attorney for the mission Indians. He later recounted to the *Los Angeles Herald* that he had investigated Rocha's claim and had decided that "whatever title he might have had was extinguished forever, and I so reported to the department." "Terrible Wrongs," *Los Angeles Herald*, 3.
37. Lewis was born in 1863. For biographical information, see Larson, "Finding Aid."
38. See *supra*.
39. Dumke, "Boom of the 1880s," 99.
40. Lake Mohonk Conference of Friends of the Indian, *Proceedings*, 80.
41. Byrne v. Alas, 16 P. 523, 528 (Cal. 1888). This decision was later overturned by the U.S. Supreme Court. See Botillier v. Dominguez, 130 U.S. 238 (1889); Barker v. Harvey, 181 U.S. 481 (1901).
42. Lake Mohonk Conference of Friends of the Indian, *Proceedings*, 81–83.
43. U.S. Board of Indian Commissioners. *Twenty-Second Annual Report of the Board of Indian Commissioners*, 188.
44. Attorney General of the United States, *Annual Report 1893*, 142. Similarly, in an April 6, 1892, letter to Lewis from Charles Painter, head of the Indian Rights Association, Painter related that at both the office of the attorney general and the commissioner of Indian affairs in Washington, DC, he had been informed that "it belonged to the duties of [Lewis's] office, without further instruction to take proper steps for the defense of the San Felipe Indians." Frank D. Lewis Papers, Autry Museum, Braun Library, MS 552.
45. See, e.g., Attorney General of the United States, *Annual Report 1897*, 218–20; Attorney General of the United States, *Annual Report 1893*, 142–43.
46. Frank D. Lewis to U.S. Commissioner of Indian Affairs, September 2, 1892, Case No. 31, Letter No. 32822, RG 75, NA.
47. Lake Mohonk Conference of Friends of the Indian, *Proceedings*, 80.
48. U.S. attorney general to Frank D. Lewis, special attorney for mission Indians, April 1, 1892, Frank D. Lewis Papers, Autry Museum, Braun Library, MS 552.

49. Lake Mohonk Conference of Friends of the Indian, *Proceedings*, 110–11 (reprinting the *Report of the Committee on Legal Assistance to the Mission Indians, 1891*).
50. Frank D. Lewis to U.S. Commissioner of Indian Affairs, October 17, 1892, Letter No. 37571, RG 75, NA, FTBMI Archive Doc. 80856.
51. See *supra*.
52. In his letter to the commissioner, Lewis also expressly credits a Mr. J. Alexander Forbes, Keeper of the Mexican Archives in the U.S. Surveyor General's office at San Francisco, who aided his investigations by furnishing deeds from the Mexican era that documented grants to the Indians. These deeds first came to light in 1880. Frank D. Lewis to U.S. Commissioner of Indian Affairs, October 17, 1892, Letter No. 37571, RG 75, NA, FTBMI Archive Doc. 80856. See "Judge R. M. Widney's Say," *Los Angeles Herald*, 7.
53. William F. Stone, Commissioner, Department of the Interior, General Land Office, to Commissioner of Indian Affairs, November 25, 1892, RG 75, NA. In February 1892, a commissioner of the General Land Office had rendered an opinion to several others interested in challenging the de Celis patent, rejecting arguments that the patent was fraudulent and erroneous in designating boundaries for the tract. According to the commissioner, "Notwithstanding the arguments for a suit, I am of the opinion that the case is stale, and that, in view of the failure on the part of the government to have patents to other private land claims in California, vacated by process of law, there is little probability that a chancery suit in the case at bar could be successfully maintained." Thos. H. Carter, Commissioner, Department of the Interior, General Land Office, to Secretary of the Interior, February 19, 1892, RG 75, NA, 6–7. The secretary of the interior received this opinion and concurred that proceedings to annul the patent should not be instituted. John W. Noble, Secretary of the Interior to Commissioner, General Land Office, June 10, 1892, RG 75, NA. However, this particular request to the General Land Office did not raise the question of competing Indian rights, and the Office did not address them.
54. Frank D. Lewis to U.S. Commissioner of Indian Affairs, October 17, 1892, Letter No. 37571, RG 75, NA, FTBMI Archive Doc. 80856. Apparently, the petition to the commission had requested confirmation of only fourteen leagues, but the commission, and later the courts, wound up confirming and patenting to the grantees a tract of over 116,000 acres, or twenty-six square leagues. Frank D. Lewis to U.S. Commissioner of Indian Affairs, October 17, 1892, Letter No. 37571.
55. Frank D. Lewis to U.S. Commissioner of Indian Affairs, October 17, 1892, Letter No. 37571, RG 75, NA, FTBMI Archive Doc. 80856.

56. Frank D. Lewis to U.S. Commissioner of Indian Affairs, October 17, 1892, Letter No. 37571, RG 75, NA, FTBMI Archive Doc. 80856.
57. See chapter 4.
58. Frank D. Lewis to U.S. Commissioner of Indian Affairs, October 17, 1892, Letter No. 37571, RG 75, NA, FTBMI Archive Doc. 80856.
59. Frank D. Lewis to U.S. Commissioner of Indian Affairs, October 17, 1892, Letter No. 37571, RG 75, NA, FTBMI Archive Doc. 80856.
60. Frank D. Lewis to U.S. Commissioner of Indian Affairs, October 17, 1892, Letter No. 37571, RG 75, NA, FTBMI Archive Doc. 80856.
61. Frank D. Lewis to U.S. Commissioner of Indian Affairs, October 17, 1892, Letter No. 37571, RG 75, NA, FTBMI Archive Doc. 80856.
62. Frank D. Lewis to U.S. Commissioner of Indian Affairs, October 17, 1892, Letter No. 37571, RG 75, NA, FTBMI Archive Doc. 80856.
63. Frank D. Lewis to U.S. Commissioner of Indian Affairs, October 17, 1892, Letter No. 37571, RG 75, NA, FTBMI Archive Doc. 80856.
64. The text of that deed is quoted in "Rogerio Rocha's Lands," *Los Angeles Herald*.
65. Frank Lewis, U.S. Special Attorney for Mission Indians to the U.S. Attorney General, March 20, 1896.
66. L. H. Valentine to Frank Lewis, December 3, 1895, Frank D. Lewis Papers, Library of the Southwest Museum, Pasadena, CA, FTBMI Archive Doc. 80838.
67. "Rogerio Rocha's Lands," *Los Angeles Herald*.
68. "Rogerio Rocha's Lands," *Los Angeles Herald*.
69. "Rogerio Rocha's Lands," *Los Angeles Herald*.
70. "Rogerio Rocha's Lands," *Los Angeles Herald*, 5. This story also notes the Special Message that President Grover Cleveland sent to Congress on January 17, 1896, asking Congress to extend the period of time within which the United States could sue to recover lands held under land patents acquired through fraud. "Grover Cleveland, 24th President of the United States: 1893–1897, Special Message, January 17, 1896," The American Presidency Project, accessed May 15, 2019, https://www.presidency.ucsb.edu/documents/special-message-669. According to the *Herald* story, a prominent Los Angeles attorney, Zachariah Montgomery, had recently gone to Washington, DC, petitioning the president to focus on reopening grants erroneously confirmed by the California Land Claims Commission, specifically mentioning the de Celis grant of San Fernando Mission lands—the very lands from which Rocha had been expelled.
71. Lewis's attorney in the libel action against the *Herald* was Shirley C. Ward, his predecessor as special attorney for the mission Indians and, according to a later

story in the paper, "instrumental in the filing of the suit." "Terrible Wrongs," *Los Angeles Herald*, 3.

72. "Action for Libel," *Los Angeles Herald*. The *Herald*'s story noted that it had not identified Lewis as the source of "treachery" and that other attorneys had also represented Rocha before Lewis became involved. During that earlier time, the paper observed, Rocha "was deprived of his property and the unfortunate man's rights languished when others besides Lewis acted in a legal capacity for him. . . . But while previous to the attorneyship of Mr. Lewis, Rocha as the result of either treachery, incompetency, or negligence was dispossessed of his lands in the San Fernando Valley, it was not until Mr. Lewis became the government attorney that his rights to those lands were finally extinguished by a quit claim deed."
73. "Terrible Wrongs" *Los Angeles Herald*, 3.
74. "There Was a Trust Deed," *Los Angeles Herald*, 5; "An Action for Libel," *Los Angeles Herald*.
75. Maria Felicitas was the daughter of Pastor Cano. Valentine was mistaken, because Paster Cano was not among the forty petitioners in 1843. See SFR Baptisms #02068a and #02068 and appendix B, "List and Analysis of the Forty Petitioners."
76. SFR Baptisms #01440, #01597, and #2931.
77. "He Never Had Any Title," *Los Angeles Herald*, 3.
78. "Hon. Frank D. Lewis' Fee," *Los Angeles Herald*.
79. "Hon. Frank D. Lewis' Fee," *Los Angeles Herald*.
80. Frank Lewis, U.S. Special Attorney for Mission Indians, to the Attorney General, March 20, 1896 Frank D. Lewis Papers, Library of the Southwest Museum, Pasadena, California.
81. See chapter 4.
82. Letter from Thos. H. Carter, Commissioner, Department of the Interior, General Land Office, to Secretary of the Interior, February 19, 1892, RG 75, NA, at 6.
83. Mathes, *Helen Hunt Jackson*, 117.
84. This point is strongly suggested in a statement by assistant commissioner of Indian affairs, Edgar B. Merritt, submitted to the House Subcommittee on Indian Affairs in 1922. Referencing the work of C. E. Kelsey, commissioned by the United States to identify lands for California Indians over the first decades of the twentieth century, Merritt stated that it would have been "impracticable to ask Congress to appropriate money to buy developed lands at a thousand

dollars an acre, such as you can buy in California, because we knew in advance that Congress would not give us money for that purpose." "Indian Tribes of California," Hearings before a Subcommittee on Indian Affairs, House of Representatives, 67th Cong. 2d Sess., April 28 and 29, 1922 (Part 2).

85. Lindley and Widney, *California of the South*, 199–200 (quoting an 1883 letter from Helen Hunt Jackson to the Commissioner of Indian Affairs).
86. Frank D. Lewis to U.S. Commissioner of Indian Affairs, October 17, 1892, Letter No. 37571, RG 75, NA, FTBMI Archive Doc. 80856.
87. See chapter 3; Johnson, "Indians of Mission San Fernando," 260. See appendix B, "List and Analysis of the Forty Petitioners."
88. Translated heading of Record of Proceedings attached to Letter from Frank D. Lewis to U.S. Commissioner of Indian Affairs, October 17, 1892, Letter No. 37571, RG 75, NA, FTBMI Archive Doc. 80856.
89. Translated letter from Joaquin, Alcalde of Mission San Fernando to His Excy the General (Governor Micheltorena), April 10, 1843, FTBMI Archive Doc. 80858, attached to Letter from Frank D. Lewis to U.S. Commissioner of Indian Affairs, October 17, 1892, Letter No. 37571, RG 75, NA, FTBMI Archive Doc. 80856.
90. Translated letter from Micheltorena, Governor to Friar Blas Ordaz, May 3, 1843, FTBMI Archive Doc. 80867, attached to Letter from Frank D. Lewis to U.S. Commissioner of Indian Affairs, October 17, 1892, Letter No. 37571, RG 75, NA, FTBMI Archive Doc. 80856.
91. Translated letter from Micheltorena.
92. See chapter 7.
93. See affidavit of deputy sheriffs Will A. Hammel and M. Agiurre, July 30, 1887, quoted in Painter, "Conditions of Affairs," 86–87.
94. Rocha had no surviving children.
95. See chapter 4.
96. "Little Interviews: Straws on the Currents of Public Opinion," *Los Angeles Times*, 4 (Deputy Sheriff Aguirre).
97. "Terrible Wrongs," *Los Angeles Herald*.
98. Translated affidavit of Rogerio Rocha, quoted in Painter, "Conditions of Indian Affairs," 87–88.
99. Horatio Nelson Rust, Notes, "Rugerego of San Fernando," undated, Horatio Nelson Rust Papers, RU 500, HL, 1.
100. See chapter 4.
101. Frank D. Lewis to U.S. Commissioner of Indian Affairs, October 17, 1892, Letter No. 37571, RG 75, NA, FTBMI Archive Doc. 80856.

CHAPTER 6

1. Water and Power Associates, "San Fernando Valley Communities"; Smith, "History of the San Fernando Valley," 154, showing population of 3,281 as of 1910.
2. Jorgensen, *San Fernando Valley*, 115.
3. The population of Los Angeles more than doubled between 1905 and 1915, from two hundred thousand to five hundred thousand, as the Southern California aqueduct brought water from the Owens Valley and electric rail service reached into the San Fernando Valley. Much of the San Fernando Valley, though not the city of San Fernando, was incorporated into Los Angeles in 1915. Jorgenson, *San Fernando Valley*, reprinting "The Rejuvenation of San Fernando," 120–21, 157.
4. Eugenia Mendez, her maternal grandmother, headed a large family in Tejon. 1900 U.S. Census, Township 3, Kern, CA, Roll 87, Page 20A, Enumeration District 0022, FTBMI Archive Doc. 80887.USC.
5. 1920 U.S. Census, Oxnard, CA, Roll T625_154, Page 11B, Enumeration District, 264, Image 202, FTBMI Archive Doc. 80874.USC.
6. 1920 U.S. Census, Soledad, CA, Roll T625_118, Page 5B, Enumeration District 609, Image 10571930, FTBMI Archive Doc. 80877; United States Census, Soledad, CA, Roll 172, Page 5A, Enumeration District 1513, Image 1184.0, FTBMI Archive Doc. 80875.USC.
7. The 1940 census shows Josefa living with husband Isidoro, adjacent to Frances and her family. 1940 U.S. Census, San Fernando, CA, Roll T627_251, Pages 17A and 17B, Enumeration District 19–658, FTBMI Archive Docs. 80876.USC, 80878.USC.A.
8. See Smith, *This Land Was Ours*. See discussion of the Del Valle grant in chapter 3.
9. SCVTC/College of the Canyons Foundation, "Story of Henry Mayo Newhall."
10. Charlie Cooke, Rudy Ortega Sr., and Rudy Ortega Jr., interview by Gelya Frank (part 1), May 27, 2008, FTBMI Archive Doc. 80305.INT, 5 (Charlie Cooke).
11. For a detailed account and photos, see Nichols, *Images of America*.
12. Only the 1906 San Francisco earthquake was worse.
13. Newhall, *Newhall Ranch*, 83–88. Pointing out that Newhall land was the single biggest recipient of monetary compensation for losses suffered in the dam disaster, nearly $750,000.
14. Charlie Cooke, Rudy Ortega Sr., and Rudy Ortega Jr., interview by Gelya Frank (part 2), May 27, 2008, FTBMI Archive Doc. 80306.INT, 14–15 (Charlie Cooke).
15. Cahuenga is less than fifteen miles to the southeast of San Fernando.
16. Angie Campero, Joe Campero, and Rudy Ortega Jr. (tribal members), interview by Gelya Frank, May 11, 2008, FTBMI Archive Doc. 80317.INT, 9–13 (Angie Campero).

17. Angie Campero, Joe Campero, and Rudy Ortega Jr. (tribal members), interview by Gelya Frank, 13–15. In the San Fernando barrio on the south side of the railroad tracks, "For years, this side of town saw no improvements. Trees went in north of the tracks while the barrio streets went unpaved. Sidewalks were nonexistent." Jorgensen, *San Fernando Valley*, 159.
18. See chapter 4.
19. Rudy Ortega Sr., interview by Gelya Frank, May 9, 2008 (part 1), FTBMI Archive Doc. 80312.INT, 2; Ernest John Ortega, interview by Gelya Frank, May 9, 2008, FTBMI Archive Doc. 80314.INT.
20. Jorgensen, *San Fernando Valley*, 156.
21. Rudy Ortega Sr. interview, May 9, 2008 (part 1), FTBMI Archive Doc. 80312. INT, 3.
22. Rudy Ortega Sr. interview, 26–27.
23. The facility was then known as the Pacific Branch of the Home for Disabled Volunteer Soldiers.
24. Kathryn Shirley Traba and Kathryn Gonzales, interview by Gelya Frank, May 3, 2008, FTBMI Archive Doc. 80321.INT, 31 (Kathryn Shirley Traba).
25. Rudy Ortega Sr. interview, May 9, 2008 (part 1), FTBMI Archive Doc. 80312. INT, 24.
26. Dorothy Newman and Verne Newman Jr. and Glenn Newman, interview by Gelya Frank, May 2, 2008, FTBMI Archive Do. 80308, 17 (Verne Newman Jr.).
27. California Senate Journal, February 11, 1852, 105–6, reprinted in "Indian Tribes of California," Hearings before a Subcommittee of the Committee on Indian Affairs, House of Representatives, 67th Congress, 2nd Session, April 28–29, 1922, 265.
28. See Madley, *American Genocide*.
29. See Shipek, *Pushed into the Rocks*.
30. See chapters 4 and 5.
31. This antagonism is recounted in Jorgensen, *San Fernando Valley*, 154–61.
32. David Salazar Sr., Stanley Salazar, Rudy Ortega Sr., Rudy Ortega Jr., and Dave Salazar, interview by Gelya Frank, February 22, 2008 (part 1), FTBMI Archive Doc. 80323.INT, 23 (Rudy Ortega Jr.).
33. David Salazar Jr., interview by Gelya Frank, May 3, 2008, FTBMI Archive Doc. 80322.INT, 2–3.
34. Kathryn Shirley Traba and Kathryn Gonzales interview, FTBMI Archive Doc. 80321.INT, 4 (Kathryn Shirley Traba).
35. Jimmy Ortega and Darlene Villasenor, interview by Gelya Frank, March 1, 2008, FTBMI Archive Doc. 80316.INT, 3 (Darlene Villasenor).

36. Beverly Folkes, interview by Duane Champagne, June 1, 2016, FTBMI Archive Doc. 91122.INT, 5.
37. Charlie Cooke, Rudy Ortega Sr., and Rudy Ortega Jr. interview (part 1), FTBMI Archive Doc. 80305.INT, 22.
38. Charlie Cooke, Rudy Ortega Sr., and Rudy Ortega Jr. interview, 8.
39. Jimmy Ortega and Darlene Villasenor interview, FTBMI Archive Doc. 80316. INT, 12 (Jimmy Ortega).
40. Thompson v. Doaksum, 68 Cal. 493 (1886); Harvey v. Barker, 126 Cal. 262 (1899). The U.S. Supreme Court ultimately backed the state court's rulings. Barker v. Harvey, 181 U.S. 481 (1901).
41. Anderson v. Matthews, 174 Cal. 537 (1917).
42. C. E. Kelsey, *Report of the Special Agent for California Indians to the Commissioner of Indian Affairs* (March 21, 1906), reprinted in "Indian Tribes of California," Hearings before a Subcommittee of the Committee on Indian Affairs, House of Representatives, 67th Congress, 1st Session (March 23, 1920), 12.
43. Piper v. Big Pine School District, 193 Cal. 664 (1924). See also McDowell, "Landless Indians of California," 52, noting that as of 1919 prejudice against Indians in public schools was not so strong as in the past.
44. State statutes authorizing discrimination against Native American and Asian American students were not repealed until 1947. Sosa, "Fragmented Diversity," 8.
45. Kelsey, *Report of Special Agent for California Indians*, 14: "In more localities a very curious race prejudice, different from that against Asiatics, militates against their employment."
46. Dorothy Newman, Verne Newman Jr., and Glenn Newman interview, FTBMI Archive Doc. 80308.INT, 9–10 (Verne Newman Jr.): "In the 1940s San Fernando was composed of whites, Hispanics, and Native Americans of different . . . tribes. . . . And to say, you know, does somebody look Indian? You could say, yeah, they looked Mexican, they looked Spanish, they looked brown compared to looking white. And that's part of what was going on with this community in the 30s and 40s." Verne Newman Jr. is the great-grandson of Antonio Maria Ortega, progenitor of the present-day Ortega lineage.
47. "Many Convicted," *San Fernando Sun*; "Mexican Shot by Officers," *San Fernando Sun*. Both articles identify the part of the city of San Fernando referred to as "Sonoratown."
48. Angie Campero interview, FTBMI Archive Doc. 80317.INT.
49. Mendez v. Westminster School District of Orange County, 64 F.Supp. 544 (S.D. Cal. 1946), aff'd, 161 F.2d 774 (9th Cir. 1947) (en banc). That was seven years

before the Supreme Court's 1954 opinion in *Brown v. Board of Education*, 347 U.S. 483 (1954).

50. Ovnick, "Three Pioneer Women's Memories," 61–62.
51. Theodore Garcia Sr. and family members Ted Garcia Jr. and Katherine Villa, interview by Duane Champagne, July 12, 2008, FTBMI Archive Doc. 80302. INT, 14 (Ted Garcia Jr.).
52. "Ku Klux Klan," *San Fernando Valley Times*, 1; Larralde and Griswold del Castillo, "San Diego's Ku Klux Klan 1920–1980," *The Journal of San Diego History*, pointing out that Los Angeles elected a Klan leader as mayor in 1928 and served as Klan headquarters in the western United States in the 1940s.
53. David Salazar Sr., Stanley Salazar, Rudy Ortega Sr., Dave Salazar, and Rudy Ortega Jr. interview (part 1), FTBMI Archive Doc. 80323.INT, 15–16 (Stanley Salazar); Charlie Cooke, Rudy Ortega Sr., and Rudy Ortega Jr. interview (part 1), FTBMI Archive Doc. 80305.INT, 9 (Charlie Cooke).
54. Beverly Folkes interview, FTBMI Archive Doc. 91122.INT, 61–65.
55. Victoria Stokes, interview by Gelya Frank, May 10, 2008, FTBMI Archive Doc. 80307.INT, 12; Dorothy Newman, Verne Newman Jr., and Glenn Newman interview, FTBMI Archive Doc. 80308.INT, 43 (Verne Newman Jr.).
56. Rudy Ortega Sr., interview by Duane Champagne, December 4, 2007 (part 1), FTBMI Archive Doc. 80310.INT, 7.
57. Rudy Ortega Sr., interview by Duane Champagne, 10.
58. Charlie Cooke, Rudy Ortega Sr., and Rudy Ortega Jr. interview (part 1), FTBMI Archive Doc. 80305.INT, 18 (Charlie Cooke).
59. Dorothy Newman, Verne Newman Jr., and Glenn Newman interview, FTBMI Archive Doc. 80308.INT, 17 (Verne Newman Jr.).
60. David Salazar Sr., Stanley Salazar, Rudy Ortega Sr., and Rudy Ortega Jr. interview (part 2), FTBMI Archive Doc. 80324.INT, 1 (Stanley Salazar).
61. David Salazar Sr., Stanley Salazar, Rudy Ortega Sr., and Rudy Ortega Jr. interview (part 1), FTBMI Archive Doc. 80324.INT, 17–18 (Stanley Salazar).
62. David Salazar Sr., Stanley Salazar, Rudy Ortega Sr., and Rudy Ortega Jr. interview (part 1), 18 (Stanley Salazar).
63. Rudy Ortega Sr. interview, May 9, 2008 (part 1), FTBMI Archive Doc. 80312. INT, 8.
64. Rudy Ortega Sr. interview, 8.
65. Rudy Ortega Sr. interview, December 4, 2007 (part 1), FTBMI Archive Doc. 80310.INT, 7. Rudy Ortega Sr., interview by Gelya Frank, April 3, 2008, FTBMI Archive Doc. 80318.INT, 18. According to Rudy Ortega Sr., born in 1936, there were only three Tataviam speakers during his grandfather's time.

66. Rudy Ortega Sr. interview, May 9, 2008 (part 1), FTBMI Archive Doc. 80312. INT, 5; Rudy Ortega Sr. interview, April 3, 2008, FTBMI Archive Doc. 80318. INT, 18.
67. Rudy Ortega Sr. interview, December 4, 2007 (part 2), FTBMI Archive Doc. 80311.INT, 10.
68. Rudy Ortega Sr. interview, May 9, 2008 (part 1), FTBMI Archive Doc. 80312. INT, 18; Jimmy Ortega and Darlene Villasenor interview, FTBMI Archive Doc. 80316.INT, 3 (Darlene Villasenor). "So it was the Native language which his father [Estanislao] knew, but probably didn't speak around in public because, again, of that fear of being put on a reservation, I think." Rudy Ortega Sr. interview, 9–10.
69. Jimmy Ortega and Darlene Villasenor interview, FTBMI Archive Doc. 80316. INT, 9–10 (Darlene Villasenor).
70. David Salazar Jr. interview, FTBMI Archive Doc. 80322.INT, at 7–8.
71. David Salazar Jr. interview, 5, 14.
72. Rudy Ortega Sr. interview, December 4, 2007 (part 1), FTBMI Archive Doc. 80310.INT, 32.
73. Charlie Cooke, Rudy Ortega Sr., and Rudy Ortega Jr. interview (part 1), FTBMI Archive Doc. 80305.INT, 22 (Charlie Cooke).
74. Victoria Stokes interview, FTBMI Archive Doc. 80307.INT, 12.
75. Victoria Stokes interview, 23–24.
76. Beverly Folkes interview, FTBMI Archive Doc. 91122.INT, 7.
77. Beverly Folkes interview, 29.
78. Beverly Folkes interview, 7–8.
79. Beverly Folkes interview, 8.
80. David Salazar Sr., Stanley Salazar, Rudy Ortega Sr., Dave Salazar, and Rudy Ortega Jr. interview (part 1), FTBMI Archive Doc. 80323.INT, 8 (David Salazar Sr.).
81. David Salazar Sr., Stanley Salazar, Rudy Ortega Sr., Dave Salazar, and Rudy Ortega Jr. interview (part 1), 9 (David Salazar Sr.).
82. Gordon, *TIQ SLO'W*, 42.
83. A. L. Kroeber, "Shamans of the California Indians," n.d., A. L. Kroeber Papers, 1869–1962, BANC, General History Reel 78, 1.
84. The voter registration list of 1932 for San Fernando city precincts nos. 2 and 9 show members of the Ortiz lineage living in very close proximity to members of the Ortega lineage, such as Vera Salazar and her family and two sons of Antonio Maria Ortega, Eulogio and Louis. See FTBMI Archive Docs. 80800.VRCA, 80939.VRCA.

85. Mary Garcia and family, 1940 U.S. Census, San Fernando, California, April, 2, 1940, Roll: T627_251, page 1B, Enumeration District 19–658; Francis Garcia and family, 1940 U.S. Census, San Fernando, California, April 15, 1940, Roll T627_251, page 17B, Enumeration District 19–659.
86. David Salazar Sr., Stanley Salazar, Rudy Ortega Sr., and Rudy Ortega Jr., interview by Gelya Frank, February 22, 2008 (part 2), FTBMI Archive Doc. 80324. INT, 4; Rudy Ortega Sr., interview by Duane Champagne, December 4, 2007 (part 2), FTBMI Archive Doc. 80311.INT, 10.
87. Gordon, *TIQ SLO'W*, 262.
88. Rudy Ortega Sr. interview, December 4, 2007 (part 1), FTBMI Archive Doc. 80310.INT, 26.
89. Rudy Ortega Sr. interview, 29.
90. Rudy Ortega Sr. interview, May 9 2008 (part 1), FTBMI Archive Doc. 80312. INT, 12.
91. Rudy Ortega Sr. interview, May 9, 2008 (part 2), FTBMI Archive Doc. 80313. INT, 7.
92. Rudy Ortega Sr. interview, December 4, 2007 (part 1), FTBMI Archive Doc. 80310.INT, 1–2; Rudy Ortega Sr. interview, May 9, 2008 (part 1), FTBMI Archive Doc. 80312.INT, 8–9. Unfortunately, although there were some records of these events, especially for the 1940s, all were lost or destroyed either accidentally or because of household moves.
93. Rudy Ortega Sr. interview, May 9, 2008 (part 1), FTBMI Archive Doc. 80312. INT, 18.
94. Rudy Ortega Sr. interview, December 4, 2007 (part 2), FTBMI Archive Doc. 80311.INT, 23.
95. Rudy Ortega Sr. interview, May 9, 2008 (part 2), FTBMI Archive Doc. 80313. INT, 23–24:

> Gelya Frank, Interviewer: So he [Estanislao Ortega] was helping people. What happened if somebody passed away and they didn't have the money for the funeral expenses? What would happen? Rudy Ortega Sr.: "I think my dad used to spread the word around to the people and see if they can donate any part of their money. I heard him say once that even fifty cents if you had nothing else to give. Fifty cents would be a lot of help for the people. So he used to. And then one of my step-brothers . . . he used to go to the bars and collect money. Even though they weren't related to us, whoever passed away, he said, 'Oh, my cousin passed away. Can you help me with some money?' They would give him five dollars at the bar because they were already drinking and they didn't know. So

> they'd give five dollars. He'd come back with a hundred, two hundred dollars to my dad and give it to the people that they needed it there in the funeral. Or he would give it to the funeral home in place of giving it to the deceased's family. He would give it to the funeral home."

96. Rudy Ortega Sr. interview, May 9, 2008 (part 1), FTBMI Archive Doc. 80312. INT, 46.
97. David Salazar Sr., Stanley Salazar, Rudy Ortega Sr., Dave Salazar, and Rudy Ortega Jr. interview (part 2), FTBMI Archive Doc. 80323.INT, 1 (Stanley Salazar). See also Theodore Garcia Sr., Ted Garcia Jr., and Katherine Villa interview, FTBMI Archive Doc. 80302.INT, 19. According to Ted Garcia Jr.,

> [If someone was in financial need] I think it's probably just people that was there [at lineage gatherings in Newhall or San Fernando] they would kick in whatever they could, you know, help out whatever way they could. They might bring clothes or they might, you know, they might bring food or they might just give knowledge to help them out, you know, somebody needs this, somebody needs that, okay, let's help them out. We'll see what we can give to them. So, like I said, it was . . . there's always a reason for it.

98. David Salazar Sr., Stanley Salazar, Rudy Ortega Sr., Dave Salazar, and Rudy Ortega Jr. interview (part 1), FTBMI Archive Doc. 80323.INT, 18 (Stanley Salazar).
99. See *supra*, this chapter.
100. Beverly Folkes interview, FTBMI Archive Doc. 91122.INT, 1.
101. Rudy Ortega Sr. interview, December 4, 2007 (part 1), FTBMI Archive Doc. 80310.INT, 30–31.
102. She is quoted in Rudy Ortega Sr. interview, 26.
103. Rudy Ortega Sr. interview, December 4, 2007 (part 2), FTBMI Archive Doc. 80311.INT, 9–10.
104. Rudy Ortega Sr. interview, 9–10, 30.
105. Rudy Ortega Sr. interview, 12–13.
106. Rudy Ortega Sr. interview, 15–16; Rudy Ortega Sr. interview, December 4, 2007 (part 1), FTBMI Archive Doc. 80310.INT, 27.
107. Rudy Ortega Sr. interview, December 4, 2007 (part 2), FTBMI Archive Doc. 80311.INT, 13.
108. Rudy Ortega Sr. interview, 13; Rudy Ortega Sr. interview, December 4, 2007 (part 1), FTBMI Archive Doc. 80310.INT, 3.

109. For photos of Frances, identified as "Chief Frances," see https://scvhistory.com/scvhistory/lt0100.htm (visited July 3, 2019). A history of leadership among the Garcia lineage is provided in Worden, "Santiago Garcia Adobe."
110. See this chapter, *infra*.
111. Charlie Cooke, Rudy Ortega Sr., and Rudy Ortega Jr. interview (part 1), 23 (Charlie Cooke); Charlie Cooke, Rudy Ortega Sr., and Rudy Ortega Jr., interview by Gelya Frank, May 27, 2008 (part 2), FTBMI Archive Doc. 80306.INT, 11 (Charlie Cooke).
112. Beverly Folkes interview, FTBMI Archive Doc. 91122.INT, 25.
113. Beverly Folkes interview, 25.
114. Gordon, *TIQ SLO'W*, 51. For photos of Mary, identified as "Chief Mary Cooke Garcia," see https://scvhistory.com/scvhistory/ff5102.htm (visited July 3, 2019).
115. Gordon, *TIQ SLO'W*, 51.
116. Beverly Folkes interview, FTBMI Archive Doc. 91122.INT, 11; David Salazar Sr., Stanley Salazar, Rudy Ortega Sr., and Rudy Ortega Jr. interview (part 2), FTBMI Archive Doc. 80324.INT, 2 (Stanley Salazar).
117. Beverly Folkes interview, FTBMI Archive Doc. 91122.INT, 11.
118. Rudy Ortega Sr. interview, December 4, 2007 (part 1), FTBMI Archive Doc. 80310.INT, 1.
119. Rudy Ortega Sr. interview, 2.
120. Dorothy Newman, Verne Newman Jr., and Glenn Newman interview, FTBMI Archive Doc. 80308.INT, 23–25 (Verne Newman Jr.).
121. David Salazar Sr., Stanley Salazar, Rudy Ortega Sr., Dave Salazar, and Rudy Ortega Jr. interview (part 1), FTBMI Archive Doc. 80323.INT, 4 (David Salazar Sr.).
122. Ernest John Ortega interview, FTBMI Archive Doc. 80314.INT, 7; Beverly Folkes interview, FTBMI Archive Doc. 91122.INT, 4.
123. Funeral Guest Book, funeral of Estanislao (James) Ortega, Noble Chapel, San Fernando, CA, FTBMI Archive Doc. 80475.Noble.
124. Funeral Guest Book, funeral of Estanislao (James) Ortega.
125. Because Miguel Raphael was only a stepbrother to Joseph Ortiz, progenitor of that lineage, he and his descendants were not eligible for tribal membership.
126. For a discussion of this treaty process, see chapter 4.
127. Act of May 18, 1928, Pub. L. 70–423, 70th Cong., 1st Sess., Ch. 624.
128. See Madley, *American Genocide*.
129. Editorial, "Owed for Seventy Years," *Fresno Republican*, January 13, 1922, reprinted in Hearings before a Subcommittee of the Committee on Indian Affairs, House of Representatives, 67th Cong., 2nd Sess., April 28 and 29, 1922 (Part 2), 201.

130. Act of May 18, 1928, 45 Stat. 602, § 7, and as amended by 46 Stat. 259 (1930). A further amendment in 1948 gave the secretary one year and some funding to revise the roll in order to remove listed individuals who had died since it was finalized in 1933 and to include their descendants born since that date. 62 Stat. 1166.
131. Act of May 18, 1928, 45 Stat. 602, § 7.
132. In addition to the reservations provided in the treaties, the Indians were promised goods, including agricultural implements, the estimated value of which had been placed at $1.8 million, as well as schools and instructors. See, "Indians of California," Hearing before a Subcommittee of the Committee on Indian Affairs, House of Representatives, 69th Cong., 1st Sess., May 5, 1926 at 10–11 (testimony of Rep. Clarence Lea).
133. See *infra*. As California attorney general Robert Kenny wrote in 1944, in limiting the recovery to treaty-based lands and promises, and in setting a value for the treaty lands, Congress went further in limiting recovery than it had in any previous claims legislation. "It appears to be the only case where a ceiling was placed on the amount of the award. In all other cases the courts were given full latitude to fix the amount of the award in accordance with the facts adduced and the terms of the jurisdictional acts." Kenny, *Claims of California Indians*, 87.
134. Act of May 18, 1928, 45 Stat. 602, § 6. The act specifically prohibited payment of attorneys' fees to the state of California, but did allow for payment of other litigation costs out of the judgment. Act of May 18, 1928, § 5.
135. Act of May 18, 1928, 45 Stat. 602, § 6, *as amended by* 64 Stat. 196 (1950), § 2.
136. See chapter 5.
137. The three reservations were Tule River in the Central Valley, Round Valley in Mendocino County, and Hoopa Valley in Humboldt County.
138. See Miller, "Secret Treaties," 39.
139. Miller, 44–45.
140. Kelsey, *Report of the Special Agent for California Indians*, 15.
141. Among other problems, the Indian agents and associated federal officials were often corrupt, using their assignments as springboards for enrichment at the Indians' expense. See, e.g., Frank and Goldberg, *Defying the Odds*, 232–33, describing fraudulent practices that removed land from the Tule River Indian Reservation; Castillo, "Euro-American Exploration," 110–11. Writing of reservation conditions during the 1860s, Professor Benjamin Madley is more explicit: "Confinement to federal reservations was a death sentence for many of the state's Indian people, whether they were starved to death, worked to death, shot, hanged, massacred, or died of sickness there." Madley, *American Genocide*, 306–7.
142. Kelsey, *Report of the Special Agent for California Indians*, 15.

143. Kelsey, 15.
144. Kelsey, 13.
145. Kelsey, 23.
146. Miller, "The Secret Treaties with California's Indians," 45; "Report on the Landless Indians of California by Malcolm McDowell," December 31, 1919, U.S. Fifty-First Annual Report of the Board of Indian Commissioners to the Secretary of the Interior (1920), 58–59 (listing all the purchases).
147. Kelsey, *Report of the Special Agent for California Indians*, 16. Kelsey's Report also noted that "this action [reservations for Southern California Indians] came late, as usual, and there was very little land of any value remaining in the public domain which could be given to the Indians." Kelsey, 16. For the Fernandeño Indians, there was no public land at all available in Los Angeles County, a major reason why they had never been provided a reservation.
148. "Report on the Landless Indians of California by Malcolm McDowell," December 31, 1919, U.S. Fifty-First Annual Report of the Board of Indian Commissioners to the Secretary of the Interior (1920), 51.
149. "Report on the Landless Indians of California by Malcolm McDowell," 55.
150. "Indian Tribes of California," *1922 Hearings*, 142 and 154.
151. The resolution is quoted in "Indian Tribes of California," 155.
152. Anderson v. Matthews, 174 Cal. 537 (1917).
153. "Indian Tribes of California," *1922 Hearings*, 153.
154. "Indian Tribes of California," *1922 Hearings*, 153.
155. "In 1919, the board established auxiliaries which were small Indian organizations that acted on the local level and raised funds for the board through memberships and special events. The Indian Board of Cooperation assisted Indians on many issues over the next decades. By May 1924, the board boasted 88 auxiliaries, with a membership of 10,400. (California Indian Herald, 1924:2) While Indians could belong to the auxiliaries, the board was made up of Whites. Most of the funds the board used for operation were obtained from Indians who paid between four and six dollars each to be members. Thus, much of the cost of financing the early land claims case came from Indians themselves." Online Archives of California, available at http://www.oac.cdlib.org/findaid/ark:/13030/c82f7pw6/ (visited July 3, 2019).
156. "Indian Tribes of California," *1922 Hearings*, 153.
157. "Indian Tribes of California," 154.
158. "Indian Tribes of California," *1926 Hearing*, 22.
159. "Indian Tribes of California," 252.

160. "Indian Tribes of California," 37.
161. Dr. C. Hart Merriam argued for including all the Indians of California, based in part on the difficulty of identifying the treaty-making tribes and their descendants. "Indian Tribes of California," 50–52.
162. The two contrasting approaches are illustrated by the bills introduced in the House in 1926 by two different members of Congress from California, John Raker and Florence Kahn. "Indian Tribes of California," 1–5.
163. Estimates ranged from $.50 to $5.00 per acre. "Indian Tribes of California," 16–17, 61.
164. "Indian Tribes of California," 57–60.
165. "Indian Tribes of California," 15–16.
166. "Indian Tribes of California," 59–60.
167. Meriam, *Problem of Indian Administration.*
168. 25 U.S.C. § 461 et seq.
169. The report also had an impact on other future legislation affecting California Indian country. It claimed, for example, that because California tribes were widely scattered across the state, federal administration of Indian affairs was too difficult, and therefore it would be better to authorize state jurisdiction within California Indian country. In 1953, Congress enacted Public Law 280, which authorized the state of California to exercise criminal and civil jurisdiction over Indians within reservations in California as well as several other states. See Carole E. Goldberg, "Public Law 280," 535–94.
170. Meriam Report, 805. See generally Wilkins, *Hollow Justice*, 41–42.
171. Meriam Report, 807.
172. Kenny, *Claims of California Indians*, 40.
173. For an account of the proceedings, see Kenny, *Claims of California Indians*. Kenny was attorney general of California from 1943 to 1947, and therefore represented the Indians of California at the time of the ultimate resolution of the case in the Court of Claims.
174. Indians of California, 102 Ct. Cl. 837 (1944).
175. Stewart, "Litigation and Its Effects," 706.
176. 64 Stat. 196 (1950), § 2.
177. Bills to increase the amount of the award by raising the price to be paid for the lands promised in the eighteen treaties from $1.25 per acre to $5.70 per acre were introduced into the House and the Senate in 1937 but failed of passage. S. 17779 and H.R. 5243, 75th Cong., 1st Sess. (1937).
178. "Indians Tribes of California," *1926 Hearing*, 12.

179. "Indians Tribes of California," 12–13. See also Stewart, "Litigation and Its Effects," 707. These lands were the subject of later claims filed under the Indian Claims Commission Act of 1946. See *infra.*
180. Kenny, *Claims of California Indians*, 40.
181. See, e.g., "California Indians May Get Justice," *Los Angeles Times*, 21.
182. Theodore Garcia Sr., Ted Garcia Jr., Rudy Ortega Jr., and Katherine Villa interview, FTBMI Archive Doc. 80302.INT, 19 (Rudy Ortega Jr.).
183. Singleton, "Surviving Urbanization," *Wicazo Sa Review*, 49–59.
184. National Archives—Pacific Region Catalog, Finding Aid RG 75 BIA CA Vol. 3, at 55: "In many cases a committee of elderly native Americans acted as witnesses to the authenticity of claims and to the fact of claimants being recognized as persons of California Indian descent."
185. See *supra.*
186. Rudy Ortega Sr. interview, May 9, 2008 (part 1), FTBMI Archive Doc. 80312. INT, 29. An 1860 report of the secretary of the interior pronounced: "Some reservation retreats, must be prepared for the reception of those who cannot obtain employment from our citizens, and thus become vagrants and nuisances to the community. Such Indians might be removed by force, if necessary, to the reservations, and there compelled to labor." FTBMI Archive Doc. 50011.A.UCLA.
187. Theodore Garcia Sr., Ted Garcia Jr., and Katherine Villa interview, FTBMI Archive Doc. 80302.INT, 19 (Ted Garcia Jr.): "Well, back then the way we understand how the Garcia's family were on the '28 Judgment was Fred Cooke. When they posted that not too many people knew how to read a newspaper or identify. Many of them refused to do it. So when they came around it was a matter of the families going to . . . go and register." Rudy Ortega Sr. interview, May 9, 2008 (part 1), FTBMI Archive Doc. 80312.INT, 30. (In this passage, he mistakenly identifies Josephine [Josefa] Garcia as married to Fred Cooke. Fred was married to Josephine's daughter, Frances.)
188. Rudy Ortega Sr. interview, May 9, 2008 (part 1), FTBMI Archive Doc. 80312. INT, 28.
189. Charlie Cooke, Rudy Ortega Sr., and Rudy Ortega Jr. interview (part 1), FTBMI Archive Doc. 80305 2–3 (Charlie Cooke).
190. Theodore Garcia Sr., Ted Garcia Jr., and Katherine Villa interview, FTBMI Archive Doc. 80302, 20 (Rudy Ortega Jr.).
191. See note 161, *supra*, and accompanying text.
192. Frances Garcia Cooke, Application for enrollment with the Indians of the State of California under the Act of May 18, 1928, RG 75, NA, 1928 Applications #11022, FTBMI Archive Doc. 40064.DC.

193. Applications for enrollment with the Indians of the State of California under the Act of May 18, 1928, RG 75, NA, 1928 Applications: Delia Cooke (Martinez) (#11014); Lida Manriquez (#11015); Manuel J. Cooke (#11016); Mary Cooke (#11017), FTBMI Archive Docs. 40056.DC, 40057.DC, 40058.DC, 40059.DC. There were slight variations. Some wrote "San Fernando Mission Indians" and others "San Fernando Mission Tribe." Lida Manriquez was the only one who failed to name Rogerio Rocha as captain.
194. Applications for enrollment with the Indians of the State of California under the Act of May 18, 1928, RG 75, NA, 1928 Applications: Margaret Ward (#11018); John Valenzuela (half-blood petition, #11019); Louis Valenzuela (half-blood petition, #11020); Paul Valenzuela (half-blood petition, #11021), FTBMI Archive Docs. 40060.DC, 40061.DC, 40062.DC, 40063.DC. Petra died in 1930.
195. Clara Maude Callis, Application for enrollment with the Indians of the State of California under the Act of May 18, 1928, RG 75, NA, 1928 Application #11059, FTBMI Archive Doc. 40065.DC.
196. See chapter 4 at notes 86–88 and 133–145.
197. For a schematic presentation of the various tribal names associated with these lineages, see appendix C.
198. Rudy Ortega Sr. interview, May 9, 2008 (part 1), FTBMI Archive Doc. 80312.INT, 30.
199. David Salazar Sr., Stanley Salazar, Rudy Ortega Sr., Dave Salazar, and Rudy Ortega Jr. interview (part 1), FTBMI Archive Doc. 80323.INT, 17 (Stanley Salazar): "In the 1926 [*sic*] California Judgment Act, my grandma was very influential in that . . . from the twenties."
200. Quoted by Beverly Folkes in Beverly Folkes interview, FTBMI Archive Doc. 91122.INT, 20.
201. According to Rudy Ortega Sr., "In 1932, they came out, the government wanted all the Native Americans to be registered and in those days there was a rumor, everybody was talking, don't register because they want to send you to a reservation, so don't register at all, because that's how they're going to find out where you live and they're going to come out and pick you up and take you. So nobody registered, my people never registered." Rudy Ortega Sr. interview, April 3, 2008, FTBMI Archive Doc. 80318.INT, 3; see also Ernest John Ortega interview, FTBMI Archive Doc. 80314.INT, 2–3.
202. Rudy Ortega Sr. interview, May 9, 2008 (part 1), FTBMI Archive Doc. 80312.INT, 28–29: "There was a rumor, I don't know who started it in the Valley, that said don't register because the government wants to put you all in the reservation and keep you there and take you away from the town. . . . I don't know who

started the rumor. But wherever it started, it started spreading out fast. Because that's when the Bureau of Indian Affairs was trying to get everybody registered."

203. Jimmy Ortega and Darlene Villasenor interview, FTBMI Archive Doc. 80316. INT, 3 (Jimmy Ortega, Estanislao's son).
204. Rudy Ortega Sr. interview, May 9, 2008 (part 1), FTBMI Archive Doc. 80312. INT, 32.
205. See *supra*, discussion of sublineages within Ortega lineage.
206. José Ortiz, Application for enrollment with the Indians of the State of California under the Act of May 18, 1928, RG 75, NA, 1928 Applications, #11171, FTBMI Archive Doc. 80126.DC.

CHAPTER 7

1. Rudy Ortega Sr., interview by Gelya Frank, May 9, 2008 (part 1), FTBMI Archive Doc. 80312.INT, 34–37.
2. David Salazar Sr., Stanley Salazar, Rudy Ortega Sr., and Rudy Ortega Jr., interview by Gelya Frank, February 22, 2008 (part 2), FTBMI Archive Doc. 80324. INT, 8, 14–15, 19–22; David Salazar Sr., Stanley Salazar, Rudy Ortega Sr., Dave Salazar, and Rudy Ortega Jr., interview by Gelya Frank, February 22, 2008 (part 1), FTBMI Archive Doc. 80323.INT, 2–7 (David Salazar Sr.) (all).
3. David Salazar Sr., Stanley Salazar, Rudy Ortega Sr., Dave Salazar, and Rudy Ortega Jr. interview (part 1), FTBMI Archive Doc. 80323.INT, 17–20; see chapter 6.
4. Dorothy Newman and Verne Newman Jr. and Glenn Newman, interview by Gelya Frank, May 2, 2008, FTBMI Archive Doc. 80308.INT, 44–45 (Verne Newman Jr.); David Salazar Sr., Stanley Salazar, Rudy Ortega Sr., and Rudy Ortega Jr., interview (part 2), FTBMI Archive Doc. 80324.INT, 5 (Dave Salazar Sr.); Rudy Ortega Sr. interview by Gelya Frank, May 8, 2008 (part 2), FTBMI Archive Doc. 80313.INT, 3; Rudy Ortega Sr., interview by Gelya Frank, April 3, 2008, FTBMI Archive Doc. 80318.INT, 12–14.
5. Rudy Ortega Sr., interview by Duane Champagne, December 4, 2007 (part 1), FTBMI Archive Doc. 80310.INT, 37–40.
6. Rudy Ortega Sr. interview, April 3, 2008, FTBMI Archive Doc. 80318.INT, 18–19.
7. Rudy Ortega Sr. interview, December 4, 2007 (part 1), FTBMI Archive Doc. 80310.INT, 1, 9, 26.
8. David Salazar Sr., Stanley Salazar, Rudy Ortega Sr., Dave Salazar, and Rudy Ortega Jr. interview (part 1), FTBMI Archive Doc. 80323.INT, 4 (Stanley Salazar).
9. The term *band* was used to refer to those with ancestors from lineages brought to San Fernando Mission.

10. Steve Ortega, interview by Gelya Frank, May 6, 2008, FTBMI Archive Doc. 80303.INT, 2. See also Rudy Ortega Sr. interview, December 4, 2007 (part 1), FTBMI Archive Doc. 80310.INT, 2; Rudy Ortega Sr. interview, April 3, 2008, FTBMI Archive Doc. 80318, 4; Rudy Ortega Sr. interview, May 9, 2008 (part 1), FTBMI Archive Doc. 80312.INT, 7–8.
11. Appendix D depicts the different names associated with the nonprofit and tribal groups at different time periods.
12. Rudy Ortega Sr. interview, December 4, 2007 interview (part 1), FTBMI Archive Doc. 80310.INT, 21–24.
13. See Parish History, St. Ferdinand Church and School, since 1902, available at http://stferdinandchurch.org/about/parish-history (visited July 8, 2019).
14. Rudy Ortega Sr. interview, December 4, 2007 (part 1), FTBMI Archive Doc. 80310.INT, 4–5.
15. Rudy Ortega Sr. interview, May 9, 2008 (part 1), FTBMI Archive Doc. 80312. INT, 7–8.
16. See chapter 6. The roll was carrying out the mandate of the 1928 California Jurisdictional Act, which provided some compensation to California Indians for lands promised in the eighteen unratified treaties of 1851–52.
17. Rudy Ortega Sr. interview, December 4, 2007 (part 1), FTBMI Archive Doc. 80310.INT, 39.
18. Letter from Edward A. Ortega to BIA Area Office, Sacramento, CA, Received October 14, 1968, FTBMI Archive Doc. 80289.OTC, 43–46, 111, Edward Arnold Ortega, AN-036449, Aka Rudy or Rudolph J. Ortega F-20457. "Applicant . . . failed to establish that he is either the father, mother, brother, sister, uncle, or aunt of a person whose name appears on the roll approved 5/16/1933."
19. SFR Baptism #0849 (Tiburcio Cayo); SFR Baptism #2908 (Jose Juan Leyva).
20. For discussion of language loss in the twentieth century, see chapter 6 at pages 182–83.
21. Heizer, *Hugo Reid's Letters*, 9.
22. Harrington, "San Fernando Bells Ring Again," 64–66.
23. Rudy Ortega Sr. interview, December 4, 2007 (part 1), FTBMI Archive Doc. 80310.INT, 21–24; Rudy Ortega Sr., interview by Gelya Frank, May 9, 2008 (part 2), FTBMI Archive Doc. 80311.INT, 24–26. Some years later, in the 1990s, this name was adopted by John Valenzuela and some other San Fernando Mission descendants.
24. Letter from William D. Oliver, Acting BIA Area Director, to Mr. Rudy Ortega, September 28, 1971, FTBMI Archive Doc. 00036.FTO, 1; Jacobs, "Cave Drawings Reveal Chumash Indians Past," *Los Angeles Times*, 1–2; Lubas, "Mission

Indians," *Los Angeles Times*, 4; Jacobs, "Indians May Press Claim," *Los Angeles Times, Valley News*.

25. Rudy Ortega Sr. interview, December 4, 2007 (part 1), FTBMI Archive Doc. 80310, 21–24.
26. Rudy Ortega Sr. interview, 28.
27. Rudy Ortega Sr. interview, 27.
28. Rudy Ortega Sr. interview, 39; Ortega Jr, "New Century, Photo 2000," *Tarahat: The People*, 1, 5; Theodore Garcia, Sr. and family members Ted Garcia Jr. and Katherine Villa, interview by Duane Champagne, July 12, 2008, FTBMI Archive Doc. 80302.INT, 15, 27, 31–32, 41–42 (all).
29. A. L. Kroeber, "Statement of Native Land Use," A. L. Kroeber Papers, 1869–1972, BANC 2049. Berkeley, CA, Bancroft Library, University of California Berkeley, 1951, 10–11, Reel 151.
30. Rudy Ortega Sr. interview, May 8, 2008 interview (part 2), FTBMI Archive Doc. 80313.INT, 4, 10–11, 15; David Salazar Sr., Stanley Salazar, Rudy Ortega Sr., and Rudy Ortega Jr. interview (part 2), FTBMI Archive Doc. 80324.INT, 5, 14, 19–21.
31. David Salazar Sr., Stanley Salazar, Rudy Ortega Sr., and Rudy Ortega Jr. interview (part 2), FTBMI Archive Doc. 80324.INT, 5 (David Salazar Sr.).
32. David Salazar Sr., Stanley Salazar, Rudy Ortega Sr., Dave Salazar, and Rudy Ortega Jr. interview (part 1), FTBMI Archive Doc. 80323.INT, 2 (Stanley Salazar). For more comments on lineage community and gatherings, see David Salazar Sr., Stanley Salazar, and Rudy Ortega Jr. interview (part 2), FTBMI Archive Doc. 80324.INT, 4, 6 (David Salazar Sr.); Victoria Stokes, interview by Gelya Frank, May 10, 2008, FTBMI Archive Doc. 80307.INT, 25–27, 40; Jimmie Ortega interview by Gelya Frank, March 21, 2008, FTBMI Archive Doc. 80316. INT, 17, 33.
33. Gordon, *TIQ SLO'W*, 54.
34. Gordon, 54–55.
35. Gordon, 53.
36. See chapter 4.
37. Gordon, *TIQ SLO'W*, 53.
38. Gordon, 53–54.
39. "December 16, 1961," *Signal*, A4.
40. Gordon, *TIQ SLO'W*, 57.
41. "Indians to Confer," *Los Angeles Times*, SF6: "Members of the San Fernando Mission Indians, an organization of descendants of the Mission, will meet Sunday at noon at Brand Park, 15174 San Fernando Mission Road, to organize a July 4 meeting with the Chuma(sh) Indians of Santa Inez."

42. See Fixico, *Termination and Relocation*; Weibel-Orlando, *Indian Country, L.A.*
43. "San Fernando Mission Indians Fair Booth, 1970s," Fernandeno/Tataviam Tribe, Oviatt Library Digital Collections, San Fernando Valley History Digital Library, California State University, Northridge, available at https://digital-collections.csun.edu/digital/collection/SFVH/id/3422/rec/1 (visited July 19, 2019).
44. "Chief Little Bear and Several Fernandeno tribe members," Fernandeno/Tataviam Tribe, Oviatt Library Digital Collections, San Fernando Valley History Digital Library, California State University, Northridge, available at https://digital-collections.csun.edu/digital/collection/SFVH/id/3432/rec/21 (visited July 19, 2019); "Mission Indian Youth," *Valley News*, 5.
45. "Van, Toys, Food Gifts," *Valley News*, 8; "San Fernando Mission Indians," *Valley News and Green Sheet*, 1.
46. "Fernandeno/Tataviam Tribe Members, February 24, 1974," San Fernando Digital Library, California State University, Northridge, University Library, available at https://digital-collections.csun.edu/digital/collection/SFVH/id/3414/rec/6 (visited July 19, 2019) (photo includes California state senator Alan Robbins); "Snake Dance" *Los Angeles Times, San Fernando Valley*, 1.
47. "Dancing by Indians," *Valley News*, 4; "56 Indian Children," *Los Angeles Times*, 14.
48. "Tribe Opens Petition Drive," *Los Angeles Times*, SF2.
49. Hansen, "Land Reparations," *Los Angeles Times*, 4.
50. Fatehi, "Tribal Cultural Resources Management," 58–98; Gordon, *TIQ SLO'W*, 73–264.
51. For an explanation of the legal operation of termination policy, see Newton et al., *Cohen's Handbook*, 89–91.
52. For the results of a major investigation of the impact of termination, see Staff of the American Indian Policy Review Commission, 94th Cong., *Task Force Report Ten.*
53. Daly, "American Indian Freedom Controversy," 15, 119–21, 135–37, 149–50.
54. See Newton et al., *Cohen's Handbook*, 165–66.
55. American Indian Policy Review Commission, *Final Report*, 8.
56. As amended over time, these regulations can be found at 25 Code of Federal Regulations § 83. For critique of the regulations, see Newton et al., *Cohen's Handbook*, 159–60.
57. 62 Stat. 683, 60 Stat. 1049 (1946). For a sustained critique of this effort, see Wilkins, *Hollow Justice*, 71–125.
58. See chapter 6.
59. See Stewart, "Litigation and Its Effects," 707.
60. Stewart, 708.

61. Public Law 90–507, 82 Stat. 860 (1968).
62. See chapter 6 at notes 187–197 and 206.
63. Rudolf John Ortega, Folder #20457, Application # 36449, 8/4/1968, BIA, Sacramento, CA, FTBMI Archive Doc. 80289.OTC, 43–46.
64. Gordon, *TIQ SLO'W*, 54; "Data Offered," *Los Angeles Times*, 54.
65. Letter from Rudolph J. Ortega to Bureau of Indian Affairs, Sacramento Area Office, Sacramento, CA, October 11, 1963. "I have never had a reply from you on the application that I made in 1950 and I would like to know if I have a roll number and if so, what is the number." Received October 15, 1963, Bureau of Indian Affairs, Sacramento Area Office, Sacramento, CA. Enrollment was rejected because Ortega ancestors had not signed up for the 1933 roll. See FTBMI Archive, Doc. 80289.OTC, 111–19, 123.
66. See chapter 6 at notes 198–205.
67. Rudolf John Ortega, Folder #20457, Application #36449, 8/4/1968, BIA Area Office, Sacramento, CA; Peter O. Lemos, Folder #204457, Application #971617, 6/21/1969, BIA Area Office, Sacramento, CA; Evelyn Ortega, Folder #20457, Application #36450, 8/4/1969; BIA Area Office, Sacramento, CA; Daniel Edward Ortega, Folder #20457, Application #36451, 8/4/1969, BIA Area Office, Sacramento, CA; and others. See FTBMI Archive Doc. 80289.OTC, 43–92.
68. See chapter 6 at notes 187–197 and 206.
69. Lubas, "Mission Indians," 4.
70. Letter from Rudy Ortega, Tribal Coordinator, San Fernando Mission Indians to Robert H. Finch, Counselor to the President, White House, Washington, DC, October 6, 1971. Letter from Robert H. Finch to Mr. Ortega, Tribal Coordinator, San Fernando Mission Indians, The White House, Washington, DC, November 26, 1971, 1–2. See FTBMI Archive, Doc. 00059.FTO, 1–2; Doc. 80301.FTI, 9.
71. Rudy Ortega Sr. interview, December 4, 2007 (part 1), FTBMI Archive Doc. 80310.INTI, 26.
72. Letter from Rudy Ortega, San Fernando Mission Indian Band to William D. Oliver, Acting Area Director, BIA, Sacramento CA, regarding "the possibility of establishing a new reservation," September 28, 1971, FTBMI Archive Doc. 00036.FTO, 1–7. See also Letter from Robert H. Finch to Rudy Ortega, November 26, 1971, FTBMI Archive Doc. 00053.FTO, 1–2.
73. "Indian Land Claims," *Los Angeles Times*, SF3.
74. "Indian Land Claims," *Los Angeles Times*. See also Hansen, "Land Reparations," *Los Angeles Times*, 4; "Rudy Ortega," *Los Angeles Times*, SF3.
75. Rudy Ortega Sr. interview, May 9, 2008, (part 1), FTBMI Archive Doc. 80312.INT, 8–10, 18.

76. Jacobs, "Indians Call Land Claims Conference," *Valley News and Green Sheet*, 1, 10.
77. Rudy Ortega Sr. interview, May 9, 2008 (part 2), FTBMI Archive Doc. 80313. INT, 7–8.
78. Whiteman, "Mission Indian Council," *Valley News and Green Sheet*; "Indian Culture Center," *Los Angeles Times*.
79. Rudy Ortega Sr. interview, May 8, 2008 (part 2), FTBMI Archive Doc. 80313. INT, 9–10.
80. Rudy Ortega Sr. interview, 9.
81. Letter from Rudy Ortega to Norman L. Sahmaunt, Enrollment Officer, BIA, February 1, 1972, Sacramento, CA, FTBMI Archive Doc. 80289.OTC, 136–39. In early 1972, Rudy Ortega was working as a community outreach worker at Indian Lodge, an alcohol prevention program in Los Angeles. The letter to Sahmaunt as well as documentation of Rudy Ortega's position as a community outreach worker can be found in 1972 California Judgment Fund File No. 20457 for Edward Ortega, attached to a letter from James J. Fletcher, superintendent of the Southern California agency of the Bureau of Indian Affairs to Rudy Ortega Sr., August 12, 2008, FTBMI Archive Doc. 80289.OTC, 106, 111.
82. "Indians Invited," *Valley News and Green Sheet*, February 18, 1972, FTBMI Archive Doc. 80654.A.FTO, 6; "Intertribal Indian Club," *Los Angeles Times*, 6; Jacobs, "Indians May Press Claim," *Los Angeles Times, Valley News*, 1, 14.
83. "Data Offered," *Los Angeles Times*, 2; "Party Schedule for Needy Children," *Los Angeles Times*, 9; "Also on the Bill Will be Rudy Ortega and his San Fernando Valley Inter-Tribal Indians dancers. Youths Aid Lions Club with Show," *Van Nuys News*, May 12, 1972, 46; "Indian Council Plans Party for Children Dec. 22 . . . The San Fernando Valley Indian Inter-Tribal Council will hold its annual Christmas party for children of the community" *Valley News*, December 15, 1972, 39; "Inter-Tribal Council," *Valley News*, 25.
84. Letter from William E. Final, Area Director to Edward Arnold (Rudy) Ortega, Folder 20–457, Applicant #D36449, May 26, 1972, BIA Sacramento Area Office, FTBMI Archive Doc. 80301.FTO, 7. There were two payment accounts, the 1944 award and the 1964 award. Rudy qualified for both rolls, others may have qualified for one or another.
85. Gordon, *TIQ SLO'W*, 54.
86. The SFVIT received a state of California nonprofit code, C0690342, and a nonprofit name, *San Fernando Valley Inter-Tribal, Inc*. See FTBMI Archive Doc. 80991.SFVITINC.
87. Bramstedt, "Corporate Adaptations," 90–91.

88. Minutes, Rudy Ortega, Commissioner, present, Los Angeles City/County Native American Indian Commission, June 13, 1977, FTBMI Archive Doc. 80301.FTO, 12–13; Jacobs, "5 Valley Indians Seek Seat," *Valley News*, 32. See also FTBMI Archive Docs. 91121, 32, and 91121.VNN.
89. Letter from Rudy Ortega to Bob Swain, December 20, 1978, FTBMI Archive Doc. 80301.FTO, 16; Meeting Minutes, Rudy Ortega, Chairperson, Los Angeles Urban Indian Health Center, Board of Directors Meeting, February 15, 1979, FTBMI Archive Doc. 80301.FTO, 17.
90. "Indian Culture Center," *Valley News*, 12. Attendees included Cahuilla silversmiths, members of the San Fernando Valley Inter-Tribal Council, and the Inter-Tribal dancers, and the event featured fry bread.
91. Carole Rubinoff to Shirley Hendrix, Bureau of Indian Affairs, Sacramento, CA, referencing "a beautiful Indian pow wow . . . at Kennedy High School in August," October 10, 1977; Fernandeño Tataviam Band of Mission Indians, Tribal Offices, San Fernando, CA, Tribal Archive, Document 80301.M.FTO, 16.
92. Leach, "Indian Children Visit Ancestral Site," *Daily News*, January 5, 1985, FTBMI Archive Doc. 80301.P.FTO; McCarry, "Tribes Question Which Will Bury Ancestors," *Los Angeles Times*, *Valley News*, 10; McCarry, "Indian Tribes," *Los Angeles Times*, J4. Charlie Cooke and about twenty-five Chumash and Fernandeño attended the meeting.
93. Rudy Ortega to Whom It May Concern, January 10, 1986, San Fernando Valley Inter-Tribal Inc. 11640 Rincon Ave., San Fernando, CA, FTBMI Archive Doc. 80290.OTC, 5.
94. Stassel, "His Language Lost," *Los Angeles Times*, B4 ("grandson Rudy Ortega Sr. who is chairman of the Fernandeño Tataviam Tribal Council"); Stassel, "Rita Rivera," *Los Angeles Times*, B12 ("she helped revive the Fernandeño-Tataviam Tribal Council to represent people with Tataviam roots attempting to get federal recognition"); Cordova, "Local Indians Vie for Status," *Signal*, A1; Kondo, "Splintered Tribe Seeks Federal Recognition," *Los Angeles Times*, B3 ("what he most dreams of is federal recognition for his Fernandeno/Tataviam tribe"); Klein, "Native Americans Fight for Cemetery," *Signal*, A1, A3, B12 ("Fernandeno Tataviam Tribe"); Clarke, "Celebrate American Indian Culture!," *Signal*, E15 ("aka Rudy J. Ortega Sr. chief of the Fernandeño-Tataviam tribe since 1971"); Cordova, "Local Indians Vie for Status," *Signal*, A1, A4 ("In the 1950s, he—Ortega Sr.—organized the San Fernando Mission Indians, and in 1968 he started the San Fernando Valley Inter-Tribal Council. In 1995, he established the current organization").

95. "Calendar and Tribal Council Meetings," *Tarahat: The People*, 4; Fernandeño/Tataviam Tribe, Tribal Members Meetings, Minutes to the Meetings, June 22, 1996; July 27, 1996; August 10, 1996; September 14, 1996; March 1, 1997; June 28, 1997; November 22, 1997. See FTBMI Archive Docs. 80580.FTTC, 1; 90052.FTT, 1–2; 90053.FTT, 1; 90054.FTT, 1–2; 90055.FTT, 1–2; 90056.FTT, 1; 90057.FTT, 1; 90058.FTT, 1; 90059.FTT, 1.
96. Alegria, "An Opportunity to Share their Heritage," *San Fernando Valley Sun*, ca. 2001, FTBMI Archive Doc. 00098.FTO.
97. Public Law 102–416 (1992). See Fernandeño Tataviam Tribal Government, "An application for an ANA grant," Resolution, certified by Rudy Ortega Sr., Tribal Chairman, January 11, 2003, FTBMI Archive Doc. 00066.FTO, 3–4.
98. Alegria, "An Opportunity to Share Their Heritage," *San Fernando Valley Sun*, ca. 2001, FTBMI Archive Doc. 00098.FTO.
99. Rudy Ortega Sr. interview, December 2007 (part 1), FTBMI Archive Doc. 80310.INT, 14–15.
100. Over, "Chanting, Music, Dance," *Malibu Times: Newspaper Magazine Online*.
101. Fernandeño/Tataviam Band of Mission Indians (History) (2005), FTBMI Archive Doc. 00066.FTO, 2.
102. Fernandeño/Tataviam Band of Mission Indians (History) (2005), 2, 4. See discussion at notes 81–83, *supra*.
103. Memorandum, Rudy Ortega Jr., "Combined Tribe and Nonprofit Council," April 18, 2009, FTBMI Archive Doc. 80594.FTTO, 1–2.
104. Memorandum, Rudy Ortega Jr., 1.
105. Bostwick, "Garcia Legacy," *Antelope Valley Press*, C8; Chief Little Bear, "Applauding Our Achievements," *Tarahat: The People*, 1, 3.
106. This discussion continued for several years, until the organization known as Pukúu was formed in 2006. See text at notes 122–123, *infra*.
107. Fernandeño/Tataviam Band of Mission Indians (History), Tribal Offices, San Fernando, CA, Tribal Archive, 2005, 2–3.
108. "Forming the Tribal Constitution," *Tarahat: The People*, 1, 5.
109. Constitution of the Fernandeño Tataviam Band of Mission Indians (2002), FTBMI Archive Doc. 80449.FTBMI.
110. FTBMI Archive Docs. 90121.FTBMI, 90122.FTBMI, 90123.FTBMI, 90124.FTBMI, 90125.FTBMI, 90126.FTBMI, 90127.FTBMI, 90128.FTBMI.
111. Rudy Ortega Sr. interview, December 2007 (part 1), FTBMI Archive Doc. 80310.INT, 8, 20; Steve Ortega interview, FTBMI Archive Doc. 80303.INT, 18–20.
112. See chapter 1.

113. Steve Ortega interview, FTBMI Archive Doc. 80303.INT, 19–20.
114. "Updates: Senate Bill And Resolutions," *Tarahat: The People*, 1, 6; Constitution of the Fernandeño Tataviam Band of Mission Indians (2002), FTBMI Archive Doc. 80449.FTBMI, 6–10; Kathy Salas and Betty Salas interview by Gelya Frank, May 11, 2008, FTBMI Archive Doc. 80315.INT, 8 (Kathy Salas).
115. Theodore Garcia Sr. and family members Ted Garcia Jr. and Katherine Villa interview, FTBMI Archive Doc. 80302.INT, 34–35.
116. Chief Little Bear, "Marching Forward," *Tarahat: The People*, 2.
117. Gordon, *TIQ SLO'W*, 265; "Chief Mary Cooke Garcia: Tataviam Culture," SCVhistory.com, FTBMI Archive Doc. 80793.SCVTV, at 1.
118. See appendix C, which includes detailed information about the progenitors, including their associated precontact villages.
119. FTBMI Archive Doc. 80449.FTBMI.Constitution, at 14–15.
120. FTBMI Archive Docs. 00076.FTO, 00084.FTO, 00062.FTO.
121. FTBMI Archive Doc. 00066.FTO.
122. Minutes, Tribal Senate Meeting, August 28, 2008, item 3, Nonprofit Council ("Now the Nonprofit is separated to expand and focus on the cultural and social awareness of the native community."), FTBMI Archive Doc. 90066.FTTS.
123. Services offered by Pukúu are described at http://www.pukuu.org/services (visited July 16, 2019).

APPENDIX A

1. King, "Ethnographic Overview," 48–49. See also SFR Baptism #02029.
2. See U.S. Census, 1850, Los Angeles, CA, roll M432_35, page 21B, image 48, FTBMI Archive Doc. 80802.USC. See also King, "Ethnographic Overview," 48–49.
3. King, "Ethnographic Overview," 48–49.
4. King, 46.
5. King, 43.
6. King, 43.
7. King, 44.
8. King, 44–45.
9. King, 44–45.
10. King, 46.
11. King, 46.
12. King, 46–47.
13. King, 46–47.
14. King, 46.

15. King, 46.
16. King, 46.
17. U.S. Census, 1850, Los Angeles, CA, roll M432_35, page 22A, image 49, FTBMI Archive Doc. 80803.USC; U.S. Census, 1860, Los Angeles, page 25, FTBMI Archive Doc. 80414.USC.
18. Hartnell, *Diary and Copybook*, 46–47.
19. Rancho San Vicente y Santa Monica, available at https://en.wikipedia.org/wiki/Rancho_San_Vicente_y_Santa_Monica (visited September 17, 2019).
20. See Gabrielino Tongva Springs Foundation, available at http://gabrielinosprings.com/wpsite/ (visited September 17, 2019).
21. See King, "Ethnographic Overview," 45–46.
22. King, 47.
23. King, 47.
24. King, 47.
25. King, 47.
26. King, 47.
27. King, 47.
28. King, 47.
29. King, 47.
30. King, 48.
31. King, 48.
32. King, 48.
33. See also King, "Ethnographic Overview," 48–53.
34. King, 50–51; Heizer, *Hugo Reid's Letters*, 9.
35. King, "Ethnographic Overview," 50–51.
36. King, 50, 108.
37. See chapter 3; FTBMI Archive Doc. 40009.Q.DC.
38. See chapter 4; L. H. Valentine to Frank Lewis, December 3, 1895, Frank D. Lewis Papers, Library of the Southwest Museum, Pasadena, CA, FTBMI Archive Doc. 80838.
39. "Terrible Wrongs," *Los Angeles Herald*, 3.
40. Latta, *Saga of Rancho El Tejón*, 203.
41. Latta, 133–35 (as told by J. J. Lopez). See FTBMI Archive Doc. 40009.Q.DC.
42. See Johnson, "Indians of Mission San Fernando," *Southern California Quarterly*, 262.
43. In 1854, an assistant to Thomas J. Henley, superintendent of Indian affairs in California, submitted a report on the Sebastian (Tejon) Reservation to the commissioner of Indian affairs, referencing and quoting from articles published

on June 17, 1854, and June 24, 1854, in the *Los Angeles Star*, which named the captains on that reservation. Letters Received by the Commissioner of Indian Affairs, 1824–1880, NA, M-234, Roll #34, CA Superintendency, FTBMI Archive Docs. 40080M.DC and 40080L.DC.

44. Johnson, "Indians of Mission San Fernando," 263–64.
45. See Report from assistant to Thomas J. Henley to Commissioner of Indian Affairs, FTBMI Archive Docs. 40080L.DC and 40080.M.DC (naming captains at Tejon).
46. Hartnell, *Diary and Copybook*, 44.
47. Latta, *Saga of Rancho El Tejón*, 218.
48. Johnson, "Indians of Mission San Fernando," 286n37.
49. See Report from assistant to Thomas J. Henley to Commissioner of Indian Affairs, FTBMI Archive Doc. 40080L.DC.
50. Johnson, "Indians of Mission San Fernando," 262–63.
51. Hudson, *The Breath of the Sun* (Banning, CA: Malki Museum Press, 1979), 99.
52. See Report from assistant to Thomas J. Henley to Commissioner of Indian Affairs, FTBMI Archive Doc. 40080M.DC.
53. Latta, *Saga of Rancho El Tejón*, 129.
54. U.S. Census, 1850, Los Angeles County, CA, FTBMI Archive Doc. 80380.B.USC.
55. See *Field Notes on the Fernandeno*, Papers of John Peabody Harrington in the Smithsonian Institution, 1907–1957, Autry National Center, Braun Library, Los Angeles, CA, FTBMI Archive Doc. 00329.A.SW; L. H. Valentine to F. D. Lewis, December 27, 1895, Autry National Center, Braun Library, Los Angeles, CA, FTBMI Archive Doc. 91179.VAL.
56. See chapter 4.
57. Johnson, "Indians of Mission San Fernando," 261; U.S. Census, 1850, Los Angeles County, CA, FTBMI Archive Docs. 80380.B.USC and 80802.USC.286.288.
58. Latta, *Saga of Rancho El Tejón*, 129.
59. See document 40009.Q.DC.
60. Latta, *Saga of Rancho El Tejón*, 129.
61. See Report from assistant to Thomas J. Henley to Commissioner of Indian Affairs, FTBMI Archive Docs. 40080L.DC and 40080.M.DC (naming captains at Tejon).
62. Johnson, "Indians of Mission San Fernando," 263.
63. See Report from assistant to Thomas J. Henley to Commissioner of Indian Affairs, FTBMI Archive Doc. 40080L.DC.
64. Johnson, "Indians of Mission San Fernando," 264.
65. "Terrible Wrongs," *Los Angeles Herald*, 3.

66. Horatio Nelson Rust, Notes, "Rugerego of San Fernando," undated, Horatio Nelson Rust Papers, RU 500, HL, 1.
67. See chapter 4.
68. "Terrible Wrongs," *Los Angeles Herald*, 3; "Little Interviews: Straws on the Currents of Public Opinion," *Los Angeles Times*, 4; *Field Notes on the Fernandeno*, Papers of John Peabody Harrington in the Smithsonian Institution, 1907–1957, Autry National Center, Braun Library, Los Angeles, CA, FTBMI Archive Doc. 00329.A.SW; J. P. Harrington Papers: Kitanemuk, NMNH-Harrington_mf3_r98_0686, FTBMI Archive Doc. 80811.Eugenia; Johnson, "Indians of Mission San Fernando," 270–72; Frank D. Lewis to U.S. Commissioner of Indian Affairs, October 17, 1892, Letter No. 37571, RG 75, NA, FTBMI Archive Doc. 80856, 2.
69. Librado, *Eye of the Flute*, 31, 91, 93, 139.
70. "Terrible Wrongs," *Los Angeles Herald*, 3.
71. Documents U.S. Census, 1850, Los Angeles County, CA, Schedule I, p. 23, Dwelling 293, July 1, 1850, FTBMI Archive Doc. 80108.A.USC.
72. See chapter 3.
73. See Deed for Encino, Roman, Roque, Tiburcio and Francisco, July 14, 1835, with reference to 1843 deed or grant given by Governor Micheltorena. Carpenter, "Rancho Encino," 12–13.
74. Walker and Hudson, *Chumash Healing*, 44–55.
75. See chapter 4.
76. See chapters 4 and 5.
77. FTBMI Archive Doc. 91150.PLC.
78. FTBMI Archive Doc. 80291.LPC.
79. See this appendix, numbers 83 and 87.
80. See this appendix number 54.
81. See chapter 6.
82. See chapter 6.
83. See chapter 6.
84. See Application for enrollment with the Indians of the State of California under the Act of May 18, 1928, RG 75, NA, Margaret Ward (#11018), FTBMI Archive Doc. 40060.A.DC.; FTBMI Archive Doc. 90707.OTC.
85. See Gordon, *TIQ SLO'W*, 50–54. For further information regarding Mary's ancestry, see "Birth Certificate: Caroline Francis Garcia," available at https://scvhistory.com/scvhistory/tlp2301.htm (visited November 3, 2019).
86. See chapter 7 and appendix D.
87. Photographs of the ceremony are at FTBMI Archive Docs. 80783.FTO, 80784.FTO, 80785.FTO, 80786.FTO, 80787.FTO, 80788.FTO, and 80788.FTO.

88. For a history of Charlie Cooke's life and activities, see Gordon, *TIQ SLO'W*.
89. John Valenzuela, interview by Leon Worden, available at http://www.scvhistory.com/scvhistory/signal/newsmaker/sg071104.htm (visited September 20, 2019).
90. Gordon, *TIQ SLO'W*, 18, 50–54, 224, 265–68, 274, 285, 300.
91. Bostwick, "Garcia Legacy," *Antelope Valley Press*, C8; Chief Little Bear, "Applauding Our Achievements," *Tarahat*, 1–3.
92. David Salazar Sr., Stanley Salazar, and Rudy Ortega Jr. interview (part 2), FTBMI Archive Doc. 80324.INT, at 18 (Rudy Ortega Jr.).

APPENDIX B

1. The list of petitioners is attached to Letter from Frank D. Lewis to U.S. Commissioner of Indian Affairs, October 17, 1892, Letter No. 37571, RG 75, NA, FTBMI Archive Doc. 40009.Q.DC.
2. Johnson, "Indians of Mission San Fernando," 261, table 4.
3. See Report from assistant to Thomas J. Henley to Commissioner of Indian Affairs, FTBMI Archive Docs. 40080L.DC and 40080.M.DC (naming captains at Tejon).
4. Johnson, "Indians of Mission San Fernando," 263.
5. See J. P. Harrington Papers: Kitanemuk, NMNH-Harrington_mf3_r98_0686, FTBMI Archive Doc. 80811.Eugenia.
6. "Terrible Wrongs," *Los Angeles Herald*, 3: "My father was a captain of my people. His name was Jerman. He never went away. . . . Then after my father died I became the captain, as all my people recognized me as such. I do not remember how long this was when I became captain of my people."
7. Rogerio confirmed that his father Jerman (or German) lived past the mission period. See "Terrible Wrongs," *Los Angeles Herald*, 3.
8. See U.S. Census, 1850, Los Angeles County, CA, January 29, 1850, p. 22, household 289, FTBMI Archive Doc. 80803.USC.288.289.
9. See U.S. Census, 1860, San Buenaventura Township Santa Barbara, CA, p. 14, household 73, FTBMI Archive Doc. 80809.USC (showing Jose and Leandra). Rufino Leyba was the godfather of Efren, Jose Juan's father (SFR Baptism #00803).
10. See Application for enrollment with the Indians of the State of California under the Act of May 18, 1928, RG 75, NA, Robert Addington and family (#11248), FTBMI Archive Doc. 40067.DC.
11. U.S. Census, 1850, Los Angeles County, January 29, 1850, p. 22, household 289, FTBMI Archive Doc. 80380.D.USC.
12. U.S. Census, 1860, Los Angeles County, FTBMI Archive Doc. 91181.USC.1860. numbers.

13. U.S. Census, 1850, Los Angeles County, January 29, 1850, p. 22, household 289, FTBMI Archive Doc. 80380.D.USC.

APPENDIX C

1. This chart focuses on progenitors discussed or mentioned in the book.
2. Josefa also later married William Gardner and Antonio Gutierrez, both non-Native.
3. James/Jim Garcia married Maria Miranda from Tejon/Topipabit, and their descendants are now associated with the Tejon Indian Tribe.
4. This chart focuses on progenitors discussed or mentioned in the book.
5. At the time of her marriage to Fernando Ortega, she was a widow, having married Benigno (Cabuepet/Cahuenga) in 1845. Benigno died sometime around 1860. None of her children with Benigno survived to adulthood.
6. This chart focuses on progenitors discussed or mentioned in the book.
7. Yabit is a village associated with San Gabriel Mission, not San Fernando.

APPENDIX D

1. For discussion of the significance of these names, see chapter 6 at notes 187–197 and 206. Only two of the three lineages currently participating in the FTBMI applied for inclusion in this roll. The Ortega lineage, demonstrating their political autonomy, opted not to apply.
2. See chapter 6 at notes 105–108.
3. See chapter 7 at note 93.
4. See chapter 7 at notes 109–115 and Tribal Constitution of the Fernandeño Tataviam Band of Mission Indians, chapter 1, article 1, describing the tribe as "a participatory union of clans, families, and persons descended from the original people of the Fernandeño Tataviam traditional villages, rancherias, and of Mission San Fernando."
5. See chapter 7 at notes 122–123.

GLOSSARY

1. See Bean and Smith, "Gabrielino," 538.
2. Engelhardt, *San Fernando Rey*, 26.
3. See Johnson and Earle, "Tataviam Geography and Ethnohistory," 191–214.

BIBLIOGRAPHY

GUIDE TO ARCHIVAL SOURCES

BANC	Bancroft Library, University of California, Berkeley
RG 75, NA	Record Group 75 (Records of the Bureau of Indian Affairs), National Archives of the United States
LPC	Archives of La Plaza Church, Los Angeles, CA
HL	Huntington Library, San Marino, CA
Braun Library	Autry National Center, Los Angeles, CA (formerly at Southwest Museum)
CMD	Santa Bárbara Mission Archive-Library, Santa Barbara, CA

All references to mission-era baptisms, marriages, and burials (e.g., SFR Baptism #_____) are from the Early California Population Project of the Huntington Library, San Marino, CA (2006), available at https://www.huntington.org/ecpp. SFR refers to Mission San Fernando Rey

BOOKS

Alexander, Jeffrey C. *Theoretical Logic In Sociology*. 4 vols. Berkeley: University of California Press, 1986.

Anderson, John. *A Circle Within the Abyss*. Kootenai, ID: AmDes Press, 2000.

Anderson, John. *The Fox Jumps and Renews Life: Spiritual Rebirth in Native American Cosmology*. Kootenai, ID: AmDes, 1994.

Anderson, John. *Kuta Teachings: Reincarnation Theology and the Chumash Path of the Dead.* Kootenai: AmDes, 2002.

Anderson, Kat. *Tending the Wild: Native American Knowledge and the Management of California's Natural Resources.* Berkeley: University of California Press, 2005.

Attorney General of the United States. *Annual Report of the Attorney-General of the United States for the Year 1893.* Washington, DC: Government Printing Office, 1893.

Attorney General of the United States. *Annual Report of the Attorney-General of the United States for the Year 1897.* Washington, DC: Government Printing Office, 1897.

Avina, Rose H. *Spanish and Mexican Land Grants in California.* San Francisco: R. and E. Research Associates, 1973.

Bancroft, Hubert Howe. *History of California, Vol. III: 1825–1840.* San Francisco: A. L. Bancroft, 1885.

Bancroft, Hubert Howe. *History of California, Vol. V: 1846–1848.* Santa Barbara: Wallace Hebberd, 1886.

Banner, Stuart. *How the Indians Lost Their Land: Law and Power on the Frontier.* Cambridge: Harvard University Press, 2007.

Bean, Lowell John. *Mukat's People: The Cahuilla of Southern California.* Berkeley: University of California Press, 1972.

Bean, Lowell John, and Thomas C. Blackburn, eds. *Native Californians: A Theoretical Retrospective.* Ramona, CA: Ballena, 1976.

Beechey, Captain F. W., R.N. *Narrative of a Voyage to the Pacific and Beering's Strait to Cooperate with the Polar Expeditions: Perform in His Majesty's Ship Blossom under the Commend of Captain F. W. Beechey, R. N. in the Years 1825, 1826, 1827, 1828, Vol. II.* Westminster: J. B. Nichols and Son, 1831.

Bell, Horace. *Reminiscences of a Ranger: Early Times in Southern California.* Norman: University of Oklahoma Press, 1999.

Blackburn, Thomas. *December's Child: A Book of Chumash Oral Narratives.* Berkeley: University of California Press, 1975.

Brewer, William H. *Up and Down California in 1860–1864.* Berkeley: University of California Press, 2003.

Caughey, John Walton, ed. *The Indians of Southern California in 1852: The B. D. Wilson Report and a Selection of Contemporary Commentary.* Lincoln: University of Nebraska Press, 1995.

Cipolla, Craig N., ed. *Foreign Objects: Rethinking Indigenous Consumption in American Archaeology.* Tucson: University of Arizona Press, 2017.

Cleland, Robert Glass. *The Cattle on a Thousand Hills: Southern California, 1850–1880.* San Marino: Huntington Library, 1941.

Coronel, Antonio. *Tales of Mexican California.* Edited by Doyce B. Nunis Jr. Santa Barbara: Bellerophon Books, 1994.

Costo, Rupert, and Jeannette Henry Costo, eds. *The Missions of California: A Legacy of Genocide.* San Francisco: Indian Historian, 1987.

Dakin, Susanna Bryant. *The Lives of William Hartnell.* Stanford: Stanford University Press, 1949.

Dakin, Susanna Bryant. *A Scotch Paisano in Old Los Angeles: Hugo Reid's Life in California, 1832–1852 Derived from His Correspondence.* Berkeley: University of California Press, 1959.

Dana, Richard Henry. *Two Years Before the Mast.* Boston: Fields Osgood, 1869.

DuBois, Constance Goddard. *The Condition of the Mission Indians of Southern California.* Philadelphia: Office of the Indian Rights Association, 1901.

Engelhardt, Zephyrin. *The Missions and Missionaries of California.* Vol. 1. San Francisco: James H. Barry, 1908.

Engelhardt, Zephyrin. *The Missions and Missionaries of California.* Vol. 2. San Francisco: James H. Barry, 1912.

Engelhardt, Zephyrin. *The Missions and Missionaries of California.* Vol. 3. San Francisco: James H. Barry, 1913.

Engelhardt, Zephyrin. *The Missions and Missionaries of California.* Vol. 4. San Francisco: The James H. Harry, 1913.

Engelhardt, Zephyrin. *San Fernando Rey: The Mission of the Valley.* Chicago: Franciscan Herald, 1927.

Engelhardt, Zephyrin. *San Gabriel Mission and the Beginnings of Los Angeles.* Chicago: Franciscan Herald, 1927.

Faracher, John Mack. *Eternity Street: Violence and Justice in Frontier Los Angeles.* New York: W. W. Norton, 2016.

Fixico, Donald Lee. *Termination and Relocation: Federal Indian Policy, 1945–1960.* Albuquerque: University of New Mexico Press, 1990.

Frank, Gelya, and Carole Goldberg. *Defying the Odds: The Tule River Tribe's Struggle for Sovereignty in Three Centuries.* New Haven: Yale University Press, 2010.

Garner, Brian, A., and Henry Campbell Black. *Black's Law Dictionary*, 10th ed. Eagan, MN: Thomson West, 2014.

Gordon, Mary Louise Contini. *TIQ SLO'W: The Making of a Modern Day Chief.* Tucson: Amethyst Moon, 2013.

Guest, Francis F. *Fermin Francisco Lasuén (1736–1803): A Biography.* Washington: American Academy of Franciscan History, 1973.

Gunther, Vanessa Ann. *Ambiguous Justice: Native Americans and the Law in Southern California, 1848–1890.* East Lansing: Michigan State University Press, 2006.

Haas, Lisbeth. *Conquests and Historical Identities in California, 1769–1936.* Berkeley: University of California Press, 1995.

Hackel, Steven W. *Children of Coyote, Missionaries of Saint Francis: Indian-Spanish Relations in Colonial California 1769–1850.* Chapel Hill: University of North Carolina Press, 2005.

Hansen, Woodrow James. *The Search for Authority in California.* Oakland: Biobooks, 1960.

Hartnell, William Edward Petty. *The Diary and Copybook of William E.P. Hartnell: Visitador General of the Missions of Alta California in 1839 and 1840.* Spokane, WA: Arthur H. Clark, 2004.

Hegel, G. W. F. *The Philosophy of History.* Mineola, NY: Dover, 1956.

Heizer, Robert F. *The California Indians vs. the United States of America, HR 4497: Evidence Offered in Support of Occupancy, Possession, and Use of Land in California by the Ancestors of Enrolled Indians of California.* Socorro, NM: Ballena, 1978.

Heizer, Robert F. *The Eighteen Unratified Treaties of 1851–1852 Between the California Indians and the United States Government.* Berkeley: Archaeological Research Facility, Department of Anthropology, University of California, 1972.

Heizer, Robert F., ed. *Handbook of North American Indians, Vol. 8: California.* Washington: Smithsonian Institution, 1978.

Heizer, Robert F., ed. *The Indians of Los Angeles County: Hugo Reid's Letters of 1852.* Highland Park, TX: Southwest Museum, 1968.

Hoffman, Ogden. *Reports of Land Cases Determined in the United States District Court for the Northern District of California: June Term, 1853 to June Term, 1858, Inclusive.* San Francisco: Numa Hubert, 1862.

Hudson, Travis, and Earnest Underhay. *Crystals in the Sky: An Intellectual Odyssey Involving Chumash Astronomy, Cosmology and Rock Art.* Menlo Park, CA: Ballena, 1978.

Hyer, Joel R. *We Are Not Savages: Native Americans in Southern California and the Pala Reservation, 1840–1920.* East Lansing: Michigan State University Press, 2001.

Hyslop, Stephan G. *Contest for California: From Spanish Colonization to the American Conquest.* Norman, OK: Arthur H. Clarke, 2012.

Jackson, Helen Hunt. *A Century of Dishonor: A Sketch of the United States Government's Dealings with Some of the Indian Tribes.* New York: Harper and Brothers, 1881.

Jackson, Helen Hunt. *Ramona: A Story.* Boston: Roberts Brothers, 1888.

Jackson, Helen Hunt, and Abbot Kinney. *Report on the Condition and Needs of the Mission Indians in California.* Washington: Government Printing Press, 1883.

Jackson, Robert H., and Edward Castillo. *Indians, Franciscans, and Spanish Colonization: The Impact of the Mission System on California Indians.* Albuquerque: University of New Mexico Press, 1995.

Johnson, John R. *Ethnohistoric Overview for the Santa Susana Pass State Historic Park Cultural Resources Inventory.* Sacramento: Department of Parks and Recreation, 2006.

Johnston, Bernice. *California's Gabrielino Indians.* Los Angeles: Southwest Museum, 1962.

Jorgensen, Lawrence, ed. *San Fernando Valley: Past and Present.* Los Angeles: Pacific Rim Research, 1982.

Kenny, Robert W. *History and Proposed Settlement: Claims of California Indians.* Sacramento: State Printing Office, 1944.

Kirkewood, Burton. *History of Mexico.* Westport: Greenwood, 2000.

Kroeber, A. L. *Handbook of the Indians of California.* New York: Dover, 1927.

Lake Mohonk Conference of Friends of the Indian. *Proceedings of the Fifth Annual Meeting of the Lake Mohonk Conference of Friends of the Indian.* Philadelphia: Sherman, 1887. Document can be found at https://babel.hathitrust.org/cgi/pt?id=uc1.a0012443123&view=1up&seq=1.

Langsdorff, G. H. *Voyages and Travels in Various Parts of the World During the Years 1803, 1804, 1805, 1806, and 1807.* London: Henry Colburn, 1813.

Latta, Frank F. *Saga of Rancho El Tejón.* Santa Cruz: Bear State Books, 1976.

Lewis, Alice Bradbury, Marie E. Spellmeyer, Francis Platt Frankhouse, Kate Maclay Hubbard, Isabella Rice Granger Maclay, Olive Rose De Remer, Elinor Merrill Craig, and Ellie Colegrove Ingham, *The Valley of San Fernando.* San Fernando: Daughters of the American Revolution, 1924.

Librado, Fernando. *Breath of the Sun: Life in Early California as Told By a Chumash Indian to John P. Harrington.* Edited by Travis Hudson. Banning, CA: Malki Museum, 1979.

Librado, Fernando. *The Eye of the Flute: Chumash Traditional History and Ritual as Told by Fernando Librado Kitsepawit to J.P. Harrington.* Santa Barbara: Santa Barbara Museum of Natural History, 1977.

Lightfoot, Kent G. *Indians, Missionaries, and Merchants: The Legacy of Colonial Encounters on the California Frontiers.* Los Angeles: University of California Press, 2005.

Lindley, Walter, and J. P. Widney. *California of the South: Its Physical Geography, Climate, Resources, Routes of Travel, and Health-Resorts, Being a Complete Guide-Book to Southern California.* New York: Appleton, 1888.

Link, Tom. *Universal City: North Hollywood: A Centennial Portrait: An Illustrated History.* Chatsworth, CA: Windsor, 1991.

Madley, Benjamin. *An American Genocide: The United States and the California Indian Catastrophe.* New Haven: Yale University Press, 2016.

Mathes, Valerie Sherer. *Helen Hunt Jackson and Her Indian Reform Legacy.* Austin: University of Texas Press, 1990.

McCawley, William. *The First Angelinos: The Gabrielino Indians of Los Angeles.* Banning, CA: Malki Museum Press, 1996.

McLendon, Sally, and John Johnson. *Cultural Affiliation and Lineal Descent of Chumash Peoples in the Channel Islands and the Santa Monica Mountains.* National Park Service: Archaeology and Ethnography Program, 1999.

Meriam, Lewis. *The Problem of Indian Administration.* Baltimore: Johns Hopkins University Press, 1928.

Merriam, C. Hart. *Studies of California Indians.* Berkeley: University of California Press, 1962.

Milles, Antonio, and Richard Slobodin, eds. *Amerindian Rebirth: Reincarnation Belief Among Native North Americans and Inuit.* Toronto: University of Toronto Press, 1994.

Monroy, Douglas. *Thrown Among Strangers: The Making of Mexican Culture in Frontier California.* Berkeley: University of California Press, 1990.

Newhall, Ruth. *The Newhall Ranch: The Story of the Newhall Land & Farming Company.* San Marino, CA: Huntington Library, 1958.

Newton, Nell Jessup, Robert T. Anderson, Bethany R. Berger, Carole E. Goldberg, John P. Lavelle, Judith V. Royster, Joseph William Singer, and Kevin Washburn. *Cohen's Handbook of Federal Indian Law.* New Providence, NJ: LexisNexis, 2012.

Nichols, John. *Images of America: St. Francis Dam Disaster.* Charleston, SC: Arcadia, 2002.

Office of Indian Affairs. *Annual Report of the Commissioner of Indian Affairs.* Washington, DC: Government Printing Office, 1883.

Panich, Lee M. *Narratives of Persistence: Indigenous Negotiations of Colonization in Alta and Baja California.* Tucson: University of Arizona Press, 2020.

Panich, Lee M., and Tsim D. Schniede. *Indigenous Landscapes and Spanish Missions: New Perspectives from Archeology and Ethnohistory.* Tucson: University of Arizona Press, 2014.

Parsons, Talcott. *Societies: Evolutionary and Comparative Perspectives.* Upper Saddle River, NJ: Prentice Hall, 1966.

Pauley, Kenneth E., and Carol M. Pauley. *San Fernando Rey De Espana: An Illustrated History.* Spokane, WA: Arthur H. Clark, 2005.

Phillips, George Harwood. *"Bringing Them Under Subjection": California's Tejon Indian Reservation and Beyond, 1852–1864*. Lincoln and London: University of Nebraska Press, 2004.

Phillips, George Harwood. *Chiefs and Challengers: Indian Resistance and Cooperation in Southern California, 1769–1906*. Norman: University of Oklahoma Press, 2014.

Phillips, George Harwood. *Vineyards and Vaqueros: Indian Labor and the Economic Expansion of Southern California, 1771–1877*. Spokane, WA: Arthur H. Clark, 2010.

Pico, Pio. *Don Pio Pico's Historical Narrative*. Edited by Marten Cole and Henry Welcome. Glendale, CA: Arthur H. Clark, 1973.

Robinson, W. W. *Lawyers of Los Angeles: A History of the Los Angeles Bar Association and of the Bar of Los Angeles County*. Los Angeles: Los Angeles Bar Association, 1959.

Robinson, W. W. *The Story of the San Fernando Valley*. Los Angeles: Title Insurance and Trust Company, 1961.

Rockwell, John A. *A Compilation of Spanish and Mexican Law, in Relation to Mines, and Titles to Real Estate, in Force in California, Texas and New Mexico*. New York: J. S. Voorhics, 1851.

Salomon, Carlos Manuel. *Pío Pico: The Last Governor of Mexican California*. Norman: University of Oklahoma Press, 2010.

Sandos, James A. *Converting California: Indians and Franciscans in the Missions*. New Haven: Yale University Press, 2004.

Sanger, Kay. *When the Animals Were People*. Banning, CA: Malki Museum Press, 1983.

Shipek, Florence. *Pushed Into the Rocks: Southern California Indian Land Tenure 1769–1986*. Lincoln: University of Nebraska Press, 1988.

Shuck, Oscar Tulley, ed. *History of the Bench and Bar of California*. Los Angeles: Commercial Printing House, 1901.

Smith, Claire, ed. *Encyclopedia of Global Archaeology*. New York: Springer, 2013.

Smith, Wallace E. *This Land Was Ours: The Del Valles & Camulos*. Ventura, CA: Ventura County Historical Society, 1977.

Stewart, Maria Helena. *Los Encino's Past and Present*. Encino: Quality Printers, 1965.

Strong, William Duncan. *Aboriginal Society in Southern California*. Berkeley: University of California Press, 1929.

Thomas, D. H., ed. *Columbian Consequences: Vol. I, Archaeological and Historical Perspectives on the Spanish Borderlands West*. Washington, DC: Smithsonian Institution, 1989.

Trafzer, Clifford E. *The People of San Manuel Indian Reservation*. Patton, CA: San Manuel Band of Mission Indians, 2002.

United States. American Indian Policy Review Commission. *Final Report.* Washington, DC: Government Printing Office, 1977.

United States. Board of Indian Commissioners. *Twenty-Second Annual Report of the Board of Indian Commissioners.* Washington, DC: Government Printing Office, 1891.

United States Congress House Committee on Indian Affairs. *Indian Tribes of California: Hearings Before a Subcommittee of the Committee on Indian Affairs, Second Session.* Washington, DC: Government Printing Office, 1920.

United States Congress House Committee on Indian Affairs. *Indian Tribes of California: Hearings Before a Subcommittee of the Committee on Indian Affairs, Volume 2.* Washington, DC: Government Printing Office, 1922.

United States Congress House Committee on Indian Affairs. *Indian Tribes of California: Hearings on H.R. 8036 and H.R. 9497.* Washington, DC: Government Printing Office, 1926.

Walker, Phillip, and Travis Hudson. *Chumash Healing: Changing Health and Medical Practices in an American Indian Society.* Banning, CA: Malki Museum Press, 1993.

Weber, MSGR Francis J., ed. *The Mission in the Valley: A Documentary History of San Fernando, Rey de España.* Santa Barbara, CA: Kimberly, 1995.

Weber, Max. *The Protestant Ethic and the Spirit of Capitalism.* New York: Oxford University Press, 2011.

Weibel-Orlando, Joan. *Indian Country, L.A.: Maintaining Ethnic Community in Complex Society.* Urbana and Chicago: University of Illinois Press, 1991.

Wetmore, Chas A. *Report of Chas A. Wetmore, Special Commissioner of Mission Indians of Southern California.* Washington, DC: Government Print Office, 1875.

Wilkins, David E. *Hollow Justice: A History of Indigenous Claims in the United States.* New Haven: Yale University Press, 2013.

BOOK CHAPTERS

Bean, Lowell John. "Introduction." In *Aboriginal Society in Southern California*, edited by William Duncan Strong, xiv–xix. Banning, CA: Malki Museum Press, 1987.

Bean, Lowell John. "Social Organization in Native California." In *Native Californians: A Theoretical Perspective*, edited by Lowell J. Bean and Thomas C. Blackwell, 99–124. Ramona, CA: Ballena, 1976.

Bean, Lowell John, and Charles R. Smith. "Gabrielino." In *Handbook of North American Indians, Volume 8: California*, edited by Robert F. Heizer, 541–44. Washington, DC: Smithsonian Institution, 1978.

Bean, Lowell John, and Sylvia Brakke Vane. "Cults and Their Transformation." In *Handbook of North American Indians, Volume 8: California*, edited by Robert F. Heizer, 668. Washington, DC: Smithsonian Institution, 1978.

Blackburn, Thomas C., and Lowell John Bean. "Kitanemuk." In *Handbook of North American Indians, Volume 8: California*, edited by Robert F. Heizer, 565–66. Washington, DC: Smithsonian Institution, 1978.

Castillo, Edward D. "The Impact of Euro-American Exploration and Settlement." In *Handbook of North American Indians, Volume 8: California*, edited by Robert F. Heizer, 105. Washington, DC: Smithsonian Institution, 1978.

Caughey, John Walton. "Introduction." In *The Indians of Southern California in 1852: The B. D. Wilson Report and a Selection of Contemporary Commentary*, edited by John Walton Caughey, ix–xxxv. Lincoln: University of Nebraska Press, 1995.

Champagne, Duane. "The Cultural and Institutional Foundations of Native American Conservatism." In *Social Change and Cultural Continuity Among Native Nations*, edited by Duane Champagne, 25–65. Lanham, MD: AltaMira, 2007.

Danchevskaya, Oksana. "Concept of Soul Among North American Indians." In *Where No One Else Has Gone Before: Proceedings of the Ninth Native American Symposium*, 90–91. Durant: Southeastern Oklahoma State University, 2012.

De Vitoria, Francisco. "The First Relectio." Reproduced in translation in *Vitoria: Political Writings*, edited by Anthony Pagden and Jeremy Lawrence, 231–92. Cambridge: Cambridge University Press, 1991.

Heizer, Robert F. "Mythology: Regional Patterns and History of Research." In *Handbook of North American Indians, Volume 8: California*, edited by Robert F. Heizer, 656–57. Washington, DC: Smithsonian Institution, 1978.

Hoover, R. L. "Spanish-Native Interaction and Acculturation in the Alta California Missions." In *Columbian Consequences: Vol. I, Archaeological and Historical Perspectives on the Spanish Borderlands West*, edited by D. H. Thomas, 395–406. Washington, DC: Smithsonian Institution, 1989.

McDowell, Malcolm. "Report on the Landless Indians of California." In *Fifty-First Annual Report of the Board of Indian Commissioners to the Secretary of the Interior for the Fiscal Year Ended June 30, 1920*, by U.S. Board of Indian Commissioners. Washington, DC: Government Printing Office, 1920.

Panich, Lee M. "Indigenous Vaqueros in Colonial California: Labor, Identity, and Autonomy." In *Foreign Objects: Rethinking Indigenous Consumption in American Archaeology*, edited by Craig N. Cipolla, 187–203. Tucson: University of Arizona Press, 2017.

Panich, Lee M. "Mission Archaeology in North America." In *Encyclopedia of Global Archaeology*, edited by Claire Smith, 4955–60. New York: Springer, 2013.

Sandos, James A. "Social Control Within Missionary Frontier Society: Alta California 1769–1821." In *Choice, Persuasion and Coercion: Social Control on Spain's North*

American Frontiers, edited by Jesus F. de la Teja and Ross Frank, 262–64. Albuquerque: University of New Mexico Press, 2005.

Stewart, Omer C. "Litigation and Its Effects." In *Handbook of North American Indians, Volume 8: California,* edited by Robert F. Heizer, 707. Washington, DC: Smithsonian Institution, 1978.

Weber, Max. "Politics as a Vocation." In *From Max Weber: Essays in Sociology,* edited by H. H. Gerth and C. Wright Mills, 77–128. New York: Oxford University Press, 1946.

Wilson, B. D. "The Indians of Southern California in 1852." In *The Indians of Southern California in 1852: The B. D. Wilson Report and a Selection of Contemporary Commentary*, edited by John Walton Caughey, 1–69. Lincoln: University of Nebraska Press, 1995.

JOURNAL ARTICLES, WEBSITES, ARCHIVES

Alegria, Andrea. "An Opportunity to Share Their Heritage, Fernandeño Tataviam Band of Mission Indians Will Conduct the Blessings at the Day of the Dead Festival." *San Fernando Valley Sun.* FTBMI Archive Doc. 00098.FTO.

American Indian Policy Review Commission. *Final Report.* Washington, DC: Government Printing Office, 1977.

American Presidency Project. "Grover Cleveland, 24th President of the United States: 1893–1897, Special Message, January 17, 1896." Accessed May 15, 2019. https://www.presidency.ucsb.edu/documents/special-message-669.

Anna, Timothy E. "The Rule of Agustin de Iturbide: A Reappraisal." In *Journal of Latin American Studies* 17, no. 1 (May 1985): 79–110.

Apostol, Jane. "Horatio Nelson Rust: Abolitionist, Archaeologist, Indian Agent." *California History* 58, no. 4 (1979): 304–15.

Avocado Memories. "From *The History of San Fernando Valley,* by Frank M. Keffer, Van Nuys, 1934" and "From *Burbank History* by Author Jackson Mayers, PhD, 1975." Accessed May 13, 2019. http://wesclark.com/am/providencia.html.

Bakersfield California. "Century-Old Native of Kern County Is Called." May 15, 1928, 1.

Blackburn, Thomas C. "Ethnohistoric Descriptions of Gabrielino Material Culture." In *UCLA Archaeological Survey Annual Report* (1963):1–42.

Bostwick, Charles F. "Garcia Legacy Still Ripples Through Littlerock." *Antelope Valley Press*, February 27, 2013, C8.

Bramstedt, Wayne G. "Corporate Adaptations of Urban Migrants: American Indian Voluntary Associations in the Los Angeles Metropolitan Area." PhD diss., University of California, Los Angeles, 1977.

Bynum, Lindley. "Governor Don Felip De Neve." *Historical Society of Southern California* 15, no. 1 (1931): 57–62.

California Genealogy and History Archives, Rootsweb. "C. R. Rinaldi, Los Angeles County, CA, Biographies." Accessed May 13, 2019. http://sites.rootsweb.com/~cagha/biographies/r/rinaldi-c-r.txt.

Carpenter, Bruce R. "Rancho Encino: Its Historical Geography." Master's thesis, University of California, Los Angeles, 1948.

Chief Little Bear. "Applauding Our Achievements." *Tarahat: The People*, no. 1 (April 1999): 1, 3.

Chief Little Bear. "Marching Forward." *Tarahat: The People* 3, no. 1 (February–April, 2004): 2.

Clarke, Margie Anne. "Celebrate American Indian Culture!" *Signal* (Santa Clarita, CA), September 27, 2002, E7.

Cordova, Blanca E. "Local Indians Vie for Status." *Signal* (Santa Clarita, CA), May 14, 2000, A1.

Daly, Heather Marie. "American Indian Freedom Controversy: Political and Social Activism by Southern California Mission Indians, 1934–1958." PhD diss., University of California, Los Angeles, 2012.

DeBow, J. D. B. *Report on the Seventh Census of the United States.* Washington, DC: Robert Armstrong, Public Printer, 1853. https://www.census.gov/library/publications/1853/dec/1850a.html.

De Celis, Eulogio F. "Card of Thanks." *Los Angeles Times*, November 29, 1885, 5.

De Celis, Eulogio F. "The Indians' Side of the Controversy." *Los Angeles Times*, November 24, 1885, 4.

De Victoria, Franciscus. *The First Relectio, On the Indians Lately Discovered* (1539). Accessed September 30, 2019. https://www.constitution.org/victoria/victoria_4.htm.

Dubois, Constance Goddard. "Religious Ceremonies and Myths of the Mission Indians." *American Anthropologist* 7, no. 4 (Oct.-Dec., 1905): 620–29.

Dumke, Glenn. "The Boom of the 1880s in Southern California." *Southern California Quarterly* 76, no. 1 (1994): 99–114

Ellison, William Henry. "The Federal Indian Policy in California, 1846–1860." Master's thesis, University of California, Berkeley, 1913.

FamilySearch. "United States Census, 1860." Accessed July 20, 2019. https://familysearch.org/ark:/61903/1:1:MDKD-QQD

Fatehi, Kimia. "Tribal Cultural Resources Management: A Case Study of the Fernandeño Tataviam Band of Mission Indians." Master's thesis, UCLA, 2017.

Fernandeño Tataviam. "Rogerio Rocha, San Fernando." Accessed May 13, 2019. http://www.tataviam-nsn.us/heritage/tribal-captains/rogerio-rocha-san-fernando/.

Fernandeño Tataviam Band of Mission Indians. "Territory and Brief Ethnohistory of the Fernandeño Tataviam Band of Mission Indians." Accessed July 30, 2019. https://scvhistory.com/scvhistory/ftbmi_ethnohistory2016.pdf.

Figueroa, Jose. "Provisional Regulation for the Secularization of the Missions of Upper California." *The Los Angeles Star*, August 9, 1834.

Fold3 by Ancestry. "1860 U.S. Federal Census—Population." Accessed July 20, 2019. http://www.fold3.com.

Frith, Eric. "The Rebellion Against the Mission of the Saintly Prince of the Archangel, San Gabriel of the Temblors, 1785," 2014. Accessed July 3, 2019. https://www.kcet.org/history-society/the-rebellion-against-the-mission-of-the-saintly-prince-the-archangel-san-gabriel-of.

Goldberg, Carole E. "Public Law 280: The Limits of State Jurisdiction over Reservation Indians." *UCLA Law Review* 22 (1975): 535–94.

Greene, Betty Patchin. "The Alcaldes of California." *Saudi Aramco World* 27, no. 6 (1976): 26–29.

Haas, Lisbeth. "Emancipation and the Meaning of Freedom in Mexican California." *Boletín* 20, no. 1 (Fall 2003): 16–17.

Haas, Lisbeth. "War in California, 1846–1848." *California History* 76, no. 2/3 (Summer/Fall, 1997): 331–55.

Hackel, Steven W. "Sources of Rebellion: Indian Testimony and the Mission San Gabriel Uprising of 1785." *Ethnohistory* 50, no. 4 (2003): 643–69.

Hackel, Steven W. "The Staff of Leadership: Indian Authority in the Missions of Alta California." *William and Mary Quarterly* 54, no. 2 (1997): 346–76.

Hansen, Kenneth. "Indians Claim Share of Land Reparations." *Los Angeles Times*. July 2, 1970, 4.

Harrington, Marie E. Review of *The Mission in the Valley. A Documentary History of San Fernando Rey de España*, by Francis J. Weber. *Southern California Quarterly* 59, no. 3 (1977): 313–15.

Harrington, Mark R. "San Fernando Bells Ring Again." *Masterkey* 20, no. 2 (March 1946): 64–66.

Hoopes, Alban W., and George W. Barbour. "The Journal of George W. Barbour, May 1, to October 4, 1851: II." *Southwestern Historical Quarterly* 40, no. 3 (Jan. 1937): 247–61.

Hudson, Travis. "A Rare Account of Gabrielino Shamanism from the Notes of John P. Harrington." *Journal of California and Great Basin Anthropology* 1, no. 2 (1979): 356–61.

Hudson, Travis, and Thomas C. Blackburn. "The Integration of Myth and Ritual in South-Central California: The Northern Complex." In *Journal of California Anthropology* 5 (1978): 225–50.

Huntington Library. "Early California Population Project." Accessed September 27, 2019. https://huntingtonlibrary.libguides.com/ecpp.

Jacobs, Julie. "Cave Drawings Reveal Chumash Indians Past." *Los Angeles Times*, January 28, 1971, 1.

Jacobs, Julie. "5 Valley Indians Seek Seat." *Valley News* (Van Nuys, CA), May 19, 1977, 32.

Jacobs, Julie. "Indians Call Land Claims Conference." *Valley News and Green Sheet* (Van Nuys, CA), October 10, 1972, 1.

Jacobs, Julie. "Indians May Press Claim on Rocketdyne Test Site." *Los Angeles Times, Valley News*, August 17, 1971, 1.

Jacobs, Julie. "Indian Points Out Error on Los Encino Brochure." *Valley News and Green Sheet* (Van Nuys, CA), July 27, 1972.

Johnson, John R., "Ethnohistory of the Tejon Indian Tribe." 2016. https://static1.squarespace.com/static/544b30c0e4b0023e70482546/t/5a8c9000e2c483d3b9f533b1/1519161349611/Tejon+Tribe_Ethnohistory_JJohnson_2016.pdf.

Johnson, John R. "The Indians of Mission San Fernando." *Southern California Quarterly* 79, no. 3 (Fall 1997): 249–90.

Johnson, John R., and David D. Earle. "Tataviam Geography and Ethnohistory." *Journal of California and Great Basin Anthropology* 12, no. 2 (1990): 191–214.

King, Chester. "Ethnographic Overview of the Angeles National Forest Tataviam and San Gabriel Mountain Serrano Ethnohistory." Arcadia: U.S. Department of Agriculture, 2004.

King, Chester. "Japchibit Ethnohistory." Los Angeles: Topanga Anthropological Consultants. September 2003.

Klein, Liane. "Native Americans Fight for Cemetery." *Signal* (Santa Clarita, CA), March 26, 2001, A1.

Kondo, Annette. "Splintered Tribe Seeks Federal Recognition." *Los Angeles Times*, May 30, 2000. https://www.latimes.com/archives/la-xpm-2000-may-30-me-35590-story.html.

Kroeber, A. L. "Map from Alfred L. Kroeber's *Handbook of the Indians of California*." Washington, DC: Smithsonian Institution, 1925. Accessed July 3, 2019. http://cla.berkeley.edu/language-maps.php.

Kroeber, A. L. "A Mission Record of the California Indians: San Fernando" (1908). Accessed July 3, 2019. http://www.sacred-texts.com/nam/ca/mrci/mrci06.htm.

Kroeber, A. L. *The Nature of Land-Holding Groups in Aboriginal California*. Accessed July 28, 2019. http://digitalassets.lib.berkeley.edu/anthpubs/ucb/text/ucas056-003.pdf.

Kroeber, A. L. "Two Myths of the Mission Indians of California." *The Journal of American Folklore* 19, no. 75 (Oct.–Dec., 1906): 309–21.

Larralde, Carlos M., and Richard Griswold del Castillo. "San Diego's Ku Klux Klan 1920–1980." *The Journal of San Diego History* 46, nos. 2–3 (Spring/Summer 2000).

Larson, Holly Rose. "Finding Aid to the Frank Dunham Lewis Papers MS.553." Online Archive of California. Accessed May 15, 2019. http://www.oac.cdlib.org/findaid/ark:/13030/c8959jrx/entire_text/.

Leach, Eric. "Indian Children Visit Ancestral Site." *Daily News*, January 5, 1985.

Lopez Adobe. "George K. Porter and San Fernando." Accessed August 24, 2015. https://lopezadobe.wordpress.com/2015/08/24/george-k-porter-and-san-fernando.

Lopez Adobe. "Gerónimo and Catalina López and the 1850 Federal and 1852 State Censuses." Accessed February 5, 2013. https://lopezadobe.wordpress.com/2013/02/05/geronimo-and-catarina-lopez-and-the-1850-federal-and-1852-state-censuses/.

Los Angeles Herald. "An Action for Libel." January 28, 1896.

Los Angeles Herald. "The Early Practices: How the Mission Indians Were Dealt With. The Fraud and Deception." March 1, 1896, 4.

Los Angeles Herald. "He Never Had Any Title; What Mr. Lewis Thinks of Rogerio Rocha's Rights; Got a Deed All the Same; 'Justice' Makes a Proposition to Judge Widney Worthy of Consideration." February 5, 1896, 3.

Los Angeles Herald. "Hon. Frank D. Lewis' Fee; The Indian Land Association Hired Several Lawyers; Was Lewis One of Them?; The President of the Association Says Positively That He Was When He Was the Government Attorney for the Mission Indians Appointed to Protect Their Rights." February 7, 1896.

Los Angeles Herald. "Judge R. M. Widney's Say Regarding Rogerio Rocha's Claims to Mission Lands." March 23, 1896, 7.

Los Angeles Herald. "Mission Indians: Hon. J. Shirley Ward's Final Report on Them." September 14, 1887, 10.

Los Angeles Herald. "The Mission Indians: The Story of Their Wrongs and the Remedy Proposed—A Practical View of the Indian Question." November 10, 1875.

Los Angeles Herald. "One Who Knows the Record: Writes Interestingly about the Wrongs of Rogerio Rocha." March 23, 1896, 7.

Los Angeles Herald. "Roger Rocha's History: Senator Del Valle's Tale." January 29, 1896, 8.

Los Angeles Herald. "Rogerio Rocha's Lands." January 24, 1896, 5.

Los Angeles Herald. "Rogerio Rocha's Lands; A Tale of Injustice Done an Indian; Deeded His Rights Away," January 21, 1896.

Los Angeles Herald. "Rogerio Rocha's Rights." February 17, 1896, 6.

Los Angeles Herald. "A Story of the Terrible Wrongs that Have Been Put Upon Rogerio Rocha; Turned Out of His Home with His Bedridden Wife in a Blinding Rainstorm to Die; Afterward Proposed to Erect a Theological Seminary on the Land Obtained by This Cruel Eviction." February 2, 1896, 3.

Los Angeles Herald. "There Was a Trust Deed; Attorney Lewis Gave It to Rogerio Rocha." January 25, 1896, 5.

Los Angeles Herald. "Wrongs of Rogerio Rocha." March 1, 1896, 4.

Los Angeles Star. "Finis." April 24, 1869.

Los Angeles Star. "Indian Affairs." September 13, 1856.

Los Angeles Star. "The Indians Again." March 24, 1860.

Los Angeles Star. "The Indians of Southern California: Report of Hon. B. D. Wilson, 1852 to the Superintendent of Indian Affairs (No. IV)." August 8, 1868.

Los Angeles Star. "The Indians of Southern California: Report of Hon. B. D. Wilson, 1852 to the Superintendent of Indian Affairs (No. VI)." August 22, 1868.

Los Angeles Star. "The Indians of Southern California: Report of Hon. B. D. Wilson, 1852 to the Superintendent of Indian Affairs (No. VII)." August 29, 1868.

Los Angeles Star. "Interesting Facts Concerning the Mission San Fernando." June 21, 1851.

Los Angeles Star. "Los Angeles County Indians: Letter No. IV." March 6, 1852.

Los Angeles Star. "Los Angeles County Indians: Letter No. V2I, Births and Burials." March 27, 1852.

Los Angeles Star. "Report of Honorable B. D. Wilson to the Superintendent of Indian Affairs." July 25, 1868.

Los Angeles Times. "Back to Rancho." January 18, 1988, 1.

Los Angeles Times. "Briefs." July 14, 1887, 4.

Los Angeles Times. "California Indians May Get Justice," November 8, 1928, 21.

Los Angeles Times. "Data Offered on Funds For Indians." May 4, 1972, 2.

Los Angeles Times. "56 Indian Children Prepare to Dance." September 5, 1970, 14.

Los Angeles Times. "Golden Secret in His Grave." March 1904, A7.

Los Angeles Times. "Indian Culture Center Meeting Slated Sunday." January 29, 1973.

Los Angeles Times. "Indian Land Claims Will Be Discussed." October 31, 1971, SF3.

Los Angeles Times. "Indians to Confer." June 26, 1970, SF6.

Los Angeles Times. "Intertribal Indian Club to Be Formed." February 14, 1972, 6.

Los Angeles Times. "Little Interviews: The San Fernando Indians." November 22, 1885, 1.

Los Angeles Times. "Little Interviews: Straws on the Currents of Public Opinion." November 17, 1885, 4.

Los Angeles Times. "The Mission Indians: The Manner of Their Treatment a Shame to Civilization." February 17, 1882, 2.

Los Angeles Times. "Party Schedule for Needy Children." December 17, 1972, 9.

Los Angeles Times. "Rudy Ortega President of the San Fernando Mission Indians." October 31, 1970, SF3.

Los Angeles Times. "The San Fernando Indians: Statement by Judge Widney as to Their Eviction." September 12, 1886, 1.

Los Angeles Times, San Fernando Valley. "Snake Dance, Practiced by San Fernando Mission Indians." June 17, 1971, 1.

Los Angeles Times. "Tribe Opens Petition Drive for Monument." February 18, 1971, SF2.

Los Encinos State Historic Parks. "Brief History of Vicente De La Ossa and Family." Accessed June 29, 2019. http://historicparks.org/documents/DeLaOssaHistory.pdf.

Lubas, Kenneth. "Mission Indians Try to Safeguard Cave Paintings of Their Ancestors." *Los Angeles Times*, January 31, 1971, 4.

Masters, Nathan. "A Tale of Two Isaacs." Ventura Boulevard. Accessed May 13, 2019. http://www.ourventurablvd.com/May-June-2014/A-Tale-of-Two-Isaacs/.

McCarry, T. W. "Indian Tribes to Demand Reburial of Ancestors." *Los Angeles Times*, February 7, 1985, J4.

McCarry, T. W. "Tribes Question Which Will Bury Ancestors." *Los Angeles Times, Valley News*, February 4, 1985, 10.

McFarland, Jas P. "Arrival of Lieut. Beale." *Los Angeles Star*, May 7, 1853.

Miller, Larissa K. "The Secret Treaties with California's Indians." *Prologue: The Journal of the National Archives* 45, nos. 3–4 (September 2013): 38–45.

Munro, Pamela. "Topanga, Cahuenga and Tujunga—Sounds from a Rediscovered Local Language." UCLA Newsroom. Accessed October 15, 2019. http://newsroom.ucla.edu/stories/topanga-cahuenga-and-tujunga-sounds-from-a-rediscovered-local-language.

Norton, Victoria Carrillo. "My Ancestors." Somos Primos. Accessed May 13, 2019. http://www.somosprimos.com/sp2007/spdec07/spdec07.htm.

Office of Federal Acknowledgment. "Final Determination Against Acknowledgment of The Juaneño Band of Mission Indians." Accessed July 12, 2019. https://www.federalregister.gov/documents/2011/03/21/2011-6470/final-determination-against-acknowledgment-of-the-juaneo-band-of-mission-indians-acjachemen-nation.

Official California Legislative Information. "Official History of California Legislation: Chapter 2, Law and Order." http://www.leginfo.ca.gov/pdf/2011/2011_Cal_Legi_Ch_02.pdf.

Online Archives of California. Accessed July 3, 2019. http://www.oac.cdlib.org/findaid/ark:/13030/c82f7pw6/.

Ortega, Rudy, Jr. "New Century, Photo 2000," *Tarahat: The People* 1, no. 2 (May–July, 2000): 1, 5.

Over, Dercum. "Chanting, Music, Dance Celebrate Chumash Heritage." *Malibu Times: Newspaper Magazine Online*, May 3, 2000. http://www.malibutimes.com/news/article_75babd79-35be-5160-872a-1387469cb3b6.html.

Oviatt Library Digital Collections, San Fernando Valley Historical Digital Library. California State University, Northridge. "Fernandeño/Tataviam Tribe." Accessed July 19, 2019. https://digital-collections.csun.edu/digital/collection/SFVH/id/3361/rec/1.

Ovnick, Merry. "Three Pioneer Women's Memories of the San Fernando Valley, 1860s–1930s." *Southern California Quarterly* 97, no. 1 (Spring 2015): 29–68.

Painter, Charles C. "The Condition of Indian Affairs in Indian Territory and California: A Report." Indian Rights Association, 1887.

Painter, Charles C. "A Visit to the Mission Indians of California." Indian Rights Association, 1887.

Preston, William L. "Portents of Plague From California's Protohistoric Period." Ethnohistory 29 (2002): 69–121.

Preston, William L. "Serpent in Eden: Dispersal of Foreign Diseases into Pre-Mission California." *Journal of California and Great Basin Anthropology* 18 (1996): 2–37.

Pukúu. "Services." Accessed July 16, 2019. http://www.pukuu.org/services.

RayBourn, Cari. "'The People' in the Beginning." Accessed July 3, 2019. https://www.csustan.edu/sites/default/files/honors/documents/journals/Edgings/ThePeople.pdf.

Sandos, James A. "Between Crucifix and Lance: Indian-White Relations in California 1769–1848." *California History* 76, nos. 2–3 (1997): 196–213.

San Fernando Sun. "'Interesting History of Memory Garden Given by Local Woman,' as told by Mrs. J. C. Maclay." June 21, 1927, 7.

San Fernando Sun. "Many Convicted." February 2, 1915.

San Fernando Sun. "Mexican Shot by Officers." February 12, 1915.

San Fernando Valley Times. "Ku Klux Klan Met in North Side Foothills." April 13, 1939, 1.

San Francisco Call. "Claims He Was Libeled." January 28, 1896, 4.

SCVHistory.com. "Diseño of Rancho San Francisco, Natural History Museum of Los Angeles County." Accessed July 20, 2019. https://scvhistory.com/scvhistory/lw2570a.htm.

SCVTC/College of the Canyons Foundation. "Story of Henry Mayo Newhall and the Newhall Foundation." Accessed July 3, 2019. https://scvhistory.com/scvhistory/cocsilverspur041115.htm.

Schuetz-Miller, Mardith. "Biofile of Building Artisans Who Worked on the Northern Spanish Border Lands of New Spain and Early Mexico." Tucson: National Park Service, n.d., ca. 2006.

Signal (Santa Clarita, CA). "December 16, 1961: On this day two dozen locals with Native American heritage met in the Hart Cafeteria to form the San Fernando Mission Indians Association . . . Charles Cooke was named president and his brother Alvin named vice-president. The group addressed compensation for loss of land." December 16, 2001, A4.

Singleton, Heather Valdez. "Surviving Urbanization: The Gabrieleño, 1850–1928." *Wicazo Sa Review* 19, no. 2 (Fall 2004): 49–59.

Smith, Clifford M. "The History of the San Fernando Valley with Special Emphasis on the City of San Fernando: A Thesis Presented to the Department of History, University of Southern California." Master's thesis, University of Southern California, 1930.

Son of DeWitt Colony Texas. "Plan of Iguala and Treaty of Cordova." Accessed April 3, 2019. https://web.archive.org/web/20090826173709/http://www.tamu.edu/ccbn/dewitt/iguala.htm#annul.

Sosa, Herbert R. "Fragmented Diversity: School Desegregation, Student Activism, and Busing in Los Angeles, 1964–1982." PhD diss., University of Michigan, 2013. Accessed July 3, 2019. https://deepblue.lib.umich.edu/bitstream/handle/2027.42/97911/hsosa_1.pdf?sequence=2.

Southern California Quarterly. Unsigned review of *The Indians of Southern California in 1852*, by John Walton Caughey, ed. 35, no. 2 (1953): 183–84.

Staff of the American Indian Policy Review Commission, 94th Congress. *Task Force Report Ten, Report on Terminated and Non-Federally Recognized Indians*. Washington, DC: Government Printing Office, 1976.

Stassel, Stephanie. "His Language Lost, His Legacy Lives On." *Los Angeles Times*, September 1, 1997, B4.

Stassel, Stephanie. "Rita Rivera; Elder of Tataviam Tribe Helped Revive Her Heritage." *Los Angeles Times*, July 13, 2001, B12. https://www.latimes.com/archives/la-xpm-2001-jul-13-me-21847-story.html.

St. Ferdinand Catholic Church and School. "Parish History." Accessed July 8, 2019. http://stferdinandchurch.org/about/parish-history.

Tarahat: The People. "Calendar And Tribal Council Meetings." No. 1 (April 1999): 4.

Tarahat: The People. "Forming The Tribal Constitution." Vol. 1, no. 3 (August–October 2000): 5.

Tarahat: The People. "Updates: Senate Bill And Resolutions," Vol. 3, no. 1 (February–April, 2004): 1, 6.

Temple, Thomas Workman II. "Toypurina the Witch and the Indian Uprising at San Gabriel." *Masterkey* 32, no. 5 (1958): 136–52.

Valley News (Van Nuys, CA). "Dancing by Indians Set for Fiesta." April 25, 1971, 4.

Valley News (Van Nuys, CA). "Indian Council Plans Party For Children Dec. 22." December 15, 1972, 39.

Valley News (Van Nuys, CA). "Indian Culture Center to Hold Grand Opening." December 1, 1974, 12.

Valley News (Van Nuys, CA). "Inter-Tribal Council Sets Yule Party for Children." October 26, 1972, 25.

Valley News (Van Nuys, CA). "Mission Indian Youth Prepare Own Costumes." September 4, 1970, 5.

Valley News (Van Nuys, CA). "Van, Toys, Food Gifts Sought for Mission Indians." December 8, 1970, 8.

Van Nuys News (Van Nuys, CA). "Also on the Bill Will Be Rudy Ortega and His San Fernando Valley Inter-Tribal Indians dancers. Youths Aid Lions Club with Show," May 12, 1972, 46.

Van Nuys News (Van Nuys, CA). "Indian Dancers Perform Today." April 16, 1972.

Van Nuys News (Van Nuys, CA). "Youths Aid Lions Club with Show." May 12, 1972, 50.

Valley News and Green Sheet (Van Nuys, CA). "Indians Invited to Valley Meeting at Mission Park." February 18, 1972, 6.

Valley News and Green Sheet (Van Nuys, CA). "The San Fernando Mission Indians and the Inter-Tribal Indians Will Join the Marchers, Continuing Their Participation in the Parade Since Its Inception. Veterans from 4 Wars to be in Sylmar Parade." November 10, 1972, 1.

Water and Power Associates. "San Fernando Valley Communities: Name Origins and Brief History." Accessed July 3, 2019. https://waterandpower.org/museum/Community_Name_Origins_SFV.html.

Whiteman, Fran. "Mission Indian Council Forms with Definite Goals in Mind." *Valley News and Green Sheet*, (Van Nuys, CA) January, 1972.

Widney, R. M. "The San Fernando Indians." *Los Angeles Times*, November 28, 1885, 3.

Wikipedia. "Pico House." Accessed May 13, 2019. https://en.wikipedia.org/wiki/Pico_House.

Wilson, B. D. "General Observations." *Los Angeles Star*, August 1, 1868.

Worden, Leon. "Prime Valencia Real Estate, $2 an Acre." SCV History, June 7, 1995. http://www.scvhistory.com/scvhistory/signal/worden/lw060795.htm.

Worden, Leon. "Santiago Garcia Adobe, Little Rock Creek," Scv History, 2014. Accessed November 3, 2019. https://scvhistory.com/scvhistory/lw2628.htm.

Wood, William. "The (Non-)Extinguishment of Aboriginal Title in California." Master's thesis, University of California, Los Angeles, 2006.

Wood, William. "The Trajectory of Indian Country in California: Rancherias, Villages, Pueblos, Missions, Ranchos, Reservations, Colonies, and Rancherias." *Tulsa Law Review* 44, no. 2 (2008): 317–64.

CASES

Anderson v. Matthews, 174 Cal. 537 (1917)

Barker v. Harvey, 181 U.S. 481 (1901)

Botillier v. Dominguez, 130 U.S. 238 (1889)

Brown v. Board of Education, 347 U.S. 483 (1954)

Byrne v. Alas, 16 P. 523 (Cal. 1888)

De Celis v. United States, Case No. 343, U.S.D.C., S. D. CA (1855)

Harvey v. Barker, 126 Cal. 262 (1899)

Indians Of California, 102 Ct. Cl. 837 (1944)

Johnson v. McIntosh, 21 U.S. 543 (1823)

Mendez v. Westminster School District of Orange County, 64 F. Supp. 544 (S.D. Cal. 1946), *aff'd* 161 F.2d 774 (9th Cir. 1947)

Piper v. Big Pine School District, 193 Cal. 664 (1924)

Porter v. Geronimo Lopez, Case No. 04278, LAACR, HL (1878)

Porter v. John Doe Palo, Case No. 04280, LAACR, HL (1878)

Porter v. John Doe Rogerio, Case No. 04279, LAACR, HL (1878)

Porter v. Rinaldi, Case No. 04713, LAACR, HL (1878)

Thompson v. Doaksum, 68 Cal. 493 (1886)

Thompson v. Los Angeles Farming & Milling Co., 180 U.S. 72 (1901)

Thompson v. United States, 8 Ind. Cl. Comm. 1 (1959)

United States v. Ritchie, 58 U.S. 525 (1854)

United States v. Vicente de la Osa, Case No. 379, U.S.D.C., S. D. CA (1857)

United States v. Workman, 68 (1 Wall.) 745 (1864)

Urbano, Odon, and Manuel v. United States, Case No. 392, BANC

INDEX

aboriginal rights/title, 100–106, 132–33, 142, 152, 169, 241

aboriginal society, 100–106, 133, 152, 169, 295n58

aboriginal territories, 194, 222

acculturation, 76

Achoicominga, 56–57

Act for the Government and Protection of Indians, 100–101, 109

Act to Ascertain and Settle the Private Land Claims, 104

adaptation, 13, 15–16, 18, 96, 98, 138, 142, 171, 186, 205, 242–43

adobe apartments, 57

Advisory Council on California Indian Policy (AICCP), 229

advocacy groups, non-Indian, 196

agents, 55, 113, 128, 202; federal, 9, 102, 142, 145, 151; Indian, 110, 123, 147–49, 153–56, 159, 198, 241–42; treaty, 102, 105

agriculturally based pueblos, 72–73

AICCP. *See* Advisory Council on California Indian Policy

Alalxiyepsh (healer), 314n100. *See also* Alipaz, Maria Rita

alcaldes, 68, 80, 283; economic relations managed by, 95; as elected leadership title, 167; Francisco, V., as, 85; Indian, 53–56, 67, 291n21; Mexican system of, 321n175; mission friars supporting, 140; Raphael Maria as, 256n85; Reyes, J. F., as, 63; San Fernando Mission elections of, 61; tribal-wide political regime of, 91

Alipaz, Maria Rita, 116, 120, 134, 167, 174, 267, 312n67; Benigno marriage to, 4–8, 64, 80–81, 85–86, 114, 139; children of, 63–64, 140, 317n134; grandparents to, 46; as healer, 122, 314n100; land grant of, 139; as progenitor, 278–79; property taxes of, 124. *See also* Rita

allotments, of land, 50, 70, 193–94, 199

Alta California, 4, 50, 54–56, 70, 90

alter, restored, 7

Alvarado, Juan, 75, 306n79

American Indian Policy Review Commission, 222

ancestral lands, 100, 145, 242

ancestral ties, 312n67

angry spirits, 41

'antap (form of religion), 32, 314n100

antipoverty programs, 221

Apache Indians, 218

Arriola, Rosaria (Rose), 66, 174, 262, 280. *See also* Ortiz, Rosario or Rose

assimilate, 18, 50, 59, 70, 91, 111

auxiliary organizations, 338n155

Baca, Judy, 52
Baja California territory, 70
band, 9–16, 283, 342n9. *See also* Fernandeño Tataviam Band of Mission Indians; Mission Indian Band; San Fernando Mission Band
baptism, 55, 58–59, 92, 315n103; California Indian Roll records for, 222–23; in Catholic Church, 141; of Leyva, M. J., 137–38, 320n166; lineage members for, 189; mission records of, 24; multiculturalism and, 53; San Fernando Mission records of, 209, 211, 233, 245–65, 311n56; of Xaviera, 63
Barbour, George W., 102–103
Barker v. Harvey case, 105
Barragan, Miguel, 302n17
Battle of Providencia, 82
Beale, Edward F., 113, 123, 258, 262
bear ceremonies, 229–31
Benigno: goldfields for, 122; marriage of, 4–8, 64, 80–81, 85–86, 114, 139; as son of one of forty petitioners, 85–86
Berns, Angie, 232
bicentennial commemoration, 229
bilateral kinship, 98, 210
Bishops, 4, 53, 59, 79
blessings ceremonies, 235
Board of Land Commissioners, 89, 104–106, 109, 132, 160, 165, 309n27
Branciforte, Viceroy, 54
Brewer, William H., 111
Brooks, Isabel Villegas, 76
Brunson, A., 152, 323n19
Brunson and Wells (law firm), 149
Buendia de Capistrano, Felicita, 164. *See also* Felicita(s)
Bureau of Indian Affairs, 202, 222, 224
burial ceremonies, 38–39, 42–43
Burro Flats, 34, 220
Bustamante, Anastasio, 79
bylaws, 208–9

Cahuenga (*Place of the Hill*), 6, 22, 47, 64–66, 329n15
Cahuilla, 22–23, 32, 38, 79, 175, 253, 293n28, 295n58
California: Act for the Government and Protection of Indians in, 100–101, 109; constitutional convention of, 92–94, 99; first census in, 113–14; immigration to, 120; Indians of, 192–93, 197–98; Mexican rule in, 79; missionaries in, 43–45; missions established in, 51; public school discrimination in, 179; real estate boom in, 120; secularization among Indian missions in, 69–70; Spain occupying, 50; statehood granted to, 97; state law policies in, 109–110; taxes in, 55; Tejon Indian Tribe of, 312n64; territory of, 3; treaty rejection in, 103; U.S. control of, 8, 321n175; white male citizen voting in, 99
California Indian Land Settlement Roll (1933), 210, 222–27
California Indians, 93–94, 197; Court of Claims and, 339n169; enrollment of, 318n141, 341n193; land claims process of, 105–106, 327n84
California Indians Jurisdictional Act (1928), 192, 197–200, 223, 337n130, 343n16
California Land Claims Act, 112, 129, 316n125
California Land Commission, 120. *See also* Board of Land Commissioners
California Mission Indians, 14–15
Californio Liberals, 69–70, 73–75, 79–83
Callis, Clara Maude, 201, 278, 341n195
Camilo, 255
Camilo, Gregorio, 163–64, 255
Campero, Angie, 174, 179
Campo de Cahuenga, 90
Camulos village, 237
Cano, Pastor (Josefo), 86, 119, 134, 164, 327n75
Capistrano, Jesus, 134
captains, 8, 80, 283–84; forty petitioners listed by, 304n45; of Garcia lineage, 212,

214; hereditary leaders as, 21–22; land grants negotiated by, 86; leadership, 186; as lineage leaders, 24–25; names of, 245–65, 305n55; Rocha as, 132, 201
Carter, Thos. H., 325n53
caste, 90, 285
Catholic Church/religion, 87, 91, 95, 141–42, 229, 301n1; centrists support of, 69; ceremony of, 63; Mary Immaculate, 224; in Mexican economy, 82–83; SFMI in, 67; social gatherings at, 189–90, 209; this-worldliness and, 53
Caucasian influence, 295n58
Cayo, Paula, 6, 63, 135, 279
Cayo, Tiburcio, 46, 62–63, 80, 210, 229, 278
ceded lands, 49–50, 102, 112
celestial beings, 40
census, U.S., 113–14, 204–5, 315n103, 318n148
centrists, 69–70, 94–95
A Century of Dishonor (Jackson), 147
ceremonies: annual bear, 229–31; of baptism, 58–59; blessings, 235; burial, 38–39, 42–43; Catholic, 63; children learning, 34–35; coming-of-age, 34, 39–40; commemoration, 77–78, 131, 141, 143, 260; Cooke, Charlie, performing, 230; eagle, 41; funeral, 130–31; Garcia, T. Jr., blessing, 235; Indian festivals as, 6–7; lineage leaders conducting, 31–32, 48; for marriage, 190–91; at San Fernando Mission, 76; shamans devoted to, 32; spiritual, 143; in villages, 31
Chaguayabit, 22, 25, 28, 46, 57
Cheney, W. A., 152–53
Chief Little Bear. *See* Ortega, Rudy Sr.
chiefs, 23, 295n58. *See also* captains
children, 34–35, 41, 63–64
Christianity: festivals for, 76–77; Indians adoption of, 55–56, 66, 78; lineages and conversion to, 55–56; Mission Indians acceptance of, 67–68; in religion, 32, 78; this-worldly view and, 44–45, 47–48; world views and, 52, 68. *See also* Catholic Church
Chumash, 131, 284; dancers from, 219; death transformation of, 44; Garcia lineage as, 210; language of, 3, 20–21, 45, 57; Naiyait elder of, 29–30; pictograph art of, 34; rebirth beliefs of, 36–37; in San Fernando Valley, 37; SFMI meeting with, 344n41; Tataviam intermarrying with, 5–6; villages speaking, 24–25
Chumash Indian Museum, 230
citizenship, 54, 69–72, 76, 78, 82; emancipated Indians and, 90–92; granting of, 94; through secularization, 307n4; tribal bonds and, 322n9
clans, 19–24, 27–28, 66, 79, 229, 295n58
Cleland, Robert Glass, 109, 119
Cleveland, Grover, 326n70
coalition of Fernandeño lineages, 9, 12, 13, 16, 27, 48, 94, 135, 211, 216, 223, 225, 238–40, 243, 288, 321
collective asset, 30–31
Collett, Fredrick, 195
colonial law, 69, 99–100, 209, 304n48
colonization, 14, 49–53, 110–13
coming-of-age ceremony, 34, 39–40
commemoration ceremony, 77–78, 131, 141, 143, 260
Commissioner of Indian Affairs, 102–3, 158, 160, 169, 194, 324n44
Committee on Legal Assistance to the Mission Indians, 156
communities, 118, 148, 209; agriculturally based pueblo, 72–73; Chaguayabit, 28; kinship, 18–20, 42, 85, 98, 143, 242; lineage of, 27–29, 141; multiethnic, 16, 66, 187, 211; multilineal, 211, 239; regional, 28–31; San Fernando Valley liaison meetings for, 188
community outreach, 347n81
Compromise of 1850, 97
Congress, of Mexico, 4, 72–74, 286, 302n8, 307n4
Congress, U.S., 92; Act to Ascertain and Settle the Private Land Claims from, 104; dispossession from, 101; Public Law

Congress, U.S. (*continued*)
90–507 passed by, 222; Public Law 280 from, 339n169; termination bill from, 221–22; treaties and legislation from, 192
conscious spirit, 35
conservatives, 69–70, 74, 79, 88, 94
constellations, 41–42
constitution, 26–27; California convention for, 92–94, 99; documents about, 231–33; FTBMI adopting, 232; Mexico adopting, 70, 307n4; tribal council forming, 231
continuity, 48, 145, 183, 238, 242; of lineages, 11, 87; among Mission Indians, 291n19; of premission period, 21; of religion, 78; of traditional leadership systems, 15
Cooke, Alvin, 215, 223
Cooke, Charlie, 178, 181, 183–85, 214, 278; California Indian Land Settlement roll and, 223; ceremony performed by, 230; as Garcia lineage captain, 215, 230; at Los Encinos Park, 232; at Newhall Land's River Village development site, 233
Cooke, Cy, 172, 185
Cooke, Frances Garcia, 172, 178, 185, 189, 199–200
Cooke, Fred, 199–200
Cooke, Manuel, 201
Coolidge, Calvin, 195
Coronel, Antonio, 75, 147, 163
Cosme (Benigno's father), 6, 80, 167
Cota, Francisco Tinoque, 112
Cota, Kawana, 112
Cota, Pablo, 134
Cota, Teofila, 112
court case, 145–46, 150–51
Court of Claims, 194–97, 339n169
cowboys (*vaqueros*), 111
culture: Indigenous peoples preserving, 13; land and resources of, 220; political activities and, 229–31; of SFMI, 75–79; sustaining, 182–91; of Ventureño Chumash, 45–46, 137
Cupertino, Jose, 320n162
death, life and, 44
de Borica, Diego, 53
debt, 93
de Celis, Eulogio, 88–89, 106, 116, 128, 151; affidavit from, 323n23; ex-San Fernando Mission and, 108, 115; land granted to, 241; lands sold to, 114; patent challenged of, 166, 325n53; property taxes paid by, 132–33; as San Fernando landowner, 108
de Celis, Eulogio, F., 115, 128, 316n124
deeds, 161–63, 313n78, 325n52
de la Osa, Vicente, 116, 121–22
Del Valle, Don Antonio, 75
demographics, of Los Angeles, 119
demurrer, 133
depression, economic, 197
detribalize, 91
Diaz, Ed, 224
Diego, Garcia, 79
differentiation, 13–14, 58, 66–69, 94–96, 139, 142–43, 239–40
discrimination, 138, 177–82
disenfranchisement, 97
dispossession, 139–41, 146, 154, 241–43, 307n4; from California Land Claims Act, 112; of California Mission Indians, 14–15; Congress joining in on, 101; of Fernandeño lineages, 114, 136; land claims leading to, 106; by Mexican law, 142; of Mission Indians, 79; of Rancho Ex-Mission San Fernando, 88–89; secularization and, 84; Spanish colonization and Indian, 49–53; state-sponsored, 97
dispute resolution, 28
dream spirit, 35–36
dream state, 35–36
droughts, 119–20
Durán, friar, 72, 84
dying-god theme, 38, 41

eagle ceremony, 41
economy, 4; alcalde's managing, 95; depression of, 197; hardship of, 203–4; of Mexico, 82–83; rancho owners for, 111; of regional communities, 29–31;

secularization and mission-based, 110; Southern California's changing, 136; from territory, 10–11
Efren, 270, 277
ejectment lawsuit, 133
the elders, 35
emancipation, 67; of Mission Indians, 72–73, 90–92, 195; secularization and, 72–74, 95; of SFMI, 306n79; of Urbano, 253; of workers, 70
employment. *See* work
Encarnacion, Maria, 47, 64–65
Engelhardt, Zephyrin, 23, 38, 50
enrollment, 228–29, 318n141, 341n193, 346n65
epidemic, 142
Escorpion, 64, 80, 117–18, 129, 130–31
Estanislao (1792-?), 137, 257–59, 262, 269, 304n45
Eugenia, 39, 64, 76–77, 80, 85, 118, 168, 251, 256, 262, 269, 273–74, 277, 301n52. *See also* Mendez, Eugenia
Eulogio de Celis v. United States, 310n33
evictions, 143, 161–62, 171, 262, 317n138; from ancestral territories, 145; of Fernandeño, 154–55; from Rancho Cienega, 169; of Rancho Ex-Mission San Fernando occupants, 135; of Rocha, 130, 133, 152–53, 168, 317n138; of San Fernando Mission, 138; tax foreclosures and, 136; treaty rejections causing, 103
Excerpts from the Writings of A. L. Kroeber (Kroeber), 292n15
exogamy, 139

Fall, Albert, 195
Farias, Valentin Gomez, 72
Farm Homestead Association, 127
farming life, 147
federal claims process (1928 California Indians Jurisdictional Act), 189, 194–95
federal government, 177–78, 205, 221–22
federal recognition, 145, 211, 216, 226–27; of Fernandeños, 170; of FTBMI, 10–11, 16, 242; lawsuit and, 165; Ortiz, Joseph, application for, 203–204; termination blocking, 221–24
fee simple, 84–85, 127, 147, 221
Felicita(s), 134–35, 137–38, 164, 255, 262, 327n75. *See also* Buendia de Capistrano, Felicita
Felis de Burrows, Maria de los Angeles, 124, 127–29
Fernandeño, 284; in American period, 91–92; California Indians Jurisdictional Act and, 198–200; cultural site protection by, 220; detribalizing, 91; discrimination and prejudice faced by, 177–82; eviction of, 154–55; federal recognition of, 170; godmother in, 118; Harrington introducing, 300n25; land claims of, 155–56; with land grants, 113; land loss of, 135–36; Land of the Dead travels of, 41; language of, 92, 290n8; Lewis and cause of, 158–59; lineage members of, 92, 98, 114, 136, 143–44, 190–91, 198–99, 211; political challenges facing, 191–204; powwows with, 219; secularization not accepted by, 67–68; spirits of dead with, 42; spiritual tradition of, 141; square league won by, 167; Tejon Reservation relocation of, 199; treaty negotiators with, 146; tribal baptism of, 92; tribe interconnectedness of, 191; wage laborers of, 136
Fernandeño-Gabrieleño, 3, 40–43
Fernandeño Mission Indians, 319n151
Fernandeño Tataviam Band of Mission Indians (FTBMI), 113, 233–36; ancestors of, 17; constitution adopted by, 232; family lineages making up, 174–77; federal recognition of, 10–11, 16, 242; lineage identities of, 238–39; nonprofit arm of, 243; prior recognition of, 11; self-governing lineages of, 241; tribal affairs of, 13; U.S. petitioned by, 9–10; villages of, 19
Fernandeño Tataviam Tribal Council (FTTC), 227–29
Fernandeño Tataviam Tribe, 228–31

Figueroa, 306n78, 307n4
Final, William E., 347n84
fire dance, 38–39
501(c)(3) nonprofit organization, 231
floods, 119–20, 173–74
Folkes, Beverly, 183–84, 229
food, 30, 42
Forbes, J. Alexander, 325n52
forced differentiation, 142
foreclosures, 109
forty petitioners, 91, 98, 164, 255–56; Benigno as one of, 85–86; captains listing, 304n45; land grant to, 89, 134–35, 167, 257–60, 267–75; Pico, P., and, 114; Rancho Ex-Mission San Fernando dispossession and, 88–89; Rocha and, 130–35; from San Fernando Mission, 80–82; for square league, 257–58
foster care, 10
Franciscans, 50, 53, 56, 87, 216, 284–85
Francisco, Vicente, 85
Francisco Pablo, 135, 318n148
Frank, Gelya, vii, 324n95
friars, 50, 87–88, 106, 141, 216; definition of, 284–85; Durán, 72, 84; Ibarra and Ordaz as, 4; Indian alcalde elections by, 67; Indians view by, 45–46, 70; mission, 140; Mission Indians control by, 74–75, 82; in pueblos, 62–63; Respuesta response of, 61–62; at San Fernando Mission, 57–61, 92, 314n101; Spanish, 71–72
FTBMI. *See* Fernandeño Tataviam Band of Mission Indians
FTTC. *See* Fernandeño Tataviam Tribal Council
fundraising, 237
funeral ceremony, 130–31

Gabrieleño, 3, 41, 285, 287, 300n25. *See also* Fernandeño-Gabrieleño
Garcia, Catalina Leyva, 321n168
Garcia, Frances, 138, 183, 215
Garcia, Isidora, 136, 138, 172–73, 175, 191, 279. *See also* Ortega, Isidora
Garcia, Isidoro, 140, 173, 277, 321n168
Garcia, Josefa Leyva, 64, 173, 186, 189, 191, 200, 210, 216, 277
Garcia, Manuela, 202
Garcia, Mary Cooke, 173, 191, 201, 228, 234, 278; as lineage captain, 190, 210, 212, 214; San Fernando Valley move of, 212
Garcia, Ted, Jr., 200, 229, 232; blessing ceremony by, 235; interview of, 325n97, 340n187; as lineage captain, 234–35, 237; Pacoima meeting attended by, 215
Garcia, Ted, Sr., 179, 191, 210, 214, 228–29
Garcia lineage, 85, 132, 185–86, 202, 223, 277–78; captains of, 212, 214; as Chumash, 210; Cooke, Charlie, as captain of, 215, 230; federal claims process of, 189; members of, 191; Paulina ancestry of, 64–65; progenitor of, 46–47, 118, 172, 305n69
Gardner, William, 172, 201
genealogy charts, 223
genocide, 177
Gente de Razon, 285
Genu (1768–1803), 25
geography, 242
George K. Porter et al. v. C. R. Rinaldi et al., 128, 315n112, 316n119, 317n133
George K. Porter et al. v. Geronimo (Lopez) et al., 316n114, 316n120, 317n125
George K. Porter et al. v. John Doe Palo et al. (Pablo Cota), 318n146
George K. Porter et al. v. John Doe Rogerio et al., 133, 323n25
Godey, Alexander, 123, 280
Godey, Jose Abelardo, 123. *See also* Ortiz, Joseph
godfather (padrino), 258, 268, 270, 273, 312; Garcia, Isidoro, as, 140; spiritual guidance from, 63; surname honoring, 137
godmother (madrina), 135, 137–38, 249–50, 257, 273; in Chumash lineage, 80; in Fernandeño community, 118; spiritual guidance from, 63
godparent, 87, 258, 268

goods promised, in treaties, 337n132
governments, pueblo, 88, 94
governor, 72, 75; Micheltorena as, 4, 79–80, 82; Pico, P., as, 4, 107
grandfather, 181–83
Great Dragon, Ku Klux Klan, 180
Gutiérrez, Antonio, 75, 172

Haas, Lisbeth, 290n13, 291n21
Hackel, Steven, 15, 301n41
Harding, Warren, 195
Harmer, Alexander, 73
Harrington, John, 39, 64, 116–17, 131, 242; linguistic names from, 300n25; Naiyait statement from, 29; Olivas and, 200
healer (*Alalxiyepsh*), 261–62, 312n71, 314n100
healing powers, of plants, 184–85
health conditions, of Indians, 119–20
Heizer, Robert, 78
Henley, Thomas J., 351n43
hereditary leaders, 21–22
Herrera, Jose Joaquin de, 87–88
historical Indian tribe, 242
Homaliwo village, 131
human symbol pictograph, 33
hunter gathers, 49–50, 67, 95
Hyer, Joel, 109

Ibarra, Francisco, 4, 71
identity, languages and, 20–21
idolatry, 60–61
immigration, to California, 120
independence, 87, 143, 200, 203, 301n1; Christian conversion and Indian, 55–56, 66; Indian readiness for, 70; lineages, 21–23, 27, 55–56; from Spain, 4
Indian Board of Cooperation, 195, 338n155
Indian Claims Commission, 92, 104, 315n103
Indian Claims Commission Act (1946), 222
Indian Defense Association, 195
Indian Gaming Regulatory Act (1988), 11
Indian New Deal, 196
Indian Rights Association, 153–54, 162
Indians, 285–86; advocacy groups of non-, 196; agents for, 110, 123, 147–49, 153–56, 159, 198, 241–42; agriculturally based pueblo communities of, 72–73; alcaldes of, 53–56, 67, 291n21; of Alta California, 55–56; Americans marrying, 98; Apache, 218; auxiliary organizations for, 338n155; of California, 192–93, 197–98; Christianity adoption by, 55–56, 66, 78; as citizens, 54; discrimination against, 179; disenfranchisement of, 97; Federal Government removal of, 177–78; festivals, 6–7; friars view of, 45–46, 70; health conditions of, 119–20; idolatry practiced by, 60–61; independence readiness of, 70; Indigenous tribes, 13, 147, 182–83; land claim process of, 103–9, 309n27; Land Claims Act for, 129; land grants to, 79, 97, 304n48; land of, 55, 87–90; land rights of, 104–5; languages of, 20–21, 314n101, 333n68; of Los Angeles County, 21, 23–24; missions left by, 4–5; mistreatment of, 146–47; Navajo, 218; new parish for, 4; pagan, 55; personal salvation of, 45; possessory rights of, 100; prejudice against, 331n43; pueblos of, 50, 53–54, 62, 69–70, 87–90, 95, 106, 209, 307n4; pure blood, 203–4; rancherias of, 194; Rancho Cienega rights of, 169–70; Rancho Encino co-owners as, 120–21; registration advice for, 200, 202–3, 341n201, 341n202; San Fernando Mission and removal of, 66–67; San Fernando Mission community of, 85; of San Fernando Valley, 44–45; self government for, 54, 90; slave markets for, 99; of Southern California, 17–20, 101; Spanish colonization and dispossession of, 49–53; square league rights of, 169–71; starvation of, 193; this worldly orientation of, 47–48; traditional world views of, 95–96; unbaptized, 58; U.S. federal funds for, 155; U.S. relationship with, 145

Indigenous tribes, 13, 147, 182–83
injustice, to Mission Indians, 161
inspectors, 147, 193, 253
institutional differentiation, 13–14, 58, 66–69, 94–96, 139, 142–43, 204, 239–40

Jackson, Helen Hunt, 109, 147–50, 161, 166
Jackson-Kinney report, 156
Joaquin, Pedro, 80
Jose Jesus, 137, 164–65, 320n162
Jose Maria (?–1840), 25, 245, 252, 254, 257–58
Jose Rosario, 122, 315n103, 315n106. *See also* Ortega, Antonio Maria
Juana Josefa, 46
Juan Maria (1778–1831), 46, 63, 279
judgment program, 202

Kawana (?–1873), 64
Kelsey, C. E., 193–94, 327n84, 338n147
Kenny, Robert, 103, 337n133
Kinney, Abbott, 109, 149–50
kinship communities, 18–20, 42, 85, 98, 143, 242. *See also* lineages
Kish, 287
Kitanemuk, 43, 229, 234, 250; 'antap of, 32; definition of, 285; dying-god them of, 37–38, 41; language of, 3, 20–21, 37–38, 46, 57; as patrilineal, 24–25; rebirth beliefs of, 35; Treaty of Tejon signed by, 101–102, 112; world views of, 37–40
Kitsepawit, Fernando Librado, 131. *See also* Librado, Fernando
Kolb, Sam, 215
Komivitam, 297n102
Kroeber, A. L., 212, 242, 292n15, 294n46, 295n58; historical observations of, 185; lineage leaders explained by, 25; San Fernando lineages and, 142; tribelets from, 19
Kuehl, Sheila, 232
Ku Klux Klan, 180, 332n52

Lake Mohonk Conference, 154, 158
land: allotments of, 193–94; ceded tracts of, 49–50; commission granting leagues of, 325n54; cultural resources and, 220; de Celis granted, 241; farming life with, 147; Fernandeño's loss of, 135–36; per acre prices of, 339n177; for reservations, 338n147; in San Fernando Valley, 154; Southern California Indians asset of, 30–31; U.S. patents for, 326n70
land claims: California Indians process of, 105–6, 327n84; dispossession from, 106; of Fernandeño, 155–56; Indians process of, 103–9, 309n27; Triunfo, J. A., and, 316n125; U.S. appeal of, 108
land grants, 75, 241; of Alipaz, M. R., 139; in American period, 113; *Barker v. Harvey* and, 105; Camilo, 255; captains negotiating, 86; deeds and, 325n52; Escorpion, 117; fee simple, 84–85; Fernandeños with, 113; to forty petitioners, 89, 134–35, 167, 257–60, 267–75; to Indians, 79, 97, 304n48; Los Encinos, 174; Mexican, 148–49, 152, 156–58, 166–67, 172, 286; from Micheltorena, 5–6, 80–81, 167, 267–75; Pico, P., issuing, 84–85, 89, 108–9, 304n48, 310n35; at San Fernando Mission, 5, 83, 86; secularization and, 72; of Spain, 287; of square league, 84, 267–75, 289n4; Triunfo, J. M., awarded, 80, 116–17, 123–29, 139; Urbano, 252
landholdings, 4, 82, 105, 114–15, 120
Land of the Dead, 36–37, 41–43, 45. *See also* underworld
land rights, 104–5, 109, 323n30, 327n72
land sale, 89, 106
languages, 289n1; of Chumash, 3, 20–21, 45, 57; of Fernandeño, 92, 290n8; Indian, 20–21, 314n101, 333n68; Indigenous, 182–83; of Kitanemuk, 3, 20–21, 37–38, 46, 57; of San Fernando Mission Indians, 210–11; of Tataviam, 3, 20–21, 37–38, 46, 63–64, 116, 182, 186; of Ventureño, 20
Lankershim Ranch Land and Water Co., 157
Lasuén, Fermin, 53–56
laws, from Spain, 54

lawsuits, 126–27, 133–34, 165, 316n124, 316n125
Lea, Clarence, 197
Lea, Luke, 102
leadership, 15, 186, 233–34
league, 118, 159–61, 255, 260–61, 290; commission granting land in, 325n54; Fernandeños tribe winning square, 167; forty petitioners for square, 257–58; Indian rights to square, 169–71; land grants with square, 84, 267–75, 289n4; Micheltorena grants land by, 5–6, 80–81, 167; Pico, P., grants land by, 84, 89; Rancho Encino as square, 115
Leandra, 80, 112, 114, 118, 137–40, 262, 270, 274, 277, 312n67, 320n159, 320n162, 354n9. *See also* Leyva, Leandra
legal system, 99–101, 142
Leocadia (1760–1837), 46
Leonis, Espiritu, 171. *See also* Santo, Maria del Espiritu
Leonis, Miguel, 129, 172
Lewis, Frank D., 155–57, 170, 242; fees paid to, 165; Fernandeño cause and, 158–59; investigation, 159–60; libel suit filed by, 162; Meserve corroborating story of, 164; Painter's letter to, 324n44; Rocha's quitclaim deed to, 161; as treachery source, 327n72; trustee role abuse by, 161–62
Leyva, (Maria) Josefa (also Josephine and Josefina), 64–65, 130, 136–38, 140, 172–73, 186, 191, 200–201, 216, 262–63, 277, 320n166, 329n7, 355n2. *See also* Garcia, Josefa Leyva
Leyva, Jose Juan, 47, 64, 130, 137–38, 210, 320n162, 320n164
Leyva, Leandra, 47, 64. *See also* Leandra
libel action, 162, 165, 326n71
Librado, Fernando, 17, 29–30, 49, 69, 97, 260. *See also* Kitsepawit, Fernando Librado
Lightfoot, Kent, 15
lineage captain, 215, 230; Cooke, F. G., as, 199–200; Garcia, M. C., as, 190, 210, 212, 214; Garcia, T. Jr., as, 234–35, 237; Ortega, A. M., as, 201; Ortega, R. Jr., as, 207–8, 231; Ortega, R. Sr., as, 219; Ortiz, J., as, 185; Rocha as, 151
lineage leaders, 24–25, 87, 140; ceremonies conducted by, 31–32, 48; conflicts negotiated by, 26; of San Fernando Mission, 245–65; traditional knowledge of, 142; treaties response of, 191–92
lineage members: for baptisms, 189; of Fernandeño, 92, 98, 114, 136, 143–44, 190–91, 198–99, 211; leadership of, 186; progenitor of, 13; spirits and, 28, 31; tribal identity of, 189–90; in villages, 24, 29; world views, 68
lineages, 3; band used for, 342n9; Christian conversion and, 55–56; collective names in, 23; community of, 27–29, 141; continuity of, 11, 87; definition of, 286; of Fernandeño Tataviam Band, 174–77, 238–39; gatherings of, 212–13; identifying, 210–11; independent, 21–23, 27, 55–56; kin-based, 58; loyalty to, 27; as ministate, 26–27; original family ending of, 25; Pimu, 86; regional network of, 140; of San Fernando Mission, 11–14, 62–66, 86–87, 95–96, 202, 204–5; self-government of, 27, 66, 241; territory governed by, 22, 286; Tujubit, 130, 132; voluntary coalition of, 239–40. *See also* kinship communities
linguistic names, 300n25
llabero (keeper of the keys), 252–53, 286
lodge, 21–22, 24
Lopez, Catalina, 76–77, 123
Lopez, Francisco, 116
Lopez, Geronimo, 76, 122–23, 137, 315n104
Lopez, J. J., 138, 204, 315n103
Lopez, Pedro, 3, 76, 116, 162, 315n104
Lopez, Setimo, 116–17. *See also* Orticimo
Lopez Adobe, 130–31, 319n158
Lopez Canyon, 155, 172
Lopez Station, 124–25, 128–29, 134
Los Angeles, 174–75, 218, 242, 308n8, 329n3

Los Angeles County: aqueduct, 174–75, 329n3; demographics of, 119; Indians of, 21, 23–24; mission Indians in, 111; treaties in, 103; tribes with territory in, 23
Los Angeles Herald, 162–65, 327n72
Los Encinos land grants, 174
low-wage workers, 171

Maclay, Charles, 125–27, 130, 150, 154, 178; lawsuits filed by, 133–34
Maclay-Porter acquisition, 125–26
Madley, Benjamin, 307n92, 337n141
Manriquez, Lida Cooke, 201, 278
Manso, Juan, 86
Manuel Chari (son), 129
Marcelina, 117–18
Maria Manuela, 118
marriage, 22, 25, 138, 294n37; of Alipaz, M. R., and Benigno, 4–8, 64, 80–81, 85–86, 114, 139; ceremonies for, 190–91; mixed, 63, 98; of Ortega, A. M., 140
Martinez, Della Cooke, 191, 201, 278
Mary Immaculate Catholic Church, 224
mayordomo, 3, 76, 122, 204, 286
McCawley, William, 32
Mendez, Eugenia, 65, 329n4. *See also* Eugenia
Menendez, Juan Jose, 172
Meriam, Lewis, 196
Meriam Report, 196
Merriam, C. Hart, 287, 339n161
Merritt, Edgar B., 327n84
Meserve, Edwin A., 164
Mexican-American population, 179–81
Mexican-American War (1846), 8, 87–90
Mexican Land Grant, 113, 152, 172, 286
Mexican War of Independence, 61–62
Mexico: alcaldes system of, 321n175; American colonization and, 110–13; California ruled by, 79; Catholic Church and economy of, 82–83; centrists in, 95; Congress of, 4, 72–74, 286, 302n8, 307n4; conservatives from, 69–70; constitution of, 70, 307n4; dispossession by law of, 142; emancipated Indians and, 90; land grants with, 148–49, 152, 156–58, 166–67, 172, 286; liberals in, 82, 88, 94; Micheltorena leaving for, 82; Mission lands and laws of, 98, 106; president of, 72, 79; pueblos, 85, 99; secularization policies of, 70–72, 84, 301n1; U.S. landholders from, 120–21; violence against people from, 310n41
Micheltorena, Manuel, 88–89, 127, 159; as governor, 4, 79–80, 82; land grants from, 5–6, 80–81, 167, 267–75; Mexico destination of, 82
Miguel Raphael, 185, 191, 336n125
Milky Way, 36–37
ministate, 26–27, 241
missionaries, 50; adobe apartments built by, 57; in Alta California, 54–55; in California, 43–45; Indian land protected by, 55; Indian pueblo honored by, 53; parish and, 53; Rancho San Francisco resisted by, 303n27; role of, 301n41; from Spain, 56; Tataviam observations of, 43
mission-based economy, 110
Mission Indian Band, 211
Mission Indian Club, 208–11
Mission Indian Relief Act (1891), 166, 177, 193
Mission Indians, 14–15, 215, 319n151; in Alta California, 90; Christianity acceptance and, 67–68; continuities among, 291n19; dispossession of, 79; emancipation of, 72–73, 90, 195; friars control of, 74–75, 82; Indians leaving, 4–5; injustice to, 161; in Los Angeles, 111; pueblos of, 50, 54; secularization and rights of, 74, 93–94; Spanish secularization of, 67–68; on territory, 49–50
Mission land: Mexican laws and, 98, 106; in San Fernando Valley, 125–26; secularization and, 79, 83, 88–89
Mission San Fernando Rey de Espana, 16, 56–57
money equivalency, 31

Montesdeoca, Demetrio, 87–88
Moran, Dorothy, 191
multiculturalism, 12, 18, 52–53, 68, 78
multidimensional social action theory, 13
multiethnic communities, 16, 66, 187, 211
multilineal communities, 211, 239
multiple spirits, 35
multiracial, 211
multitribal club, 187, 211, 287
Murphy, Jessie, 179

Naiyait (Chumash elder), 29–30
Native Americans. *See* Indians
natural disasters, 119
Navajo Indians, 218
neophytes, 71, 256, 286, 298n120
Nerea, Maria Ygnacio, 270, 277
Newhall (Ranch and town), 136, 172–73, 216, 329n13
Newhall Land's River Village development site, 233
Newman, Kathryn Ortega, 176, 181–82, 191, 207, 279
Newman, Verne, Jr., 181, 331n46
Newsom, Gavin, 16
Nicolas Jose (Sibapet lineage), 51–53
Noble, John W., 325n53
Nonprofit Council, 233, 236
nonprofit organization, 188, 226–27, 230–34, 236–40, 243
Northern California Indian Rights Association, 193
Nú, 253, 293n28
nuclear families, 18–19

Odon (chief), 117
Office of Federal Acknowledgment, 242
Olivas, Jose Juan, 137, 200
Ordaz, Blas, 4, 80
Orpheus myths, 42
Ortega, Antonio Maria, 134–36, 174–78, 186, 208; census records of, 315n103; epidemic survived by, 142; healing knowledge to, 122; judgment program enrollment and, 202; as lineage captain, 201; Lopez Station and, 124; marriage of, 140; Newman, V., relation to, 331n46; Ortega lineage from, 64, 279; Rocha's farm and, 317n134; Tataviam language known by, 182–83. *See also* Jose Rosario
Ortega, Edward A., 343n18
Ortega, Ernie, 231
Ortega, Estanislao (James), 176–79, 182–83, 186–88, 191, 202, 207, 263–64, 279, 333n68, 334n95
Ortega, Eulogio, 175–76, 279
Ortega, Fernando, 8, 64, 122
Ortega, Isidora, 186, 194–95, 198, 202, 279. *See also* Garcia, Isidora
Ortega, Larry, 19
Ortega, Luis, 175–76, 279
Ortega, Luis Eduardo, 64, 122–24, 136, 174, 186, 279
Ortega, Rudy Jr., 178, 212; at Camulos village, 237; community outreach by, 347n81; as lineage captain, 207–8, 231; mission club bylaws created by, 208–209; at Newhall Land's River Village development site, 233; payment accounts of, 347n84; as SFMB leader, 216, 224; SFVII from, 225–27; tribal activities interest of, 231
Ortega, Rudy Sr. (Chief Little Bear), 187–88, 190–91, 232, 279; at Burro Flats rock art site, 220; funeral of, 8–10; grandfather comments of, 181–83; Indian registration from, 200, 202–3, 341n201, 341n202; interview of, 324n95, 332n65; as lineage captain, 219; San Fernando Inter-Tribal dancers with, 218–19; SFMB name from, 211, 343n23; as tribal coordinator, 230; writing as Rudolph J. Ortega, 346n65
Ortega, Sally, 175–76. *See also* Verdugo, Sally Ortega
Ortega lineage, 85, 174, 198, 202, 278–80; California Indian Land Settlement and,

Ortega lineage (*continued*)
223; captain leadership of, 186; from Ortega, A. M., 64; Ortiz lineage close to, 333n84; progenitor of, 45–46, 167; of San Fernando Mission, 62–64
Orticimo, 134. *See also* Lopez, Setimo
Ortiz, Helen, 213, 229, 280
Ortiz, Joseph, 124, 138, 174, 179, 185, 203–204, 280
Ortiz, Miguel, 124, 138
Ortiz, Miguel Raphael, 185, 191
Ortiz, Rosaria (Rose), 47, 129, 136, 280. *See also* Arriola, Rosaria (Rose)
Ortiz lineage, 64–66, 167–68, 174, 188–89, 280, 333n84
other-worldly, 143

Pacoima meeting, 215, 224–25
pagan Indians, 55
Painter, C. C., 153–54, 164, 324n44
Palma, Josepha Leonisa, 119, 134
pan-Indian, 225–26, 237, 286–87; interethnic communities and, 189; powwows, 217–20, 229
Papabubaba, Francisco (Rita's father), 6–8, 63, 80, 85, 114–15, 279
parish, 59, 70–72, 74, 141, 229; communities, 209; Indian's, 4; missionaries and, 53; priests, 302n8
partition lawsuit, 316n124
patents, 104–105, 160, 166, 325n53, 326n70
Path of the Dead, 36
patrilineal, 24–25, 57, 85, 98
Paulina (1773–?), 46
Pavasikwar, 297n102
Payéras, friar, 62
Pedro Joaquin, 80, 258, 260, 267, 290, 299, 304n45
per capita distribution, 205
per capita payment, 192
Perfecta, Maria Rafaela (also Cañedo and Arriola), 116, 123, 129, 262, 280, 312n67
persistence, 91, 240, 291n18, 291n21; cultural, 15–16, 18, 48; institutional, 68; of traditional leadership systems, 15. *See also* resistance
personal salvation, 45
Phillips, George Harwood, 292n5, 301n41, 321n175
Pico, Andres, 86, 126–28
Pico, Pio, 82–83, 106; forty petitioners and, 114; as governor, 4, 107; land grants issued by, 84–85, 89, 108–9, 304n48, 310n35; league of land granted by, 84, 89; Rancho Ex-Mission San Fernando sold by, 89; Spanish friar distrust of, 71–72
Pico House, 316n122
pictographs, 33–34
Pimu (Pimubit) lineage, 86, 119, 137, 202, 238, 250, 255
place name, 22, 287, 289n1, 290n8
Place of the Hill (Cahuenga), 22
Place of the Old Woman (Tujunga), 22
Plan of Iguala, 307n4
plants, healing powers of, 184–85
politics, 91, 191–204, 229–31, 233–34
Pomposa, 131, 141, 260
pope, power of, 49, 298n1
population decline, 61
Porter, Benjamin, 316n117
Porter, George, 125–27, 130, 133, 150, 154
Porter Ranch, 316n117
Portilla, Pablo de la, 73
Portola expedition, 28
possessory rights, of Indians, 100
post-traumatic stress disorder, 175
powwows, pan-Indian, 217–20, 229
prejudice, 177–82, 331n43
Price, Hiram, 109, 149
prickly pear cactus, 30–31
prior recognition, 9–11, 145–46, 170
private property ownership, 84, 147
The Problem of Indian Administration (Meriam Report), 196
progenitor: ancestors, 139, 277–80; of Garcia lineage, 46–47, 118, 172, 277–78, 305n69; of lineage members, 13; of

Ortega lineage, 45–46, 167, 278–80; of Ortiz lineage, 47, 167–68, 280
property protection, 144
property rights, 93
property taxes, 120–21, 129, 168–69, 260; of Alipaz, M. R., 124; for California Indians, 93; de Celis, E., paying, 132–33; Indian land rights and, 109
public domain, 104–5, 192, 338n147
Public Law 90-507, 222
Public Law 280, from Congress, 339n169
public school discrimination, 179
pueblos, 67–68, 83–86, 104–5, 241, 283; agriculturally based, 72–73; friars in, 62–63; governments, 88, 94; of Indians, 50, 53–54, 62, 69–70, 87–90, 95, 106, 209, 307n4; Mexican, 85, 99; missionaries honoring Indian, 53; of Mission Indians, 50, 54; secularization and, 94–95; self-government of, 50, 54, 69, 72, 99, 209; Spanish colonization and, 49–50; Spanish-Mexican government and, 73; territory's government of, 59–60
Pukúu, 236–38, 240, 265, 281, 349n106, 350n123

Qua-o-ar (creator), 40
quit claim deed, 161–63

Rafael (1769–1841), 245
railroads, 126, 136
Raker, John, 195
Ramirez, Jesus, 134
Ramirez, Teresa, 134
Ramon, 80, 84, 277
Ramona, 147. *See also* Jackson, Helen Hunt
Ramos, James, 236
rancherias, 72, 194, 232, 245; baptisms at, 55; chief of, 23; fire dance at, 38–39; institutional relations in, 48; personal services in, 60; as small villages, 111
Rancho Cahuenga, 81, 85
Rancho Cienega, 118, 130, 168–70
Rancho El Escorpione. *See* Escorpion
Rancho Encino, 6–7, 115–16, 313n73; de la Osa acquiring, 121–22; Folkes at, 183–84; Indian co-owners of, 120–21; Rita heir to, 8
Rancho Ex-Mission San Fernando, 88–89, 130, 135, 157, 160
rancho owners, 111
Rancho San Francisco, 75–76, 172–73, 303n27
Rancho Tejon, 113
Rancho Tujunga, 85–86, 99, 113, 116. *See also* Tujunga
Raphael Maria, 256n85
ratification, 177
real estate, boom in, 120
rebellion, of San Gabriel Mission, 56
rebirth, 35–37, 44, 143
recognition, 16, 91, 140, 143, 284; government-to-government, 208; prior, 9–11; through representation, 146–70; U.S. sought for, 111. *See also* federal recognition
recovery claims, 227n133
redemption, 145
regional communities, 28–31
Reid, Hugo, 22–23, 31, 41, 77–78, 210
religion, 12, 14, 17, 32, 43–45, 48, 50, 53, 60, 67, 74, 78, 92, 95, 143, 290n13
Report of the Attorney General of the United States, 158
Report on the Condition and Needs of the Mission Indians of California, 149
reservations: confinement of, 337n141; public domain land and, 338n147; Sebastian (Tejon), 123, 351n43; Southern California Indian, 239; Tejon, 199; from treaties, 197, 340n186; Tule River Indian, 337n141
resistance, 13–14, 16, 18, 43, 48, 68, 73, 75–76, 126, 142–43. *See also* persistence
Respuesta, 60–62
resurrection, 40
Reyes, Angela, 122
Reyes, Juan Francisco, 63

Reyes, Pedro, 122
right of preemption, 309n24
Rinaldi, C. R., 125–26
Rita (1830–1866?) (also Maria Rita), 4–8, 85–86. *See also* Alipaz, Maria Rita
Rivera, Rita, 231
Rivera (also Valenzuela), Petra Garcia, 200, 277–78
Rocha, Rogerio, 87; as captain, 132, 201; case sensationalized of, 145–46, 150–51; as Catholic Church participant, 142; drawing of home, 163; Escorpion home to, 118; Escorpion left by, 130–31; eviction of, 130, 133, 152–53, 168, 317n138; forty petitioners and, 130–35; land rights of, 323n30, 327n72; Lewis quitclaim deed from, 161; as lineage captain, 151; mixed marriage and, 98; Ortega, A. M., and farm of, 317n134; as pauper, 162; as petitioner, 167; property protection of, 144; survival of, 155; taxes paid by, 168; ten-acre farm of, 168–69; tribal connections and, 201–202; Ward, S., on claim of, 324n36; Widney working against, 165
Rocketdyne property, 220
Rodriguez, Christina Ortega, 176, 202, 207, 279
Rodriguez, Ed, 202
Romero, Joaquin, 118
Roosevelt, Franklin, 196–97
Roque, 84, 115
Rosaria Arriola (1840–1911), 47, 66, 174
Ross, Erskine, 133
Rust, H. N., 153–55, 159, 170, 172, 323n27

Sahmaunt, Norman, 224
Salazar, Dave, Jr., 178
Salazar, Dave, Sr., 183–84, 213
Salazar, Manuel, 176
Salazar, Stanley, 114, 180, 182, 188, 214
Salazar, Vera Ortega, 187–89, 213, 225, 229; enrollment discouraged by, 202; grandson of, 182–83; husband of, 176; ridicule of, 178–80; tribal relations sustained by, 207
Salazar, Vivian, 176
Salvador (1758–1813), 46
Samuel, 79–80, 313n78
sanctions, 26–27
Sandos, James, 15, 290n13
sand painting, 39
San Felipe Indians, 324n44
San Fernando Farm Homestead Association, 127–28
San Fernando Inter-Tribal Indian, 218–19
San Fernando Mission: alcalde elections at, 61; alter restored of, 7; ancestors living at, 215–16; baptismal records of, 209, 211, 233, 245–65, 311n56; bicentennial commemoration of, 229; boundary of, 71; cemetery of, 9; census and lineages of, 204–5; ceremonies at, 76; Christian festivals at, 76–77; de Celis, E., and, 108, 115; diverse lineage of, 11–12, 14; 1856 sketch of, 5; eviction of, 138; fall of, 82–84; forty petitioners from, 80–82; friars at, 57–61, 92, 314n101; Garcias lineage of, 64–65, 186; Indian community at, 85; Indian removal and, 66–67; land grant at, 5, 83, 86; legal rights of, 142; lineage leaders of, 245–65; lineages of, 62–66, 86–87, 95–96, 202; Ortegas lineage of, 62–64; Ortiz, H., in garden of, 213; Ortizes lineage of, 64–66; panoramic view of, 132; Pico, A., at, 126; population decline of, 61; pure blood Indians of, 203–4; for rent, 84; Samuel granted acres to, 79–80, 313n78; secularization and, 110–11; south side barrio of, 320n17; surviving lineages of, 12–13; Takic dialect in, 57; this-worldly maintained by, 61; Tomearunasjum buried at, 25; villages of, 12, 18; wedding day at, 3–4, 8
San Fernando Mission Association, 216
San Fernando Mission Band (SFMB): bylaws created for, 208–9; membership of, 188–89; Ortega, R. Jr., leader of, 216,

224; Ortega, R. Sr., name of, 211, 343n23; tribal member records of, 209–210
San Fernando Mission Indians (SFMI): in Catholic Church, 67; Chumash Indians meeting with, 344n41; culture of, 75–79; emancipation of, 306n79; employment for, 110; landholdings of, 114–15; languages of, 210–11; natural disasters attacking, 119; Pacoima meeting of, 224–25; powwow booth of, 217; Wells as attorney of, 149–50
San Fernando Mission Indians Council, 225
San Fernando Valley, 11–12, 22; acres bought in, 127; Chumash people in, 37; community liaison meeting in, 188; development of, 111; discrimination in, 179, 181–82; Garcia, M. C., moving to, 212; Indians of, 44–45; land in, 154; Los Angeles aqueduct and, 174–75, 329n3; low-wage workers in, 171; Mexican-American population in, 179–81; Mission land in, 125–26; parish communities in, 209
San Fernando Valley Inter-Tribal Incorporated (SFVII), 225–27, 230
San Gabriel Mission, 50–53, 56, 108
San Juan Capistrano Mission, 291n21
San Luis Rey Mission Indian, 215
Santa Anna, Antonio Lopez de, 72, 82
Santa Barbara Mission, 73
Santa Clarita Valley, 216
Santo, Francisco del Espiritu, 64, 112
Santo, Maria del Espiritu, 129, 171–72, 257, 270. *See also* Leonis, Espiritu
Santos, Jose de Todos, 65. *See also* Triunfo, Jose Miguel
Sebastian Military Reserve, 112
Sebastian (Tejon) Reservation, 123, 351n43
secularization: of Alta California, 4, 54; among California Indian missions, 69–70; Catholic Church and, 141; centrists and liberal, 95; citizenship through, 307n4; dispossession and, 84; emancipation and, 72–74, 95; Fernandeños not accepting, 67–68; Indian Claims Commission findings on, 92; land grant and, 72; Mexican policies toward, 70–72, 84, 301n1; mission-based economy and, 110; Mission Indians rights and, 74, 93–94; mission lands and, 79, 83, 88–89; pueblos and, 94–95; San Fernando Mission and, 110–11; of Santa Barbara Mission, 73; Solá efforts toward, 62; Spanish colonial laws of, 69, 209; Spanish legislature passing law for, 59–60, 62, 67–69, 94, 97; struggles over, 74–75
Seelye, Julius, 322n9
self-government, 83–84, 93–94, 221–22, 243; of Indian pueblos, 50, 54, 69, 72, 99, 209; for Indians, 54, 90; lineages with, 27, 66, 241
Sepulveda, Ygnacio, 134
Serra, friar, 50
Serrano, 229, 250–51, 274, 285, 287; ceded lands of, 102; dying-god theme of, 38; of Kitanemuk language, 46, 57; Nú used by, 253; Tomearsaxabia and, 255
seven sisters, 41–42
sexual relations, 43
SFMB. *See* San Fernando Mission Band
SFMI. *See* San Fernando Mission Indians
SFVII. *See* San Fernando Valley Inter-Tribal Incorporated
shamans, 23, 32, 40
Shipek, Florence, 309n27
Sibapet lineage, 51–53
slavery, 97, 99, 308n8
smallpox epidemic, 119
social action theory, 48
social change, 13–14
social gatherings, 189–90, 209
social hierarchy, 11
Solá, Pablo Vicente de, 62
soul, 35–36, 40–41
Southern California: economy changing of, 136; Indian people of, 17–20, 101; Reid's Indian observations of, 22–23; territory in, 19; Toloache Cults of, 290n13; tribal communities in, 148

Southern California Indians, 22–23; dream and spirit of, 40; dying-god theme of, 38; land as collective asset of, 30–31; multiple immortal spirits of, 44; reservation, 239; termination bill struggles of, 221; world levels of, 40, 44; world views of, 17–18
Southern Pacific railway, 126
Spain: California occupied by, 50; colonization by, 49–53; land grant of, 287; laws from, 54; Mexican independence from, 4; missionaries from, 56; Pico, P., friar distrust and, 71–72; pueblos and, 49–50, 73; secularization and colonial laws of, 209; secularization law passed by, 59–60, 62, 67–69, 94, 97
Spanish-Mexican government, 73, 97
special commissioner report, 146, 322n5
spirits, 35–36, 63; angry, 41; Fernandeño with dead, 42; Land of the Dead burial with, 42–43; lineage members and, 28, 31; shaman's power from, 23; Southern California Indian, 40, 44
spiritual ceremonies, 141, 143
spirituality, 36, 39, 41
square league. *See* league
starvation, 193
state laws, 109–10
Stokes, Victoria, 183
Stone, William F., 325n53
summer solstice, 37, 43
Supreme Court, U.S., 99–100, 105
surnames, 46, 210

Taapu, village of, 45–46, 62–64
Takic dialect, 19–21, 24, 57, 287
Tapia, Refugia Ortega, 176, 207, 279
Tataviam, 190, 208, 227, 229, 287; ceded land of, 102; Chumash intermarrying with, 5–6; dwelling pictograph of, 33; dying-god theme of, 41; Estanislao chief of, 137; language of, 3, 20–21, 37–38, 46, 63–64, 116, 182, 186; missionaries observations of, 43; in Newhalll, 172; Ortega, A. M., knowing language of, 182–83; as patrilineal, 24–25; Takic dialect of, 57; Tomiear leader in, 25, 35; villages of, 19; white people punishing, 181; world views of, 37–40. *See also* Fernandeño Tataviam Band of Mission Indians
taxes, 111, 114, 116; in California, 55; de Celis, E., paying property, 132–33; foreclosures because of, 136; property, 93, 109, 120–21, 124, 129, 132–33, 168–69, 260; Rocha paying, 168
Tejon Indian Tribe, 46–47, 311n56, 312n64
Tejon Ranch, 204
Tejon Reservation relocation, 199
Teller, Henry, 148
Temple, Thomas Workman, 315n103
Teofila (1799–1819), 64
Teresa, 62–63, 278, 318n148
termination policy, 221–22
Territorial Assembly, 54, *71*, 79, 84, 86
territory, 73; abandonment of, 103–4; of Achoicominga, 56; of Alta California, 70; ancestral, 145, 242; of Baja California, 70; Cahuenga name of, 66; of California, 3; ceded lands of, 102; economic development from, 10–11; Indian missions on, 49–50; Indigenous tribes living on, 147; lineages governing, 22, 286; Los Angeles County tribes with, 23; Mission Indians on, 49–50; pueblo government for, 59–60; in Southern California, 19
testimonial witnesses, 289n4
this-worldly, 44–45, 47–50, 53, 61, 143
Thom, Cameron, 133
Tiburcia (1755–1837), 45, 298n120
Toloache Cults, 290n13
toloache plant, 34–35, 39
to-me-arr' (Tomear), 25, 77, 255
Tomearsaxabia, 255
Tomearunasjum (1767–98), 25
Tongva, 287
Toypurina, 52–53
Traba, Shirley Newman, 178

traditional knowledge, 142
transmigration, 44
treaties: agents for, 102, 105; California Jurisdictional Act and, 343n16; California's opposition to, 103; Congressional legislation and, 192; evictions from rejecting, 103; Fernandeño's negotiators with, 146; goods promised in, 337n132; lineage leaders response to, 191–92; in Los Angeles County, 103; per acre prices in, 339n177; process of, 101–103; recovery claims from, 227n133; reservations from, 197, 340n186; U.S. negotiators of, 241–42. *See also* unratified California treaties
Treaty 4, of U.S., 111–12
Treaty of Cordova, 307n4
Treaty of Guadalupe Hidalgo, 90, 99, 114, 179, 241
Treaty of Tejon, 101–102, 112, 289n4
tribelet, 19, 22, 92, 104, 242, 288
tribes, 230–31; affairs, 13; affiliation, 198; baptism, 92; bonds, 322n9; communities, 148; concept of, 294n46; connections, 201–202; government, 236, 302n15; identity, 189–90; lands, 101; legal assistance, 158; lineage, 226–27; members, 209–210; names, 223; relations, 207; senate, 233
Triunfo, Ildefonso (Yldefonso), 85, 116, 123, 127
Triunfo, Jose Antonio (Antonio), 85, 116, 127, 316n125
Triunfo, Jose Miguel, 47, 66, 81, 85, 312n67; as deed cosigner, 313n78; land grant awarded to, 80, 116–17, 123–29, 139; land sold by, 129. *See also* Santos, Jose de Todos
trust deed, 163–64
trustee, 160–62, 165
trust in land, 4, 10, 50, 56, 58, 70, 79, 81, 83–85, 87–90, 93, 97, 99, 100, 105–6, 111, 132, 141, 145–46, 167, 221, 241, 304n48
Tujubit lineage, 22, 57, 118, 130, 132, 139–40, 168–69, 259–60, 277. *See also* Tujunga
Tujunga (*Place of the Old Woman*), 22, 25, 64, 98, 112, 118, 130, 132, 168–89, 238, 312n67. *See also* Rancho Tujunga; Tujubit lineage
Tule River Indian Reservation, 337n141
tutelage, 66, 70

underworld, 40. *See also* Land of the Dead
United States (U.S.): aboriginal rights denied by, 241; California control by, 8, 321n175; census in, 113–14, 204–205, 315n103, 318n148; Congress of, 92, 101, 104, 192, 221–22, 339n169; federal funds from, 155; Fernandeño in period of, 91–92; FTBMI petition to, 9–10; Indians marrying people from, 98; Indians relationship with, 145; land claim appeal by, 108; land grants in period of, 113; land patents in, 326n70; Mexican-American population and, 179–81; Mexican-American War of, 8, 87–90; Mexican landholders in, 120–21; Mexico and colonization of, 110–13; public domain lands of, 104–105, 192; recognition sought from, 111; Supreme Court of, 99–100, 105; Tejon treaty with, 101–102, 112, 289n4; Treat 4 of, 111–12; treaty negotiators of, 241–42; tribal government participation in, 302n15
unratified California treaties, 103–105, 111–12, 177, 191, 193–94, 200, 241, 263, 289n4, 343n16
Upper Van Norman reservoir, 116, 125
upper world, 44
Urban Indian centers, 221
Urbano (1745–1812), 117–18, 252–53
Urbano Chari (??), 80, 118, 129

Valentine, L. H., 161
Valenzuela, John, 201, 278, 318n141, 341n194
Valenzuela, John W., 264, 278, 343n23
Valenzuela, Jose Jesus, 172, 277
Valenzuela, Louis, 201, 278, 341n194
Valenzuela, Paul, 201, 278, 341n194

Valenzuela, Petra. *See also* Rivera, Petra Garcia
Vallejo, Mariano, 71, 74, 91
vaqueros (cowboys), 111
Ventureño, 98, 117, 142, 168, 288; 'antap in, 32; of Chumash language, 3, 20–21, 45, 57; Indian language of, 20; Rancho Escorpion captain and, 80
Ventureño Chumash, 20–21, 210; coming-of-age ceremony of, 34; culture of, 45–46, 137; multiple spirits in, 35; religion and, 43; spiritual journey of, 41; Tapuu village of, 62–64; world view of, 35–38
Verdugo, Sally Ortega, 174–76, 203, 279–80, 293n185. *See also* Ortega, Sally
Vicente Francisco, 64, 80
Victoria, Franciscus de, 298n1
villages, 5–7, 15–16, 20–23, 28; Camulos, 237; ceremonies in, 31; Chumash-speaking, 24–25; conflicts between, 26; Homaliwo, 131; lineage members in, 24, 29; rancherias as small, 111; of San Fernando Mission, 12, 18; of Taapu, 45–46, 62–64; of Tataviam, 19
Villasenor, Darlene, 333n68
violence, against Mexicans, 310n41
Vischer, Edward, 126
Vito (1793–1845), 245
voting rights, 93, 99, 179, 211

wage laborers, 136
Ward, John S., 147
Ward, Margaret, 201
Ward, Shirley C., 324n36
wealth, 37
Wells, G. Wiley, 149–52, 154, 165, 170, 242
Wetmore, Charles, 97, 146
white male citizens, 99
Widney, R. M., 133, 154, 162–65, 323n30
Wilson, B. D., 110, 113, 319n156
Wilson, Woodrow, 194
winter solstice, 36–37
Wood, William, 104
work, 58–62, 67–68, 99, 110; emancipation and, 70; low-wage, 171; wage laborers in, 136
Work, Hubert, 196
world levels, 44
world views, 11–12, 147; Christianity and, 52, 68; of Fernandeño-Gabrieleño, 40–43; of Kitanemuk, 37–40; lineage members, 68; religion's continuity and, 78; social action theory and, 48; of Southern California Indians, 17–18; of Tataviam, 37–40; traditional Indian, 95–96; of Ventureño Chumash, 35–38
writ of possession, 152–53

Xaviera, Francisca, 46, 63, 279
Xaviera, Francisco, 25, 80, 245

Ygnacia, Maria, 137

Zenona (1751–?), 46

ABOUT THE AUTHORS

Duane Champagne is a member of the Turtle Mountain Band of Chippewa from North Dakota. He is professor emeritus of sociology, law, and American Indian studies at University of California, Los Angeles. Champagne has authored or edited more than 125 publications. His research interests focus on issues of social and cultural change in historical and contemporary Native American communities. His most recent book is *Indigenous Nations Within Modern Nation States: Integration and Autonomy*.

Carole Goldberg is distinguished research professor of law and Jonathan D. Varat distinguished professor of law emerita at University of California, Los Angeles, specializing in Native American tribal law and federal Indian law. She is also chief justice of the Hualapai Tribe in Arizona. Her numerous publications include the most influential treatise on federal Indian law, a widely used casebook on the subject, and articles and books that address issues such as tribal sovereignty, criminal justice, child welfare, and repatriation. As one of President Barack Obama's three appointees to the Indian Law and Order Commission, she co-authored its 2013 report *A Roadmap for Making Native America Safer: Report to the President and Congress of the United States*.